A Garland Series

AMERICAN INDIAN ETHNOHISTORY

North Central and Northeastern Indians

compiled and edited by

DAVID AGEE HORR
Brandeis University

Indians of Illinois and Indiana

ILLINOIS, KICKAPOO, AND POTAWATOMI INDIANS

Joseph Jablow

Garland Publishing Inc., New York & London

1974

Library of Congress Cataloging in Publication Data

Jablow, Joseph.
  Illinois, Kickapoo, and Potawatomi Indians.

  (American Indian ethnohistory: North central and
northeastern Indians)
  At head of title: The Indians of Illinois and Indiana.
  Report presented before the Indian Claims Commission,
petitioners' exhibit no. 133, docket no. 313, 315 et al.
  1. Illinois Indians. 2. Kickapoo Indians.
3. Potawatomi Indians. I. United States. Indian Claims
Commission. II. Title. III. Title: The Indians of
Illinois and Indiana. IV. Series.
E99.I2J32   970.4'73   74-2278
ISBN 0-8240-0805-7

E
99
.I2
J32

Contents

*Garland Publishing has repaginated this work (at outside center) to facilitate scholarly use. However, original pagination has been retained for internal reference.

6

Publisher's Preface

The Garland American Indian Ethnohistory series presents original documents on the history and anthropology of many American Indian tribes and groups who were involved in the Indian Claims actions of the 1950s and 1960s. These reports were written to be used as evidence in legal proceedings to determine the aboriginal rights of various Indian groups to certain geographical regions or areas within the United States. In each case, the Indian Claims Commission issued a set of findings which are an important historical outcome of the proceedings and of the reports.

The Garland volumes include, as background material, introductory sections on the Indian Claims actions and the gathering of the ethnohistorical materials by Ralph A. Barney, Chief of the Indian Claims Section of the Department of Justice since its inception in 1946, and Robert A. Manners, Professor of Anthropology at Brandeis University. Both were professionally involved in several cases and Dr. Manners has published on the Claims actions.

Each volume also contains a brief introductory historical sketch of the tribe or group which is representative of the kind of information available at the time of the Claims actions. Much of this material was summarized in a 1650-page document (House Report No. 2503), published in 1953 by order of the House of Representatives committee investigating the Bureau of Indian Affairs. In addition to summaries on history and population, the massive government report included maps which gave the 1950 location of the various American Indian groups, largely on reservations, as well as the estimated original range occupied by the group or tribe in question. This material appears in the Garland volumes in abridged form, since it gives a picture of the kind of information available to the United States government in the 1950s on which it might have based decisions concerning the

PREFACE

American Indians had the Indian Claims actions not taken place. In addition, these brief introductory sections will help orient the general reader to the groups covered by the ethnohistorical reports.

The reports in this series have been organized into logical groupings for maximum efficiency of use. Short reports have been bound together into single volumes by tribe or by geographical area when several tribes are represented by a single report, with Commission findings bound at the end of the pertinent volume. In those cases where many reports pertain to the same group or area they may comprise several volumes which are numbered consecutively. When several volumes deal with the same set of claims, the findings appear in the final volume of that set of interrelated reports. It should be noted that, since this series is intended to present these ethnohistorical materials as documents, the reports are reproduced *verbatim*, with no additions, deletions, or other editing by the compiler of the series or the original authors.

Within the body of the reports, reference is often made to exhibit numbers. These refer to other material accepted as evidence, often in the form of excerpts from existing publications or other documents pertaining to the tribes in question. This material is not included in the volumes themselves, although a bibliography of these items usually appears in the report. These exhibits are on file in the Indian Claims Commission offices in Washington, D.C., or in the National Archives.

General Nature and
Content of the Series

The formal reports contained in this series represent only part of the evidence amassed in the 370-odd court actions assigned separate docket numbers by the Indian Claims Commission. Almost since the outset, those involved with the Indian Claims' activities have voiced the opinion that the specifically researched ethnohistorical studies should not simply be filed away in some federal depository though this did become the case with these reports. The present series is the result of careful searching through more than 600 unindexed file drawers in the Indian Claims Commission, the National Archives, and elsewhere, sometimes even in the papers of the originally participating scholars.

Each claims action was an adversary proceeding with a particular Indian tribe or group as plaintiff and the United States Government, represented by the Indian Claims Section of the Justice Department, as defendant. Each side collected evidence on the nature of aboriginal use and occupancy of particular areas in order to determine which Indian groups were entitled to compensation for lands taken by the United States, either by treaty or otherwise, and just what lands were in question. Once this phase of the action was settled, the proceedings moved on to the question of the value of the lands at the time they were taken from the Indians. It is with the title phase of the Claims proceedings that the present series is concerned. Therefore the numerous appraisals of economic value are omitted.

Claims to title were settled on the basis of several types of evidence presented during hearings before the Indian Claims Commission. The expert testimony submitted included verbal and written reports by anthropologists, archaeologists, and historians. During the early days of the Commission, virtually all such testimony was oral and is preserved only in the official court transcripts. Later on, the Government required its expert witnesses to submit formal written reports. The lawyers for the plaintiffs did not initially make this a requirement so that, for some cases, reports are available on the Government side but not for the Indians. Finally, the Commission did require all ethnohistorical reports to be submitted by both sides in written form. The title page of each individual report indicates whether it was submitted as an exhibit for the plaintiff (sometimes called claimant, petitioner or intervenor) or the defendant.

Since the formal reports were subject to examination by the Commissioners and by the opposing lawyers, they were carefully prepared. The specific nature of the reports did mean that some topics often included in an ethnography might be excluded. In the California cases, for example, some well-researched reports on pottery making and other craft industries were not used. On the other hand, data on political structure, kinship and property inheritance rights, and many other such topics, were often considered because they did bear upon how rights to property and power were determined within a group and the question of how the Indians originally used the land. Once the evidence was submitted and examined in the hearings, the Commissioners issued a set of Findings and Opinions, which, by themselves, are important historical documents.

The Garland series includes only the formal ethnohistorical reports and the title findings of the Commission since the entire documentation of the Claims actions is so voluminous. The lengthy hearing transcripts are uneconomic to reproduce without editing and our purpose is to present unedited documents as actually *used*. The transcript of the Kiowa-Comanche case is included because of its unique nature. The transcripts are all on file either in the Indian Claims Commission or the National Archives, and may be consulted there.

The content of this series was determined solely by those ethnohistorical reports submitted to the Commission. Therefore, American Indian tribes and groups not involved in Claims actions are not represented for various reasons. For example, the Indians of the northeastern and eastern United States had lost most of their lands prior to the establishment of the country in 1776. In other instances, the tribe no longer existed in 1946 or did not submit a claim. In some cases claims were submitted, but were denied before a report was commissioned for that tribe.

The reports for the various areas covered by the Claims Act have been approached in somewhat different ways. When possible, they deal with individual tribes or named groups. This does not mean that in such cases there were no overlapping claims; however, the overall tribal situation was not so complex as to prevent an initial identification of tribal groups with specific geographic areas. By contrast, in some areas such as the eastern and north central regions, reports tend to focus on Royce areas rather than individual tribes because the aboriginal claims situation often involved recurring movement through the region by many different tribes over a relatively short time period. In these regions treaties ceding certain lands to the United States were often signed by several different tribes or perhaps only by certain parts of some of the tribes involved. Here the area reports *in toto* form an almost jigsaw-puzzle-like solution to the enormously complex tribal relationships. The Royce Area maps and designations were published in Bureau of American Ethnology, Annual Report, vol. 18, no. 2, 1896-7.

David Agee Horr

11

The Indian Claims Commission

Prior to the creation of the Indian Claims Commission by the Act of August 13, 1946 (60 Stat. 1049; 25 U.S.C. § 70 et seq.), no tribe of Indians could bring a suit against the United States without the special permission of Congress. This was a cumbersome and wholly unsatisfactory procedure. By the 1946 Act, Congress created a special judicial tribunal to "hear and determine" claims by Indian tribes in an effort to settle, once and for all, the claims of the Indians. The Act is unique in the true sense of the word. Never before has any government generally opened the doors of its courts to the claims of its aborigines. The Commission is authorized to consider claims by any "tribe, band or identifiable group of American Indians" that the United States in its previous dealings had not always carried out its treaty obligations, had imposed treaties upon them against their wishes, had failed to pay them adequately for their land, had failed to account properly for the expenditure of their tribal funds and, in many instances, had not been "fair and honorable" in their dealings with them.

The tribes had five years within which to file their claims and, after adjudication, they could have the Commission's decisions reviewed by the United States Court of Claims and by the Supreme Court of the United States. The Congress imposed one important limitation: the Commission could render only a money judgment in favor of the tribes. It could not return any land to them which might have been taken wrongfully, nor could it give them any land to supply a land base.

The present volumes deal with only one of the multi-faceted aspects of Indian claims litigation: the area of land occupied by the tribes prior to the coming of the white man into the area in general, or the area occupied by a particular tribe for "a long time" prior to its acquisition by the United

States, or their dispossession by the whites.

The land problem was confounded by different concepts inherent in the nature of the disparate cultures. The culture of the Europeans who discovered and later settled this continent was basically legalistic, particularly where land was concerned. Land was the subject of "ownership" either by the monarch or his subjects, and "titles" were the capstone of such ownership. "Ownership" in the sense of a legal right was unknown to the Indian. As Justice Black said in *Shoshone Indians* v. *United States*, 324 U.S. 335, 357 (1945):

> . . . Ownership meant no more to them than to roam the land as a great common, and to possess and enjoy it in the same way that they possessed and enjoyed sunlight and the west wind and the feel of spring in the air. Acquisitiveness, which develops a law of real property, is an accomplishment only of the "civilized."

When the Europeans "discovered" the North American continent they found it inhabited by the Indians and the question of their rights aroused a great moral debate. Charles V of Spain sought the advice of the theologian Franciscus de Victoria, primary professor of sacred theology in the University of Salamanca, who suggested that since the aborigines "were true owners, before the Spaniards came among them, both from the public and private point of view," they should be treated with to secure cessions of their lands. This view obviously could not prevail if the European monarchs owned the land and could parcel it out to their subjects.

The matter came to a head in 1823 when Chief Justice John Marshall decided the famous case of *Johnson* v. *McIntosh*, 21 U.S. (8 Wheat.) 453. In 1775 the Piankeshaw Indians had sold a tract of land to various individuals. However, in 1818, the United States sold and patented the same land to William McIntosh. Thus the contest was which deed was valid. From a long and detailed examination of the history of Indian relations in this country, Chief Justice Marshall concluded that the legal title was in the United

States Government and that the tribes had no right to sell and convey the land (at least, without governmental consent).

However, the Indians could not be ignored, particularly in the early days when they were numerically far stronger than the few settlers huddled along the coast. From this developed the theory that while the legal "title" was in the discovering nations and later in the United States, the Indians had a right of possession based on what was characterized as their "aboriginal title."

More than thirty years ago, long before the creation of the Indian Claims Commission, the Supreme Court had occasion to lay down the rule, which was later adopted by the Commission, as to what was necessary to establish Indian title. In *United States* v. *Santa Fe Pacific R. Co.*, 314 U. S. 339, 345 (1941), the Court said:

> Occupancy necessary to establish aboriginal possession is a question of fact to be determined as any other question of fact. If it were established as a fact that the lands in question were, or were included in, the ancestral home of the Walapais in the sense that they constituted a definable territory occupied exclusively by the Walapais (as distinguished from lands wandered over by many tribes), then the Walapais had "Indian title". . . .

15

The determination of the "question of fact" of the aboriginal or original Indian title is what the ethnographic studies in these volumes, and the findings and the opinions of the Commission are all about. The anthropologists have dug up the facts to the extent that they were able to do so. Based on these facts the Commission has made its determination of the areas of land occupied by the various tribes under their original title or their later occupancy, and it is on the basis of these determinations of the areas of aboriginal title that these cases then go forward to determine the amount of recovery by the several tribes.

Quite understandably much of the "evidence" consists of deductions made by the witnesses from the frequently meager hard facts available and, of necessity, the determinations of the Commission are based on this type of evidence. While the boundaries of the areas exclusively and actually used and occupied may not always be correct, they represent in most instances a fair approximation of the areas occupied by the various tribes aboriginally or for "a long time" on the dates when the United States acquired the land or they were permanently dispossessed of it. All in all, it has been a difficult job well done.

I cannot close this brief introduction without expressing my admiration for the many scholars on both sides who so diligently sought out the facts to present to the Commission. They did a magnificent job for which all other scholars and interested laymen should be grateful. My personal acquaintance with them has been an outstanding experience.

I am also personally happy to see these ethnographic studies and the decisions of the Commission published instead of being buried in the National Archives. They will contribute greatly to our knowledge of the American Indian.

16

Ralph A. Barney

Introduction to the
Ethnohistorical Reports
on the Land Claims Cases

The research reports and the findings contained in this compilation may prove, in the long run, to have contributed little to resolving the massive economic and social problems which confront today's Native Americans. However, it is most unlikely that any of the diligent and often dedicated sponsors of the movement that led, in 1946, to the passage of the Indian Claims Commission Act ever had such lofty expectations. What is more likely is that the proponents of the legislation, as Ralph Barney observes in his introductory remarks, had simply hoped to "clean up the mess," to put an end to the stream of suits and claims against the federal government, each of which had required Congressional approval before it could be brought to trial. But the "mess" was not so easily resolved. Some cases have been settled. Others have been heard, adjudicated and appealed to higher courts. A few, like that of "the Indians of California," may be reopened.

But when, and if, all of the claims have been resolved in the courts, the government will not have succeeded in pacifying the claimants nor in satisfying their demands for decent compensation. In short, the Act has not fulfilled even the minimal goal of putting an end to Native American claims against the United States Government.

In light of the relatively meager benefits that have so far accrued to Native Americans as a consequence of the Act of 1946, it might seem almost callous to draw attention now to the richness of the by-product of that Act as represented in the 118 volumes in this series. For whatever one may feel about the intended benefits of the Act, it is clear that the

INTRODUCTION TO THE REPORTS

scholarly fallout is stunning indeed. The materials presented in these volumes include a concentrated body of ethnohistorical research data and adversary findings unique in the record of cultural historiography and, so far as I know, in the annals of jurisprudence.

Literally hundreds of people were involved in the research and litigation that led to these reports and findings. Thousands of interviews were conducted. Extensive archaeological surveys were made. Large quantities of previously "unknown" or unexamined agency and other files, personal correspondence, photographs, diaries, and so on were uncovered and their contents incorporated in the reports. Regular archival and library resources were examined and reexamined with a thoroughness that would not have been possible without the support that both claimants and the defendant were able to provide. Then there were the adversary proceedings, which, though patently unpleasant to most of the experts, did provide an even more effective check on the quality of the research product than the customary scholarly scrutiny of one's colleagues. For where there is litigation, the experts on both sides have probably reviewed much, if not all, of the same data. Moreover, the litigous circumstances place a premium on revealing inaccuracies and/or slipshod research methods.[1]

Finally, I would like to emphasize that another apparent by-product of the Act and the research and hearings that followed its implementation may be detected in the effect that this research and its attendant litigation have had on the thinking of many Native Americans now pressing for improved economic, social and political conditions for *all* Indians in the United States. Thus, if the working-out of the Act has made only minor contributions to the welfare of a

18

[1] Some ethnohistorical and legal problems confronted by the plaintiffs' and defendant's experts and attorneys were explored at a 1954 symposium on the Claims Act (see *Ethnohistory 2,4*, pp. 287-375). The participants were Ralph A. Barney, Chief of the Indian Claims Section, Lands Division, Dept. of Justice; Donald C. Gormley of the law firm of Wilkinson, Boyden, Cragun & Barker; and anthropologists Verne Ray, Julian Steward, A. L. Kroeber, J. A. Jones and Nancy Oestreich Lurie.

INTRODUCTION TO THE REPORTS

handful of American Indians, it has apparently had a much more salutary effect on their thinking about the welfare of *all* Native Americans. For the "time immemorial" and the "exclusive occupancy" strictures of the Act resulted, in many ways, in pitting group against group to the detriment of all.[2] In most cases, the occupancy and/or use claims of one group conflicted, at least in part, with those of another or several other groups of Indians.[3] Where such joint use or occupancy was proved to the satisfaction of the Commission, none of the claimants benefitted, thus demonstrating (as I have been told by several Native Americans) the perils of division and intra-Indian competition and, by implication, the likely advantages of pan-Indian cooperation in future endeavors, political as well as legal.

This "unforeseen consequence" of the research and litigation, of the claims and counter-claims, has certainly been among the factors that have helped to persuade those Native Americans who were not already convinced of the pitfalls as well as the potential virtues of a revived "tribalism" of the need for a more unified, a pan-Indian approach to their problems. These volumes can only help to bolster the case for such unity and, thus, perhaps to enhance the political impact of Native Americans in the United States.

Robert A. Manners

[2] In this respect, the claim of "The Indians of California" is exceptional because an earlier case had laid the groundwork whereby a number of different groups (culturally and linguistically) were permitted to combine all of their separate land-use-and-occupation claims into one. If the Act had allowed *all* American Indian plaintiffs to combine their claims in this manner (and to share equally in the awards), and if they had been willing to do so, the resultant claims, litigation and decisions might have been, at the very least, quite interesting. . . . i.e., "The Indians of the United States vs. the United States Government for just compensation for the taking of all lands (less land held in existing reservations) between the Atlantic and the Pacific Oceans."

[3] A striking example, with which I am familiar, are the overlapping Navaho, Hopi, Walapai, Havasupai claims.

Editor's Note

In terms of the numbers of tribes involved in overlapping claims, the area of the upper Great Lakes and Ohio Valley is the most complicated of all the Indian Claims Commission actions. At the time of the founding of the new United States government following the Revolution, many Indian tribes and groups had been dislodged from their earliest locations along the lower Great Lakes and the Eastern Seaboard, and many of these groups had moved across the mountains into the old Northwest Territories. Here, they encountered already existing Indian groups, and by the time of the Treaty of Greeneville in 1795 many Indian tribes and groups were contesting these lands with the advancing whites and with each other. By the mid-1800s, most of the Indians in this area had moved west of the Mississippi River, though some groups remained.

In trying to sort out this most complicated Claims situation, reports were written around Royce areas, in an attempt to determine exactly which Indian groups had how much claim to particular regions. It will therefore be useful for the reader to refer to the volume containing the Royce report, although recent scholarship has shown that some of Royce's original boundaries were incorrectly drawn.

In general, then, the individual reports for this area do not concentrate on the history of a particular tribe. However, taken together, they provide the most detailed study available of the history and interrelations of the many Indian tribes in this area. It should be noted that the Chippewa claims were so extensive that most of the reports concerning their lands have been grouped in a series of volumes.

D.A.H.

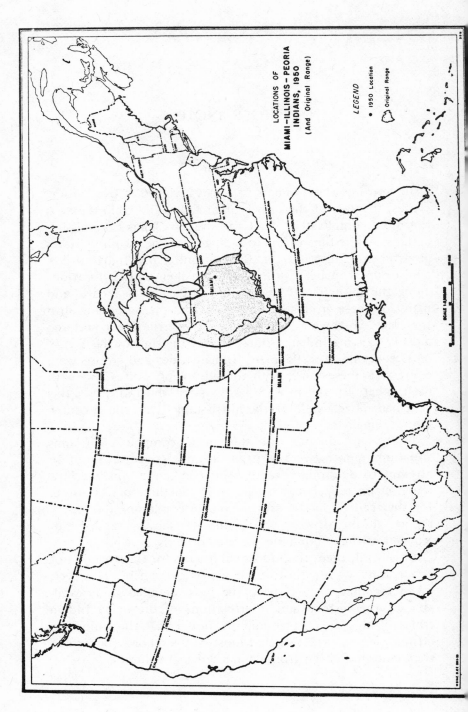

LOCATIONS OF
MIAMI−ILLINOIS−PEORIA
INDIANS, 1950
(And Original Range)

LEGEND

• 1950 Location

Original Range

SCALE 1:14,500,000

22

"MIAMI (? Chippewa: *Omaumeg*, 'people who live on the peninsula'). An Algonquian tribe, usually designated by early English writers as Twightwees (twa^{n}h twa^{n}h, the cry of a crane.— Hewitt), from their own name, the earliest recorded notice of which is from information furnished in 1658 by Gabriel Druillettes (Jes. Rel. 1658, 21, 1858), who called them the Oumamik, then living 60 leagues from St Michel, the first village of the Potawatomi mentioned by him; it was therefore at or about the mouth of Green bay, Wis. Tailhan (Perrot, Memoire) says that they withdrew into the Mississippi valley, 60 leagues from the bay, and were established there from 1657 to 1676, although Bacqueville de la Potherie asserts that, with the Mascoutens, the Kickapoo, and part of the Illinois, they came to settle at that place about 1667. The first time the French came into actual contact with the Miami was when Perrot visited them about 1668. His second visit was in 1670, when they were living at the headwaters of Fox r., Wis. In 1671 a part at least of the tribe were living with the Mascoutens in a palisaded village in this locality (Jes. Rel. 1671, 45, 1858). Soon after this the Miami parted from the Mascoutens and formed new settlements at the s. end of L. Michigan and on Kalamazoo r., Mich. The settlements at the s. end of the lake were at Chicago and on St Joseph r., where missions were established late in the 17th century, although the former is mentioned as a Wea village at the time of Marquette's visit, and Wea were found there in 1701 by De Courtemarche. It is likely that these Wea were the Miami mentioned by Allouez and others as being united with the Mascoutens in Wisconsin. The chief village of the Miami on St Joseph r. was, according to Zenobius (Le Clerq, 11, 133), about 15 leagues inland, in lat. 41°. The extent of territory occupied by this tribe a few years later compels the conclusion that the Miami in Wisconsin, when the whites first heard of them, formed but a part of the tribe, and that other bodies were already in n. e. Illinois and n. Indiana. As the Miami and their allies were found later on the Wabash in Indiana and in n. w. Ohio, in which latter territory they gave their name to three rivers, it would seem that they had moved s. e. from the localities where first known within historic times. Little Turtle, their famous chief, said: 'My fathers kindled the first fire at Detroit; thence they extended their lines to the headwaters of the Scioto; thence to its mouth; thence down the Ohio to the mouth of the Wabash, and thence to Chicago over L. Michigan.' When Vincennes was sent by Gov. Vaudreville in 1705 on a mission to the Miami they were found occupying principally the territory n. w. of the upper Wabash. There was a Miami village at Detroit in 1703, but their chief settlement was still on St Joseph r. In 1711 the Miami the Wea had three villages on the St Joseph, Maumee, and Wabash. Kekionga, at the head of the Maumee, became the chief seat of the Miami proper, while Ouiatenon, on the Wabash, was the headquarters of the Wea branch. By the encroachments of the Potawatomi, Kickapoo, and other northern

23

tribes the Miami were driven from St Joseph r. and the country n. w. of the Wabash. They sent out colonies to the e. and formed settlements on Miami r. in Ohio, and perhaps as far e. as the Scioto. This country they held until the peace of 1763, when they retired to Indiana, and the abandoned country was occupied by the Shawnee. They took a prominent part in all the Indian wars in Ohio valley until the close of the war of 1812. Soon afterward they began to sell their lands, and by 1827 had disposed of most of their holdings in Indiana and had agreed to remove to Kansas, whence they went later to Indian Ter., where the remnant still resides. In all treaty negotiations they were considered as original owners of the Wabash country and all of w. Ohio, while the other tribes in that region were regarded as tenants or intruders on their lands. A considerable part of the tribe, commonly known as Meshingomesia's band, continued to reside on a reservation in Wabash co., Ind., until 1872, when the land was divided among the survivors, then numbering about 300.

*   *   *   *   *   *   *

It is impossible to give a satisfactory estimate of the numbers of the Miami at any one time, on account of confusion with the Wea and Piankashaw, who probably never exceeded 1,500. An estimate in 1764 gives them 1,500; another in the following year places their number at 1,250. In 1825 the population of the Miami, Eel Rivers, and Wea was given as 1,400, of whom 327 were Wea. Since their removal to the W. they have rapidly decreased. Only 57 Miami were officially known in Indian Ter. in 1885, while the Wea and Piankashaw were confederated with the remnant of the Illinois under the name of Peoria, the whole body numbering but 149; these increased to 191 in 1903. The total number of Miami 1905 in Indian Ter. was 124; in Indiana, in 1900, there were 243; the latter, however, are greatly mixed with white blood. Including individuals scattered among other tribes, the whole number is probably 400.

The Miami joined in or made treaties with the United States as follows: (1) Greenville, O., with Gen. Anthony Wayne, Aug. 3, 1795, defining the boundary between the United States and tribes w. of Ohio r. and ceding certain tracts of land; (2) Ft Wayne, Ind., June 7, 1803, with various tribes, defining boundaries and ceding certain lands; (3) Grouseland, Ind., Aug. 21, 1805, ceding certain lands in Indiana and defining boundaries; (4) Ft Wayne, Ind., Sept. 30, 1809, in which the Miami, Eel River tribes, and Delawares ceded certain lands in Indiana, and the relations between the Delawares and Miami regarding certain territory are defined; (5) Treaty of peace at Greenville, O., July 22, 1814, between the United States, the Wyandot, Delawares, Shawnee, Seneca, and the Miami, including the Eel River and Wea tribes; (6) Peace treaty of Spring Wells, Mich,. Sept. 8, 1815, by the Miami and other tribes; (7) St Mary's, O., Oct. 6, 1818, by which the Miami ceded certain lands in Indiana; (8) Treaty of the Wabash, Ind., Oct. 23, 1826, by which the Miami ceded all their lands in Indiana, n. and w. of Wabash and Miami rs.; (9)

Wyandot village, Ind., Feb. 11, 1828, by which the Eel River Miami ceded all claim to the reservation at their village on Sugar Tree cr., Ind.,; (10) Forks of Wabash, Ind., Oct. 23, 1834, by which the Miami ceded several tracts in Indiana; (11) Forks of the Wabash, Ind., Nov. 6, 1838, by which the Miami ceded most of of their remaining lands in Indiana, and the United States agreed to furnish them a reservation w. of the Mississippi; (12) Forks of the Wabash, Ind., Nov. 28, 1840, by which the Miami ceded their remaining lands in Indiana and agreed to remove to the country assigned them w. of the Mississippi; (13) Washington, June 5, 1854, by which they ceded a tract assigned by amended treaty of Nov. 28, 1840, excepting 70,000 a. retained as a reserve; (14) Washington, Feb. 23, 1867, with Seneca and others, in which it is stipulated that the Miami may become confederated with the Peoria and others if they so desire."

Source: *Handbook of American Indians, Part 1*, pp. 852–854.

MIAMI AND ILLINOIS POPULATION

"This is a group of small Algonquian tribes made up of the Miami and the remnants of the Wea, Piankashaw, and Peoria. The number enumerated in 1930 was 284, as compared with 360 in 1910. Of these, 173 in 1930 were located in Ottawa County, Oklahoma, and 47 in Indiana. Only 21 of this group of tribes (17 in Oklahoma and 4 in Indiana) were returned as full blood."

Source: *The Indian Population of the United States and Alaska*, 1930, p. 38.

SELECTED REFERENCES ON THE MIAMI
AS OF 1952

(Including the Miami proper, the Piankashaw, and the Wea)

Andrews, H. A. Quapaw Subagency Ten Year Program Report. 1944. 31 pp. (Bureau of Indian Affairs.)

Kinietz, W. V. The Indian Tribes of the Great Lakes. Occasional Contributions from the Museum of Anthropology of the University of Michigan, Ann Arbor, Vol. V, pp. 161–225, 1940.

Krzywicki, Ludwik. Primitive Society and its Vital Statistics. London, 1934. pp. 460–1.

Murdock, Geo. P. Ethnographic Bibliography of North America. 1941. p. 89.

Trowbridge, C. C. Meearmeear Traditions. Ed. W. V. Kinietz. Occasional Contributions from the Museum of Anthropology of the University Michigan, Ann Arbor, Vol. VII, pp. 1–91, 1938.

Wright, Muriel H. A Guide to the Indian Tribes of Oklahoma. Norman, 1951. Eel River Indians, p. 155, Miami pp. 182–3, Wea pp. 254–5.

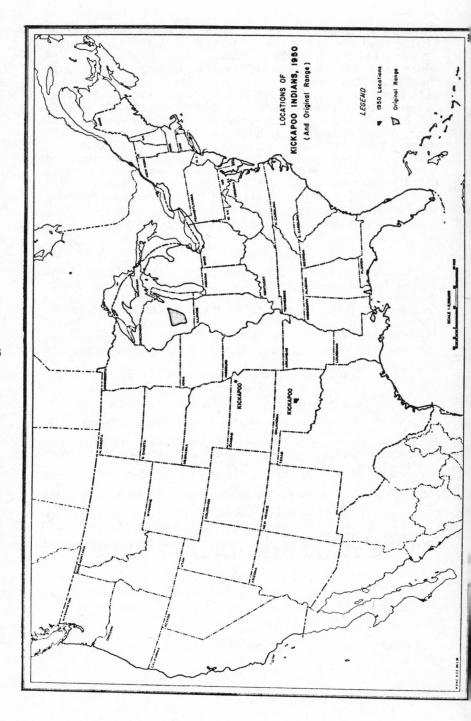

LOCATIONS OF
KICKAPOO INDIANS, 1950
(And Original Range)

LEGEND

▼ 1950 Locations

Original Range

KICKAPOO

KICKAPOO

26

"The people of this tribe, unless they are hidden under a name not yet known to be synonymous, first appear in history about 1667–70. At this time they were found by Allouez near the portage between Fox and Wisconsin rs. Verwyst (Missionary Labors, 1886) suggests Alloa, Columbia co., Wis., as the probable locality, about 12 m. s. of the mixed village of the Mascouten, Miami, and Wea. No tradition of their former home or previous wanderings has been recorded; but if the name Outitchakouk mentioned by Druillettes (Jes. Rel. 1658, 21, 1858) refers to the Kickapoo, which seems probable, the first mention of them is carried back a few years, but they were then in the same locality. Le Sueur (1699) mentions in his voyage up the Mississippi, the river of the Quincapous (Kickapoo), above the mouth of the Wisconsin, which he says was 'so called from the name of a nation which formerly dwelt on its banks.' This probably refers to Kickapoo r., Crawford co., Wis., though it empties into the Wisconsin, and not into the Mississippi. Rock r., Ill., was for a time denominated the "River of the Kickapoos," but this is much too far s. to agree with the stream mentioned by Le Sueur. A few years later a part at least of the tribe appears to have moved s. and settled somewhere about Milwaukee r. They entered into the plot of the Foxes in 1712 to burn the fort at Detroit. On the destruction of the Illinois confederacy, about 1765, by the combined forces of the tribes n. of them, the conquered country was partitioned among the victors, the Sauk and Foxes moving down to the Rock r. country, while the Kickapoo went farther s., fixing their headquarters for a time at Peoria. They appear to have gradually extended their range, a portion centering about Sangamon r., while another part pressed toward the e., establishing themselves on the waters of the Wabash, despite the opposition of the Miami and Piankashaw. The western band became known as the Prairie band, while the others were denominated the Vermilion band, from their residence on Vermilion r., a branch of the Wabash. They played a prominent part in the history of this region up to the close of the War of 1812, aiding Tecumseh in his efforts against the United States, while many Kickapoo fought with Black Hawk in 1832. In 1837 Kickapoo warriors to the number of 100 were engaged by the United States to go, in connection with other western Indians, to fight the Seminole of Florida. In 1809 they ceded to the United States their lands on Wabash and Vermilion rs., and in 1819 all their claims to the central portion of Illinois. Of this land, as stated in the treaty, they 'claim a large portion by descent from their ancestors, and the balance by conquest from the Illinois nation, and uninterrupted possession for more than half a century.' They afterward removed to Missouri and thence to Kansas. About the year 1852 a large party left the main body, together with some Potawatomi, and went to Texas and thence to Mexico, where they became known as 'Mexican Kickapoo.' In 1863 they were joined by another dissatisfied party from the tribe. The Mexican band proved a constant

27

source of annoyance to the border settlements, and efforts were made to induce them to return, which were so far successful in 1873 a number were brought back and settled in Indian Ter. Others have come in since, but the remainder, constituting at present nearly half the tribe, are now settled on a reservation, granted them by the Mexican government, in the Santa Rosa mts. of e. Chihuahua."

Source: *Handbook of American Indians, Part 1*, pp. 684–685.

KICKAPOO POPULATION

"This is a small but well-known tribe formerly living in Wisconsin, but now located in the Kickapoo Reservation in Brown County, Kansas, and in Lincoln and Pottawatomie Counties, Oklahoma. The number enumerated in 1930 was 523, as compared with 348 in 1910. Perhaps as many more are located in the State of Chihuahua in Mexico. Of the Kickapoo in Kansas, only 14.7 percent were returned as full blood, but of those in Oklahoma, 95.0 percent were so returned."

Source: *The Indian Population of the United States and Alaska*, 1930, p. 38.

28

SELECTED REFERENCES ON THE KICKAPOO
AS OF 1952

Affairs of Mexican Kicking Kickapoo Indians. Report. (To accompany S. Res. No. 261, 59th Cong.) (Washington, Govt. Print. Off., 1907.) (60th Cong., 1st sess. Senate. Rept. 5.)

Affairs of the Mexican Kickapoo Indians. Hearings before the subcommittee of the Committee on Indian Affairs, United States Senate. Wash-ing n, Govt. Print. Off., 1907.

Affairs of the Mexican Kickapoo Indians. Hearings before the subcommittee of the Committee on Indian Affairs, United States Senate. Washington, Govt. Print. Off., 1908. (60th Cong., 1st sess. Senate. Doc. 215.)

Affairs of the Mexican Kickapoo Indians. Hearing before the subcommittee of the Committee on Indian Affairs, United States Senate. (Washington, Govt. Print. Off., 1908.)

Bruce, H. E. Potawatomi (Kansas) Ten Year Program Report. 1944. 62 pp. (Bureau of Indian Affairs).

Gilmore, Thos. R. Shawnee Agency Ten Year Program Report. 1944. 17 pp. (Bureau of Indian Affairs).

Jones, W. Kickapoo Ethnological Notes. American Anthropologist, n. s. Vol. XV, pp. 332–5, 1913.

Krzwicki, Ludwik. Primitive Society and its Vital Statistics. London, 1934. pp. 406–7.

Mooney, J. and Jones, W. Kickapoo. Bulletin of the Bureau of American Ethnology, Vol. XXX, i, pp. 684–6, 1907.

Murdock, Geo. P. Ethnographic Bibliography of North America. 1941. p. 89.

Spaulding, R. Potawatomi Ten Year Program Summary. 1944. 11 pp. (Bureau of Indian Affairs).

Treaty stipulations with Kickapoo Indians. Feb. 13, 1908. (Washington, Govt. Print. Off., 1908.) (60th Cong., 1st sess. Senate. Doc. 350.)

Wright, Muriel H. A Guide to the Indian Tribes of Oklahoma. Norman, 1951. Kickapoos pp. 166–9.

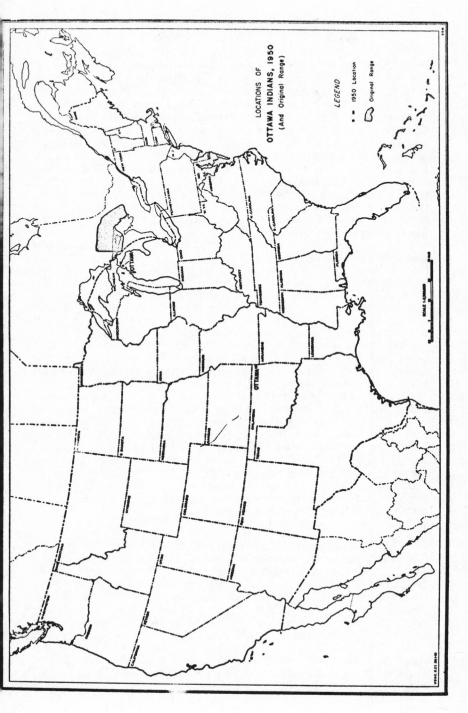

LOCATIONS OF
OTTAWA INDIANS, 1950
(And Original Range)

LEGEND

• — 1950 Location

⬭ — Original Range

SCALE 1:4,500,000

29

"The two tribes (i. e., the Ottawa and Hurons) lived together until about 1700, when the Hurons removed to the vicinity of Detroit, while a portion of the Ottawa about this time seems to have obtained a foothold on the w. shore of L. Huron between Saginaw bay and Detroit, where the Potawatomi were probably in close union with them. Four divisions of the tribe were represented by a deputy at the treaty signed at Montreal in 1700. The band which had moved to the s. e. part of the lower Michigan peninsula returned to Mackinaw about 1706. Soon afterward the chief seat of a portion of the tribe was fixed at Waganakisi (L'arbre Croche), near the lower end of L. Michigan. From this point they spread in every direction, the majority settling along the e. shore of the lake, as far s. as St. Joseph r., while a few found their way into s. Wisconsin and n. e. Illinois. In the n. they shared Manitoulin id. and the n. shore of L. Huron with the Chippewa, and in the s. e. their villages alternated with those of their old allies the Hurons, now called Wyandot, along the shore of L. Erie from Detroit to the vicinity of Beaver cr. in Pennsylvania. They took an active part in all the Indian wars of that region up to the close of the War of 1812. The celebrated chief Pontiac was a member of this tribe, and Pontiac's war of 1763, waged chiefly around Detroit, is a prominent event in their history. A small part of the tribe which refused to submit to the authority of the United States removed to Canada, and together with some Chippewa and Potawatomi, is now settled on Walpole id. in L. St. Clair. The other Ottawa in Canadian territory are on Manitoulin and Cockburn ids. and the adjacent shore of L. Huron.

All of the Ottawa lands along the w. shore of L. Michigan were ceded by various treaties, ending with the Chicago treaty of Sept. 26, 1833, wherein they agreed to remove to lands granted them on Missouri r. in the n. e. corner of Kansas. Other bands, known as the Ottawa of Blanchard's fork of Great Auglaize r., and of Roche de Bouef on Maumee r., resided in Ohio, but these removed w. of the Mississippi about 1832 and are now living in Oklahoma. The great body, however, remained in the lower peninsula of Michigan, where they are still found scattered in a number of small villages and settlements.

*   *   *   *   *   *   *

"The Ottawa entered into numerous treaties with the United States as follows: Ft. McIntosh, Jan. 21, 1785; Ft. Harmar, Ohio, Jan. 9, 1789; Greenville, Ohio, Aug. 3, 1795; Ft. Industry, July 4, 1805; Detroit, Mich., Nov. 17, 1807; Brownstown, Mich., Nov. 25, 1808; Greenville, Ohio, July 22, 1814; Spring Wells, Mich., Sept. 8, 1815; St. Louis, Mo., Aug. 24, 1816; on the Miami, Ohio, Sept. 29, 1817; St. Mary's, Ohio, Sept. 17, 1818; L'Arbre Croche and Michilimackinac, Mich., July 6, 1820; Chicago, Ill., Aug. 29, 1821; Prairie du Chien, Wis., Aug. 19, 1825; Green Bay, Wis., Aug. 25, 1828; Prairie du Chien, Wis., July 29, 1829; Miami Bay, Ohio, Aug. 30, 1831; Maumee, Ohio, Feb. 18, 1833; Chicago, Ill.,

Sept. 26, 1833; Washington, D. C., Mar. 28, 1836; Council Bluffs, Iowa, June 5 and 17, 1846; Detroit, Mich., July 31, 1855, and Washington, D. C., June 24, 1862.

"The population of the different Ottawa groups is not known with certainty. In 1906 the Chippewa and Ottawa on Manitoulin and Cockburn ids., Canada, were 1,497, of whom about half were Ottawa; there were 197 Ottawa under the Seneca School, Okla., and in Michigan 5,587 scattered Chippewa and Ottawa in 1900, of whom about two-thirds are Ottawa. The total is therefore about 4,700."

Source: *Handbook of American Indians, Part 2*, pp. 170–171.

SELECTED REFERENCES ON THE OTTAWA
AS OF 1952

Andrews, H. A. Quapaw Subagency Ten Year Program Report. 1944. 31 pp. (Bureau of Indian Affairs).
Holst, J. H. A Survey of the Indian Groups in the State of Michigan. 1939. 26 pp. (Bureau of Indian Affairs).
Kinietz, W. V. The Indian Tribes of the Western Great Lakes. Occasional Contributions from the Museum of Anthropology of the University of Michigan, Vol. X, pp. 226–307, 1940.
Krzywicki, Ludwik. Primitive Society and its Vital Statistics. London, 1934. pp. 464–5.
Mooney, J., and Hewitt, J. N. B. Ottawa. Bulletin of the Bureau of American Ethnology, Vol. XXX, ii, pp. 167–72, 1910.
Murdock, Geo. P. Ethnographic Bibliography of North America, 1941. p. 104.
Perrot, N. Memoir on the Manners, Customs, and Religion of the Savages of North America. Indian Tribes of the Upper Mississippi Valley. Ed. E. H. Blair. Cleveland, Ohio. Vol. I, pp. 25–272, 1911.
Wright, Muriel H. A Guide to the Indian Tribes of Oklahoma. Norman, 1951. Ottawa, pp. 200–2.

31

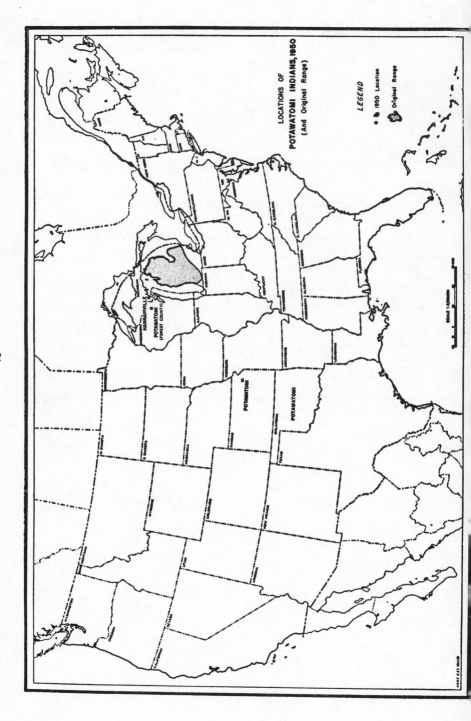

LOCATIONS OF
POTAWATOMI INDIANS, 1950
(And Original Range)

LEGEND

● 1950 Location

◉ Original Range

32

". . . After the conquest of the Illinois, about 1765, they took possession of the part of Illinois lying n. e. of the country seized by the Sauk, Foxes, and Kickapoo, at the same time spreading eastward over southern Michigan and gradually approaching the Wabash. At the treaty of Greenville, in 1795, they notified the Miami that they intended to move down upon the Wabash, which they soon afterward did, in spite of the protests of the Miami, who claimed that whole region. By the beginning of the 19th century they were in possession of the country around the head of L. Michigan, from Milwaukee r. in Wisconsin to Grand r. in Michigan, extending s. w. over a large part of n. Illinois, e. across Michigan to L. Erie, and s. in Indiana to the Wabash and as far down as Pine cr. Within this territory they had about 50 villages. The principal divisions were those of St Joseph r. and Huron r., Mich., Wabash r., and the Prairie band of Potawatomi in Illinois and Wisconsin.

The Potawatomi sided actively with the French down to the peace of 1763; they were prominent in the rising under Pontiac, and on the breaking out of the Revolution in 1775 took arms against the United States and continued hostilities until the treaty of Greenville in 1795. They again took up arms in the British interest in 1812, and made final treaties of peace in 1815. As the settlements rapidly pressed upon them, they sold their land by piece-meal, chiefly between the years 1836 and 1841 and removed beyond·the Mississippi. A large part of those residing in Indiana refused to leave their homes until driven out by military force. A part of them escaped into Canada and are now settled on Walpole id. in L. St Clair. Those who went w. were settled partly in w. Iowa and partly in Kansas, the former, with whom were many individuals of other tribes, being known as Prairie Potawatomi, while the others were known as Potawatomi of the Woods. In 1846 they were all united on a reservation in s. Kansas. A part of them was known as the Keotuc band. In 1861 a large part of the tribe took lands in severalty and became known as Citizen Potawatomi, but in 1868 they again removed to a tract in Indian Ter. (Oklahoma), where they now are. The others are still in Kansas, while a considerable body, part of the Prairie bands, is yet in Wisconsin, and another band, the Potawatomi of Huron, is in lower Michigan.

The tribe probably never greatly exceeded 3,000 souls, and most estimates place them far below that number. The principal estimates give them about 1,500 in 1765, 1,750 in 1766, 2,250 in 1778, 2,000 in 1783, 1,200 in 1795, 2,500 in 1812, 3,400 in 1820, and 1,800 in 1843. The last estimate does not include those who had recently fled to Canada. In 1908 those in the United States were reported to number 2,522 distributed as follows: Citizen Potawatomi in Oklahoma, 1,768; Prairie band in Kansas 676; and Potawatomi of Huron, in Calhoun co., Mich., 78. A few besides these are scattered through their ancient territory and at various other points. Those in British territory

33

are all in the province of Ontario and number about 220, of whom 176 are living with Chippewa and Ottawa on Walpole id. in L. St. Clair, and the remainder (no longer officially reported) are divided between Caradoc and Riviere aux Sables, where they reside by permission of the Chippewa and Munsee.

The Potawatomi have participated in the following treaties with the United States: Ft Harmar, Ohio, Jan. 9, 1789; Greenville, Ohio, Aug. 3, 1795; Ft Wayne, Ind., June 7, 1803; Ft Industry, Ohio, July 4, 1805; Grouseland, Ind., Aug. 21, 1805; Detroit, Mich., Nov. 17, 1807; Brownstown, Mich., Nov. 25, 1808; Ft Wayne, Ind., Sept. 30, 1809; Greenville, Ohio, July 22, 1814; Portage des Sioux, Mo., July 18, 1815; Spring Wells, Mich., Sept. Sept. 8, 1815; St Louis, Mo., Aug. 24, 1816; Miami, Ohio, Sept. 29, 1817; St Mary's, Ohio, Oct. 2, 1818; Chicago, Ill., Aug. 29, 1821; Prairie du Chien, Wis., Aug. 19, 1825; Wabash, Ind., Oct. 16, 1826; St Joseph, Mich, Sept. 19, 1827; Green Bay, Wis., Aug. 25, 1828; St Joseph River, Mich., Sept. 20, 1828; Prairie du Chien, Wis., July 29, 1829; Camp Tippecanoe, Ind., Oct. 20, 1832; Tippecanoe River, Ind., Oct. 26 and 27, 1832; Chicago, Ill., Sept. 26, 1833; Lake Maxeeniekuekee, Ind., Dec. 4, 1834; Tippecanoe River, Ind., Dec. 10, 1834; Potawattomie Mills, Ind., Dec. 16, 1834; Potawattimie Mills, Ind., Dec. 16, 1834; Logansport, Ind., Dec. 17, 1834; Turkey Creek Prairie, Ind., March 26, 1836; Tippecanoe River, Ind., Mar. 29 and Apr. 11, 1836; Indian Agency, Ind., Apr. 22, 1836; Yellow River, Ind., Aug. 5, 1836; Chippewanaung, Ind., Sept. 20, 22, and 23, 1836; Washington, D. C., Feb. 11, 1837; Council Bluffs, Iowa, June 5 and 17, 1846; Kansas River, Kan., Nov. 15, 1861; Washington, D. C., Feb. 27, 1867."

Source: *Handbook of American Indians, Part 2*, pp. 290–291.

POTAWATOMI POPULATION

"This tribe, when first known, inhabited what is now the Lower Peninsula of Michigan. Later they moved to the Upper Peninsula and then gradually to the south and west to their present locations in Kansas and Oklahoma. The tribe is widely scattered. The greatest concentration is in Jackson County, Kansas, where 573 were enumerated. There were 347 Potawatomi in Pottawatomie County, Oklahoma, and 288 in Forest County, Wisconsin. Indians were returned as Potawatomi from 19 different states, from New York to California. The total number enumerated in 1930 was 1,854, as compared with 2,440 in 1910. Of the total number in 1930, 38.0 percent were returned as full blood. The largest proportion of full bloods was in the Wisconsin band, the Oklahoma and Kansas Potawatomi being mainly of mixed blood."

Source: *The Indian Population of the United States and Alaska*, 1930, p. 39.

Selected References on the Potawatomi
AS OF 1952

Bruce, H. E. Potawatomi Agency Ten Year Program Report. 1944. 62 pp. (Bureau of Indian Affairs).

Cavell, C. Great Lakes Agency Ten Year Program Report. 1944. 257 pp. (Bureau of Indian Affairs).

Gilmore, Thomas R. Shawnee Agency Ten Year Program Report. 1944. 17 pp. (Bureau of Indian Affairs).

Great Lakes Ten Year Program Summary. 1944. 54 pp. (Bureau of Indian Affairs).

Kryzyicki, Ludwik. Primitive Society and Its Vital Statistics. London, 1934. pp. 467–9.

Mooney, J. and Hewitt, J. N B. Potawatomi. Bulletin of the Bureau of American Ethnology, Vol. XXX, ii, pp. 289–93, 1910.

Murdock, Geo. P. Ethnographical Bibliography of North America. 1941. p. 90.

Skinner, A. The Mascoutens or Prairie Potawatomi Indians. Bulletins of the Public Museum of the City of Milwaukee, Vol. VI, pp. 1–411, 1924–1927.

Tiedke, K. E. A Study of the Hannahville Indian Community, Menominee County, Michigan. 1949. 29 pp. (Bureau of Indian Affairs).

Wright, Muriel H. A Guide to the Indian Tribes of Oklahoma. Norman, 1951. Potawatomi pp. 214–18.

A STUDY OF INDIAN TRIBES
IN ROYCE AREAS 48, 96-A,
110, 177 AND 98, ILLINOIS
AND INDIANA, 1640-1832

by
Dr. Joseph Jablow
Brooklyn, New York
June 1967

37

TABLE OF CONTENTS

39

40

INTRODUCTION

The purpose of this study is to ascertain the relationship of Illinois, Kickapoo, and Potawatomi Indians to certain areas of Illinois and Indiana. It was undertaken at the request of attorneys representing the following Indian groups before the Indian Claims Commission of the United States: the Kickapoo Tribe of Oklahoma, the Kickapoo Tribe of Kansas, the Peoria Tribe of Oklahoma (the present tribal organization of the Peoria, Kaskaskia, Wea, and Piankeshaw Indians), the Citizen Band of Potawatomi, and the Prairie Band of Potawatomi. These Indians have claims arising out of cessions made by their predecessor groups in Illinois and an adjoining part of Indiana as delineated in the following Royce Areas: 110, 96a, 48, 177, 98 (Royce, 1899, maps 17, 18, 19).

The study has been organized in the following manner:

a) the relevant data are arranged and discussed in chronological sequence.

b) the report is divided into a series of sections covering varying periods of time; some of the time divisions are arbitrary, employed for convenience in analyzing the data, while some are made at points which culminated in changes, such as treaties, or new conditions, such as warfare.

c) A summary and conclusions from the data precede the detailed presentation.

Section I (1640–1673) deals with the initial period of recorded contact in Wisconsin, where Kickapoo and Potawatomi were located, and where parties of Illinois who came to Wisconsin to trade were met by European observers.

Section II (1673–1680) adduces data which indicate the outline of the

41

Illinois tribal area and identifies the location of their villages.

Section III (1680–1687) describes the influence of La Salle's plans upon the Illinois and other Indians, and it includes an account of Iroquois hostilities against the Illinois which were probably induced by La Salle's activities in the area.

Section IV (1687–1703) discusses the changes in village locations of Illinois groups, influenced by early French plans of trade and development.

Sections V (1703–1715) and VI (1715–1730) reveal the continuing French impact on intertribal relations resulting in a proliferation of hostilities. The Illinois supported the French in periodic warfare with the Fox, who were in turn supported by the Kickapoo and their Mascouten confreres.

Section VII (1730–1750) covers a period in which Kickapoo and Mascouten are first found in villages on the Wabash and the upper Illinois River.

Section VIII (1750–1763) deals with the impact on the Illinois Indians of French trade and settlement on the Mississippi. By the end of the period Kickapoo (with Mascouten) and Potawatomi have moved into the traditional Illinois tribal area.

Section IX (1763–1777) covers the period of British hegemony until the inception of the American war of independence.

Section X (1777–1795) encompasses the years ending with the treaty of Greenville entered into between the United States government and various Indian tribes concerning the lands northwest of the Ohio River.

Section XI (1795–1819) is the period during which most of the treaties of cession were made.

The final section (1819–1832) concerns only Potawatomi in connection with the cession made in 1832.

SUMMARY AND CONCLUSIONS

The Illinois

From at least as early as 1640 until approximately the middle of the eighteenth century the major portion of the state of Illinois was inhabited and exploited by various tribes of Illinois Indians. Since in the course of time portions of the aboriginal Illinois tribal area came to be controlled by Kickapoo and Potawatomi Indians, discussion of the first century covered by this study focuses largely, but by no means exclusively, on the Illinois Indians and on the context of historical forces which motivated their southerly orientation and movement within this area.

The first direct observations of the Illinois in their villages derive from 1673 to 1674. The records indicate that before the arrival of La Salle in the area at the beginning of 1680 Illinois Indian tribes were spread from the northern Illinois River southward as far as the Ohio.

These early European visitors reported a large village comprising several groups (or parts of them) of Illinois Indians situated on the upper Illinois River. Other villages and camps were visited southward along the Illinois and on the Mississippi rivers some miles above the mouth of the Ohio. By the end of the seventeenth century the Illinois tribes had occupied village locations from about 150 miles up the Kankakee River at least as far south as the mouth of the Kaskaskia River on the Mississippi, where Kaskaskia Indians established themselves in 1703, after moving from Lake Peoria, where the Peoria tribe of Illinois remained.

From 1710 to 1730 the Illinois were engaged in hostilities with the Fox at various times, as were other Indians, and on several occasions the Illinois participated in campaigns of the French against the same intransigent foe. Because the Kickapoo and Mascouten were allies of the Fox, the

Illinois had become embroiled with them also. But in 1730 an apparently lasting peace was effected between Illinois and Kickapoo. Despite periodic involvement in hostilities, Illinois villages continued to be occupied along the Illinois and Mississippi rivers, and their hunting apparently extended from Starved Rock in the north, to the Ohio-Wabash area in the southeast.

The end of the French and Indian Wars also saw the end of Illinois tribal influence in the northern reaches of their traditional area. From the outset of the eighteenth century the Illinois had been attracted to French trade along the American Bottom of the Mississippi. By 1763 their villages were mainly located in the same area, and their hunting became increasingly constricted within the southern half of Illinois.

After 1797 the Peoria tribe of the Illinois were mainly to be found west of the Mississippi. Kaskaskia, however, remained in the Illinois territory east of the Mississippi River.

The Kickapoo

The earliest reported contacts with Kickapoo Indians occurred in Wisconsin. Prior to 1734 there is no record of Kickapoo or Mascouten (generally found in association with, and apparently absorbed by, the Kickapoo) in or on the border of the area under study. In 1734 Kickapoo are reported on the Illinois River and on the Wabash near the French post of Ouiatanon, on the northwest side of the river a few miles below Lafayette.

Although the main Kickapoo village was then reported to be on the upper Illinois River, there are no subsequent accounts of this village location. On the Wabash, however, a Kickapoo village was occupied opposite a large Wea village on the southeast shore, until it was destroyed by General Scott in 1790. Kickapoo and Mascouten continued to be identified with locations west and southwest of Ouiatanon, and to utilize the Wabash River area.

44

As of 1764, Kickapoo hunting took them as much as 225 miles from their village near Ouiatanon. In subsequent years reports relate Kickapoo and Mascouten to various locations in the Illinois country, including the Illinois, Kankakee and Iroquois Rivers. As of 1790, Kickapoo appear to have been established for some years in the prairies of central Illinois, and they had villages on the Sangamon River and its affluents.

Until their treaty of cession in 1819, Kickapoo maintained their position in Illinois. The main focus of Kickapoo settlement and subsistence activity was in central Illinois within an area bounded on the north by the Illinois and Kankakee Rivers; and on the west by the Illinois River and a small segment of the Mississippi between the Illinois and Missouri Rivers. The southern boundary of Royce Area 110, at about the latitude of the mouth of the Illinois River, seems to be a reasonable approximation of the southern Kickapoo range, while the Illinois-Indiana border roughly approximates the extent of their eastward range. As suggested below in the summary and conclusions on the Potawatomi, a Kickapoo boundary within Royce Area 177 might reasonably be located west of the state line, and within Royce Area 98, east of the state line.

45

The Potawatomi

Potawatomi claims are concerned only with Royce Area 177 in northeastern Illinois, and Royce Area 98 on the Wabash River. Potawatomi utilization of these areas is first reported in the second helf of the eighteenth century.

In 1763 the Kankakee River and the Illinois River as far down as Starved Rock were referred to as the chief Potawatomi hunting ground. In subsequent years Potawatomi activity in the northeastern portion of Illinois, and in Area 177 in particular, seems to have been more intensive and

extensive than that of the Kickapoo whose orientation was toward central
Illinois. Potawatomi were dispersed along the Kankakee River and its
affluents, a center of activity peripheral to the area of Kickapoo activity.
If it is necessary to draw a line between Potawatomi and Kickapoo territories
in Area 177, the Kankakee River, the Iroquois River, and Spring Creek—a
branch of the Iroquois—would provide a reasonable approximation.

With respect to Area 98, by the year 1778 a group of Potawatomi was
established on the Tippecanoe River in Indiana, the northeastern boundary of
Area 98. A few documents of special interest appear to refer to this group.
A 1790 report mentions a band of Potawatomi who lived near the Wea, one of
the Miami tribes. As noted above, there was a Wea village on the Wabash, a
few miles below the site of Lafayette. In 1795 an army officer going up the
Wabash observed land in the vicinity of the Tippecanoe River under cultivation
by Potawatomi and Wea Indians. In 1796 a chief of the Potawatomi of
St. Joseph declared that, by reason of the friendship of the Miami, "a part
of our nation has been permitted to live and hunt at, and near the
Thopincanos [Tippecanoe]". Earlier, in 1789, Kickapoo Indians, visited by
an American emissary on the Wabash, apparently at or near their village in
the vicinity of Quiatanon, referred to the Wea as "the owners of their
[Kickapoo] lands".

The evidence of Wea-Potawatomi and of Wea-Kickapoo association does
not indicate where boundary lines may be drawn. As between the Kickapoo and
Potawatomi the reference to Pine Creek in the Potawatomi cession treaty of
1818 implies that a line may be drawn somewhere between that creek and the
Vermillion River, the southwestern boundary of Area 98 and the site of a
Kickapoo village.

I - 1640-1673

The earliest references to the Illinois, Kickapoo and Potawatomi are found in the period 1640-1660. Of the three, the Illinois then had the largest population, and were referred to most frequently.

The first published reference to the Illinois appears in the Jesuit Relations in the report submitted by Father Le Jeune for the year 1640. He states that beyond the Menominee, upon the shores of "the second fresh-water sea" (Lake Michigan) dwell the Winnebago, in the neighborhood of whom are the Sioux, Assiniboin, Illinois, Maskouten and Potawatomi (JR 18:231). Le Jeune goes on to say that the names of these "nations" who are among those situated beyond the St. Lawrence and "the great lakes of the Hurons on the North" were given him by Nicolet, who visited them "for the most part in their own country." Thus, the earliest references to the Illinois are not based upon direct observation. The information is derived from individuals who, like Nicolet, and Radisson and Groseillers, had either met them "in their own country" or learned about them from other Indians (ibid. pp. 231-233; pp. 260-1 last paragraph).

47

During the period covered by The Relation of 1640, or shortly before, the Illinois are said to have virtually exterminated the Winnebago, near the shores of Green Bay, in retaliation for the latter's treachery after the Illinois had come to their aid following a series of Winnebago misfortunes (Blair 1: 295-300; JR 54: 237; JR 55:183).

In his account of the events of 1642 Lalemant, discussing the journey of Jogues and Raymbault to the Sault, says that they "obtained information about a great many other sedentary nations" including the Sioux, who are engaged in "continual wars" with the Cree, Illinois, "and other great nations who inhabit the same country" (JR 23: 225-227). It is not, however, entirely clear that it is the Sioux alone who are at war with the Cree, Illinois, and others, although the context lends some degree of plausibility to such meaning. Occasional hostilities between Sioux and Illinois at this time do not seem unreasonable in view of later direct evidence of such relations between them.

The foregoing data, then, suggest the likelihood that in the time period around 1640 the Illinois were, or had been, engaged in hostilities, with the Sioux on the one hand and the Winnebago on the other, in the areas of the upper Mississippi River and Green Bay.

The anonymous author of the Relation of 1657-58 includes information provided by Father Gabriel Dreuillettes whose sources were again probably Radisson and Grosseilers as well as Indians from the upper country. This account makes reference to fourteen "nations" whose locations and directions are generally described in relation to a point of orientation which is a village of Potawatomi that Dreuillettes named Saint Michel. The location of this village is not given in the report, but Thwaites says that "it was apparently at some point on the west shore of Lake Michigan" (JR 45: 324, fn 21). Dreuillettes says further that the Potawatomi had for neighbors a group of Ottawas and, also "Nagaouichirinionck", the latter of whom Thwaites considers "a band of Illinois" (idem). Thwaites' location of the Potawatomi village on the west shore of Lake Michigan (or Green Bay) seems reasonable in view of the statements by Dreuillettes that the Winnebago "are but a very short distance" from it, and that the Mascouten and Fox are "about three days' journey inland, by water. . ." (ibid. p. 247).

Of all the groups to which Dreuillettes makes reference the Illinois is the largest, for "it is computed at fully 20,000 men and sixty villages, making about a hundred thousand souls in all. It is seven days' journey

48

Westward from St. Michel" (ibid. p. 247). In the circumstances these figures cannot, of course, be accepted literally, but they probably reflect the relative size of the Illinois population as compared with the other groups mentioned in this source.

Perrot's sojourn in the western country began in 1665. While his "Memoire" makes reference to events, especially the Iroquois wars, which took place before this date, he includes only material which, he says, the "early relations" of these events omitted, "and which I have learned from the lips of the old men among the Outaoua tribes" (Blair, 1916, 1:151). It may be assumed, therefore, that the following information about past events was obtained from Indian informants.

What he reports to be "the first acquaintance" of the Illinois with the Iroquois is described by Perrot. He writes that after putting the Hurons and the Nipissings to flight, the Iroquois turned upon the Ottawa in the Green Bay area in 1653. After making efforts over a period of two years, the Iroquois failed to subdue their intended victims. The attackers then divided themselves in two parties and left. One of them was soon defeated by a combination of Chippewa and two other Algonkian groups (ibid. p. 153). The main Iroquois force went southwest into buffalo country where they killed the women and children of "a small Illinoet village", while the men ran for assistance to "other Illinoet villages, who were hunting at various places in that vicinity. . ." In Perrot's words the Illinois "utterly defeated" the Iroquois after the latter had killed the women and children of an Illinois "village" or encampment (ibid. pp. 153-157). This encounter probably took place in 1655 or 1656 and it may have initiated a period of hostile relations which continued intermittently until some time towards the close of the seventeenth century. It was undoubtedly the Iroquois, abetted

49

unintentionally by a French policy which was designed to urge their allies to war against the Iroquois, who contributed in significant measure to the ultimate decline of Illinois power.

From "two Frenchmen", undoubtedly Radisson and Groseillers, who, after two years in the northwest, returned in August 1656 with an Ottawa trading flotilla of fifty canoes loaded with furs, it was learned that among the "many nations surrounding" the Winnebago, the Illinois "their neighbors, comprise about sixty villages;. . ." (JR 42:221).

In July 1660 a Jesuit (Dreuillettes?) met on the Saguenay River a group of eighty Indians among whom was a leader, or chief, who had passed the summer of 1658 and the following winter on the shores of Lake Superior. This man told the Father that "the whole length of its coast is lined with Algonkin nations, fear of the Iroquois having forced them to seek there an asylum" (JR 45:217-19).

When the priest returned to Quebec later in the summer (1660) he met "two Frenchmen" (Radisson and Groseillers) who had just arrived from the upper country, having "passed the winter on the shores of Lake Superior, . . ." During their journeyings in that region they visited "the remnants of the Hurons of the Tobacco Nation" who had fled from the Iroquois to take refuge among the Illinois, situated "six days' journey beyond the lake toward the Southwest." There, on the banks of a "beautiful River, large, wide, deep, . . . they found the great Nation of the Alimiwec, which gave them a very kind reception. This Nation comprises sixty villages--. . ." (JR 45:235).

This information concerning sixty villages of Illinois repeats what the "two Frenchmen" had previously revealed on their return from the upper country in 1656 (see JR 42:221 above). Now, however, the likelihood is that the Illinois are located in the Mississippi River area, whereas in

50

1640 the Illinois were vaguely identified as "neighbors" of the Winnebago.
They do not, however, confirm Perrot's account of Illinois-Iroquois hostilities in the area west or southwest of the Great Lakes. That the Iroquois
were making incursions into the Western Great Lakes at this time as reported
by Perrot, is confirmed by what the converted Indian told the priest on the
Saguenay River, i.e., that "all the Nations surrounding the Bay" had given
him presents to take "to the French and Algonkins of these regions, -- to
attract them to their Bay, in order that they might all fortify themselves
there against the Iroquois,--" (JR 45:233).

    At first, the Potawatomi, apparently, were the primary customers of
the Ottawa middlemen who sold them European articles which they had obtained
from the French (La Potherie in Blair, 1911, 1:303). Subsequently, at the
time that Perrot made his first visit among the Potawatomi who "dwelt at the
foot of [Green Bay]," they were guided by an Ottawa to Montreal in order to
engage in direct trade with the French (ibid. p. 309). Upon the return of
this expedition, the Potawatomi "sent deputies in every direction to inform
the Islinois, Miamis, Outagamis [Fox], Mashoutechs, and Kikabous that they
had been at Montreal, whence they had brought much merchandise; they besought
those tribes to visit them and bring them beavers. Those tribes were too far
away to profit by this at first;..." (ibid. p. 316-17). The Fox, responding
to this invitation to trade, settled for the winter thirty leagues (75 miles)
from Green Bay in a village of over six hundred cabins. In the spring they
informed the Sac, at the northern end of Green Bay, of their new settlement
(ibid. p. 317). The following summer "fifteen cabins of Islinois" in
addition to Miami, Mascouten, and Kickapoo "came toward the bay" and "made
their clearings thirty miles away, beside the Outagamis, toward the south."
(ibid. p. 321).

51

Temple suggests that this event occurred "about the year 1666" (Temple, 1958, p. 13). After planting their crops the newcomers went on a bison hunt, which must have taken them generally south and west.

Assuming, as Temple seems to think, the year of this movement to the Green Bay area to be 1666 we may look at what the Jesuits tell us happened during 1666-7. Allouez writes in his Journal that the Potawatomi country lies along Lake Michigan (JR 51:27). The country of the Fox "lies Southward [Southeast from Chequamequon] toward" Lake Michigan (ibid. p. 43). The Sac are "wandering and scattered in the forests,. . ." (ibid. p. 45).

Of the Illinois, Allouez says that he understands them "only slightly, because I have talked with them only a very little" and that "their country" is "more than sixty leagues [150 miles] hence [from Chequamequon] toward the south, beyond a great river--. . . these people are hunters and warriors, using bows and arrows, rarely muskets, and never canoes. They used to be a populous nation, divided into ten large Villages; but now they are reduced to two, continual wars with the Nadouessi [Sioux] on one side and the Iroquois on the other having well nigh exterminated them" (JR 51:47).

Allouez was at the St. Esprit mission at Chequamegon Bay on Lake Superior from 1665 to 1667 where, he says, most of the people never saw Europeans before. Although he did not visit the Illinois area he preached to eighty members of the tribe who carried the word of Christ "and published it with approbation to the whole country of the South;. . ." (ibid. p. 49). Although he makes this statement about the Illinois as a populous nation in the past tense it agrees with earlier references to their numbers. The number of their villages is now said to have been ten, a considerable reduction in estimate from a supposed 60. That they were now reduced to two villages, all told, does not at all agree with later direct evidence.

Hostilities with the Iroquois are confirmed from 1655 on; occasional hostilities with the Sioux earlier are referred to in the sources and are definite at a later time (See JR 23:225-7 above, and data of La Salle below). Marquette, in about 1670, said that the Illinois "were formerly at war with the Nadouessi [Sioux], but made peace with them some years ago, which I confirmed, in order to facilitate their coming to la Pointe,--where I am going to await them, that I may accompany them into their Country" (JR 54:191). But that they were "well-nigh exterminated" was, as Mark Twain said of the report of his death, exaggerated.

In fact, Father Claude Dablon, writing of the peoples connected with the St. Esprit Mission on Chaquamegon Bay in 1669-70, informs us, still without direct evidence, that "the Ilinois, tribes extending toward the South, have five large Villages, of which one has a stretch of three leagues, the cabins being placed lengthwise. They number nearly two thousand souls, and repair to this place from time to time in great numbers, as Merchants, to carry away hatchets and kettles, guns, and other articles that they need..." (JR 54:167). While the Illinois seem to have come to Chequamegon regularly to trade, this was not the case with the Sioux who, because of the "extensive warfare" they wage "with our Hurons and with some other Nations of those Regions" came to Chequamegon "only in small numbers" (idem).

53

Father Marquette, in a letter to the Father Superior of Missions, writes that "the Illinois are distant from la pointe [Chequamegon Bay] thirty days' journey by land, by a very difficult route, and live by themselves, Southwestward from the point of saint Esprit" (ibid. p. 185). If Marquette's information respecting distance and direction is correct, then the Illinois might have been, at this time some distance west of the Mississippi River as Temple (1958, p. 13) and Hyde (1962, p. 135) seem to believe. Such a conclusion from the data can only be highly inferential, and seems, in large part, to have been perpetuated by Father Tailhan, the original editor of Perrot's Memoire, who wrote that "the war between the Iroquois and the Illinois [1656-1667] brought on the ruin of the latter people, and those who escaped took refuge beyond the Mississippi" (Blair, 1911, 1:155). As Hunt (1960, pp. 145-6) points out, there is no "reliable mention" in the liter-ature of a conflict between the Illinois and Iroquois during this period "of sufficient proportions to have driven the numerous and powerful Illinois across the Mississippi River."

What might appear to lend support to the contention that the Illinois at this time were west of the Mississippi is Marquette's statement later on in his letter: "When the Illinois come to la Pointe, they cross a great river which is nearly a league in width, flows from North to South, and to such a distance that the Illinois, who do not know what a Canoe is, have not yet heard any mention of its mouth" (JR 54:189). But if they travelled by land, as Marquette says, the route on the west side of the river might have been safer, thus accounting for the statement that they cross a great river. And in arriving at, and departing from, Chequamegon Bay their direction could very well have been southwest as Marquette says it was (ibid p. 185). But he also says that the Sioux "are toward the Southwest from the Mission of St. Esprit" (ibid. p. 191). If, as seems likely, in coming to Chequamegon the Illinois had to pass through Sioux territory, then the two tribes were in amity at the time. In fact Marquette specifically says that they made peace some years ago (idem). In this connection a Jesuit map accompanying the Relation of 1670-71 is of some importance (JR 55: facing p. 94). Running southward from "La Pointe du Esprit" (Chequamegon Bay) is a straight dotted line which ends at the cartouche in the lower left hand corner. This line,

according to the inscription, is the "Road to the Illinois at 150 leagues
[375 miles] toward the South." We can hardly take this line literally, but
it is obvious that due south, or southwest, the Mississippi must be crossed.
Furthermore, if this line represents, in fact, a route regularly traversed
by the Illinois, then they probably had a peaceful understanding with the
Sioux.

The point of the foregoing discussion is that on the basis of
Marquette's statement, the Illinois were not necessarily located west of the
Mississippi, although they probably made crossings of that river in journey-
ing to Chequamegon Bay.

Marquette also says that en route to the Illinois "One passes the
Nation of the Ketchigamins, who live in the interior, constitute more than
twenty large cabins. ..." and fear the Illinois. "One goes on then to the
[Miami], and, after crossing great prairies, reaches the Illinois, who are
mainly gathered in two Villages, containing more than eight or nine thousand
souls" (ibid, p. 185-187).

It is interesting to observe how two documents, each from the pen of
a different author, written at about the same time (1670?) make reference to
the Illinois with contradictory data. Dablon, quoted above (JR 54:167), gives
the Illinois five villages, and a population of about two thousand, whereas
Marquette makes reference to two villages and 8-9,000 people. Although
neither of these Fathers was a personal observer, Marquette would seem to be
the more reliable of the two because he had direct contact with the Illinois
who traded at Chequamegon Bay. He was still learning the language, however,
and was using, probably Ottawa, interpreters. The number of Villages is
consistent with the information of Allouez who preceded Marquette at the St.
Esprit Mission. But Marquette's information might have come from Allouez

55

(JR 51:47). Dablon, on the other hand, was writing from Sault St. Marie.

Marquette states, further, that "the Illinois are warriors and take a great many Slaves, whom they trade with the Outaouaks for Muskets, Powder, Kettles, Hatchets and Knives" (JR 54:191). It is not entirely clear why the Illinois should have traded captives rather than beaver for the desired European goods, but this was obviously a commodity acceptable to the Ottawa. A reasonable explanation might be that rich sources of Beaver were available to the Ottawa both through their own hunting and from trade with others in their more immediate area. If they avoided warfare, insofar as possible, in order to keep secure their middleman position by as wide a range of friendly relations as they could effect, then a trade for captives would replace whatever losses they might suffer from occasional forays of enemies; and it also relieved them from the necessity of intensifying hostilities too greatly by retaliatory attacks. There were alternative ways of obtaining satisfaction by peaceful means if they were concerned to minimize hostilities disruptive of their trade. Furthermore, the captives obtained in trade could have provided a labor supply useful in their trading ventures while they were at the same time a source of additional numerical strength for the protection of the group.

56

I have not explored the nature of Sioux-Ottawa relations, but if, as Marquette states with regard to the Sioux, "All the nations of the Lake make war on them, but with little success" then this may be a partial explanation of the Ottawa need for captives. That the Sioux dominated the area west of the Great Lakes is clear from Marquette's request that the Sioux permit him free passage in the autumn to visit the Illinois. The Sioux assented, but they informed Marquette that they would come to his Mission in the autumn "to hold council with the Illinois and talk with me" (ibid. p. 193). It is

possible that the Sioux were concerned over the prospect of the French
establishing themselves among the Illinois and becoming a source of strength
to the latter. In view of subsequent developments, through the medium of
LaSalle's enterprises in the Illinois area, the fears of the Sioux were
probably justified, for by 1680 the Sioux and the Illinois are engaged in
hostilities while at the same time the latter are under devastating attack
from the east by the Iroquois (see below).

It is quite clear from a letter of Allouez, who came to Green Bay,
where he founded the Mission of St. Francis Xavier in December of 1669, that
the Sioux were the dominant force in Wisconsin at that time. Upon his arrival
at the south end of Green Bay he found several villages in the area, in one
of which were living Sac, Fox, Potawatomi and Winnebago (JR 54:205). He
subsequently visited: a village of Potawatomi on the east side of Green Bay;
Sac on Little Fox River; Fox on the Wolf River; Mascouten on the Upper Fox
River; and, beyond the latter, Miami and Kickapoo (ibid.p. 207-237). The
Kickapoo, he says, are four leagues from the Mascouten-Miami village (ibid.
p. 233).

Not only are these Wisconsin tribes in fear of the Sioux; they also
are subjected to the depredations of the Iroquois. In writing of his passage
on Lake Winnebago, Allouez notes that it "is uninhabited, on account of the
Nadouecis [Sioux], who are there held in fear" (ibid.p. 217). When he
arrived at the Fox Village he learned that the preceding month, while the
men were out hunting, eighteen Seneca attacked "six large cabins" of these
people, apparently in winter quarters, two days' journey from "the foot" of
Lake Michigan, killing all in the camp except thirty women captives (ibid.
p. 219-221). According to Allouez the Fox "are often killed by them
[Iroquois]" (ibid. p. 225). Although the Fox "withdrew to those regions to

57

escape the persecution of the Iroquois, and settled in an excellent country" they can hardly be said to have found peace; for, Allouez continues, "they are at war with the Nadouecious, their neighbors" (ibid. p. 223). Among the Mascouten, too, Allouez was told "the Nadouessious and the Iroquois are eating us;. . ." (ibid. p. 229). Both groups, Mascouten and Fox, requested the missionary to intercede for them in the interests of peace.

It seems, therefore, that the area north of the Illinois, in Wisconsin, was, to say the least, in a state of tension in 1670, with pressures being applied from east and west by the Iroquois and Sioux respectively. In this situation it is not difficult to predict that such pressures could ultimately produce a bulge to the north or to the south into which movements from the pressure zone might take place. The Wisconsin tribes, being culturally ill-adapted for life north of the Great Lakes, would, under ordinary circum-stances, not move in that direction. And, as it happens, historic opportunity arose in the area to the south. Assisting in the process of movement from the Wisconsin area southward there soon was to appear another opposite force, the attraction of French establishments in what came to be known as the Illinois country. In time, the Illinois found the flow of the tide an irresistible force. At this point, however, the Illinois, like the Wisconsin tribes, had experienced attack from both Sioux and Iroquois, but they may have had the advantage of being more distant from the home bases of those two formidable adversaries. In any event, peace had been made with the Sioux, thus insuring safe passage for the Illinois to trade at Chequamegon Bay. As for the consequences of hostilities with the Iroquois, I have already stated that, like Hunt, I found no evidence that the Iroquois attacked with sufficient force or frequency to cause an apparently populous group like the Illinois to seek refuge west of the Mississippi.

One possible source for the belief that the Illinois were west of the Mississippi has been suggested above in connection with Marquette's letter from the St. Esprit Mission. But it is Father Claude Dablon, writing at Quebec in 1671, who makes positive assertions respecting the trans-Mississippi habitation of the Illinois at that time. "Beyond that great river lie the eight Villages of the Ilinois, a hundred leagues [250 miles] from saint Esprit point; while forty or fifty leagues Westward from the latter place is found the Nation of the Nadouessi, - very populous and warlike, and regarded as the Iroquois of these regions, waging war, almost unaided, with all the other tribes hereabout" (JR 55:97). There are two points to be made about this statement. First, Dablon has revised upward the figure he gave for the number of Illinois villages the year before, which was five (JR 54:167). Second, he confirms the earlier observations of Allouez concerning Sioux hostilities against the tribes in the western Great Lakes region. Later, in the same account, he writes that the Illinois, having taken refuge on the shores of Lake Michigan from their enemies, were driven from there by the Iroquois, and "they finally withdrew to a spot seven days' journey beyond the great river" (JR 55:101). In 1657-8, it will be recalled, Dreuillettes placed the Illinois seven days west (southwest?) of the Potawatomi who were in the vicinity of Green Bay (JR 45:247).

59

Dablon's statement of the supposed total withdrawal by the Illinois to some distance beyond the Mississippi seems to be unsupported by any other source or evidence and is most likely based on the earlier one of Dreuillettes. As a matter of fact, it could be interpreted as contradictory to what Dablon himself says later in this same Relation of 1670-71, when he makes reference to "the Ilinois, who are very numerous and dwell toward the South, . . . near the great river named Missisipi. . ." (JR 55:207). This statement, taken in

context, apparently means south of Chequamegon Bay, on Lake Superior, for in
commenting on the Ottawa Dablon added that "the first who visited point saint
Esprit to trade were called Ilinois" (idem). In the very same document Dablon
makes another statement which, again, appears to conflict with the first two
quotations placing the Illinois west of the Mississippi. Discussing the
tribes in the Green Bay region, he goes on to say that "the remaining tribes,
farther distant toward the South and Southwest, are either beginning to draw
near to us, — for already the Ilinois have reached the [Green] bay mentioned
above, — or else are waiting until we can advance to them" (ibid. p. 103-105).
It is hardly necessary to make the point that this does not necessarily put
the Illinois beyond the Mississippi. In connection with Dablon's reference
to the presence of the Illinois at Green Bay, it is well to remember a quotation cited above, in which as early as 1666 some Illinois, among others from
several different groups, came to trade at Green Bay at the behest of the
Potawatomi (Blair, 1911, 1:321).

This discussion is not to be construed as an effort to reject out of
hand the notion that the Illinois, in whole or in part, could have been
located at times, during the period under discussion, west of the Mississippi.
They certainly ranged more widely than the specific locations of their villages
would indicate; and it is hardly to be doubted that from time to time they
moved through, and exploited, lands west of the Mississippi. They very
probably sojourned in that area and, on occasion, settled there, for Marquette
and Joliet in 1673 did visit Illinois villages in proximity to the west bank
of the river. But it is difficult to accept the contention that they had been
driven there from their homelands by the Iroquois. In spite of the fact that
the latter had a considerably greater supply of guns than the Illinois could
possibly have had at the time, the latter were probably sufficiently numerous

and powerful to avoid being overwhelmed by the Iroquois.

It is, nevertheless, possible that some bands of Illinois decided to move westward, but there is no need to assume that the entire tribe did. Such an inference would appear to be not unreasonable from the comments by Dablon in another part of his report. He was in the Mascouten village on the Upper Fox River, where he also found the Miami, to whom he referred earlier as "one of the Nations of the Ilinois, — being dismembered, so to speak, from the rest, to make its home in these regions" (JR 55:201). He goes on to say: "Now the Ilinois, . . . lie on the farther side of this great river, and from them those [the Miami] living here with the Fire Nation [Mascouten] separated, for the purpose of forming here a sort of transplanted colony, —" (ibid. p. 209). But a few pages later he says: "During our sojourn in this Village [of the Mascouten], twelve or fifteen men arrived there from the real country of the Ilinois, — partly to visit their relatives or their country-men, and partly to do some trading" (ibid. p. 215, italics - JJ). From what Dablon has said of the Illinois heretofore it could be that what he calls the "real country" of the Illinois lay east of the Mississippi; and what the preceding quotations could convey is that the Illinois were situated on both sides of the river. It may be recalled that Dablon has also been quoted as saying that the Illinois are situated "near the great river named Missisipi" (ibid. p. 207); and it has been stated above that two years or so later Marquette and Joliet actually found their villages on the west side of the river. It is not necessary, however, to assume that they (the Illinois) must have taken refuge there. It may well have been part of their customary range where, for various reasons, they located and sojourned from time to time at intervals over the years. At any specific time the nature of inter-tribal relations could have been a factor at work. But there is no evidence to

61

suggest that up to this time the Illinois had <u>abandoned</u> their customary lands east of the Mississippi, for any significant period, under pressure from the Iroquois.

Dablon describes his journey, in company with Allouez, to Green Bay, where they arrived September 6, 1670, and, from there, to the Mascouten village, where some of the Miami were residing with them in the same community. The residents in the vicinity of the Bay are the "four nations", Winnebago, Potawatomi, Sac, and people of "the Fork", the latter three living there "as foreigners, driven by their fear of the Iroquois from their own territories, which lie between the Lake of the Hurons and that of the Illinois [Michigan]" (ibid. pp. 183-187). Dablon learned what Allouez before him had reported concerning the widespread fear of the Iroquois and Sioux in the area and the incursions and depredations committed by them (ibid. pp. 201-3).

62

Writing at about the same time (1671) the governor of New France, de Courcelles, says that the Iroquois "are so inclined to war that they wage it not only against their neighbors, but against tribes more than six hundred leagues distant from them" (NYCD 9:79). Having exhausted the beaver in their own lands south of Lake Ontario, they drove off the Hurons on the north side of the lake, "so that it may be said the Iroquois do all their hunting at present, on our allies' lands, . . ." and take their peltries to New Netherland (ibid. p. 80).

Perhaps the motives behind Iroquois warfare are not directly germane to the problem considered here, but certainly the consequences of this activity are; and their role in causing the dispersion of tribes throughout the Great Lakes country has been extensively documented (Hunt, 1960 & Kellogg, 1925). If the economic factor in their wide-ranging hostilities was not the only one, it seems to have been dominant. One may disagree that

their primary objective was to control intertribal trade through the establishment of an exclusive middleman position between the Northeastern Indians and
the sources of supply of European goods; one may suggest that plunder of
beaver pelts from other tribes was a powerful incentive for their seemingly
indiscriminate hostilities; or that they were impelled by values connected
with honors and prestige acquired in war; or vengeance, etc. The explanations
for human behavior are rarely, if ever, simple. Nevertheless, if the French
could observe and interpret the behavior of the Indians with any reasonable
degree of clarity and insight, and if it is true that Indians were stimulated
by the new needs that were created among them through the introduction of
European goods (which nobody denies), it is not necessary to argue too hard
for what is by now a truism. If one could argue successfully that aboriginally economics was not a dominating force in Indian life, it was no longer
true after the arrival of Europeans.

63

But there is, nevertheless, the role of the French, a not unimportant
factor in the maintenance and continuation of hostilities between the Iroquois
and others. For example, deCourcelles reports that in the autumn of 1670 some
Iroquois accompanied French traders to the Ottawa, who were incensed when
they learned from the Iroquois how much cheaper than French prices were the
goods to be obtained from the Dutch (a perennial complaint). When the French
learned that the Iroquois agreed to introduce the Ottawa to the Albany trade,
they proceeded to disrupt this plan by instructing the Missionaries among
these two groups to sow discord with "speeches that the Governor put into the
mouths of the Missionaries of the two Nations in order to prevent them con-
fiding the one in the other" (NYCD 9:84-85).

In August 1672 Father Allouez arrived at the Mascouten village on the
Upper Fox River where, in addition to the Miami whom he had seen established

there in 1670 (JR 55:199-201), he also found Illinois, Kickapoo, and Wea. He writes: ". . .I counted there twenty cabins of ilinoues [Illinois], thirty large cabins of Kikabou [Kickapoo], Fifty of Machkoutench [Mascouten], Over ninety of Miamiak [Miami], [and] three Ouaouiatanoukak [Wea]" (JR 58:23). Allouez also says that the majority of the population in this community are Miami (idem). In 1670 he found only Miami with the Mascouten, at which time he wrote that "they form together more than three thousand souls, and are able to furnish each four hundred men for the common defense against the Iroquois, who pursue them even into these remote districts" (JR 55:201). The Kickapoo were then situated four leagues from this Mascouten village on the Fox River (JR 54:233).

The missionary arrived back at the St. Francis Xavier Mission at Green Bay on September 16, 1672, and he recorded the information that at Green Bay were the Potawatomi, Sac, Winnebago, Menominee, "the outaoussingouc [Ottowa?] and others. . . Deeper in the woods, toward the west" are the Fox, and others who were probably Chippewa. "Still farther to the westward, in the woods," are the Mascouten, Kickapoo, and others; "The village of the miami, . . . whither come The Ilinoue [Illinois], the Kakackiouek [Kaskaskia], Peoualen [Peoria], ouaouiatanouk [Wea], memilounioue (?), pepikoukia [Pepikokia], kilitika, mengakonkia, -- Some for a short time, Others for a longer time. These tribes dwell on the Banks of the Missisipi, and all speak the same Language" (JR 58:41-43). These seem to be all Illinois and Miami speaking groups. By the end of October all the Indians had left for the winter hunt.

This seems to be the first mention of the Kaskaskia and the Peoria, but it is not clear whether he distinguishes them from, or includes them in, the term Illinois immediately preceding. But he does mean, clearly, that they all live on the Mississippi and all speak the same language. As was

seen above some Illinois had come to Green Bay in about 1666 (Blair 1:321).
In 1670 Dablon stated that twelve or fifteen of their men visited the Mascouten
village (JR 55:215), and also that the Illinois had reached Green Bay (ibid.
pp. 103-105). Now, in 1672 we see the first relatively substantial movement
of Illinois into the area west of Green Bay (20 cabins). Other tribes seem
to be moving about in the lands into which they had fled earlier, while the
Illinois, when they are in the Green Bay area or at the Mascouten-Miami
village, have comparatively speaking, come a long way. There is little doubt
that the prime factor stimulating these movements is the desire to trade; but
there must also have been the wish to attract missionaries and, preferably,
traders into Illinois country.

In his account for the year 1673 Allouez says that the St. Francis
Xavier Mission "summons from a very great distance the Savages who dwell
beyond the Mississipi, to come and live among the Machkoutens; it calls the
Illinois from a still greater distance to come and settle in their former
country, near the lake that bears their name, six days' journey from the
Machkoutens" (JR 58:265). The use of the word "summons" here can only be the
expression of a hope, at best. And like all Jesuits in this enterprise he
knew he was writing for publication and with an eye for the attraction of
funds to carry on the good works. The good father, like all missionaries, is
hoping to gather as large a flock as he can. Apart from the names of tribes
already familiar to us from the Great Lakes southward, on the east side of the
Mississippi, no groups from "beyond the Mississippi" are known, other than the
Sioux, Assiniboin and others west of Lake Superior. If the Illinois are
called "from a still greater distance", which is six days' journey from the
Mascoutens, it does not necessarily follow that this greater distance is still
farther beyond the Mississippi. His notion of the distance of the river from

65

either Green Bay or Chequamegon on Lake Superior is quite vague. Equally vague, no doubt, was his idea of the "former country" of the Illinois, which he says is near Lake Michigan, six days' travel from the Mascouten. At any rate the "still greater distance" of the Illinois could just as well have been in a direction south and southwest of Green Bay. But it seems obvious that the Illinois have come farther than any other group associated with this Mission.

Apparently the Kaskaskia had come to the vicinity of the Green Bay mission in accordance with a promise made to Father Dablon the year before (1672) at the mascouten village. Also, "the other Illinois, called Peoualeas [Peoria], are gradually coming here to settle, in the conviction that the house of God will protect them, and keep them safer than they formerly were" (idem). Here again the assumption need not be the usual one that, having taken refuge beyond the Mississippi, they were gradually returning because they felt it was becoming safe to do so. To a missionary the house of God is a protection to all, and within its walls all are safer than outside. Thwaites, in what seems like a burst of misplaced, or exaggerated, enthusiasm interprets Allouez's comments to mean that "the Illinois tribes are flocking to that region, as well as many from the upper Mississippi" (JR 58, Preface pp. 17-18). This seems to be stretching a point. Allouez himself does not convey such an impression. Allouez, however, was keenly conscious of the wars, strifes, uncertainties of the period, not only for the Indians, but also for the French. He could easily project his feelings upon others; and what he said need not have been any more applicable to the Illinois than to any of the other groups he was familiar with. The time, in fact, was such that hardly anyone felt safe. Father Andre, among the Menominee, was in fear of his life because of the Sioux in the fall of 1673 (JR 58:289).

The Missionaries were only just beginning to meet the Illinois in any numbers, and it does not seem that they had, as yet, mastered the language. Only Marquette has recorded his effort to learn it in 1669-70. With so few missionaries and so many tribes at least part of the information about a group they saw relatively infrequently could easily become garbled. Here again, I have in mind the comments, direct or implied, concerning the purportedly enforced trans-Mississippi period of the Illinois. If Allouez and Dablon did not know the language, or had a limited command of it, they could very well have made applicable to the entire tribe what was true only of a part.

Allouez seems to have been constantly on the move between the St. Francis Xavier Mission at Green Bay, and those of St. Mark among the Fox and St. Jacques among the Mascouten and Miami. As Dablon said of him: "He has preached the gospel with much toil to a great many pagan savages, of _various nations_ and of _different languages_, . . ." (my italics - JJ). And Dablon emphasizes "the fatigues that must be undergone in going to seek them, and the diversity of Languages that had to be learned, in order to be able to preach to them;. . ." (JR 58:21). In these circumstances it is not doing the worthy and overworked Father an injustice to question the accuracy of some of his statements about a tribe which was distant from his regular missions, and representatives of which he saw only occasionally. True, he met some Illinois who came to the St. Esprit Mission at Chequamegon as early as 1665 or 1666; but Allouez had his hands full then also.

It must be said, however, that at this time (1673) Allouez took advantage of the opportunity to engage in the first relatively substantial missionary effort among the Illinois - the Kaskaskia, apparently near Green Bay, and the Peoria among the Miami at the Mascouten village. In Allouez's own words, "I have already visited the Caskaskias, and have baptized many of

67

their children; I have borne the first words of the Faith to the Peoualeas, who dwell among the Miamis, and they have listened to me with much docility. They have even begun to pray, and have promised me to come and dwell nearer to us to have the advantage of being instructed at leisure" (ibid. pp. 265-267).

While Allouez was carrying on at the southern end of Green Bay Father Louis Andre was farther north along the west shore of the bay among the Menominee and others. Andre arrived there at the end of April 1673. When the Indians left on their winter sojourn he was not in a position to accompany them "to the extreme end of Cape Illinois [Door Peninsula, east side of Green Bay]" (ibid. p. 289). Had he followed them he would "thus have had an opportunity to instruct at the same time the Illinois, the Pouteouatamis, the Oussakis [Sac], the Nessouakontoun, and a part of the Outaouasinagous" (idem). The Illinois here referred to may have been the Kaskaskia who, Allouez said, were at Green Bay; or there may have been, in addition, other parties of Illinois in the area.

When, on one of his excursions from his Green Bay Mission to minister to his outlying flocks, Allouez arrived at the Mascouten village on May 4, 1673, the only other group to which he made reference is the "very numerous" Miami, "a considerable portion" of whom he visited (JR 58:59, 63). Had members of any other tribe been there at the time he undoubtedly would have mentioned the fact. The following month, when Marquette and Joliet stopped at this village and obtained two Miami guides who led them to the Wisconsin River on their epic voyage of discovery, Marquette noted that "Here is the limit of the discoveries which the french have made, for they have not yet gone any farther" (JR 59:101). But now, apparently, "this Village Consists of three Nations who have gathered there - Miamis, Maskoutens, and Kikabous" (idem). The previous year, in August, Allouez recorded the presence here of

not only Kickapoo, but also Illinois and some Wea (JR 58:23). It does not
seem unusual for mention to be made in the warmer months of the year of the
presence of members of other tribes in this village; for it was on the Fox-
Wisconsin route from Green Bay to the Mississippi. On some early maps this
is indicated as the outward route, whereas the return route is shown extending from a point lower on the Mississippi, opposite what may be the Iowa or
the Wapsipinicon River, eastward to the Des Plaines – Chicago portage and
Lake Michigan, perhaps via the Kaskaskia village on the upper Illinois River
(Thevenot's map, 1681, in JR 59: facing p. 154; Map facing p. 228 in Kellogg,
1917).

70

II - 1673-1680

The first recorded contact of Europeans with the Illinois, and observation of the latter, in their villages, is by Marquette and Joliet. This took place on June 25, 1673 when the explorers followed a path leading from the bank of the Mississippi, "and, after walking About 2 leagues [5 miles] We discovered a village on the bank of a river, and two others on a Hill distant about half a league [1.25 miles] from the first" (JR 59:115). Marquette's account does not indicate on which bank of the Mississippi they landed before proceeding toward the villages, but his map clearly places the "Peouarea" and the "Moingouena" subgroups of the Illinois on the west side of the Mississippi on either the Des Moines or the Iowa River at about 40° latitude (Tucker, 1942, Plate V).

The village in which the two Frenchmen and their companions were entertained was Peoria (JR 59:125). When the feast was over they visited the entire village "which Consists of fully 300 Cabins" (ibid. p. 123). This information is contained in another form in a letter dated August 1, 1674 written by Dablon to his superior in France; and what he says is based on conversations he had with Joliet. According to Dablon, of the villages Marquette and Joliet saw on their travels, some "contained 300 cabins, such as that of the Ilinois, which contains over 8,000 souls" (JR 58:97). (See also Blasingham, 1956, pp. 362-3).

The map known as Joliet's Map of 1674, which may not actually have been made by Joliet (Tucker, 1942, Notes on maps, Plate IV) shows "Illinois Pouearea" on the west side of the Mississippi, followed by the note "300 cabins". North of them, along the Mississippi, are shown the Ouaouiatanon (Wea). But the Moingouena of Marquette's map are not present here. Both maps, however, denote the Kaskaskia on the upper Illinois River.

71

The Marquette journal says of the Illinois: "they are divided into _many_
villages, some of which are quite distant from that of which we speak, which
is called _peouarea_. This causes some difference in their language, which, on
the whole resembles allegonquin, so that we easily understood each other"
(JR 59:125-27; italics - JJ). The implication here seems to be that Marquette
didn't actually speak Illinois, but was able to understand it because of its
close affiliation with other Algonkian languages that he knew. We do know,
however, that he began studying the language at the St. Esprit Mission a few
years before. What he says earlier in the present account could imply that
he knew the language, for he "spoke to them first, and asked them who they
were. They replied that they were Ilinois;. . ." (ibid. p. 117). Subsequently,
near the southernmost point of their river voyage, at a village labeled
"Metchigamea" (but which was probably Quapaw, as Delanglez says in Mid-
America, 27:46) they "had to speak by signs, because none of them understood
the six languages which I spoke" (ibid. p. 153). Quapaw is a Siouan language,
and the six languages which Marquette spoke were undoubtedly Algonkian. But,
fortunately, they "found an old man who could speak a little Illinois" (idem).
At another village in the area, called "Akamsea" in the journal, they "found
a Young man who understood Ilinois much better than did the Interpreter whom
we had brought from Mitchigamea" (ibid. p. 155). This encounter among Siouan-
speaking people with two men who knew some Illinois again clearly suggests
that Marquette could speak the Illinois language.

The description given of the Illinois states that in addition to their
skill with the bow and arrow "they also use guns, which they buy from our
savage allies who Trade with our french. They use them especially to inspire,
through their noise and smoke, terror in their Enemies,. . ." who do not know
guns for they are too far west. The Illinois "are warlike, and make themselves

72

dreaded by the Distant tribes to the south and west, weither they go to procure slaves; these they barter, selling them at a high price to other Nations,
in exchange for other Wares. Those very Distant Savages against whom they
war have no Knowledge of Europeans;. . ." (ibid. p. 127). The Indian middlemen with whom the illinois were trading were probably at Chequamegon, Michilimackinac, or Sault St. Marie, and also around Green Bay. As regards their
use of captives in their trade for European goods, this is a point made a few
years earlier (1669 or 1670) by Marquette when he wrote from the St. Esprit
Mission on Chequamegon Bay (JR 54:191).

At the last village reached by Marquette and Joliet before their
return voyage up the Mississippi they learned from the "Akansea" that "the
hatchets, knives, and beads that we saw were sold to them partly by Nations
from the east, and partly by an Ilinois village situated at four days' journey
from their village westward" (JR 59:155). Just what this means has been a
subject of considerable speculation and hardly anything more. It is not
impossible that Illinois were in the area stated. And it may be, as suggested
by Delanglez, that they were the Metchigamea whose name was placed near the
Mississippi on Marquette's map, but which actually should be associated with
a village symbol on that map placed inland above the name.

73

Temple apparently does not accept Delanglez's interpretation (which
seems far more reasonable than his own) concerning the location of the
Metchigamea village four days inland from the river. Temple's own suggestion
is that "Perhaps this was a group of Cahokia or Tamaroa who had not as yet
returned to the Illinois Country after the Iroquois wars which had thrown the
Iliniwek into disorder and demoralized them" (Temple, 1958, p. 18). The
"disorder" and "demoralization" of the Illinois by Iroquois warfare is a
strictly gratuitous piling of Pelion on Ossa, devoid of documentary

foundation. It is undoubtedly an inference drawn from the known dispersal of other tribes by the Iroquois which is combined with a tradition that seems to have been founded by Father Tailhan, as was discussed above.

Is it necessary to assume that the Illinois had been driven beyond the Mississippi in a state of disorder and demoralization? The description, already quoted, of the Illinois as a warlike people, dreaded by tribes to the south and west gives a very different picture. It seems simpler to infer from the evidence at hand that the Illinois were accustomed to exploiting, at least in part, the lands west of the Mississippi for hunting, warfare, and trade on their own initiative.

On the return journey Marquette and Joliet went up the Illinois River and "found on it a village of Illinois called Kaskasia, consisting of 74 cabins" (JR 59:161). Although this reference does not locate the village, the maps of both Marquette and Joliet place it on the north bank of the upper Illinois (Tucker, 1942, Plates IV & V). Then, in a final paragraph, after having stated that the explorers arrived at Green Bay by the end of September, the account says, ". . .when I was returning, we passed through the Ilinois of Peouarea, and during three days I preached the faith in all their Cabins;. . ." (JR 59:163). This statement concerning a visit with the Peoria on the return trip may be the result of some confusion on the part of Dablon in the preparation of this account. Certainly there is no Peoria village on the Illinois River on the map of either explorer, the only Peoria location in those documents being on the west side of the Mississippi.

But if this reference, in fact, means that the explorers met this group on the Illinois River as well as on the outward voyage down the Mississippi, then Temple's interpretation of these events is suggestive. The location of the Peoria village on the Illinois, he writes, "could well have been on Lake Peoria, the home of this tribe in later years." If so, they could have "returned to their permanent villages from the summer hunt in time to harvest their corn in August or September" (Temple, 1958, pp. 18-19).

This is the kind of more or less regular trans-Mississippi movement which had probably been part of the customary Illinois pattern. It seems a violation of the Law of Parsimony to resort to the unnecessary assumption that "the Illini were probably returning to the Illinois Country before the French made contact with them, but the presence of these Europeans seems to have given them courage to face the Iroquois" (ibid. p. 19). At a later time the role of the French in support of the Illinois against the Iroquois is a factor, but not during the period under discussion.

On October 25, 1674 Marquette left the St. Francis Xavier Mission at DePere, Wisconsin on a second journey to visit the Illinois, in order to establish among them the Mission of the Immaculate Conception. He spent the night at the mouth of the Fox River, down which he had come to Green Bay. There he found the Potawatomi assembling, apparently from the village indicated on his map as being on the shore of Green Bay, east of Fox River outlet. He writes that the elders would not permit the young men to go trading among the Illinois for fear that after obtaining robes from them, and also hunting beaver, they would then leave in the spring to trade for more French goods at Montreal, thus leaving the rest of the group unprotected against possible attacks of the Sioux. Nevertheless, Marquette "learned that 5 canoes of Poutewatamis, and 4 of Ilinois, had started to go to the Kaskaskia" (JR 59:165). Obviously, these Illinois had been trading at the Potawatomi village. Later the Illinois women helped Marquette's party to complete the portage at Sturgeon Bay, and the Illinois party suggested that the French travel with them, as they were more familiar with the route.

75

Among them was "Chachagwessiou, an Illinois greatly esteemed among his nation, partly because he engages in the fur trade. . ." (ibid. p. 167). It is thus possible that there were individual Illinois who acquired prestige as specialist traders and who were, in part, responsible for making available to their countrymen the European goods they sought so eagerly. Trading journeys required considerable effort, and time away from the rest of the group. These were not undertaken by everyone; and those who did, not only received a profit, but probably thanks in addition. In this connection Marquette makes an interesting comment. About the middle of December (1674), while wintering at the Chicago portage, he writes: "Chachagwessiou and the other Ilinois left us, to go and join their people [presumably at the Kaskaskia village on the upper Illinois River] and give them the goods that they had brought, in order to obtain their robes. In this they act like the traders, and give hardly any more than do the French" (ibid, p. 175).

Along the west short of Lake Michigan, en route to the Chicago River, they met "maskoutens, to the number of 8 or 9 cabins, who had separated from the others in order to obtain subsistence" (ibid, p. 171). They also encountered "3 ilinois who had come from the village" located, no doubt, on the upper Illinois (idem). And shortly before Chachawessiou and the other Illinois left, Marquette writes, "Several Ilinois passed yesterday, on their way to carry their furs to Nawaskingwe", an Illinois who was among those travelling with Marquette from Green Bay (ibid, p. 175). Apparently, these Indians, who were eager to obtain tobacco from Marquette for beaver skins, wanted the advantage of trading with Nawaskingwe before he arrived at the village.

Marquette was forced to winter near the Chicago portage because of illness. Several times he was visited by Illinois who brought food, as did one of two French traders, situated 18 leagues away, probably near the

Illinois village. In addition one of his companions went to the latter place
and to the traders for provisions. Marquette, however, does not seem to be
quite sure of how far he was from the village. At one point he says "Jacque
arrived from the Ilinois village, which is only six leagues from here;. . ."
(ibid. p. 175). Then, referring to three Illinois who, on behalf of the
elders, had brought provisions, Marquette writes that "they had come a
distance of 20 leagues" (idem). Refusing their request for powder he says
that "I did not wish them to begin war with the Muiamis" (idem). There is no
other reference to hostility between the two groups at this time.

It seems that during the first half of February some of the Illinois
were on their way to the Potawatomi, probably to trade, for Marquette states:
"out of a cabin of Ilinois, who encamped near us for a month, a portion have
again taken the road to the Poutewatamis, and some are still on the lake-
shore, where they wait until navigation is open. They bear letters for our
Fathers of St. Francois" (ibid. p. 179).

According to Dablon, Marquette finally arrived at the Illinois village
on April 9 or 10, 1675. There, the audience to which he preached on one
occasion "was Composed of 500 chiefs and elders, seated in a circle around
the father, and of all the Young men, who remained standing. They numbered
more than 1,500 men, without counting the women and children, who are always
numerous, -- the village being composed of 5 or 600 fires" (ibid. p. 189).

In his Relation of 1675 Dablon writes that the St. Francis Xavier
Mission, near Green Bay, "is a sort of center for a great many nations dwelling in its vicinity" (JR 59:219). It is Father Allouez who is in charge of
the Fox and Mascouten; and of the Mascouten village Dablon says: "there are
as many as twelve tribes, speaking three different languages, and comprising
no less than twenty thousand souls, gathered in this village alone" (ibid.

77

p. 221). This is a rather remarkable assemblage of people in one village, and the priest must be referring either to its population at the time of writing or he may mean that such numbers can be found there at certain times. Although as many as five tribes have previously been found in this village, this is the first time that twelve are referred to. As stated earlier, this village seems to have been a point of concentration during the warmer months of the year. The possible reasons for this concourse of groups may be connected with the trade around the lakes, the protection it offered against war parties of Sioux or Iroquois, and the proximity of the Green Bay Mission.

The Mission of St. Jacques at this village includes, according to Father Allouez in a 1674 report, in addition to the Mascouten, "Kikabouas, Miamis, and other tribes, . . ." (idem). Then he goes on to say: "This mission would require 2 missionaries on account of the 2 nations who dwell in it, who speak 2 different languages; and because of the multitude of people who are continually arriving, in great numbers, to take up their abode in it" (ibid. p. 225). It seems clear from these quotations that while only the Mascouten and Miami actually reside in this village the other tribes resort to it, at least partly, for the reason that the Jesuits have established a chapel there. The more or less regular presence of the French probably provided a kind of sanctuary, and perhaps those who had been converted were attracted there periodically. It is doubtful that Allouez can mean that the number of people who keep coming there take up permanent "abode in it." But Thwaites, the editor of the Jesuit Relations, seems to think that this increase in population was caused by an influx of "refugees from many tribes" (ibid. p. 19). There seems to be nothing in the context of Allouez's remarks to warrant the statement made by Thwaites.

In the autumn of 1674, subsequent to his sojourn at the Mascouten

village, Allouez went to his mission of St. Marc among the Fox on Wolf River.
He followed them for 40 leagues (100 miles) on their hunt for beaver and deer
through the forests. When they returned to the village he spent two months
of the winter with them (ibid. pp. 225-227). His statement that they were in
constant danger, either of hunger or of being captured and burned by their
enemies (ibid. pp. 227-229) was certainly borne out the following winter
(1675-6) when not only were Illinois "killed by the Nadoessis," but some also
died of disease. In addition to these troubles "the ihilinois made raids upon
them, and Carried off others into captivity" (JR 60:199-201).

It is, perhaps, in this connection that some statements made by Perrot
in his Memoire, where chronology is so often difficult to unravel, may be
pertinent. He refers to the building of the fort by Frontenac in the summer
of 1673, but, as usual, does not give the date, which, fortunately, we know.
He then writes: "He [frontenac] summoned thither the chiefs of all the
Irroquois nations, and always maintained harmony between them and the savages
of the upper country--until some Iroquois warriors who came from Chaouanonk
[Shawnee?], where they had accomplished nothing, carried away five families
of Renards [Fox], and a chief who had gone to solicit aid in the war which
that tribe were then waging against the Illinois" (Blair 1:227). The capture
by the Iroquois of these Fox who were on their way to seek assistance against
the Illinois appears to be an event which occurred after 1673. The Illinois
raids against the Fox to which Allouez alludes occurred during the winter of
1675-6. These statements from the two sources quoted may refer to the same
series of events, and Allouez's quite specific date could, then, logically
be ascribed to Perrot's statement.

To return to the original reference to Allouez in connection with his
mission to the Fox, there is no doubt of the existence of hostilities between

79

that tribe and the Illinois during the winter of 1675–1676. La Potherie recounts a situation which, according to the context, certainly occurred at some time between 1673 and 1680. An Iroquois war party of 800 was on its way to the Green Bay region of Wisconsin; but after receiving presents of beaver skins from the Miami, Mascouten, Kickapoo, Fox, and others around Green Bay, they turned their attention elsewhere. According to La Potherie: "that army of Iroquois was divided into two; six hundred went against the Chaouanons [Shawnee], and two hundred followed the river of Chicagou [Chicago]—where they encountered some Islinois who were returning from Michilimakinak with some Outaouaks, and captured or killed nineteen of them. The Islinois, when they heard of this blow, checked their resentment; they could have gone to attack the Iroquois, but they sent to Onontio [who at the time was Monsieur de Frontenac, who had arrived in Canada in 1672], a package of beaver skins, by which they made complaint that the Iroquois had violated the peace. They said that, through fear of displeasing him, they had refrained from going to find the Iroquois and fighting them; but, nevertheless, they asked him for justice." The governor told them to defend themselves but ". . .not to set out on the war-path to encounter the enemy in their own country" (Blair 1:348–351).

Plainly, at the time the small party of Illinois and Ottawa became an Iroquois target of opportunity, the former were on their way home to the Upper Illinois River from a trade journey among the Ottawa. The embassy and present to Frontenac suggests that the time was post-Marquette, when the French were coming into the Illinois area, while the Illinois were becoming increasingly active in the trade complex around the Great Lakes. It is not improbable that the time was closer to 1680 than to 1675. The Illinois undoubtedly wished to do nothing that might deter the French from opening their country to trade.

And, as it happens, the Iroquois soon did everything they could to achieve the contrary goal.

After the death of Marquette in 1675, Father Allouez was assigned to the Illinois mission. In late October, 1676, he left Green Bay for his new post. A month earlier, Father Jean Enjalran, newly arrived from France, wrote a letter containing information he had obtained from his fellow-missionaries at Quebec, some of whom had just returned from their stations in the Great Lakes area. In a brief allusion to the mission of the Illinois he says it "consists of fifty thousand souls in a single village" (JR 60:129-131). It is not necessary to dwell upon the degree of accuracy of this figure. But, accurate or not, it would seem that the Illinois still had some reputation as a populous group.

When in the spring of 1677 Allouez arrived at the Chicago River, he was met by eighty Illinois who accompanied him to their village. Allouez then records that "it was not until the 27th of April that I was able to arrive at Kachkachkia, the great village of the Ilinois" (JR 60:159). This appellation of "great village" is used for the first time. There has obviously been a considerable increase in population here since Marquette's first visit in 1673 when he reported 74 cabins. His second visit in 1675, described by Dablon, refers to a village of "5 or 600 fires" which has been estimated at 100 to 150 cabins (Shea, 1852, p. 74).

81

Allouez says further: "I found this village largely increased since a year ago. Formerly, it was composed of but one nation, that of the Kachkach-kia; at the present time, there are 8 tribes in it, the first having summoned the others, who inhabited the neighborhood of the river Mississippi. One cannot well satisfy himself as to the number of people who Compose that village. They are housed in 351 cabins, which are easily counted, as most of them are situated upon the bank of the river" (JR 60:159).

Allouez, at the beginning of the passage quoted, implies that he was at this village the preceding year, but there is no published account of such a visit. Yet, a little later on, he states: "This is all that I was able to observe in this country, in the short time that I lived in it" (JR 60:163), which seems to have been about a month. At any rate, he was sufficiently impressed by the size of the village to use the adjective "great". Although he once reported that there were 20,000 people in the Mascouten village he never used the word "great." Although he found it difficult to venture a guess as to the number of people inhabiting it, Allouez seems to have made an exact count of the dwellings and of the Illinois subgroups present. Finally, he is specific as to the fact that it is the Kaskaskia who are the original occupants and that the other groups were "summoned" there from their habitations in the "neighborhood" of the Mississippi River. From what Allouez writes it seems that the significant factor in the choice of the location of the village was defense. As he puts it, in spite of the fact that the locale is swampy and damp, at least on the river bank side, "they delight, however, in this location, as they can easily espy from it their enemies" (ibid. p. 161).

82

At the close of this account of 1677 Allouez makes a passing reference to ". . .the war which the Iroquois intend to make against the Ilinois" (ibid. p. 167). According to Hunt (op.cit., p. 149) ". . .the Iroquois made war upon the Illinois as early as 1677, as soon as the Susquehannah menace was removed." Father Dablon, in a postscript to this Relation of Allouez makes a statement concerning a defeat inflicted upon the Iroquois by the Illinois which is chronologically elusive: "In the year after, 1678, father aloués set out on his return to that mission, to remain there two consecutive years,. . .We have since learned that the Iroquois have made an incursion thus far, but that they were defeated by the Illinois. This will go far to foment war between these nations;. . ." (JR 60:167). Two inferences may be drawn from this statement of Dablon's. First, the Iroquois incursion probably took place either in 1678 or 1679, although it could, conceivably, have occurred in 1677 after Allouez's departure from the "great" Kaskaskia village. Second, whatever the number of Iroquois raids upon the Illinois thus far, and the indications are that they were relatively infrequent, they were still not sufficiently numerous or large before 1680 for Dablon to infer, as yet, the existence of a state of war between these two groups.

The Wisconsin tribes were oriented toward Green Bay as a focus of concentration. Father Albanel, superior at the St. Francis Xavier Mission there, wrote Dablon (Relation for 1677-1678) that "from time to time, the Savages gather there from all quarters,. . ." (JR 61:71). During this period Father Allouez, who left the Kaskaskia village in May 1677, was busy among the Fox and others (ibid, p. 73).

The extent of the concentration in the regions of Green Bay is more dramatically revealed in the Relation of 1679 (written by Bigot and revised by Dablon) by the following statement concerning the Mission there at De Pere: "It forms the center of all the missions which are carried on among the neighboring peoples,—whether on the bay des puants, where there are six nations speaking two different languages; or among the outagami [Fox], where there are four nations; or among the mascoutins, who number as many as 12 nations, speaking 3 different languages, and who, when gathered together in this village, aggregate at least 20,000 souls" (ibid, p. 149). This is followed by a reference to "the large number of nations" and to "the diversity of so many languages" (idem). Later on it is said that the "six nations" on Green Bay "are distant from one another ten or fifteen leagues" (ibid, p. 155),

83

and also that Fathers Allouez and Silvy have been concerned mainly with
ministering to the Fox and Mascouten "sometimes conjointly and at other times
separately" (idem). If Allouez was engaged in these labors in 1679 it is hard
to reconcile the date with Dablon's postscript to Allouez's report on his
visit to the Kaskaskia, wherein he wrote that Allouez returned to the Illinois
mission in 1678 to remain two consecutive years. If he did go back in 1678,
then he couldn't have remained there but visited it on his "rounds" as he did
the other tribes.

III - 1680-1687

La Salle's journey into the area inhabited by the Illinois in 1679-80 enlarged considerably the historical perspective on that group through the records left by him and by members of his party. Journeying from Lake Michigan up the St. Joseph River of Michigan to the portage leading to the Kankakee River, thence down to the Illinois River, they "reached the Illinois village on the 1st of January, 1680" (Anderson, 1901, p.85). Other members of the expedition place the time of arrival "toward the close of December" (Membré, in Shea, 1852, p. 93) and December 31, 1679 (Tonty in Anderson, 1898, p. 29). The village, devoid of its inhabitants who were away on their annual winter hunt, was situated "on a somewhat marshy plain, upon the right bank of the river...." (Anderson, 1901, p. 85). It extended for a league (2.5 miles) parallel to the shore, and was a half league (.625 miles) in width (ibid. p. 195; Margry 2: 120). A careful analysis of the various documents which refer to the location of this "great Illinois village," as it came to be known, places it on the northern bank of the Illinois River between the towns of Utica and Ottawa with its eastern extremity at Twin Bluffs (Habig in Mid-America, 16:12). This was the one which Allouez earlier called "The Great village of the Illinois" and which, in their respective accounts relating to this journey, Hennepin calls "their greatest village" (Thwaites, 1903, 1: 153) and Membré "the largest Ilinois village" (Shea, op. cit. p. 93) or "the only great Illinois village..." (ibid. p. 150). La Salle, writing some time before November, 1680 refers to it as "the great village of the Illinois" (IHC 1: 5).

In the Official Narrative, compiled by his friend the Abbé Bernou from La Salle's writings, "the village contains four hundred and sixty lodges... Every cabin has four or five fires, and about every fire are one

85

or two families...." (Anderson, 1901, p. 85). Membré writes that this village was "composed of about four or five hundred cabins, each of five or six families" (Shea, op. cit. p. 93). But La Salle elsewhere says that it is "made up of about 400 huts..." (IHC 1: 5). In this connection he also gives "the names of some of the tribes composing the nation of the Illinois—(The Peoria, Kaskaskia, Tamaroa, Coiracoentanon, Chinko, Cahokia, Chepoussa, Amonakoa, Cahokia (Ooukkea), Quapaw (Acansa),..." who form this village in addition to "many [several] others..." (idem). Of the Illinois, La Salle also says, "I have reckoned up almost 1,800 fighting men..." (idem), a figure repeated in the Official Narrative (Anderson, 1901, p. 191). Membre accords this village a population "of seven or eight thousand souls" (She, op. cit. p. 150). In this he is followed by Hennepin (IHC 1: 93).

Lacking provisions because of a scarcity of game resulting from the fact that the region through which they had come had been denuded by prairie fires set in hunting, La Salle took a number of bushels of corn from the village caches. Continuing down the Illinois River the French found the Illinois encamped on both sides of the river at Lake Peoria (Anderson, 1901, pp. 87-91; Membré in Shea, op. cit. p. 94; Hennepin, IHC 1: 78-9 and in Thwaites, 1903, p. 155). This lake is "about seven leagues [17.5 miles] long, and about one wide, called Pimiteoui, meaning in their language that there are plenty of fat beasts there" (Membré, in Shea, op. cit. p. 94; Margry 2: 177; Deliette, IHC 23: 327). Here, according to Membré (Shea, op. cit. p. 94) there were several thousand Indians, although Hennepin puts it as "several thousand Men,... (Thwaites, 1903, p. 156). It seems that the habitations on this part of the river formed a winter encampment, for it was at "the great village, where the Savages' stores of Indian corn were buried" (Anderson, 1901, p. 47) and where, obviously, they

86

planted their crops.

But winter quarters at Lake Peoria had decided advantages. Apparently game in this area was plentiful, and, if Membré is correct, the name conferred by the Illinois on Lake Peoria, reflects this fact. During the summer the Illinois drained the swamps created by the overflow of the river by digging trenches, and they then collected the stranded fish (La Salle in Margry 2: 178). Furthermore, from Lake Peoria down to the Mississippi "Navigation is open at all seasons, and free from ice" (Membré in Shea, op. cit., p. 166; also Anderson, 1901, p. 147), permitting the Illinois to use their pirogues in transporting supplies of game from hunting areas to the south (see Hennepin below).

After the peaceful intent of the European intruders had been established, and they had been feasted, La Salle "called together the chiefs of the villages from both sides of the river" (Anderson, 1901, p. 91; Hennepin in IHC 1: 79). Having largely dispelled the suspicions of the Illinois, which were exacerbated by a visit from the Miamis, who although themselves allies of the Iroquois in this instance (Anderson, 1901, p. 97ff; Membré in Shea, op. cit., p. 95; IHC 23: 11; Hennepin IHC 1: 82) reinforced earlier rumors that La Salle was in league with the Iroquois, who were enemies of the Illinois, La Salle began construction of Fort Crevecoeur, in the middle of January, on the east side of the Illinois River just below Lake Peoria. This establishment was an earnest of La Salle's promise to the Illinois of protection and trade.

During the month of February, 1680, La Salle and the Illinois received visits from representatives of several tribes to the west and south. On one occasion "savages from five remote nations, [arrived] at the village,..." (Anderson, 1901, p. 137; also Hennepin in IHC 1: 90 and in Thwaites, 1903,

p. 174). There followed the "arrival of some Osages, Chicasaws, and Arkansas, who had come from the south to see the Frenchmen and to buy hatchets" (Anderson, 1901, p. 141). Hennepin writes that the latter "brought fine Furrs to barter for our Axes" (Thwaites, 1903, p. 177). And a third reference in this connection by La Salle reveals that "on the 17th of February, two chiefs of the Matoutenta [Oto] tribe, living eighty or a hundred leagues west of the Great River, came to see the Frenchmen" (Anderson, 1901, p. 143; IHC 23: 4).

There are also indications that at this time the Illinois were obtaining captives from people to the south of them, for they told La Salle of "slaves from the country near the seacoast [Gulf coast], whom they had taken in war..." (Anderson, 1901, p. 97). In addition, there came to the village "a young Illinois warrior,--one of a party returning with prisoners from the south,--" (ibid p. 137; Hennepin in IHC 1: 91 and in Thwaites, 1903, p. 175).

On February 29th Hennepin and Michel Accault set off down the Illinois River on a voyage which would take them up the Mississippi to the Sioux. Shortly after their departure, writes Hennepin, "while descending the river Seignelay [Illinois], we met on our way several parties of Islinois returning to their village in their periaguas [pirogues]... loaded with meat" (IHC 1: 95; Thwaites, 1903, p. 182). Subsequently, on March 7, about two leagues (five miles) before they came to the mouth of the Illinois River they encountered "a nation called Tamaroa or Maroa, composed of two hundred families. They would have taken us to their village lying west of the river Colbert [Mississippi], six or seven leagues [15-17.5 miles] below the mouth of the river Seignelay [Illinois] ,..." (IHC 1: 96; Thwaites, 1903, pp. 183-4).

It would appear that the Illinois were at odds with the Sioux, for the Tamaroa "seeing that we carried iron and arms to their enemies" attempted to stop the Frenchmen (IHC 1: 96). That a state of hostility existed between those two groups was borne out when Hennepin met one hundred and twenty Sioux coming down the Mississippi "with extraordinary speed to make war on the Miamis, Islinois and Maroha..." (ibid; p. 101). When, the following September, the Illinois were attacked in force by the Iroquois, a considerable body of Illinois warriors were away on an expedition against the Sioux (see below).

Early in March, 1680 La Salle left Tonty in a command at Fort Crevecoeur and, accompanied by some of his men and one Indian, began a return journey to Fort Frontenac to look after his affairs. They dragged two canoes over ice and snow along the river to the village on the upper Illinois River because La Salle wanted to send back to his fort at Lake Peoria a canoe laden with corn from this village. The Official Narrative indicated that they reached it on March 10, but "found no one from whom to buy, nor did it seem likely that anyone would return to the village at a season so inclement" (Anderson, 1901, p.151). Membré, on the other hand states that La Salle "arrived on the 11th at the great Illinois village where I then was,..." (Shea, op. cit. p. 148). Habig attempts to resolve these contradictions and other questions concerning the nature of this village in a rather suggestive essay on "The Site of the Great Illinois Village" (Mid-America, vol. 16: 3-13), in which he assumes that it was composed of several villages of Illinois subdivisions (see below).

At any rate, when La Salle "observed tracks in the snow, he thought there must be some Illinois in the neighborhood engaged in

hunting..." (Anderson, 1901, p. 151). He did in fact, meet on the following day, three Illinois, one of whom was Chassagoac "the principal chief
of the Illinois,..." (ibid p. 153) and who, apparently, was not at the
Lake Peoria encampment of Illinois during the time La Salle was there.
La Salle was thus able to send a canoe load of corn down to his fort.

Membré writes: "As by the end of February I already knew part of
their [Illinois] language,...our father superior [Gabriel Ribourde] appointed me to follow when they were about to return to their village"
(Shea, op. cit. p. 149). What is clear from this sentence is that by
the end of February Membré could speak some Illinois, but it is not at
all clear that the Indians actually did leave their winter camp at the
end of February, as Habig assumes (Mid-America, 16: 8). It could well
be that Membré went on ahead to prepare for the arrival of the Illinois
who ordinarily would not leave until the weather was suitable. The
Official Narrative of La Salle states that it did not "seem likely that
anyone would return to the village at a season so inclement" (Anderson,
1901, p. 151).

During the summer of 1680 Membré and Ribourde apparently moved
about a good deal among the Illinois, but there are no geographical
references given. All that Membré says is that they "followed our
Indians in their camps, and to the chase. I also made a voyage to the
Myamis...; Thence I went to visit other villages of the Illinois..."
(Shea, op. cit., p. 153).

Membré's remarks concerning the introduction of guns among the
Illinois is somewhat puzzling when seen in the light of earlier testimony. It would seem, however, that after having spent the better part
of a year with the Illinois his statements would be reliable. Like

Marquette earlier, he notes that they are "good archers", and he goes
on to say that "they had as yet, no firearms; we gave them some...
they have used iron implements and arms only since our arrival..."
(ibid. p. 151; also Hennepin in Thwaites, 1903, p. 156). The description of Marquette's 1673 voyage among the Illinois states that
the Illinois used guns, which they obtained from Indian middlemen,
mainly to frighten their enemies to the west of them (JR 59:127).
Then, again, Marquette writes in his journal that during the winter
of 1674-5 he refused to give powder to some Illinois because he did
not want them to start fighting the Miami (ibid. p. 177). What Membré
reports is, therefore, difficult to reconcile with Marquette's statements, especially since we know that Illinois were trading at Chequamegon
at least as early as 1667 (JR 51:47) and subsequently at Green Bay.

When La Salle's party arrived at Lake Peoria the Illinois prepared to defend themselves with bow and arrow. No guns are mentioned
as being in possession of the Illinois prior to their acquisition of
firearms from La Salle. It is, of course, possible that other Illinois
were in possession of these European weapons; but from what Marquette
said the Kaskaskia and/or the Peoria should have had them.

In referring to "the richness and fertility of the country"
Membré merely supports the contentions of all observers since the
time of Marquette. But it would be interesting to know exactly what
he had in mind when he says that the richness and fertility "gives
them fields everywhere" (Shea, op.cit., p. 151). It would appear
that he was impressed with the fact that wherever he went among the
Illinois he observed their plantings. Possibly he was referring to

91

the extensive fields in the vicinity of the "great village" on the
upper Illinois River.

While Tonty and Fathers Membré and Ribourde were at the "great
village an Iroquois force of several hundred men, accompanied by Miami
warriors, arrived in September, 1680 to make an attack (Membré in ibid.
pp. 154-6; Anderson, 1901, pp. 193-209; Margry, 2:118-124). Most of
the Illinois warriors were on expeditions elsewhere and there were few
guns and little ammunition left in the village (Tonty in Kellogg, 1917,
pp. 291-4). In spite of the efforts of Tonty and Membré, and offers
of beaver and slaves by the Illinois, the Iroquois rejected peace.
The Illinois managed to evacuate the village and sent their families
down the Illinois River to the Mississippi. The Frenchmen were forced
to leave, and they journeyed up the Illinois River while the Illinois
men joined their families down river. The Iroquois, after devastating
the village, cornfields, and burial grounds went down the left bank
of the river in pursuit of the Illinois who moved along the right bank.
At the mouth of the river the Illinois groups separated, the Kaskaskia,
Cahokia, and Chinkoa proceeding up the Mississippi, the Peoria crossing
over that river while the "Omouhoa, Corrachietanon, Moingoama, and
Chepousca" went downstream. The Tamaroa, Tapouaro, and the Espeminkia
stayed to hunt in the area, and were attacked and dispersed by the
Iroquois (Anderson, 1901, pp. 213-15; Margry, 2:134). Membré, on the
other hand, says that La Salle "learned" that "of the seventeen
Ilinois villages, the greater part had retired beyond the river Colbert
[Mississippi], among the Ozages, two hundred leagues [500 miles] from
their country, where too a part of the Iroquois had pursued them" (Shea, 1852,

p. 162). This statement appears to be substantiated in part by a memoir of
the Intendant of New France, dated November 13, 1681, which states that
". . .the Illinois having fled a hundred leagues thence [from their village],
were pursued by the Iroquois,. . ." (NYCD 9:163). The indications are that
at this time the Illinois fled across the Mississippi as a reaction to this
devastating blow.

Various reasons are suggested in different documents of the period for
the Iroquois attack upon the Illinois in 1680, but an exploration of this
question seems hardly necessary. However, one document of November, 1681, in
a discussion of this incident, suggests that, whatever the ostensible reason
[and the Iroquois offered their "assumed excuse" for their war against the
Illinois], "their true motive was. . .to force the Illinois to bring their
beaver to them, so that they may go and trade it afterwards with the English;
also, to intimidate the other nations and constrain them to do the same thing"
(idem).

93

This is a statement which seems to lend support to Hunt's thesis that
the wars of the Iroquois were motivated by their desire to control the beaver
trade as middlemen between the Europeans and other tribes in an ever widening
area which the Iroquois attempted to dominate. The middleman role may have
been an important facet of an Iroquois aspiration for control of sources of
supply of the most essential commodity in the trade with Europeans. Apparently
they were as ready to plunder the canoes bearing beaver to Montreal as they
were to force other tribes to trade through them (ibid. p. 79). And just as
readily were they prepared to wage a war of extermination in order to open the
beaver-bearing lands of other tribes to Iroquois exploitation of that particular natural resource (ibid. pp. 80 & 162-3). For, as the Iroquois themselves said in 1684 ". . .we cannot live without free Bever-hunting."

(Colden, 1958, p. 48). And again Colden, discussing the 1685 period, writes: "The Five Nations have few or no Bevers in their own Country, and are for that reason obliged to hunt at a great distance, which often occasion'd disputes with their neighbours about the Property of the Bever, in some parts of the country" (ibid. p. 57). La Salle himself recognized a kind of avariciousness on the part of the Iroquois in relation to beaver. In describing a Miami embassy to the Iroquois, seeking an alliance against the Illinois before the attack of 1680, he cites ". . .the desire for trade which the Miami deputies offered the Iroquois, who have a great passion to possess many beaver. . ." (Margry 2:219, my translation - JJ). Quite naturally the Miami offered beaver through trade. The Iroquois undoubtedly found acceptable such a peaceful incursion into new beaver country so long as they could turn a profit as middlemen. Otherwise military incursion would serve their purposes.

94   Other sources can be cited to support the statement quoted above that the primary motive of Iroquois hostilities against the Illinois was the quest for supplies of beaver. At the same time it is apparent that the French numbered the Illinois among the Indians whose production of beaver skins was considered important to the trade of Canada. In March, 1682 DeChesneau, Intendant of New France, on the basis of a series of letters received from two Jesuits and the commandant at Fort Frontenac, said: "That it is quite evident that the Iroquois, inflated by the victories they have obtained over the Illinois, propose to destroy that Nation, which is in alliance with us, and one of those from whom we obtain a great many peltries" (NYCD 9:171, italics - JJ). In May, 1682 the King issued the following instruction to La Barre who was appointed to replace Frontenac as Governor: ". . .by all means prevent the Iroquois making war on the Illinois and other tribes, neighbors to them,. . .whose furs constitute the principal trade of Canada,. . ." (ibid.

p. 167, italics - JJ). Among the abstracts of letters received by the French government from its officials in Canada during 1682 is this:

"The first design of the Iroquois has been to seize the trade by destroying our allies and those who sell us the Beaver.

"They commenced last year with the Illinois. . ." (ibid. p. 198). And from Sieur de Meulles, dated 12 November, comes the information that "the Iroquois wish to make war on the Illinois. . .Is necessitated. . .to prevent them attacking the [Illinois], without which the revenue from the Beaver would be destroyed" (ibid. pp. 198-9).

The British also recognized the importance of the Illinois trade, as did the Iroquois, for Colden writes: "The Five Nations likewise continued in War with many of the Nations, The Chictaghiks [Illinois] particularly, who yielded the most Profitable Trade to the French; and as often as they discovered any of the French carrying Ammunition towards these Nations, they fell upon them, and took all their Powder, Lead and Arms from them" (Colden, 1958, p. 46; italics - JJ).

It is a truism that the French presence in North America was rooted in the fur trade. The preceding discussion was not meant to belabor the obvious. It was merely intended to place in perspective the importance of the Illinois as producers in the system of trade relations the French were trying to develop and maintain in the face of Iroquois competition, which happened also to be grounded in the more favorable terms of trade which they received from the British and Dutch. According to the French the defeat by the Iroquois of the Illinois, Miami, and Kiskakons (Ottawa), would give them control of Michilimackinac, Green Bay, and Lakes Erie and Huron ". . .and would thereby deprive us of all the trade which is derived from that country--. . ." (JR 62:161). The natural resources of the Illinois in relation to the demands of the fur

95

trade could form a serious threat to the Iroquois once La Salle's plans for development of that area were carried into effect. The threat was the greater in view of the fact that the Illinois were probably one of the most populous, if not the most populous, tribes in the Great Lakes Region.

Although La Salle's French enemies, who feared his competition in this development of trade in the Illinois country, undoubtedly played a role in inciting the Iroquois against the Illinois, there is little, if any, doubt that the Iroquois were sufficiently astute to see the consequences of the establishment of French power in the western country through trade alliances. The Iroquois had surely cast envious eyes upon the Illinois area for some time before intensive warfare was initiated in 1680 with the devastation of the village on the upper Illinois River. The process of Illinois attribion had begun with the most serious blow dealt by the Iroquois.

In December 1680 La Salle returned with a party on a second journey to the Illinois area, found the devastated village, and went on down the Illinois River to its mouth. He counted six Illinois camping places along the way until he reached Fort Crevecoeur at Lake Peoria (Anderson, 1901, pp. 223-233).

After Tonty and the two Recollect priests left the Illinois village and ascended the river following the Iroquois assault, they stopped several leagues from the village to dry some furs and repair their canoe. According to Membré (Shea, op.cit., p. 157) they had travelled a "full eight leagues [20 miles] from the village," but Tonty estimates the distance at five leagues (12.5 miles) (Kellogg, 1917, p. 294). While Tonty and Membré busied themselves Father Gabriel went off by himself to pray but failed to return. After a fruitless search and because of indications that he might have been attacked by Indians, Membré and Tonty continued on their way. It was afterwards

96

learned that Father Gabriel had been killed by a war party of Kickapoo
(Membré in Shea, op.cit., p. 158; Tonty in Kellogg, 1917, p. 294; Anderson,
1901, p. 209; Margry 2:124). Habig, following Membré's estimate of the
distance travelled from the Illinois village, places the location of Father
Gabriel's death at the hands of the Kickapoo near the town of Seneca,
Illinois (Mid-America, 16:10).

This event occurred in September, 1680. The following November
La Salle, coming down the Kankakee River on his return to the Illinois, "on
the 23d reached a place called the Fork of the Iroquois, where the Kickapoos,
who were also at war, had recently encamped upon a hill to the number of two
hundred" (Anderson, 1901, p. 221; Margry 2:127). Reference to the Kickapoo
being engaged in warfare in this area of northern and northeastern Illinois,
was also made by Membré in his account of Father Gabriel's death. He writes:
"The Kikapous, a little nation you may observe on the west, quite near the
Winnebagoes, had sent some of their youth in war-parties against the Iroquois,
but learning that the latter were attacking the Illinois, the war-party came
after them" (Shea, op.cit., p. 158). When in December La Salle examined the
devastated Illinois village, he noticed some of the huts rebuilt "in a
different way; but he learned some time afterward that it was the work of two
hundred Kickapoos who had encamped there a few days before his arrival"
(Anderson, 1901, p. 227; Margry 2:130).

From the foregoing statements pertaining to the presence of the
Kickapoo, it is apparent that they were moving about northeastern Illinois
from approximately the middle of September through November. It is almost as
if they were scavenging amidst the destruction and confusion created by the
Iroquois.

There is one further circumstance of interest in connection with the

97

observations made by La Salle on his journey at this time. When he was going down the Kankakee from the Fork of the Iroquois to the confluence of the Des Plaines River "...he found game everywhere very abundant,--a circumstance which gave much pleasure to his men, but aroused his apprehensions, as he was unable to imagine what had prevented the Illinois from setting the prairies on fire as usual, in order to hunt the wild cattle" (Anderson, 1906, p. 221; Margry 2:127-8). It would seem that this was a region in which he would expect the Illinois to hunt. But when he first journeyed down the Kankakee in December 1679, having traversed the marshes, "...they found no game as they had expected, because there are only great open plains where nothing grows but very tall grass, which is dry at this season, and had been burnt off by the Miamis in the chase of wild cattle" (Anderson, 1901, p. 79). Presumably the area referred to here is above the confluence of the Iroquois River, and this statement may be connected with the fact that a Miami village had recently been established near the St. Joseph-Kankakee portage (Anderson, 1901, p. 77; IHC 23:11; Margry, 2:216-7).

98

By the end of January, 1681 La Salle had returned from his second Illinois journey to his fort at the mouth of the St. Joseph River of Michigan. There he found about 20 or 30 New England Indians interested in settling, under his auspices, with the Illinois or Miami (Margry 2:140; Anderson, 1901, p. 249). At about the same time a Shawnee chief came to La Salle's fort, and he too expressed interest in this proposal (Margry 2:142-3; Anderson, 1901, p. 259). In view of this development La Salle set out a third time to visit the Illinois Indians in order to determine their reaction to the idea of uniting in a community not only with these other tribes, but also with the Miami (Anderson, 1901, pp. 263-5; Margry 2:144-7?). Upon acceptance by the Illinois of this proposal, he obtained a considerable quantity of corn (100

minots) from them and returned to the mouth of the St. Joseph, where he held
a council with representatives of several eastern tribes (Anderson, 1901,
p. 271; Margry 2:148-9). La Salle convinced them of the advantages of settling in the Illinois and Miami area because of the fruitfulness of the land
with respect to soil, game, and beaver for trade (Anderson, 1901, pp. 271-3;
Margry 2:149-50).

Thus, under the aegis of La Salle, was eventually established in 1683
the grouping of tribes in the upper Illinois area represented on Franquelin's
map of 1684.

To return briefly to the preceding summary, when La Salle went back to
the Illinois in March, 1681 to seek their acquiescence to his colonization
scheme, he was undoubtedly at the "great village," although he makes no reference to it. Nevertheless, the description of his trip leaves no other alternative open. Besides, it is not likely that he could obtain 100 minots of
corn elsewhere in the area. This circumstance seems to indicate that at
least some of the Illinois returned to the village after the Iroquois attack
the preceding September. The point is raised only because in a document
written subsequent to the completion, in March, 1683, of Fort St. Louis on
Starved Rock near the "great village," La Salle makes reference to "the old
village of the Kaskaskias, abandoned by the Illinois since the rout by the
Iroquois three years ago. The news of the fort that I have built there brought
them back with others of different tribes" (Margry 2:175; translation - JJ).

Another account by La Salle only _implies_ abandonment of the village.
Speaking of the settlement in the general vicinity of this village under the
protection of the fort built by Tonty on Starved Rock in the winter of 1682-3,
La Salle writes: "The arrival of the Ciscas and Chaouenons was followed by
the _return_ (italics - JJ) of the Illinois Peoueria, Kaskaskia, Moingoana,

99

Tapouero, Coiracoentanon, Chinkoa, Chepoussa, Maroa, Kaockia and Tamaroa. All these nations were included under the name of Illinois, because they are related [allied?] and there are a number of families of each in the village of Kaskaskia (who are the true Illinois), since their villages were separated from one another by a distance of more than 100 leagues [250 miles]" (Margry 2:201; translation - JJ; see also English translation of Margry, 2:203).

Here it might be profitable to take note of the fact that in the second sentence of the preceding quotation the word "related" appears. This is my translation of the French "allié," which in other translations appears as "allied." In the context of relations between the subgroups of Illinois, "related" would seem to be a not unreasonable translation, especially in a connotation of kinship or relationship through marriage (see also J.R. 64:210 and 211 on this point). In the present excerpt, for example, La Salle clearly states that "...there are a number of families of each [of the other Illinois subgroups] in the village of Kaskaskia..." This by itself is no proof of kinship between the families of other Illinois and families of Kaskaskia. But it seems appropriate at this point to call attention to information from Deliette who arrived among the Illinois in 1687 and whom he left, after their removal to Lake Peoria (see below), in 1698 or 1699. He says: "...It should be stated that they almost all call each other relatives, and such degrees of kinship as I have just enumerated [i.e. father, mother, uncle] are often claimed by persons whom we should not even call cousins. I have seen men of eighty claim that young girls were their mothers" (IHC 23:363-4).

It is unnecessary to go into the complexities and ramifications of the kinship system, but one must also take into account the existence of fictive kinship, in which there are neither affinal nor consanguineal ties. Nevertheless, his statement "that they almost all call each other relatives,"

100

especially in the situation of geographical proximity described, lends support to the assumption that the various groups of Illinois were not merely "allied", but also "related."

If La Salle did consider the village to be abandoned after September, 1680, and not reoccupied until the spring or summer of 1683, it does not necessarily follow that it was not used or visited from time to time by at least some Illinois. Complete reoccupancy soon after the Iroquois destructiveness could, possibly, be an invitation to a second attack of a similar nature. But in view of the proposal made them by La Salle in March, 1681, they might very well have decided to wait until the settlement on the upper Illinois River, with allies secured by La Salle, was ready to be established under French protection as promised by La Salle.

Having considered La Salle's testimony on the question of the abandonment of the Illinois village, it is necessary to introduce a statement by Membré on the same subject. This priest, with Tonty and a large party of French and Indians, accompanied La Salle on his journey to the mouth of the Mississippi. Setting out from the mouth of the St. Joseph River early in January, 1682, they proceeded on down the Illinois River and, toward the end of the month, "...we traversed the great Ilinois town without finding anyone there, the Indians have gone to winter thirty leagues lower down on Lake Pimiteoui [Peoria], where Fort Crevecoeur stands. We found it in a good state, and La Salle left his orders here" (Membré in Shea, 1852, p. 166). Obviously, Membré implies that the village was unoccupied only because of the fact that the Illinois were in winter quarters lower down on the river; although, having arrived at Lake Peoria he makes no mention of their presence there. Contrary to La Salle's view, it does not appear that he considered the "great Illinois town" to have been abandoned.

101

Nevertheless, Tonty, who preceded La Salle on the return from the mouth of the Mississippi, writes that he arrived "...on the 27th [of June, 1682] at the Illinois village, which we found abandoned by reason of fear of the Iroquois" (Anderson, 1898, p. 109). But at this point the failure of the Illinois to be present is understandable. For one thing, Iroquois intentions and action in following up their initial victory was recorded in 1682. In March, at a conference attended by Jesuits and government officials in Quebec, reference was made to "...the war which there is reason to believe the Iroquois wish to continue against the Illinois, over whom they have already gained great advantages;..." (NYCD 9:169). At another conference, in October follow- ing, the view was expressed that "...when they [the Iroquois] set out this year with a body of twelve hundred men, well armed and good soldiers, it was not to be doubted that they would entirely destroy the Illinois..." (JR 62:161; also ibid. p. 151). It is thus not to be wondered at that Illinois discretion might keep them away from the village at this time.

In the second place, the Illinois undoubtedly knew that the Iroquois were in their vicinity in some strength, if only in passing on their hostile way to and from the Sioux. For in June, 1682 Tonty, coming up the Mississippi above the Ohio River, "...encountered four Iroquois, the survivors of a band of a hundred men which had been defeated by the Sioux;..." (Anderson, 1898, p. 107). Elsewhere, however, Tonty says that "In passing toward the Ouabache [Ohio] I found four Iroquois, who told us that there were 100 men of their nation coming after them..." (Kellogg, 1917, p. 304). For the Illinois, this may have put the Iroquois too close for comfort.

In the course of La Salle's descent of the Mississippi in February, 1682, both Tonty and Membré record the presence of a Tamaroa village on the east side of the river, six leagues (15 miles) below the mouth of the Missouri

102

(Tonty in Anderson, 1898, p. 64, & in Kellogg, 1917, p. 297). This "village of a hundred and eighty lodges" was unoccupied, "all the inhabitants being away hunting,..." (Anderson, 1898, p. 65). Tonty stopped briefly at this village on the return trip in June, and was received in friendly fashion only after it had been determined that he was not of a party of Iroquois (Anderson, 1898, p. 107; Kellogg, 1917, p. 304).

After the completion of the Mississippi voyage La Salle sent Tonty back to the Illinois where, during the winter of 1682-3, he constructed Fort St. Louis on Starved Rock. It was completed in March, 1683, and Tonty writes that "During the winter I gave all the nations notice of what we had done to defend them from the Iroquois...They approved of our good intentions, and established themselves, to the number of 300 lodges, at the fort--Ilinois and Miamis and Chaouanons [Shawnee]" (Kellogg, 1917, p. 305; see also Franquelin map 1684). Tonty also stated, in another document, that the Shawnee and Miami came first, and "...later the Illinois, to whom, in the month of March, 1683, I made a journey of more than a hundred leagues [250 miles] across the prairies. After I had made them great presents in behalf of M. de La Salle, ...they gave me their word that they would join us" (Relation, p. 113). It is not clear why Tonty crossed the prairies to reach the Illinois when the usual method was to go by canoe down the Illinois River. There is the possibility that his direction was westerly towards the Mississippi River and the Iowa border. We know that the Kaskaskia, Cahokia, and Chirkoa went up the Mississippi from the Illinois River after the Iroquois incursion in 1680, and it is in that area that he may have known where to find them. An alternative is a hundred leagues south to the mouth of the Kaskaskia River where the Kaskaskia went in 1700. But that was a place more easily accessible to the Iroquois to whose depredations the Illinois were not prepared to expose

103

their settlements although, according to Tonty, even after 1680 Illinois war parties were continually harrassing the Iroquois. "Not a year passes in which they [Illinois] do not take a number of prisoners and scalps" (Tonty in Kellogg, 1917, p. 303).

At any rate, it would seem, from what Tonty has said, that the Illinois joined La Salle's "colony" near Starved Rock, probably sometime after March, 1683.

La Salle was earlier quoted in connection with the arrival of the various groups of Illinois whose villages, he says, were more than 250 miles distant from each other. This seems to be a rather wide dispersal, perhaps induced by fear of the Iroquois. We do know that the Tamaroa, for one, were situated on the Mississippi, about 30 miles below the Illinois River. La Salle also states, in connection with his new "colony" that "The village of the Tamaroas alone is made up of three hundred cabins." The composition of the remaining groups who came to establish themselves here was as follows: "The village of Matchinkoa, with three hundred fires (each fire is for two families) is thirty leagues [75 miles] from the fort, where they also go, and the party of the Emissourites [Missouri], the Peanghichia [Piankashaw] Kolatica, Megancockia, Melomelinoia, who all together make up a village of two hundred to three hundred fires, have their fields at four leagues [10 miles] from the fort. The Oiatenon, numbering 35 huts have come there now, having left their villages with me" (Margry 2:201-2. All translations - JJ; see also English translation of Margry, 2:204).

In this enumeration all known groups of Illinois are accounted for, plus Wea, Piankashaw, Shawnee, Missouri, and people from several other Indian tribes or communities. While La Salle was in France, before returning to North America in 1684 to attempt to establish a colony near the mouth of the

104

Mississippi, he wrote a memoir in which he mentioned "the savages who are at Fort St. Louis, to the number of more than 4,000 warriors,..." (B.F. French, Part 1, p. 29). If this figure is reasonably accurate then the total population of the tribes assembled in the upper Illinois region comprised a rather remarkable concentration of Indian groups.

Nevertheless, this French fortification and this assemblage of Indian allies in the upper Illinois region did not prove to be a sufficient deterrent against an Iroquois war of attrition waged upon the Illinois. During the remainder of the decade official documents and correspondence refer repeatedly to the Iroquois determination to wipe out the Illinois.

In March, 1684, two hundred Iroquois besieged Fort St. Louis but were repulsed at the end of six days (Tonty in Kellogg, 1917, p. 305; see also French 1:79). Still the Iroquois continued their harrassment of the Illinois. Father Lamberville wrote in October, 1684 that "A party of 40 warriors will leave here [Onondaga] in six days to attack the Illinois whom they may find among the Chaouennons" (NYCD 9:260). In November it was reported that the Onondaga "have declared to M. de La Barre that the entire Iroquois nation reserved unto itself the power of waging war against the Illinois as long as a single one of them would remain on earth;" and it was suggested that peaceful relations between the French and the Iroquois would be "uncertain, until they be obliged to leave the Illinois undisturbed" (ibid. p. 249).

This communication of Callieres to Seignelay goes on to state: "It is reported here [Montreal] that these Iroquois have already departed to attack the Illinois, and to endeavor to exterminate them before the arrival of M. De La Salle, who, they learned, was on his way to their relief by the Grand [Mississippi] River. It would be a serious loss to us should they succeed in

105

this design, as the best allies we have among the Indians are the Illinois..."
(idem). When Denonville replaced La Barre as governor in 1685, the king instructed him that "the pride of the Iroquois must be humbled, the Illinois
and other allies who have been abandoned by Sieur de la Barre must be sus-
tained..." (ibid. p. 271); and he must also "prevent the Iroquois by all means,
waging war against the Illinois and other tribes, their neighbors,..." (ibid.
p. 272) because it disrupted the all important fur trade with these groups.
In 1686 a memoir by Denonville states: "I say nothing...of what they (the
Iroquois) have done to the Illinois, whom they spare not, having within two
years destroyed a vast number of them" (ibid. p. 298).

The Iroquois were not entirely single-minded in their purpose against
the Illinois, for in 1686 they also went against the Miami, Hurons and Ottawa
(ibid. p. 319). And in 1688 the French expressed the opinion that even if
they should succeed in concluding peace with the Iroquois, the latter would
not "forego making war on the Illinois and the other tribes to the South,..."
(ibid. p. 395). Early in the last decade of the seventeenth century, however,
Iroquois fury against the Illinois seems to have abated, and reports indicate
that the Illinois and other tribes were successful in harrassment of the
Iroquois (ibid. pp. 502, 516, 537).

The foregoing discussion supports the statement of Pease and Werner
that "...war between the Iroquois and the Illinois was quite the usual thing
in French calculations;..." (IHC 23:xi), especially so in the decade 1680-1690.

IV - 1687-1703

Henri Joutel, a member of La Salle's ill-fated expedition which sought to establish a colony near the mouth of the Mississippi, ascended that river and reached the confluence of the Illinois in September, 1687. During his voyage up the Illinois River he encountered an encampment of Kaskaskia on the bank of a river above Lake Peoria. There he met an Illinois who "told us that he belonged to a village near Fort St. Louis," and he and others accompanied Joutel's party to the fort on Starved Rock (French 1:183), after which "they returned to their own homes" (ibid. p. 184). At the fort, Joutel obtained furs to barter at Michilimackinac and received "visits of two chiefs of two nations called Cascasquia, Peroueria and Cacahouanous (Cahokia or Shawnee?). . ." (ibid. p. 185). Apparently these Illinois groups continued in residence at the "Great Village" since La Salle reported their "return" in 1683.

107

Joutel spent the winter there and took the opportunity to make observations on the richness of the country. He specifically states that "Fort St. Louis is in the country of the Illinois" and adds that "Several of the natives live in [the fort], in their huts" (ibid. p. 186). As he saw the Illinois, "the men have no other business but going to the war and hunting, and the women must fetch the game when they have killed it, which sometimes they are to carry very far to their dwellings" (ibid. p. 187). On October 27th Tonty returned to Fort St. Louis with the Illinois who accompanied him, from a French expedition against the Iroquois. When, in December, two men arrived from Montreal, having left supplies and merchandise at the Chicago River because of low water, the Shawnee chief provided forty men and women to pack the supplies back to the fort (ibid. p. 189). Obviously, the Shawnee brought there by La Salle were still in their settlement at this time. Sieur Deliette,

who arrived at Fort St. Louis in 1687 and was associated with the Illinois for
a number of years, found there ". . .a hundred families of Shawnee. But. . .
I never saw them except for two years,. . ." (IHC 23:307).

Joutel left Fort St. Louis in March 1688. On April 28 he "arrived
among the Poutouatannis which is half way to Micilimaquinay" (French 1:191).
The Potawatomi at this time continue to be associated with the Green Bay region.

In the summer of 1688 Tonty acceded to Deliette's request to be permitted "to accompany a village [band? - JJ] of Illinois who were going off on
a buffalo hunt for five weeks" (IHC 23:307). The chief of this group agreed,
and after their departure they established a "camp two leagues [5 miles] away"
near some woods where they cut poles "for their summer hunting cabin". When
Deliette inquired why "there were so few young men" he was told "that they
were out on a hunting expedition" (ibid. p. 308). This may have been only
partly true, for Deliette says later (ibid. p. 323) that in midsummer 800
Illinois men began returning in small groups from hostilities against the
Iroquois.

After this encampment had slaughtered one hundred and twenty bison they
remained for a week drying the meat (ibid. pp. 310-311). During this process
of meat preservation by the women and girls, Deliette writes, there usually
are "little hunts" by young men who may go out individually at any time "for
bucks, bears, and young turkeys, on which they feast, not failing to invite
strangers whom they have among them (a very frequent thing), such as Miami,
Ottawa, Potawatomi, Kickapoo,. and others;. . ." (ibid. pp. 312-313). Of the
groups mentioned by name, only the Miami were in proximity to the Illinois,
the rest being situated to the north in the Wisconsin, western Lake Michigan,
and the Lake Superior region.

Deliette states that "we went as much as twenty leagues [50 miles] from

the fort on this hunt,. . ." and that "more than 1200 buffalos were killed
during our hunt, without counting the bears, does, stags, bucks, young turkeys,
and lynxes" (ibid. p. 318). They returned from this hunt near mid-July; and
"From that time up to the end of September there arrived continually bands of
ten and fifteen and twenty Illinois, to the number of 800, whom the late Monsieur de Tonti had sent out at the beginning of March against the Iroquois, by
order of Monsieur the Marquis Denonville. They brought in this summer, captive
or killed, sixty men, women, and children" (ibid. pp. 323-324). This lends
confirmation to an earlier statement made in this study that by this time the
Illinois and others began dealing blows against the Iroquois. The latter,
however, were busy with hostilities directed against the French. Therefore
Tonty and la Forest in 1689 ". . .used all their address to induce as many
Illinois as possible to set out against [the Iroquois]. In this they were
fairly successful. . ." (ibid. p. 324).

109

In December of 1689 Tonty set off down the Illinois River to bring
back the survivors of La Salle's expedition and to attempt to carry out the
original purposes of that undertaking. Arriving at the mouth of the Illinois
River on the 17th of the same month Tonty found there a village of Illinois,
of which he writes: "They had just come from fighting the Osages, where they
had lost thirteen men, but brought back 130 prisoners" (Kellogg, 1917, pp. 312-
313). This "village" was probably either a temporary winter camp or, if it
consisted entirely of warriors, a rest stop in Illinois territory on the way
home.

In a "Relation concerning the Illinois. . ." which presumably includes
information up to 1690 Tonty states that: "In going up the river of the
Kankakee on which there is a village of 80 cabins of the Illinois one figures
60 leagues [150 miles]; and from there to the Miami 30 [75 miles]" (IHC 23:276).

The meaning seems to be that the Illinois village is 150 miles up the Kankakee River and that the Miami village near the St. Joseph-Kankakee portage is 75 miles beyond that of the Illinois. If this is, in fact, what Tonty means, then there may be some question about the degree of accuracy of the distances he gives. One hundred and fifty miles up the Kankakee would probably place the Illinois village well within northwestern Indiana. But what follows the sentence quoted seems to be clouded in some obscurity: "As to the Mascouten and Kickapoo they are 15 leagues [37.5 miles] inland, reckoning 200 leagues from the mouth of the Illinois River and 200 leagues from there to the Falls of St. Anthony" (ibid. pp. 276-7). The original French states that this location of the two tribes is inland from the banks of the river, presumably the Mississippi. If so, is the distance to be measured from the Falls of St. Anthony? Or from another point on the river? In any event these two groups would appear to be still in Wisconsin.

In 1691 Tonty left his nephew Deliette temporarily in command at Fort St. Louis, when the Illinois foiled an attempted attack by three hundred Iroquois. In September Deliette received a letter from Tonty saying that ". . .he was coming up with a large number of engagés, and that I should therefore sound the Illinois regarding the abandonment of their village, for which they had shown a desire because their firewood was so remote and because it was so difficult to get water upon the rock if they were attacked by the enemy. They chose the end of Lake Pimitoui, which means Fat Lake, so called on account of the abundance of game there. . . .Monsieur de Tonti arrived in the winter [1691-1692] and started the building of a large fort to which the savages might retire in case of an alarm. The following spring Monsieur de la Forest arrived also with a considerable number of engagés and of soldiers, who completed the building of it. . ." (IHC 23:326-327). This fort, which was also referred to as Fort Pimitoui, was situated ". . .on the northwest shore of Lake Peoria about a mile and a half above the outlet of the lake" (Palm, 1933, p. 14).

There are several points of interest in this quotation of Tonty. It is not unreasonable to infer that Tonty was interested in a change of location for this concentration of Illinois. The desire for such a move was probably prompted by business, trade, and political considerations. At the same time it is probable that the Illinois were already aware, or were told directly, that the French were interested in such a project. The ostensible reasons given by Deliette for the Illinois disposition to move -- need for a closer source of firewood and a more accessible water supply in case of attack -- were valid enough on the face of it. Nevertheless, had the French been willing and able to maintain their fort and to provide protection in the vicinity of Starved Rock, the Illinois would probably have remained at the "great village" or, perhaps, at a suitable location in proximity to it. Had it not been for the French fort the Illinois might have moved much earlier; or they might not even have returned to their village after the 1680 attack. On the other hand, if La Salle had not begun developing the plans he had for the Illinois country the Iroquois might not have made their attack just after La Salle began establishing himself in the Illinois area.

111

Deliette says the Illinois <u>chose</u> to remove to the Lake Peoria area down the river. This was hardly surprising. The place was a traditional wintering area, rich in game, fish, vegetation, and fertility; and La Salle had built Fort Crevecoeur there at the beginning of 1680, on his first journey. Although, the Illinois were given a free choice, as it were, the possibilities were rather severely restricted to the primary considerations of a) accessibility to lines of communication for trade, b) subsistence, and c) defense.

In the circumstances, the move to Lake Peoria down the Illinois River was the only one that made sense for all concerned. The point is, however, that the impetus for this change of locale of the upper Illinois village probably came from the French, upon whom the Illinois were beginning to become increasingly dependent, and in whose decisions, diplomacy, and economic needs their destiny was becoming more closely enmeshed. In varying degrees this was obviously true for all Indian groups under the conditions of European impact; but the Illinois were among those for whom the process began rather early in the history of Indian-European relations.

The Illinois, of course, were vitally interested in trade and, by the same token, in a close French alliance. Tonty was interested in the same things. Establishment of an entrepôt on the Illinois was advantageous in being located between Canada and the southern and western tribes, to say nothing of its advantages in connection with French interest in the mines of the region of the Mississippi and Ohio Rivers.

In 1692 Father Sebastien Rasle arrived at the newly established Illinois village, situated at the south end of Lake Peoria on the west side (north shore) of the river, to take up his missionary post (IHC 23:350). This new village, according to Deliette, was ". . .more than an eighth of a league (0.3+ miles) long. . ." (ibid. p. 362). On Lake Peoria the missionary also found the fort and trading post (Fort St. Louis or Pimitoui) built by Tonty and the engages who were brought by la Forest to staff this new installation. Referring to his arrival among the Illinois Rasle writes: ". . .I came to their first Village, which had three hundred cabins, all of them with four or five fires. One fire is always for two families. They have eleven villages belonging to their tribe" (JR 67:163).

Rasle ". . .remained two years with the Illinois, when I was recalled,. . ."

(ibid. p. 177). The account from which the quotation is taken was written in 1723. But according to Deliette: "This nation is composed of eight villages of which there are six at Pimitoui [Lake Peoria], and two others which I have never seen with them. These last are built eight leagues [20 miles] beyond the mouth of the Illinois River on the Mississippi, called Cahokia and Tamaroa, having I believe, more than sixty cabins.

"The six of which I wish to speak are the Kaskaskia, the Peoria, Moingwena, Coiracoentanon, Tamaroa, Tapouara. The Peoria and Coiracoentanon usually join [in playing lacrosse] against the four other villages because they are as numerous as the other four" (IHC 23:341-342).

Since the six "villages" were probably built in juxtaposition to form one large entity, Rasle's reference to a single community is understandable. On the other hand, Deliette's intention may have been merely to indicate that members of six subdivisions of the Illinois were living in the same village. In this connection it may be appropriate to call attention to Habig's hypothesis that at the "great village" the Illinois subdivisions probably ". . .did not mingle but settled as separate groups, one adjoining the other, though there may have been a short distance between their villages. All of these villages, taken together, constituted the Great Village, varying at different times in population as well as extent, always, however, situate in the same general neighborhood until it was destroyed by the invading Iroquois in September, 1680" (Habig, 1933, p. 4).

This hypothesis would appear to be confirmed by Deliette. He says that Missouri River tribes, such as the Osage and the Missouri, came to the Illinois to trade, and that ". . .aside from their need of hatchets, knives, and awls, and other necessary things, are very glad to keep on the good side of this nation, which is much more warlike than theirs. They never fail every

113

year to come among them and to bring them the calumet, which is the symbol of peace among all the nations of the south.

". . .Two leagues from the village to which they are going they send ahead some of their best known people to announce their arrival, how many they are, and to whom they come to sing the calument. Messengers are sent back to them with orders to tell them how many men are to lodge at the village of the Peoria, how many at that of the Kaskaskia, and so on,. . ." (IHC 23:389-390).

It would be difficult to infer from the last sentence in the foregoing quotation anything other than that the Illinois settlement at Lake Peoria was composed of identifiable aggregations or communities consisting of the Illinois subdivisions enumerated by Deliette. If this was true at the time and place under consideration there is no reason to question the existence earlier of the same settlement pattern at the erstwhile "great village", as suggested by Habig.

114

Deliette's statement that the "Peoria and Coiracoentanon are as numerous as the other four" groups of Illinois is a reminder of the reference to the 1680 period in the Official Narrative of La Salle that the Peoria are the "most populous" of the Illinois (Anderson, 1901, p. 215). But it is plain that Rasle and Deliette are in disagreement as to the total number of "villages". It may be that the size and types of grouping varied, for other names are sometimes cited which might total eleven, more or less. For example, La Salle mentions the Chepoussa, Chinkoa, Amonokoa (Margry·2:201; IHC 23:5).

The same two sources (Deliette and Rasle) are also somewhat at variance in the number of cabins and the number of "fires" in each cabin; but the difference here is probably more apparent than real. Rasle's account was

written about twenty-nine years later, after two years at Lake Peoria.
Deliette left in 1698 or 1699 after seven years at the same place. Furthermore, his memoir was probably written in 1704 at the earliest, for he refers
to "the late Monsieur de Tonti" (IHC 23:323); and he also says that "It is
four years ago this spring that I left the place" (ibid, p. 327). If Rasle's
memory served him well then his information concerning 300 cabins, each with
4 or 5 fires, may be taken as of 1694, when he left. With two families per
fire there were approximately 2,700 families. Deliette's data would be as of
1698 or 1699, four or five years later than Rasle's. According to Deliette:
"I left there something over 260 cabins, which have from one to four fires.
I put them at two on the average, and thus calculate about 800 warriors
between the ages of twenty and forty" (IHC 23:327). He does not mention the
number of families per fire, but if Rasle's figure is used there were 1,040
families, considerably less than half the number that may be extrapolated
from Rasle's information. With Deliette's superior knowledge of the culture
and language of the people, his information concerning them would be more
valid. But in the intervening years between 1694 and 1698-9, geographical
mobility might have resulted in a reduction in the number of dwellings at the
Lake Peoria village.

115

Father Gravier came to the mission at this settlement in March 1693.
He refers specifically to the presence of four villages and their chiefs,
although his discussion centers exclusively on the Kaskaskia and Peoria
(JR 64:197). In connection with the discussion above, concerning the nature
of the total community here, he writes, at one point, of "the village of the
Peouareoua" (ibid. p. 199) and also "the chiefs of all the villages" (ibid.
p. 181). In addition, he makes a reference to ". . .the other villages of
the Ilinois which are on the banks of the Mississipi River. . ." (ibid. p. 171).

In the latter case he has in mind ". . .the Tamaroua and the Kaoukia [Cahokia], who are Illinois;. . ." (ibid. p. 161).

Gravier's statement concerning four villages at Lake Peoria differs with Deliette who said there were six. Since the latter's information dated from as late as 1698 or 1699 it could simply mean that at the time of Gravier's arrival only four had as yet been erected, the others joining later.

Some idea of the distance of the cultivated fields from the villages, and the area over which they were dispersed, is derived from Gravier's journal. He writes: "As there are always people here who dwell amid the fields, at a distance of more than a league from the village, until they depart for their winter quarters, I continued my short excursions from the month of July to the 24th or 25th of September [1693]. . .I went to visit alternately those who were in their corn and squash fields. At a distance of a league from the village is a small one, on a hill whose base is bathed by a river,. . ." (ibid. p. 185). He then goes on to relate that ". . .I visited from time to time all whose fields were in that quarter. My walk always covered fully three leagues [7.5 miles], over a very good road;. . ." (ibid. p. 189).

When, on September 26, 1693, "All the people left for their winter quarters. . .excepting some old women, who remained in 14 or 15 cabins, and a considerable number of Kaskaskia. . ." the missionary tried ". . .to prevent the sick children being embarked without receiving baptism. . ."; and he ". . .followed others as far as the place of embarkation,. . ." where he spoke with "the chief of the Peouareoua. . ." (ibid. p. 189). It seems evident that at this time most, if not all, of the Peoria and, perhaps with them, or on their own, part of the Kaskaskia went on the winter hunt. Obviously the departure on this winter hunt was made in pirogues; but whether the

116

people went up or downstream is not stated. But in February 1680 Hennepin, on
his way down this river below Lake Peoria, met Illinois pirogues returning upstream loaded with bison meat from the hunt. If the direction at this time
also was south it is possible that the Illinois then went down the Mississippi
and up the Ohio to hunt on the south side of the latter river. For Deliette
says that in that region "Spring arrives a month earlier than among the
Illinois. At most there are never more than two inches of snow, which dis-
appears in two days. Although I have been there only in summer, I can speak
authoritatively owing to the knowledge which I have got from the Illinois,
most of whom go there every year to hunt" (IHC 23:394; italics - JJ).

As regards Gravier's account, whether or not the Kaskaskia and the
Peoria conducted their hunt jointly, the former, apparently, returned sooner,
probably by the end of January or early February, 1694. After noting that
the Kaskaskia came back from the hunt, and discussing his pleasure over their
receptivity to his religious ministrations, Gravier expresses the hope that
he will ". . .find the same docility among a portion of the Peouareoua on
their return from their winter quarters" (JR 64:227, 233). It is obvious also
that the chiefs of the Kaskaskia and of the Peoria differed strongly in their
attitudes toward the missionary, the former succumbing to the religious onslaught while the latter continued in adamant opposition, the people of each
reflecting the differing attitudes of their respective leaders.

Apart from the mission, the primary interest of the French was, of
course, trade. Gravier reports that in May 1693 some Illinois accompanied
two French traders to the Missouri and Osage villages ". . .with the view of
carrying on an advantageous trade with those tribes,. . ." (JR 64:161). The
following June this expedition, which had been undertaken ". . .in the expec-
tation of the great profits they would derive from the trade with the latter

117

[Osage and Missouri] came back with two chiefs from each village, accompanied by some elders and some women" (ibid. pp. 169-171).

Deliette, it may be recalled, also mentions trade with the Osage and Missouri who, after the establishment of this trade alliance on the expedition referred to by Gravier, came every year with the calumet for the trade, bringing gifts to their hosts and engaging in ceremonial and commercial exchanges (IHC 23:387-391). It is also stated by Deliette, incidentally, that porcupine quills with which the Illinois "trim their gala moccasins" are obtained from the Potawatomi and the Ottawa, which indicates that there was also a continuing trade from an earlier period with those tribes to the north (ibid. p. 339). He says, further, that "The French and Indians [at Lake Peoria]. . .even carry on a trade in lead with the Indians who came to trade with them" (ibid. p. 347).

In the summer of 1698 a company of priests and lay brothers of the Seminary of Quebec set out on a journey to establish missions among tribes on the Mississippi below the Illinois. Under the guidance of Tonty they left Michilimackinac in the middle of September, and followed the west shore of Lake Michigan. A record of this voyage was left by one of the Seminarians in the party, Father Jean F.B. de St. Cosmé, who notes the presence of particular Indian groups at various points along the way.

St. Cosmé writes that several tribes inhabit the Green Bay area, among which are the Menominee, Potawatomi, Sac, and the Fox, the latter being on the Fox River en route to the Fox-Wisconsin portage (Kellogg, 1917, p. 344). On the Lake Michigan side of Door Peninsula, and east of the southern end of Green Bay, the large Potawatomi village of long standing was in process of being depleted since the death of its chief, some of its occupants going to live on Green Bay. A small village of Potawatomi, probably situated near Manitowoc, provided shelter early in October. Reaching the Milwaukee River on

118

October 9 they stayed for two days in what was a large village consisting of
Mascouten, Fox and Potawatomi (ibid. pp. 394-5).

On October 21 the expedition reached the Jesuit Mission at Chicago,
founded in 1696 by Father Pinet (ibid. p. 346). Nearby was a village of over
150 cabins of Miami, ". . .and a league up the [Chicago] river is still
another village almost as large" (idem.). Deliette writes that after leaving
the Illinois at Lake Peoria in 1698 or 1699 ". . .I remained [four years] with
the Wea at Chicago, which is the most considerable village of the Miami, who
have been settled there for ten or twelve years,. . ." (IHC 23:392). He also
indicates that during the years between 1687 and 1704 they established villages
on the Calumet River ". . .and at the fork of the Kankakee River" (idem.).

St. Cosmé states that after they came to the Illinois River, some
unspecified distance below the Kankakee, they reached ". . .the village of
the Peangichias [Piankashaw],. . .who have for some years been settled at this
place" (Kellogg, 1917, p. 349). The Illinois left the "great village" on the
upper Illinois in the winter of 1691-1692. According to Franquelin's map of
1684 the Piankashaw were among the tribes forming La Salle's colony, and they
seem to be denoted on the upper Illinois, thus indicating that the village
observed by St. Cosmé may have continued to be occupied since about 1683, and
subsequent to the departure of the Illinois almost ten years later. Franquelin's map of 1688, however, shows the Piankashaw more clearly north of the
upper Illinois River.

About 2.5 miles above the abandoned Fort St. Louis on Starved Rock,
the party ". . .found two cabins of savages; we were consoled on finding a
woman who was a thoroughly good Christian" (ibid. p. 350). If these Indians
were Illinois it is quite probable that the christianized woman was a Kaskaskia. The Frenchmen reached the Illinois settlement at Lake Peoria on November

119

19, 1698, but the Indians ". . .were all scattered down the bank of the river for hunting" (ibid. p. 351). The few women they did see were married to Frenchmen, a process which seems to have been proceeding apace. It is worthy of note also that Cosmé says the Illinois were "down" the river; and, in fact, continuing his voyage downstream he met six encampments of them. Furthermore, the Jesuits, Binneteau and Pinet, who were ministering to the Illinois at the time, accompanied the Seminarians part way ". . .as they wished to go and spend the whole winter with their savages"; which indicates that at this time, at any rate, most, if not all, Illinois were hunting to the south of Lake Peoria (idem.).

Cosmé states that, continuing on their way from Lake Peoria, they arrived, on November 23, at the encampment of the Kaskaskia chief, Rouensa, "the most notable of the Illinois chiefs" who informed them that the Shawnee, Chickasaw, and Kakinampols [?]". . .had attacked the Kaoukias [Cahokia], an Illinois tribe about five or six leagues below the mouth of the river of the Illinois along the Miçissipi,. . ." killing ten men an taking 100 women and children prisoners (ibid. p. 351).

120

Indications that the Illinois were tending either to concentrate in, or to orient themselves toward, the southern half of Illinois and, possibly, beyond may be inferred from Cosmé's statement that they gave Rouensa some presents ". . .to induce him to facilitate our passage through the Illinois tribes, not so much for this first voyage as for the others, when we should not be so strong;. . ." (ibid. p. 352). And following this visit with the Kaskaskia chief they stopped at five more Illinois encampments along the river before they reached the Mississippi.

Their second stop was at "a small village of savages" where they spoke with a chief named "L'Ours", the Bear (idem.). On November 24 ". . .we slept

at another village of several cabins where we found one Tiret, a chief who
was formerly famous in his nation but who has since been abandoned by nearly
all his people" (idem.). The next day they left Father Pinet ". . .who remains
in this village to spend the winter, for there are a good many savages here
who pray,. . ." (idem). On November 26 they arrived at ". . .a village whose
chief was away hunting with all the young men. Some old men came to meet us,
weeping for the death of their people killed by the Chaouanons [Shawnee]. . ."
(ibid. p. 353). In view of Rouensa's information, this might have been an
encampment of Cahokia whose year round village was on the Mississippi. After
spending the night five or six leagues below this place ". . .on the 28th we
landed at a village consisting of about twenty cabins, where we saw the woman
chief" (idem). Here they found a French soldier married to one of the women,
and here, too, Father Binneteau remained for the winter. They travelled nine
more leagues (22.5 miles) finding a variety and abundance of game along the
way, and came to a camp of five cabins where they obtained some pirogues
(ibid. p. 354).

121

The expedition started down the Mississippi on December 6, and after
travelling fifteen miles, they reached a point opposite the mouth of the
Missouri, on the left (east) bank of the Mississippi, where "We camped that
day at the Kaouchias [Cahokia], who were still in grief in consequence of the
attack made upon them by the Chikachas [Chickasaw] and the Chaouanons" (ibid.
p. 355). The following day they reached the Tamarois who were camped on an
island below their village ". . .probably in order to obtain wood more easily
than in their village, which is on the edge of a prairie and some distance
away, probably through fear of their enemies" (ibid. p. 356). It is difficult
to infer just where the village might have been, at this time, although it is
known that in 1682 Tonty visited a Tamarois village on the east side of the

Mississippi the same distance below the Missouri at which St. Cosme here reports the presence of the Cahokia village. Thaumur de la Source, who was in the party with St. Cosmé, wrote that the Tamarois are ". . .eight leagues [20 miles] from the Illinois. It is the largest village that we have seen. There are about 300 cabins there" (Shea, 1861, p. 84). It is not obvious from his account that he saw the village itself to ascertain by his own count the number of cabins, but he suggests the population was substantial (see below). La Source, however, was a brief visitor, and his information does not square with reports of others quoted below.

In any event the Tamarois were not far below the Cahokia village, and, in fact, Cosme says they were "quite near" each other, so that a mission established among the Tamarois could serve both groups (Kellogg, 1917, p. 356). He says that ". . .there seemed to be a great many of them, although the majority of their people were away hunting" (idem). According to La Source "there are as many people at the Tamarois as at Kebeq" (Shea, 1861, p. 84). An additional incentive for establishing the Tamarois mission was ". . .the Mechigamias, who live a little lower down the Micissipi, and who are said to be pretty numerous"; but St. Cosme did not see the latter ". . .because they had gone into the interior to hunt" (Kellogg, 1917, p. 356). The priest thus had the idea of bringing together in one mission the Cahokia to the north of the Tamarois and the Mitchigamia to the south, all three fairly near each other along the east bank of the Mississippi, southward from the mouth of the Missouri.

It is apparent, therefore, that in the winter of 1698-1699 the major concentration of Illinois settlements was along the Illinois River southward from Lake Peoria to the Mississippi, with an enclave along the east side of the Mississippi some distance southward of the Missouri. This by no means precluded use of the interior for hunting within the bounds of the Illinois,

122

Mississippi and Wabash rivers.

In January 1699 Father Binneteau wrote a letter from his missionary post among the Illinois at Peoria to a Jesuit confrere after the departure of St. Cosme and his fellow Seminarians. After commenting on the fact of intermarriage between Frenchmen and Illinois women, a statement which is supported by la Source, who says that "many Canadians marry among the Illinois"(Shea, 1861, p. 85), Binneteau notes the further interesting fact that "Kikabous [Kickapoo] as well as Illinois are lodged around us, in order to cultivate corn in the neighborhood of our chief village" (JR 65:69). This is the only statement made with reference to the presence of the Kickapoo in the winter of 1698-9; nor is it clear whether corn had already been planted or was yet to be planted in the spring. Numbers are not stated, but in view of the obviously friendly relations their presence could have been useful also in defense. In addition, it undoubtedly meant trade and hunting in, or on the periphery of, the Illinois country for the Kickapoo whose earlier presence in the Illinois area was recorded to the north in 1680 (see Margry, English translation, 4:661).

123

Binneteau's statement that he is ". . .at present spending the winter with a portion of our savages who are scattered about. . ." may refer to the group headed by a female "chief" with whom he remained after St. Cosme's departure from that encampment (JR 65:71). He also writes that "I have recently been with the Tamarois, to visit a band of them on the bank of. . . the Missisipi. . .," and indicated that "I am to return to the Illinois of Tamaroa in the spring" (idem). Finally, he notes the method of movement of the Illinois on the winter hunt. He writes: "All walk, or proceed in pirogues, to the wintering-place. From there the most active men, women, and girls go into the interior, to seek the ox;. . ." (ibid. p. 73). The implication of "interior" here is, obviously away from the Illinois River, which, technically, might be east or west, of the river, but probably means east.

On the return journey of the Seminary priests in 1699, la Source records that while ". . .going up the Illinois River we came near being plundered by the Miamis" (Shea, 1861, p. 84); and then at Chicago they stayed with the Miami who, he says, were ". . .trying to pick a quarrel with us" (ibid. p. 85). There is no indication as to where on the river the Miami intercepted the French, although the likelihood is that it was north of Lake Peoria, a region in which there seems to have been no permanent establishments of Illinois at the time.

Some time between March 28 and May 20, 1699 the Tamarois mission was established by the Seminary of Quebec (Fortier, 1909, p. 233). Montigny, who headed the group of priests on the expedition, was among the Tamarois when he wrote early in May 1699, that the Tamarois and Cahokia ". . .make about 600 men. . .but since our arrival the Mitchigamea and the Missouris having joined them, they make [now] at least 8,000 souls" (MA 21:232, fn. 48). Tonty, in a letter dated March 4, 1700 states that the Tamarois ". . .is a village of 400 Illinois Indians" (idem). Writing in the latter part of February, 1700 from the Tamarois mission, where he arrived earlier the same month, Bergier, another Seminary priest, says: "I have counted there a hundred cabins in all, or thereabouts, of which nearly half are vacant because the greater part of the Cahokias are still in winter quarters twenty or twenty-five leagues [40-50 miles] from here up the Mississippi" (Fortier, 1909, p. 236). This means, then, that the majority of the Cahokia were probably wintering about 10-20 miles above the mouth of the Illinois River.

Bergier then goes on to say that "the village is composed of Tamarois, Cahokias, some Michigans [Michigamea] and Peorias. There are also some Missouri cabins. . ." who are there only temporarily (ibid. pp. 236-7).

124

According to this source, "The Tamarois and the Cahokias are the only ones
that really form part of this mission. The Tamarois have about thirty cabins
and the Cahokias have nearly twice that number. Although the Tamarois are at
present less numerous than the Cahokias, the village is still called Tamaroa,
. . .because the Tamarois have been the first and are still the oldest inhabitants. . .All the other nations who have joined them afterwards. . .have
been known under the name Tamarois although they were not Tamarois" (ibid.
p. 237).

It may be inferred from this excerpt that there is a special relationship between the Tamarois and the Cahokia which seems to be distinct from the
other possible combinations of Illinois subgroups. It is apparently similar
to the relationship between the Kaskaskia and the Peoria, who are most often
reported as living near each other, or jointly, or in close association, as
at Lake Peoria and, before then, on the upper Illinois. What is also interesting in this statement is that in spite of the fact that this is a village
founded by the Tamarois, there are almost twice as many cabins of Cahokia.
This implies that the population of the latter may have been, perhaps, double
the former. Certainly the number of cabins in this village differs from the
300 reported by la Source and from the 180 of Tonty in 1682; but as far as
these individuals knew they were all Tamarois. Up to now the Tamarois and
Cahokia villages had been reported separately. It seems, however, that during
1699 the priests managed to forge a close residential association between the
Cahokia and Tamarois into one community of habitations.

In the letter of Tonty, referred to above, he says that the Miami are
situated on the St. Joseph River, where La Salle reported a village in late
1679. He also writes that "there are at least 800 men settled at Fort St.
Louis" on Lake Peoria (MA 21:233), by which he means the Illinois.

125

In June 1700 Bergier reported that the Tamarois village was subject to "frequent alarms" because of enemy incursions, and he mentions an incident involving four Sioux in the vicinity who were finally captured and killed (Fortier, 1909, p. 237). Bergier also adds that ". . .the Shawnee who are enemies of the Illinois are feared" (idem).

Other tribes also felt the strong arm of the Sioux as reported by Father Marest on July 10, 1700 in a letter to LeSueur. In this case the Michigamea joined in a retaliatory effort revealed in this excerpt from Marest's letter: ". . .the Peanguichas [Piankashaw] have been routed by the Sioux and the Ayavois. They have combined with the Quicapous and some Mascoutins, Renards [Fox] and Metisigamias and are going to wreak their vengeance,. . ." (Margry Transl. 6:93; A-263; italics - JJ). The letter was received by LeSueur from three Canadians whom he met at the mouth of the Illinois River. The preceding June, on his way up the Mississippi he had stopped at the Tamarois village, which he left on July 12, 1700.

On July 30, about 100 miles above the Illinois River LeSueur "fell in with seventeen Sioux in seven canoes, going to avenge the death of three Sioux, of whom one had been burned and the others killed among the Tamaroas, a few days before his arrival at their village. As he had promised the chief of the Illinois that he would pacify the Sioux who should come to fight against his tribe, he made a present of some goods to the leader of this expedition, to induce him to turn back" (ibid. p. 94). To this proposal the Sioux leader assented.

After the failure of La Salle's plans to open the lower Mississippi Valley to French trade and settlement, they began to assume more positive form by the end of the last decade of the 17th century with the establishment, during the first half of 1699, of Iberville's post at Biloxi on the lower

126

Mississippi. As governor of Louisiana, Iberville conceived plans which
". . .like that of La Salle contemplated an extensive rearrangement of the
native tribes"; but it was not until 1702 that he set those plans down in an
"elaborate memorial" (Alvord, 1920, p. 129).

In a "Memorandum on the settlement of Mobile and the Mississippi"
Iberville's idea was to "induce the Illinois tribe to settle on the Wabash
[Ohio], - the river which will take us to the English colonies and to the
Iroquois" and, further, that "the Illinois should be informed that they must
not expect to trade with Canada in future, but must do their trade with the
posts on the Mississippi. When they see that no one will trade with them
unless they come to Wabash [the Ohio], they will come there provided a few
presents are made to the chiefs of the <u>various tribes of which the Illinois
are made up consisting of a thousand men, armed and warlike</u>" (A-261, pp.
651-2; italics - JJ). The plan also provided for a move by the Sioux to the   127
Des Moines River, and for LeSueur "to negotiate peace between them and the
Illinois, the Renards, Kikapous and Maskoutins,. . ." (ibid. p. 652).

The "civilizing" and exploitive intent of Iberville's program was
brought out in the following statement: "Having, as I proposed, placed the
Illinois at the mouth of the Wabash [Ohio], where there would be a French post,
and the Sioux at the mouth of the River Moingona [Des Moines], a hundred
leagues this side of the Wabash, to the west of the Mississippi, we shall set
those people and the others, in time, to the wool, cotton and silk trades,
and to working in the lead and other mines" (ibid. p. 654).

In discussing his proposed arrangement for a division of the fur trade
between Canada and his Mississippi colony by means of formal geographical
boundaries between the two provinces, Iberville had this to say: ". . .all
the streams falling into the Mississippi, up to their sources, and the tribes

upon them, should belong to the Mississippi [colony], as may also the whole
tribe of the Illinois, the Miamis at the fork of the Illinois River, or those
at Wisconsin, the Pegoncoquias [Piankashaw?], the Maskoutens, the Kikapous,
who number about 400 men, and the other tribes, which I do not know on those
rivers.

"Those who should be under Canada are the Indians on the rivers falling
towards Canada, such as the Miamis of Chicago, those on the R. Ahitipuat [?]
and those on the St. Joseph River; all these rivers fall into the [Lake]
Michigan" (ibid., p. 656).

According to this document, then, the several groups of the Illinois
Indians, with a complement of a thousand "warlike" men, are, presumably,
among those tribes situated on the eastern affluents of the Mississippi.
Apparently the Sioux are considered to be in a state of hostility not only
with the Illinois, but also with the Fox, Kickapoo and Mascouten. Iberville
wants the Illinois to move near the mouth of the Ohio where a French post
would be established. The Miami are said to be located on the Chicago River,
and at the Kankakee - Des Plaines confluence, while the Kickapoo and Mascouten
are associated with the Wisconsin River.

The Canadian officials and traders, for their part, wanted their
territory to extend to the Ohio River and a post to be established at the
mouth of the Wisconsin River to which, presumably, the Kickapoo and Mascouten,
among others, would bring their trade. Since the Canadians also intended to
set up "the post of the Miamis or Chicago," Iberville felt that "if they
establish a warehouse there, it is evident that all the Indians on the Illinois
river would go there, since it would be only 60 leagues [150 miles] away by
water, and less by land, and they would not think of the Mississippi." As a
result, wrote Iberville, "we need take no steps to attract the Illinois away

from their land [to the Ohio River] nor hope to obtain from them any assistance except in the direction of Canada and for the beaver trade only" (ibid.
p. 653).

In other words, Illinois action at this time would be motivated
primarily by the opportunities for trade. Should a post be established at
Chicago, Iberville would expect the Illinois to reject a move to the vicinity
of the Ohio "away from their land." The implication of this last phrase may,
perhaps, best be seen in relation to the statement above that "all the Indians
on the Illinois river would go" to Chicago to trade rather than to the
Mississippi. Since the distance to Chicago via the Illinois River is
estimated at about 150 miles, it would seem to imply that Iberville took the
vicinity of Lake Peoria as the point of departure. In this case it seems
reasonable to suppose that the lands of the Illinois would be encompassed
roughly within an arc radiating eastward from Lake Peoria as a center. The
northern end of such an arc might be in the area of the Kankakee-Des Plaines
confluence, with the southern terminus in the vicinity of the Mississippi-
Ohio region.

129

Iberville also indicates that if the Illinois are attracted to trade at
Chicago "We shall not be able to induce them to make peace with the Sioux, who
are seeking peace and have made advances to obtain it". And he seems to be
saying that continuing hostilities between Sioux and Illinois will involve
the Fox, Kickapoo and Mascouten for, as he put it, "The Renards, Kikapous and
Maskoutins will be captured again." This sentence is followed immediately by:
"We need not think of going to the country of the Sioux, as we should risk
meeting the tribes situated between the Illinois and Lake Superior, on the
east of the Mississippi, who would attack us as they have done before" (ibid.
p. 653). Whichever tribes Iberville may have had in mind, and it would appear

that the Kickapoos and Mascouten were not included among them, their location between the Illinois (river or tribe) and Lake Superior would place them in Wisconsin and, probably, northern and/or northwestern Illinois.

During 1700 there was apparently considerable disagreement among the Illinois at Lake Peoria as to their course of action in response to the new opportunities which appeared to be opened by news of the establishment of the French in Louisiana. When, in September of that year, Father Gravier visited the settlement briefly, he managed to placate the Peoria and the Moingoena, who were violently opposed to the Kaskaskia; but he did not succeed in convincing the latter to abandon their plans to relocate on the Mississippi. As Gravier tells it: "I arrived too late among the Illinois of the strait [at the southern end of Lake Peoria]. . .to prevent the migration of the Village of the Kaskaskia, which has been too precipitately made, in consequence of uncertain news respecting the Mississipi settlement. I do not think that the Kaskaskia would have thus separated from the Peouaroua _and from the other Illinois of the strait_, if I could have arrived sooner. I reached them at least soon enough to conciliate their minds to some extent, and to prevent the insult that the Peouaroua and the Mouingouena were resolved to offer the Kaskaskia and the French when they embarked" (JR 65:101; italics - JJ). Apparently, the action finally taken by the Kaskaskia had been under debate for some time, because Gravier goes on to say that there will come ". . .no good from this Separation, _which I have always opposed_,. . ." (ibid. p. 103; italics - JJ).

The Peoria, however, promised to await Gravier's return from the lower Mississippi settlement, where he was to visit Father du Rue; and Gravier said that he ". . .would never leave their Village until I should inform them to what place the great Chief [Iberville] who is at the lower end of the River

130

wished them to remove" (idem). Gravier then accompanied the Kaskaskia for four days, and went on to the Tamarois village, which he left on October 9, 1700. The Tamarois themselves were not in the village, for Gravier writes: "At 2 Leagues [5 miles] from the village I found the Tamarouha, who have taken up their winter quarters in a fine Bay, where they await the Metchigamia, — who are to come more than 60 leagues to winter there, and to form but one village with them" (ibid. p. 105). He also adds that the Cahokia ". . .have taken up their winter quarters 4 leagues [10 miles] above the village" (idem).

The "Tamarouha" village, mentioned by Gravier was where the Seminary priests established themselves in 1699. It came to be known as Cahokia; and there some Frenchmen, according to Gravier (ibid. p. 103), were also settled near the joint Tamarois-Cahokia village. It was five miles below this place on the Mississippi that the Tamarois were wintering and expecting the Michigamea to join them, while the Cahokia were encamped ten miles above the village.

131

The information provided by Gravier pertains to the autumn of 1700. From a letter written by Bergier at the Tamarois Mission on April 13, 1701, we learn a little of what happened after Gravier left the Kaskaskia and the other Illinois. Bergier writes that the Kaskaskia ". . .to the extent of about thirty cabins have established their new village two leagues below this one [Tamarois-Cahokia] on the other [west] side of the Mississippi. They have built a fort there and nearly all the French hastened there" (Fortier, 1909, p. 238). As indicated above, these French were already living near the village which came to be known as Cahokia. It is not immediately apparent why the French "hastened" to join the Kaskaskia unless they expected some definite trade advantage connected with the western Indians, or greater freedom from Canadian authority.

In addition to the French, the Tamarois chief and a part of his people crossed the river to join the Kaskaskia, and were to be followed by the rest of their people. The Cahokia remained. Bergier writes: "the Chief of the Tamarois followed by some cabins joined the Kats [Kaskaskia], attracted by Rouensae who promises them much and makes them believe him saying that he is called by the great chief of the French, Mr. d'Iberville, as Father Marest has told him.

"The remainder of the Tamarois numbering about twenty cabins are shortly going to join their chief, already settled at the Kats. So there will remain here only the Cahokias numbering 60 or 70 cabins. They are now cutting stakes to build a fort" (idem).

If Rouensa was telling the truth, that Father Marest, who went with them to their new village, said it was Iberville's wish that the Illinois move, it certainly ties in with the subsequent plans outlined by Iberville in his memorial of 1702. But Marest might have had something to do with the decision of the Kaskaskia to establish themselves on the west side of the Mississippi because of the rivalry between the Jesuits and the Seminarians. And Rouensa succeeded in influencing the Tamarois, if not the Cahokia, to join him almost immediately. With the building of a "fort", the Cahokia were obviously planning to remain on the east side of the river. Father Marest, who was with the Kaskaskia at the time of this change does not provide information to confirm or deny Bergier's statements regarding the location of their village. A letter written by Marest on November 26, 1702 is headed simply "among the ilinois On the missisipi" (JR 66:41), from which it is apparent that they were, at the time of Marest's writing, still where Bergier's letter of April 1701 placed them. Further documentary evidence adduced, and the analysis made by Palm, indicates that the Kaskaskia were located ". . .at the

132

mouth of the River Des Peres in what is now St. Louis. They remained here for about two and a half years and then left again for their more enduring settlement upon the Kaskaskia River in Randolph County, Illinois, where they arrived on April 13, 1703" (Palm, 1933, p. 14; esp. Palm, 1931, pp. 36-41).

In his letter Marest reports the arrival of Juchereau who, in accordance with Iberville's plans, was given a grant of land to set up a tannery on the Ohio River. As part of the enterprise Marest ". . .took steps for endeavoring to assemble the ilinois at wabache [Ohio River];. . ." but he felt it would be difficult to achieve (JR 66:39). He did, however, accompany Juchereau ". . .for a distance of 30 Leagues [75 miles] from my village to see roensa in his winter quarters" (idem). In view of the location of their village the Kaskaskia were most likely, but not necessarily, hunting in Missouri.

Another Iberville memorandum, dated June 20, 1702, written at approximately the same time as the previous one (see above), and entitled "Memorandum on the country of the Mississippi. . ." was again concerned with the question of obtaining a supply of hunters of bison and other animals (not beaver), in the interests of the Mississippi Colony, by relocating tribes who were accustomed to trading for beaver skins. In offering his proposals he states that the Ohio River "is not inhabited by any Indians" and that, therefore, "I should like to make the most of it, by bringing the Illinois tribe to occupy the district who would devote themselves to hunting oxen and roebucks as well as getting the skins of smaller animals, the surrounding country being full of them" (Margry, English translation, 4:660). This statement is apparently connected with the purpose of Juchereau's grant; but more important is the restatement of the plan to get the Illinois to move to the Ohio River. And once again Iberville writes: "While the Illinois are in

133

their present position, they become useless to us for any purpose since we do not wish to go on trading with them for beaver skins" (idem). The "present position" of the Illinois, as was shown in the previous Iberville memorandum, was essentially the area of the state of Illinois bounded by the Illinois, Mississippi, Ohio, and perhaps, the Wabash Rivers. But if the Illinois were to go to hunt on the Ohio from "their present district," they would, according to Iberville, "have to come a distance of 30 to 40 leagues [75–100 miles] for the hunting, in the direction of the Wabash" (ibid. p. 661). If the distance to the Ohio here given is reasonably accurate then it is probable that the reckoning was made from a point on the Mississippi, either in the vicinity of St. Louis or Cahokia. At any rate, if the Illinois settled on the Ohio, Iberville says that "we should have a thousand good armed men, including the Illinois of the West, of whom we could make use in case of need" (idem). There is no indication as to the identity of "the Illinois of the West".

134

Once the Illinois were on the Ohio River it was Iberville's plan to have the Kickapoo and Mascouten move into the area thus vacated. In this connection he gives some idea of the general situation of the latter groups in relation to the Illinois. He writes: "When the Illinois have left their country, we shall easily get the Maskoutens and the Kikapous to occupy it. That would give us 450 good men, who are now on the streams falling into the Illinois River and the Mississippi. Their only occupation is hunting for beaver skins, which they go and sell at the Bay des Puans [Green Bay] and in the Illinois country" (idem; italics - JJ).

From what Iberville said in his previous memorandum (ibid. p. 656), he associated the Mascouten and Kickapoo with the Wisconsin River region. In the present instance, however, it seems that he would include not only that

affluent of the Mississippi, perhaps, together with others, but also the
affluents of the Illinois River. Given the Illinois Indians in the area east
of the Illinois River, then Iberville implies that the Kickapoo and Mascouten
were exploiting the western affluents of the same river in northwestern
Illinois. Thus, the Kickapoo and Mascouten were probably generally within
the southern half of Wisconsin and northwestern Illinois. Such an interpretation would also fit in with their trading at Green Bay and "in the Illinois
country." In the latter case they must have traded at Peoria for, as cited
above, Kickapoo were with the Illinois at that place in the winter of 1698-
1699, as recorded by Binneteau (JR 65:69).

That the Illinois River is the area that Iberville basically had in
mind when he spoke of the Illinois leaving "their country" is revealed by a
later statement in the present document in which he specifically mentions, as
part of his scheme, placing not only the Kickapoo and Mascouten, but also the
Miami on the Illinois River. With regard to the latter he wrote: "The Miamis,
who have withdrawn from the banks of the Mississippi and gone to Chicago for
the convenience of beaver-hunting, and those at Atihipi-Catouy [?] and St.
Josephs River, would come readily and gladly to the Illinois River, where they
would be reunited with a hundred of their own tribe who are still at Wisconsin
on the Mississippi, and another hundred families who are settled at the fork
of the Illinois River" (Margry, English translation, 4:661). This statement
apparently indicates that there were Miami with the Kickapoo and Mascouten on
the Wisconsin River in addition to other Miami groups "at Atihipi-Catouy" (see
ibid. p. 656), on the St. Joseph River, Chicago, and the confluence of the
Kankakee and Des Plaines rivers. This aggregation of Miami families, incidentally, "would make another 450 men, armed with guns, who would be taken from
the beaver-trade and be set to hunt for ox-hides and the skins of roebucks,

135

stags, hinds and small animals;. . ." (ibid. p. 662).

Iberville goes on to say that "By taking these Miamis, Maskoutens and Kicapous, formerly on the Mississippi, from their present stations and placing them on the Illinois River or lower down, the beaver-trade of Canada will be relieved of fifteen thousand skins a year; [and by] "The movement of the Illinois, ten thousand;. . ." (idem).

From these comparative figures on the production of beaver skins by the Miami, Mascouten, and Kickapoo on the one hand, and the Illinois on the other, one might, conceivably, judge the relative size of the two groups of populations. There are, however, other factors about which information is lacking, that would have to be taken into consideration in an effort to arrive at reasonable conclusions regarding population size. The amount of game in each area, techniques of hunting, population distribution, nature of the terrain, are some examples of such factors. Nevertheless, it is a striking fact that (if Iberville's data are correct) the combined production of Miami, Kickapoo, and Mascouten was only half again as much as the Illinois. On this basis alone it seems reasonable to assume not only that the Illinois population was substantial, if not considerable, but also that they probably exceeded the population size of each of the three other tribes.

136

Actually, if the figures provided by Iberville on the "number of families of the Indians I speak of" are accepted together with certain group identifications, then on the basis of his estimates the Illinois population exceeded that of the Miami, Mascouten and Kickapoo combined. For "The Quicapou and Maskoutens" the number of families is 450; for "The Miamis" the figure is 500. This total of 950 families is, however, greater than the 800 families attributed to "The Illinois of the big village and Tamaroua" (ibid. p. 666). But if the 200 families of "The Medsigamea, Chepouchia,

Medchipouria" are accepted as part of the Illinois, then the combined total is 1000, an excess of 50 over the combined total of Miami, Mascouten, and Kickapoo families (idem).

These last three groups are not mentioned elsewhere in Iberville's memorandum, but it is difficult to see how they can be regarded as anything other than Illinois. The "Medsigamea" are obviously Michigamea, and the mere fact of association of two others in the same grouping with the Michigamea would imply their Illinois relationship. Nevertheless, it seems clear that Iberville's Chepouchia is the equivalent of La Salle's Chepoussa or Chepousca who are probably the Cahokia, while the Medchipouria might possibly be the Peoria.

By 1706 the Kaskaskia were clearly farther south on the Mississippi at the Kaskaskia River. Their missionary at the time was Father Mermet who, in a letter dated March 2, 1706, "Among the Cascaskias", describes his efforts to save Father Gravier who was severely wounded by a Peoria at the village on the Illinois River. In the course of his account he refers to Bergier, of the Seminary of Quebec, ". . .who was nearer to the Pewarias than we were. . ." since he was stationed at Cahokia (JR 66:57). Mermet, however, still refers to the latter place as "the Tamarrais" [Tamaroa] (idem), and since it was nearer the Peoria it follows that the Kaskaskia were below.

It is evident also from Father Mermet's letter that the French were established among the Peoria (ibid. p. 53) and that relations between the Illinois and Fox were amicable. The latter inference is derived from the fact that a Fox to whom Mermet refers as "A good Samaritan, a stranger in the village,. . ." (ibid. p. 55), was instrumental in saving Father Gravier's life, after he was wounded, by stanching the flow of blood from an artery.

137

V - 1703-1715

While the Kaskaskia were in process of settlement in their new home the Peoria were becoming affected by new developments taking place northeast of them in southeastern Michigan, where Cadillac established Detroit in 1701. In a memorandum of 19 November 1704 Cadillac states that fifteen Illinois (Peoria) were captured attempting to make an attack on Detroit where tribes were settling at his behest. At about the same time the Wea made a foray into the area, killing one Ottawa, two Hurons, and one Potawatomi. Cadillac blames Father Gravier and Sieur Deliette, both of whom he places with the Peoria (although Deliette was probably among the Wea at Chicago), for instigating these hostilities. The Illinois, however, maintained that an Ottawa chief from Michilimackinac had urged the attack against those of his tribesmen who had settled at Detroit (MPHC 33:234).

If the story told by the Illinois is to be believed, then it would seem that just as Iberville's plans for the geographical rearrangement of tribes was responsible for dissension between the Kaskaskia and Peoria, so did Cadillac's efforts to assemble the tribes at Detroit create disagreement among the Ottawa. It should be borne in mind that such internal dissensions were probably exacerbated by opposing French interests, for the Jesuits at Michilimackinac were anything but pleased by Cadillac's Detroit venture; and there was also opposition from other quarters connected with the fur trade.

On September 26, 1706 Miscouaky, the brother of an Ottawa chief residing at Detroit, came from his home at Michilimackinac to talk with Governor Vaudreuil and to complain about the hostilities of the Miami who, he

139

said, had aroused the antagonism of many of the Great Lakes tribes. In his peroration he said that he spoke ". . . in the names of all the Outavois tribes, the Poutouatamis, the Sakis, the Outagamis, the Mastrowtins [Mascouten], the Kikapous, the Ouinipigos [Winnebago], the Malominys [Menominee], the Sauteurs, the Mississaguez, all the people of the districts bordering on the lake; . . ." (ibid. p.294). According to this Ottawa statement, therefore, the Kickapoo and the Potawatomi, among others, were at this time in "the districts bordering on the lake."

After he was seriously wounded at the Peoria village, Gravier returned to France. While there he wrote a letter on March 6, 1707 in which he gave the population of the village as "about three thousand souls" and estimated the inhabitants of the Kaskaskia village at "two thousand two hundred souls" (JR 66:121-123). Whether or not he had such numbers, or any particular figures in mind Cadillac, in October, 1707, made the statement that the Illinois "tribe is a powerful one,. . ." (MPHC 33:337). Three years later Antoine Raudot, an Intendant of Canada, wrote of the Illinois as a relatively populous group when he stated that they " . . . are the most numerous of these savages" in the Illinois-Wisconsin-Lake Michigan region (Kinietz p.382). According to Raudot who was not an observer, but apparently used reliable sources, all the Illinois groups (as listed by Deliette) " . . . could muster, all assembled together, fifteen hundred warriors" (ibid. p.384).

By 1710 the Fox, assisted by the Kickapoo, were embroiled in hostilities with the Wea, Piankashaw, and the Illinois. The following year (1711) in another vain effort to maintain tribal peace Governor Vaudreuil called in the leading men of tribes from the "upper country". Although the Illinois were not present they figured in Vaudreuil's remarks to the Fox and the Kickapoo. To the Fox he said that the maintenance of peace with the Detroit tribes depended on them; and he added "I also intend the war you have with the Ilinois to be stopped, . . . And as the Kikapoos are united with you in one and the same body, I arrest their axe also by this belt, . . . I will send to the Ilinois to explain to them also my opinion, and to stay their axe from you, . . ." (MPHC 33:505). But to the Kickapoo Chief, Vaudreuil said: "I praise you, Kakikepia for having prevented your tribe from continuing the war against the Illinois. M. deTonty has assured me that you told him that your men would remain at peace in your village" (ibid.p.506).

The establishment of Louisiana, with a port at the mouth of the Mississippi, made it essential to maintain peace with, and among, the tribes and thereby keep the lines of communication open through the Illinois-Great Lakes region and the Mississippi River. In 1711 Bienville, Governor of Louisiana, expressed concern that "The Miamis and the Mascoutens who are established in the Wabash" had pillaged Frenchmen on their way down from Canada. He also 141 voiced the hope that Cadillac, at Detroit, would "try to reestablish peace between the nations that are annoying the French as they pass through and the Illinois . . .with whom it is important for us not to be at war" (MPA 3:162). The villages of the Illinois, situated along an arc extending at least from Lake Peoria and down the Mississippi to the Kaskaskia River, were in a strategic position on the French lines of communication and trade. Peace was essential for the hoped for development of mines, the intended shipment of hides from the Ohio River area, and production of grains and other edibles in the Illinois country (MPA 3:59; Winsor, 1895, PP.56-58,66; MPA 2:51-52,61-62). The Indians, however, in the first decade of the 18th century were in a rising state of ferment which soon burst forth in 1712 as the Fox War.

Writing in November, 1712 "At Cascaskias, an Illinois village" Father Gabriel Marest also recounted some of his experiences and observations from late 1710 to late 1711 (JR 66:219-295). To him "It seems that a Country as beautiful and as extensive as this ought to be overspread with well-populated Villages; nevertheless, counting our own [Kaskaskia] there are only three - . . ." the two others being the Peoria Village on the Illinois River "where there are eight or nine hundred savages; and the other [Cahokia] is on the Mississippi, 25 leagues [62.5 miles] from our Village" (ibid. p.229). Cahokia is still referred to by Marest as "the village of the Tamarouas" (ibid.p.257, 267). The Peoria village, he says, "is the largest one in these quarters" (ibid.p.265). Although he attributes a population of 8-900 to the Peoria, Father Gravier, who spent a number of years with them, wrote in 1707 that there were "about three thousand souls" (ibid.pp.121-123).

According to Marest the Kaskaskia are mostly Christianized and have become more "civilized" than the other Illinois, a circumstance "which has brought many Frenchmen to settle here" and "has conduced increasingly to intermarriage with the French" (ibid.p.231). Clearly, the process of western-ization is proceeding apace, " . . . and they are now distirguished for cer-tain gentle and polite manners that have led the Frenchmen to take their daughters in marriage" (ibid.p.241). They pursue, of course, the yearly round of planting their fields and going on the summer and winter hunts. But, in the latter connection, says Marest "Our village is the only one in which a few Savages are permitted to remain during all these journeys; many of them raise chickens and pigs, in imitation of the Frenchmen who have settled here; and these savages are exempt, for the most part, from this sort of hunting" (ibid.p.253-255). He writes also that "Cows have just been brought to us. . ." (ibid.p.291), and refers to "advantages" which "are extremely favorable to the plan that some Frenchmen have of settling in our Village" (ibid.p.293). In addition, the changing character of the life of the Kaskaskia is revealed

142

by their ownership of two grain mills by 1711, the only other one in that region being the property of the Jesuit Mission (Penicaut) in Margry 5:490, cited by Palm in Mid-America, 16:18).

Late in 1710 Marest, having received news of the dangerous illness of Bergier, went to Cahokia, where he spent eight days. Upon his return to the Kaskaskia village he found that ". . . nearly all the Savages had gone: they were scattered along the Mississippi" on their winter hunt (JR 66:259). About six leagues down the river he "found three cabins" and ministered to a sick old man (idem). "Five or six leagues farther on, I found a great number of cabins, which formed a sort of village" (idem). At this point Marest was about 27-30 miles below the mouth of the Kaskaskia River. After remaining several days he received an urgent call, and went "eighteen leagues [45 miles] still farther down the Mississippi . . ." (idem). He thus travelled a total of about 75 miles, visiting groups of Kaskaskia in their winter quarters along the river. 143

In the spring (Easter week) of 1711 Father Marest left on a journey to Michilimackinac via the Peoria village which, since the injury done to Gravier and the murder of a French soldier, had been deprived both of a missionary and of the opportunity to trade. Although some Frenchmen secretly traded with them, they were nevertheless lacking in ammunition, as a result of which ". . . in many encounters they had been beaten by their enemies, for want of powder, which was no longer furnished to them by the French;. . ." (ibid.pp. 265-267). Lacking a missionary, Christian Peorias would come to Kaskaskia. In addition to some Illinois from Cahokia, who accompanied Marest only as far as their own village, two Christian Peorias left Kaskaskia with the Jesuit. Rumors of hostile bands ranging throughout the area they were to travel were borne out by the tracks they observed en route to the Illinois

River. After two weeks in the Peoria village, where he was received with enthusiasm by all, including the chiefs, the Father ". . . resolved to go by the river Saint Joseph to the Mission of the Pouteautamis, which is under the direction of Father Chardon" (ibid. p. 279). Along the way "A party of warriors, enemies of the Illinois, rushed upon some hunters, a gunshot distance from the road that I was taking; . . ."killing one and capturing another (ibid. p. 281).

As Marest ". . . was drawing near the village of the Pouteautamis . . . Some of the Savages, . . . were sowing their fields . . ." (idem). He is definite about the fact that ". . . the Pouteautamis and the Illinois live on good terms, and visit each other from time to time" (ibid. p. 285). This amicable relationship is probably a holdover from an earlier time, for Deliette, it will be recalled, mentions the Potawatomi among visitors to the Illinois (IHC 23:313) and refers to their supplying the Illinois with porcupine quills for fancy moccasins (ibid. p. 339). This Potawatomi village was probably not far from the mouth of the St. Joseph, for Marest on his return says ". . .we ascended the river St. Joseph, in order to make a portage at 30 leagues [75 mile from its mouth" (JR 66:285).

When Marest was on his way back down the Illinois River "Many of the Savages from the village of the Peouarias came some leagues to meet me, in order to escort me and to defend me from the parties of warriors who range the forests; . . ." (JR 66:287). It is probable that these war parties were Miami, for on September 6, 1712 Vaudreuil wrote that he had sent ". . . Sieur de Vincennes to the Miamis . . . both in order to make peace between these savages and the Ilinois, and to prevent them from approaching the English as they have long wished to do" (MPHC 33:561). Nevertheless, Marest, who was writing in November,1712, refers to the possibility of trade between Kaskaskia and the Miami via the Ohio-Wabash route (JR 66:293).

Having said this it must be noted that when Father Marest left the Peoria village, en route to Kaskaskia, he and his party espied a camp of about 100 Sioux warriors ten leagues (25 miles) below Peoria, but it was " . . . judged that these Savages had struck their blow and were retreating; . . ." (ibid. pp. 289-291).

The inception of the Fox Wars, sparked by an Ottawa attack "During the winter of 1711-12 . . . upon a Mascoutin village wintering upon the St. Joseph River, . . ." (Kellogg, 1908, p. 160) embroiled the Illinois in hostilities with the Fox chiefly because of persistent Illinois loyalty to the French. The Illinois were among the six hundred warriors who saved the French and their Indian allies from extermination by the Fox and Mascouten at Detroit in May, 1712 (WHC 16:272). And it was "The head chief of the Illinois . . ." who spoke on behalf of the Indian allies and harangued the besieged Fox and Mascouten (ibid. p. 278).

145

The Illinois in this action were from the village near Starved Rock, indicating that occupation of that site had been resumed. In his report to Governor Vaudreuil on this outbreak at Detroit, Dubuisson, who was temporarily in command during the absence of Cadillac, wrote that he was sending to the Governor "the grand Chief of the Illinois of Rock Village [Starved Rock]" in hopes that Vaudreuil "will induce him to make peace with the Miamis" (ibid. p. 285). Chachagouache, the Illinois chief, was to be accompanied by Mikisabie, the Potawatomi chief, because the latter "has much influence over the mind of this Illinois chief" (idem).

Miami-Illinois amity was important to the French because, as enemies of the Fox, these two tribes would thus have available about 1500 warriors to be employed against the Fox (ibid. p. 302, 304). The peace was finally effected in 1715 (ibid. p. 313), the allies undertaking to aid the French.

This alliance was, in effect, also directed against the Kickapoo. Writing to Vaudreuil in the middle of 1712 from Michilmackinac Father Joseph Marest said he had heard "that the people of Detroit are to go and fight against the Kickapoos," to whom he and Vaudreuil refer as allies of the Fox and Mascouten (MPHC 33:559, 555, 560), all three often acting in concert (ibid. p. 556; WHC:16:310). According to one account forty families of Mascouten and Kickapoo, like the Fox, had accepted Cadillac's invitation and built a "fort" at Detroit. Other tribes were also attracted there by the new prospects of trade. When the allies of the French defeated the Fox, the Mascouten and Kickapoo retaliated against the other tribes until they were stopped by de Louvigny (WHC 16:293-5).

The repercussions of their course of action as allies of the French were soon felt by the Illinois, for during the winter of 1713-14, according to acting Governor Ramezay, "...the Fox destroyed several cabins at the Illinois..." (ibid. p. 300); and more of the kind was to follow in subsequent years. Thus, once again, as in the case of the enmity of the Iroquois, the dependence of the Illinois upon French policy brought them into conflict with yet another implacable foe. The enemies of the French became their enemies. Not long after the blow struck by the Fox, the Illinois once more felt the hand of the Iroquois. In the spring of 1715 a war party of the latter, returning from action against the Cherokee or Chickasaw, passed near Kaskaskia, killing one, wounding another, and taking eight females captive (ibid. pp. 315-16). Such events compounded other misfortunes of the Illinois such as the ravages of disease which, in the summer of 1714, was responsible for two to three hundred deaths among the Kaskaskia (Palm, 1933, p. 19).

In 1715 a French plan of action for war against the Fox involved.

146

assembling at Chicago the Illinois, Wea, Miami, and Indians from Detroit by the end of August (WHC 16:324). Because of a measles epidemic among them the Wea abandoned the project, but Longeuil who was leading them, found his way "to LeRocher [Starved Rock], among the Illinois" (idem). Ramezay's son also came to this village, and the Illinois " . . .to the number of 200, came out two Leagues [5 miles] to meet my son and carried him to their village . . . to show their joy at his arrival. He only remained there long enough to collect 450 men with whom he went to Chicagou, on Aug. 17th, . . ." but he found no one there, and the rendezvous was a failure (idem).

Subsequently, Vaudreuil reported that actually both Ramezay's son and Longeuil were taken ill and remained at Kaskaskia, while Bizaillon, an Illinois trader, and Pachot, an army cadet, led the Illinois, some Montreal Indians, and a detachment of Detroit Indians (Huron and Potawatomi), the entire complement consisting of 80 men. On receiving news that ". . . seventy huts of the Mascoutins and Quikapous, allies of the Fox Indians, . . . were hunting at a certain river" they went in pursuit, and attacked on November 20, 1715, killing over a hundred and taking 47 male captives plus women and children. Eleven days later the same allied party met and defeated 400 Fox (idem). Afterwards, Ramezay learned that the Kickapoo threw themselves upon the mercy of the French (MPHC 33:576-7; WHC 16:341).

147

In November, 1715 Ramezay and Bégon reported that about 100 coureurs escaped to Cahokia, where they joined 47 others who had previously settled there. Cahokia was described "as a retreat for the lawless men both of this Colony and of Louisiana"; and these officials recommended the building of a garrisoned fort there for the dual purpose of maintaining order among the French and "to oppose the building of forts by the English, and all the enterprises carried on by them in that territory, . . ." (WHC 16:331-2).

Thus, in 1715 in addition to the indigenous Illinois population between the mouths of the Illinois and Ohio Rivers, there was a gradual increase of French settlement in the area. In addition, there was a center of Illinois and French at Lake Peoria, while on the upper Illinois River there seems to have been a predominantly Illinois community near Starved Rock. As at Kaskaskia, the changing character of Cahokia is revealed by the presence of a grain mill and "a great many cattle" (idem), in addition to which the French "get as many slaves as they wish, on the River of the Missouris, whom they use to cultivate their land; and they sell these to the English of Carolina, with whom they trade" (idem). Earlier in the same month of November, Ramezay suggested the necessity for troops to restrain the allegiance of the Indians to prevent their trading with Carolina and Virginia traders; to restain English incursions stimulated by fur trade and discovery of mines; and, finally, to prevent unauthorized activities of Canadian coureurs de bois (ibid. p. 325). Above all, the threat of English competition was ever in the minds of French officialdom.

148

VI - 1715-1730

Early in January, 1716 Bienville conveyed information received from a trader among the Chickasaw ". . .that a big party of the Cherokee nation has been at war at the Kaskaskias, an Illinois village, and killed and took prisoners a large number of them and ten to twelve of the French inhabitants who were established at that village" (MPA 3:200). He also suggested that Cadillac was to blame for inspiring "war in all the nations established on the [Mississippi] River" (idem). In this same dispatch Bienville took occasion to note that the mouth of the Wabash ". . .was the passage-way for all the warriors of the Illinois, Miami, Chickasaw and Cherokee nations who made war on each other and who ordinarily killed and plundered all those whom they found on the way allied as well as enemies;. . ." (ibid. p. 192).

Hostilities between the Illinois and tribes to the south of them are hardly a recent phenomenon since, as indicated earlier, the Illinois had been sending war parties during the second half of the 17th century as far as the vicinity of the Gulf Coast to take captives. Iberville, in his Journal covering the period December 15, 1701 - April 27, 1702, notes that he sent three Canadian traders with two Chickasaw up to the Illinois with a demand for the return of Chickasaw prisoners and to insist that they stop making war on these allies of the French (Margry 4:520).

An unsigned "Memoir" which seems to be dated "1718" but which, on the basis of a statement contained therein (NYCD 9:890-1) might possibly have been written in 1717, makes reference to the location of several tribes with varying degrees of specificity. The Mascouten and Kickapoo are dealt with in this fashion: having located the Sac on the Fox River above the portage of the Wisconsin, the Fox are said to be 45 miles from the Sac. The statement is then made that "the Foxes are fifty leagues [125 miles], in the direction

149

of Chicagou, from the Mascoutins and the Quicapous, who reside together in a
village on the bank of a river, the name of which I forget" (ibid. p. 889).
There follows shortly the sentence: "The Quicapous and Mascoutins are not far,
perhaps fifty leagues, from Chicagous, which they must pass on their way to
Detroit or to the River St. Joseph" (idem). Neither of these sentences is a
model of clarity, but a general idea of the area in which the Mascouten and
Kickapoo may be found at this time is more easily derived from the second
quotation, which could place them on the Rock River of Illinois, as the editor
of the New York Colonial Documents seems to think (idem, fn 1). On the other
hand a location in Wisconsin is not unlikely.

As regards the Illinois who, he writes, are at war with the Fox and the
Wea, he locates their villages at Starved Rock, Lake Peoria, Cahokia, and
Kaskaskia. "The Illinois of the Rock number 400 men, and are eighty leagues
[200 miles] from the Oujatanons [Wea, on the Wabash],. . ."; they ". . .do not
kill a great deal of beaver. . ." and "they dwell on the borders of the
Illinois river. . ."; the Kaskaskia are "very numerous", raise much corn and
wheat, have three mills, in addition to "oxen, cows, hogs, horses; fowls; in
fine, every thing suitable for life" (ibid. pp. 890-1). Kaskaskia is apparently a well established community along European lines where a number of
French are in permanent residence.

150

Miami are established at the site where Fort Wayne was later erected,
while the villages of Wea, Piankashaw, Pepikokia, "Les gros", and a fifth
unidentified village are situated contiguously on the Wabash, probably below
Lafayette, Indiana (WHC 16:376). It is these groups, probably, or the Wea,
at least, who are referred to in documents of the year 1715 as the "Miami of
Ouabache" (WHC 16:312, 322, 323, 338). Still earlier, in the fall of 1711, a
letter of Bienville had stated that the Miami and the Mascouten were settled

along the Wabash, the Miami in this instance very likely being the Wea,
Piankashaw, or both (Margry 5:372).

An account written by Cadillac in 1718 places a village of Miami at
Chicago (WHC 16:361) and another on the St. Joseph near the French post
(ibid. p. 362), while Potawatomi are inhabitants of Washington Island, near
the mouth of Green Bay (ibid. p. 359). Cadillac also states that there are
no Indian villages at the south end of Lake Michigan ". . .owing to the
incursions of the Iroquois; but in the interior on the North side [to the
north?] there are several in a Westerly direction, such as the Mascoutens,
. . .Peanguiseins [Piankashaw?] Peaouarias [Peoria], Kikapoux,. . ." (ibid.
p. 362).

A report by Vaudreuil in October, 1718 indicates that although the
Fox had been quiet since the expedition against them in 1716, which resulted
in peace with the French, the Kickapoo and Mascouten allies of the Fox,
". . .have continued the war against the Ilinois, against whom they have made
incursions, as the Ilinois have against them" (ibid. p. 377). This is a
state of affairs which had been going on intermittently since 1712. Vaudreuil
urged the Fox to restrain their allies, at the same time sending ". . .
Deliette among the Ilinois expressly to put an end to this war, and to prevent
them from making any movement against the Kikapou and the Maskoutin" (ibid.
p. 378). But despite these efforts Vaudreuil had to write exactly one year
later, on October 28, 1719, that war ". . .still continues between the
Ilinois, and the Kikapous and Mascoutins, in which the Renards now find themselves involved, because the Ilinois have attacked them on various occasions
since last year, killing and taking prisoners several of that nation" (ibid.
p. 381). Vaudreuil felt that the Kickapoo, who, through the Fox, returned
captives taken from the Illinois, were interested in peace; but ". . .a band

151

of forty Ilinois, who came to make an attack, had encountered on their way the Renards, Kikapous, and Mascoutins, in the place where they were carrying on their Summer hunting together; and had been so completely surrounded and attacked that not one escaped – twenty being killed On the spot, and as many more being made prisoners" (idem).

It was rather ironic that, although the French were at peace with the Fox and their allies, warfare continued between the Mascouten and Kickapoo on the one side, and the Illinois on the other. The Fox participated in these hostilities ". . .only after having been attacked by the [Illinois], who in various encounters had killed or taken prisoners many Renard savages from 1718 Up to 1719 – while that nation was laboring to Persuade the Kickapous and Mascoutins to cease making Attacks upon the Illinois;. . ." (WHC 16:429).

At about the same time (1719) two Kaskaskia chiefs journeyed to New Orleans and received presents there from the Council of Commerce for themselves and "for the warriors of their villages" (MPA 3:260).

152

In 1720 The Fox, Kickapoo and Mascouten were still engaged in warfare with the Illinois, and were a threat to a number of other tribes (WHC 16:393). The depredations of the Fox in particular were so aggravating that "the Principal Chief of the Pouteouatamis" informed the French that if they approved "at least a thousand men, people from the lake and from the Miamis, Ouayatanons and Ilinois" were prepared to attack the Fox (idem). It would thus appear that Illinois hostilities against the Fox-Mascouten-Kickapoo alliance was part of a general pattern of response to the activities of that alliance which were being directed against other tribes also.

Then ". . .on Sept. 15, 1720, there arrived at the St. Joseph River two mascoutin chiefs with ten other Savages, who, in the name of their nation, asked the Poutouatomis of that post for permission to settle near them, saying that they wish to get away from the Renards, who always continue in their Perversity, and commit hostilities incessantly." Again, on May 2, 1721, another group of Mascouten came with their chief to make the same request of the Potawatomi who told them that their most important chiefs, together with the Kickapoo chief, Robe Blanche, must go to Montreal and confer with Vaudreuil in the matter. The French, of course, were pleased with this turn of events (ibid. pp. 398-9).

In the meantime the French, in an effort to counteract the influence of the English and Iroquois, were attempting to get the Miami to settle on the St. Joseph River and the Wea on the Kankakee. Some of each of the two groups actually made the move, and several Miami chiefs tried, nevertheless, to pursuade them to join a trading expedition to Albany. But in 1721 the few Wea who had settled on the Kankakee left when the rest refused to join them; the main body of the Miami were adamant in their refusal to settle on the St. Joseph. It would seem as if the latter wished to remain in a location more accessible to the Albany trade. Consequently, the French established a post among the Miami under the command of Dubuisson in August, 1721 (ibid. p. 399). By this time the French had already established the post of Ouiatanon on the Wabash where Dubuisson assumed command in 1721 (ibid. pp. 382, 394-5).

153

Father Charlevoix's journey took him to the St. Joseph River in August, 1721 where a garrisoned French post was situated about fifty miles above its mouth. Here he also found a Potawatomi village on the same side of the river as the fort, while a Miami village was located on the opposite side, having moved there recently at the behest of the French (Charlevoix, 1923, 2:92-3; WHC 16:394). While he was there, Indians from both villages ". . .arrived from the English colonies, whither they had been to sell their furs, and from whence they have brought back in return a great quantity of spirituous liquors" (Charlevoix, 1923, 2:98). It would seem, therefore, that the French had not quite succeeded in their purpose of removing the Miami from the attraction of English trade.

According to Charlevoix "the Mascoutins had not long since a settlement on this river, but have returned back to their own country. . ." and the Potawatomi ". . .occupied successively several posts here where they still are;. . ." (ibid. pp. 92-3). As regards the latter he says that they formerly inhabited the islands at the entrance of Green Bay, but that now they occupy only one of the smallest of them in addition to ". . .two other Villages, one on the River St. Joseph, and the other at Detroit" (WHC 16:409).

Writing of the beauty of the Fox River region of Wisconsin he states: ". . .and still more so is that which extends Southward to the River of the Illinois; but its only inhabitants are two Tribes, of very few people, the Kikapous and the Mascoutins" (idem). It is not quite clear but, nevertheless, entirely likely, that he considers the area between the Fox and Illinois Rivers to be the country of the Kickapoo and Mascouten.

The Miami, he says, ". . .are now separated into three Villages: one of these is on the River Saint Joseph; the second upon another river, which bears their name [Maumee], and flows into Lake Erie [Ft. Wayne, Indiana]; and the third upon the Ouabache River,. . .; these last are better known under the name of Ouyatanons" (idem). It is apparent by now that the Wea have probably been on the Wabash for some years.

Making his way down the Kankakee, while still above the confluence of the Iroquois, Charlevoix expressed ". . .fear of being surprized by the Sioux and Outagamies, whom the neighborhood of the Illinois, their mortal enemies, draws hither. . ." (Charlevoix, 1923, p. 183). This is an area in which

154

La Salle, forty years earlier, expected to find the Illinois on the hunt. Then the enemy was Iroquois, but now the Illinois must be on guard against inroads of the Fox and their allies. Charlevoix probably considers the Kankakee to be in the "neighborhood" of the Illinois because of the Illinois village at Starved Rock, which he visited.

The Fox River of Illinois, Charlevoix writes, ". . .proceeds from the fine country of the Mascotins" to the north (ibid. p. 184), a statement which, because of what he said above, would include the Kickapoo by implication. On an island in the Illinois River at Starved Rock he came to the first Illinois village, where he met some French traders and received a visit from the village chief (ibid. p. 186). Continuing downstream, near the outlet of Peoria Lake on the right bank of the river, he arrived at the second Illinois village on October 3, 1721 (ibid. p. 190). The river was swarming with fish, and game was plentiful on both banks. At the village were four French traders who told Charlevoix that there were four parties of Fox in the area. He had come through "an ambuscade of thirty", an equal number were in the vicinity of the village, while an additional eighty ". . .were posted lower down the river in two companies" (idem). There had already been "a sharp action in the neighborhood" with the enemy; and each side had taken a prisoner from the other (ibid. p. 191).

Charlevoix's party managed to make its way safely down to the Mississippi and came to Cahokia ". . .a village of the Caoquias and the Tamarouas, two Illinois tribes which have been united, and together compose no very numerous canton" (ibid. p. 201). Apparently half the area of the village had been undermined by the Mississippi, and the Indians were planning to move (ibid. p. 202).

Proceeding on to Kaskaskia, he writes that it is ". . .a very

155

flourishing mission, which has lately been divided into. . .two cantons of Indians instead of one. The most numerous is on the banks of the Mississippi, . . .the second village of the Illinois lies farther up the country at the distance of two leagues [5 miles] from [the French Village of Kaskaskia]" (ibid. pp. 205-6).

In this connection Palm states that in 1719 or 1720, when Boisbriant took command at the original Fort Chartres some miles above the mouth of the Kaskaskia River, he "created three villages out of the original Kaskaskia" which was five miles up the east bank of the Kaskaskia River (Palm, 1933, p. 25, fn 42; and p. 15). "The French remained on the original site, thereafter called French Kaskaskia. The Indians were divided: The Kaskaskia moved a league and a half [3.75 miles] north of their old home forming the village sauvage Kaskaskia; the Michigamea, who had been living with the Kaskaskia, settled still farther north, a half league above Fort Chartres" (Palm, 1933, p. 25 fn 42). She also refers to a French document which mentions the transfer of a Jesuit from Lake Peoria to the Michigamea in 1720, which ties in with the separation of the Michigamea from the Kaskaskia at about that time to form their own village on the Mississippi above Fort Chartres. This information also corroborates the quotation from Charlevoix cited above.

After stating that one of the Illinois subgroups bears the name "Moingana" Charlevoix writes: "the rest are known under the names of Peorias, Tamarouas, Caoquias, and Kaskasquias; these tribes are at present very much confounded, and are become very inconsiderable. There remains only a very small number of the Kaskasquias, and the two villages of that name are almost entirely composed of the Tamarouas and Metchigamias, a foreign nation adopted by the Kaskasquias, and originally settled on the banks of a small river you

156

meet with going down the Missisippi" (Charlevoix, 1923, 2:212-213). But he
appears somewhat confused here, for earlier he said that the Cahokia and
Tamaroa are "united" in one village near Cahokia. Then he states that the
two "Kaskaskia" villages are chiefly Tamaroa and Michigamea. Although some
of the latter groups might have resided temporarily, or even permanently,
with the Kaskaskia in their village, on Kaskaskia River, it seems an exaggeration to claim that it consisted mainly of others.

There are three final points of interest in Charlevoix's account.
First is his statement that the Illinois, as a whole, "are become inconsiderable" and that "only a very small number" of Kaskaskia remain; but it is
difficult to judge on what information he based this remark, for there is as
yet no other evidence to support it. By comparison with their earlier numbers
they may have become "inconsiderable". The second point concerns the fact
that "the Osages. . .depute some of their people once or twice every year to
sing the calumet among the Kaskasquias, and they are now actually here at
present" (ibid. p. 208). This brings to mind information provided by Deliette,
who wrote that Osage and other tribes came to Fort St. Louis and the Illinois
villages on Lake Peoria in the last decade of the 17th century not only to
trade, but also that "they never fail every year to come among them and to
bring them the calumet,. . . ." (IHC 23:389-390).

Finally, Charlevoix writes that the alliance of the Fox with the
Iroquois to the east, and with the Sioux to the west, has "rendered them
formidable". As a result, not only is the upper Mississippi unsafe, but
"there is not entire safety even in voyaging upon the Illinois River. . ." as
Charlevoix discovered on his way down (WHC 16:417).

Legardeur Delisle's journal of a voyage on the Mississippi and Illinois
rivers from May 23 to July 1, 1722 indicates the distribution of the Illinois

157

from Fort Chartres to Starved Rock, and alludes to the forays of the Fox in the area (Delisle, 1945, pp. 52-57). About a mile and a half up the Mississippi from the fort he and his party spent the night at the Michigamea village. A few days later, at Cahokia, Delisle gave presents to the Illinois Indians on behalf of Boisbriant, the commandant of Fort Chartres. There they learned that the Peoria village at Lake Peoria, after defeating twenty-eight Fox, had gone to join the Illinois at Starved Rock. To this place came two hundred Fox to retaliate, but they retired, after killing four persons, without attacking the entire community (ibid. pp. 52-3).

This account of Fox action against Starved Rock may possibly be a milder version of the same incident as reported by Vaudreuil in a letter dated October 2, 1723. He writes: "The Renards last year [1722] besieged The Ilinois of LeRocher. They reduced them to such extremities that they were Obliged to Sue for their lives, which the Renards granted; and, raising the siege, retired to their village" (WHC 16:429 and 418).

158

To return to Delisle, when he arrived at Pimitoui, the Peoria village, on June 9 he ". . .found no one there, as we had been told when we passed Cahokia. The Indians of this place had gone to make their village with those of the Rock, who are twenty-six leagues [65 miles] from there" (Delisle,p. 54). Arriving at his destination, Delisle found the Lake Peoria villagers among the Illinois of Starved Rock (ibid. p. 55).

On the day of Delisle's return to Fort Chartres another officer at that post, Chassin by name, wrote a letter in which he referred to Fox depredations in the area against the Michigamia and the Kaskaskia. He also noted that the Peoria had gained two victories over the Fox, killing nine the first time and twenty-eight the second (MPA 2:277). As told by Delisle, the second victory seems to be the occasion upon which the Peoria thought it advisable

to withdraw up the river to their kinsmen at Starved Rock. Chassin adds that
forty Illinois went in pursuit of a party of Sioux which had killed and captured members of a family of Canadians who came to settle in the area, probably at Kaskaskia (ibid. p. 278). This incident apparently occurred about
10 miles above the mouth of the Ohio River (d'Artaguiette, p. 66).

In 1722-23 Diron d'Artaguiette made a tour of inspection up the Mississippi and in the Illinois country for the Company of the Indies. He wrote
in April, 1723 that the Illinois ". . .are scattered about in three villages -
the Cascakias, the Mekchiquamias and the Cahokias". He notes that ". . .up
the Rivière des Ilinnois, there used to be two villages of the same nation,
the Peorias [at Lake Peoria] and the Roches [at Starved Rock], but they were
forced to abandon these villages and to withdraw to the above-mentioned villages, because of the Outagamis [Fox] nation or the Renards, who last year came
clear to their villages to attack them" (ibid. p. 71).

As we have seen, Delisle in 1722 reported the withdrawal from Lake
Peoria to Starved Rock, and also a foray of 200 Fox against the joint community thus created by the move from Peoria. But the Illinois River villages
had not as yet withdrawn to join their kinsmen in the three villages on the
Mississippi. Not even Vaudreuil, writing in October, 1723, mentions such a
withdrawal. Yet d'Artaguiette in April, 1723, is clear and specific about
such a withdrawal as an accomplished fact.

As regards the number of Illinois he writes: "the Ilinnoise Nation was
formerly numerous, but the continual wars, and principally the one against
the Iroquois,. . .have so enfeebled them that they number at present not more
than 700 warriors" (ibid. p. 71). The Michigamea, whose village is a half
league above Ft. Chartres, number "perhaps about 200 warriors" (ibid. pp. 69-
70). The Kaskaskia, he says, ". . .number about 200 warriors" (ibid. p. 68),

and he places their village on the Kaskaskia River 1/2 league (1.25 miles) above French Kaskaskia, which is ". . .2 leagues [5 miles] up this river on the left. . ." (ibid. pp. 67, 68). The third, and last Illinois village is Cahokia, situated one-eighth of a league above the French post of Cahokia, located ". . .18 leagues [45 miles] by land and 15 [37.5 miles] by water from Fort de Chartres" (ibid. pp. 81, 71). There is no statement of the number of warriors in this village although d'Artaguiette visited it and spoke to the assembled ". . .Indian chiefs of the Cahokias. . ." who were ". . .accompanied by forty of their warriors. . ." (ibid. p. 81).

During the time that d'Artaguiette was in the area (April 17–June 27, 1723) there was considerable movement by the Illinois between their villages and the French forts at Cahokia and Chartres. One reason for this activity was connected with hostilities between them and the Fox. On April 29 at Fort Chartres ". . .there arrived a party of 200 Illinois warriors, who were on their way to make war upon the Renards" (ibid. p. 75). It would be interesting to know what was their objective in view of their later contention that they acted only in self-defense against the Fox in Illinois territory (see below). The Illinois, as subsequent events proved, may have known then that a Fox war party, or parties, was in the vicinity of the Illinois and Mississippi Rivers. On May 10 "An Ilinnois Indian has informed us that the Renards were going toward the Rocher with the purpose of establishing themselves there" (ibid. p. 76). Then on May 28 two Illinois arrived at Fort Chartres with news about an encounter with the Fox. "They had set out about fifteen days ago to the number of thirty men to go to war against the Renards. They had not gone forty leagues [100 miles] from here when they were attacked by a part of the latter, who killed eleven of their men. The rest escaped" (ibid. p. 77).

A few days later fifteen Fox in two canoes attacked the canoe of two

160

French soldiers and two Cahokias not far from the mouth of the Missouri,
killing a soldier and wounding an Indian (ibid. pp. 78-9). After the middle
of June a Fox attack·upon the Cahokia village was repulsed with reinforce-
ments. Three prisoners were taken who participated in the assault upon the
French and Indians near the Missouri (ibid. pp. 82-3).

D'Artaguiette's journal also records Illinois relations both hostile
and amicable with other Indian groups. On May 19 a war party of Illinois
returned with ". . .the head and the scalp of a Chicachat [Chickasaw]" (ibid.
p. 77). Earlier d'Artaguiette reported the arrival at Fort Chartres of three
Miami and wrote: "We learned that the Wiatanons [Wea] Indians, living up
toward the head of the Riviere de Wabache, were leaving that place to go to
establish themselves at their old village of LaBabiche, which is on a little
River [Little Miami?] which empties into Lake Erie" (ibid. p. 75).

On May 2 a Cahokia came to Fort Chartres to announce that a deputation
of four Missouri Indians had arrived at his village and that members of their
tribe ". . .were going to come to pay their respects to M. Boisbriant,"
commandant of Fort Chartres. The group arrived on May 24 (ibid. pp. 75-6,
77) and departed for home on June 6 accompanied by Frenchmen who were going
among them. . ."to trade in horses and to buy skins" (ibid. p. 80).

Locating on the Mississippi between the mouths of the Illinois and
Ohio Rivers was advantageous to both the Illinois and the French. In both
cases the dual purpose of defense and trade was served. From the viewpoint
of defense the Illinois had French assistance against incursions of the Fox;
while the French were equally concerned with deployment of the Indians
against English penetration into the area (MPA 3:496). Kaskaskia was
envisioned by the French not only as an entrepot for trade but also as a
breadbasket for the province of Louisiana (see below). D'Artaguiette writes

161

that the French village of Kaskaskia ". . .is composed entirely of Farmers who live there very comfortably" and raise a fairly large amount of wheat and vegetables which is sold to the garrisons at Fort Chartres and Cahokia. They also had treadmills, and the Jesuits there had cattle (d'Artaguiette, pp. 67-68).

In spite of the fact that this area belonged to Louisiana and was supposed to receive its wares from New Orleans, that source was unreliable. Consequently, Canada supplied the manufactured goods necessary for the trade with both French and Indians. The settlers were the middlemen in the trade in foods and goods with both the French troops and the Indians. In this exchange it would appear that the Illinois were the main source of supply for the meat and furs while the Canadian traders provided the merchandise. D'Artaguiette described the situation this way:

162

"The trade of the inhabitants of the Illinois, who are Canadians, French or discharged soldiers, consists in selling their wheat and other products to the company for the subsistence of the troops, in exchange for merchandize (which they are obliged to fetch from New Orleans) which they trade to the Indians for quarters of buffalo, bear oil and other meats, which serve them for food or which they sell in exchange for merchandize. They also trade in skins, such as beaver, buck and deer, buffalo and bear skins, and other peltries, which they get very cheap from the Indians, and which they sell at a very high price to the traders who come down from Canada every spring and autumn, and who give them merchandize in exchange. For it is not necessary for them to rely upon having their needs supplied from New Orleans, whence very few convoys come, and even when they do come they bring so few merchandizes that they are not nearly sufficient to pay a part of the debts which the company is obliged to incur every year" (ibid. pp. 70-71).

French activity in this region was also centered on exploration for, and exploitation of, lead and silver mines. About 3-1/2 to 4 miles up from the Michigamea village was an establishment of forty miners under the super-vision of the company's "director of mines," who were engaged in work some distance up the Meramec River which enters the Mississippi not far below the Missouri (ibid. pp. 70, 77).

In October, 1723 Vaudreuil reported not only continued warfare between the Illinois and Fox, but also the existence of Illinois differences with the Wea. With reference to the former he writes: "The Renards, in their last fight against the Ilinois, had with them some scioux, Mascoutins, Kicapous, puants, and Sakis;. . ." adding that the Mascouten ". . .Are at present incorporated with [the Fox], while the Kicapous have always been their allies" (WHC 16:434). As regards the Wea he states that there were several occasions on which Vincennes, his commandant among the Miami and Wea, restrained the latter from engaging the Illinois in hostilities (ibid. p. 436).

163

In October, 1724 the missionaries on the St. Joseph River reported that the Fox persisted in their hostilities against the Illinois because they claimed that the Illinois failed to return captives held since the peace of 1716 (ibid. pp. 448-450). The following January (1725) DuTisné, who replaced Boisbriant as commandant at Fort Chartres, complained that the Illinois district in the province of Louisiana had been suffering from Fox raids because their trade with Canada was providing them with arms and ammunition. As he put it, "The Beaver in Their district cause this Great carnage among us;. . ." (ibid. p. 452; see also p. 462).

DuTisné's statement seems to be based on a letter from the missionaries at Kaskaskia who, charging Vaudreuil with responsibility for Fox depredations among the Illinois and the French in the area, wrote: "He seems to have no

other desire than to allow the vein of Beaver skins to flow; and, by Letting
The Renard attack us, prevent this country from being settled, and thereby to
shut off the trade between His Government and Ours" (ibid. p. 456). The
missionaries, testifying that the Illinois acted only in self defense on
their own lands, also stated that ". . .since The peace [1716], The illinois
have not left Their Lands [to wage war against the Fox, presumably]; that If
the Renards went thither, it was because they wished to attack The illinois.
The destruction of LeRocher [Starved Rock] and of Pimithony [Lake Peoria]
Are proofs of this" (ibid. p. 454). Further, they express their belief
the peace effected by DeLignery, commandant at Michilimackinac, between the
Fox and lakes tribes, such as the Chippewa, ". . .is hurtful to this province,
and will undoubtedly break up its Trade with three or four nations against
whom the renards had to defend Themselves. They will have only the illinois
to Contend with, and the French, their allies, will support Them" (ibid.
p. 455).

164

The letter from the missionaries at Kaskaskia to DuTisné at Fort
Chartres was brought by Kaskaskia and Michigamea chiefs. They also brought a
calumet to send back with the chief White Cat who had brought letters to
DuTisné from the commandants at Michilimackinac, Green Bay, and St. Joseph
River relative to the Fox insistence on return of the captives. The letters
also requested that any captives be delivered up to White Cat. The Illinois
chiefs recited to White Cat a list of attacks and killings perpetrated over
the years by the Fox at every one of the Illinois villages (ibid. pp. 456-61).
They not only accused the Fox of being the aggressors but also of inducing
". . .several nations to come and kill us. . ." asserting that ". . .the
scalp dance has Been performed around [French] scalps and ours among the
Mascoutins, quikapous, Renards, syoux, and everywhere around La bay [Green

Bay]" (ibid. p. 458). Three times towards the close of the speech of the
Illinois chiefs was reference made to the fact that the Fox and their allies
secure their guns and ammunition from the Canadian traders because the latter
are interested only in securing beaver skins. In this context the statement
is made "I admit that we do not kill as many Beavers as the People of the
lakes;. . ." (ibid. p. 462). The Illinois expressed the hope that these
"nations" would smoke the calumets they are sending to them" (ibid. p. 457).

The report of this conference refers to some of the Illinois ". . .being
away on an inland hunting expedition" (ibid. p. 458). The meaning here is
probably that the hunt took place somewhere within the present state of
Illinois.

DuTisné, in his communication referred to above, also voiced the
suspicion that the murder of five Frenchmen on the Wabash was done by the
Kickapoo (ibid. p. 451).

One month later, at the end of February, 1725, a letter sent from New
Orleans to the Company of the Indies in Paris suggested that the area under
the jurisdiction of Fort Chartres could produce the food and other necessaries
of life for ". . .all the country that is situated on the banks of the
Mississippi. . ." and that a warehouse there ". . .might eventually induce the
Foxes to make peace with us. . ." (MPA 2:412; see also d'Artaguiette, pp. 67-
8).

It is plain that warfare between the Fox and the Illinois had been
going on in more or less regular fashion even after the French made peace
with the Fox in 1716, one of the conditions being the cessation of hostilities
against the Illinois and other French allies. But by 1722 the Fox were
including the French in their attacks, especially in the Illinois area.

At the end of October,1725 Longueil and Begon reported to France the attacks by Kickapoo and Fox on the French, adding that "the latter tribe [Fox] say they will not allow the French to pass to go to the Scioux, because the trade the French would do with them would greatly reduce that which they do there themselves; also that the Renards and Scioux, acting in concert, have attacked the French who are settled among the Illinois, and that both tribes are so enraged with the Illinois that it is impossible to make them stop fighting against them, and the same with the Sakis settled at the Bay;. . ." (Margry, English translation, 6:548). Then, on June 7, 1726 the French succeeded once again in effecting a short-lived peace at Green Bay with the Fox and two of their allies, the Sac and the Winnebago (WHC 3:150-153). The French also planned, afterwards, to hold a conference at Montreal with the Fox and ". . .their allies, the Puants [Winnebago], Sauks, Kickapoos, Maskoutens and Sioux,. . ." (ibid. p. 149), for the French wanted not only a general peace, but also ". . .to put an end to the unjust war which these nations [the reference is to those in the Green Bay area] are waging against the Illinois" (ibid. p. 150; also pp. 153-4, 156, 157, 159).

166

Less than two weeks after the French-Fox peace DeLignery, writing from Green Bay, said that the Fox ". . .have still (since spring) three or four war parties upon the Illinois, to whom they were to speak against continuing the war" (ibid. p. 154). And in October Beauharnois wrote that he had learned from DeLignery that two Fox war parties had been defeated by the Illinois (ibid. pp. 159-160; see also WHC 16:463-468).

At about this time (1726) Bienville composed a memoir on Louisiana, summarizing the information available to him. He writes that the largest number of French settlers are at Kaskaskia (MPA 3:514), and that "At the Illinois there are one hundred and fifty inhabitants who have only ninety negro workmen among them" (ibid. pp. 523-4). Here it is possible to produce,

in addition to furs and minerals, a number of grains, fibers, and tobacco
(ibid. pp. 522 and 533).

With regard to the Illinois Indians he disclaims any first hand knowledge, stating that his information comes from "reliable persons". Like others
before him he writes: "The nation of the Illinois was formerly very numerous
and could put ten thousand men under arms,. . ." (ibid. pp. 532-533). He may
be reasonably close to the mark when he says further: "After many different
changes the continual war that this nation has always had has so greatly
enfeebled it that only eight hundred warriors now remain in three villages,
namely: four hundred at the Cahokias. . .; about two hundred at the
Michigameas near Fort Chartres,. . .and two hundred at the village of
Kaskaskias. . ." (ibid. p. 533).

In connection with the question of trade he writes: "The voyageurs of
Canada formerly obtained from them [the Illinois] a large number of beaver
[and] raccoon skins and skins of deer, bears and of buffaloes, but for six or
seven years the French have been obliging them to devote themselves to producing [bear] oil, tallow and meat for which they trade with them" (idem).
Bienville implies that since about 1720 the fur trade with the Illinois
declined as the trade in meat and fat rose.

He also makes some comments on the Miami who ". . .are separated into
three villages". The first, retaining the name of Miami is on the Maumee.
"The second, which is called the village of the Weas and in which there are
more than four hundred·men, is two hundred leagues up the Wabash on the left
as one goes upstream, and several leagues lower down is the new village of
Mercata or Piankashaw where there are at least one hundred and fifty men. The
voyageurs of Canada come there to trade and obtain many peltries from them. . ."
(ibid. p. 534).

167

As stated above, the latest peace made with the Fox did not long endure, and the next year, on August 20, 1727, Governor Beauharnois of Canada reported that the Fox, by continuing to send out war parties, failed to honor the peace, and therefore, made it necessary for the French to undertake war against them. Knowing where the French were weakest, the Fox directed their hostilities for the most part at the Illinois area. Beauharnois, therefore, expressed the hope ". . .that the people in Louisiana will come to this war with more ardor than the Canadians, as they are much more exposed to the incursions of the Foxes, who alarm and even kill them continually" (WHC 3:163). Convinced that the English were engaged in a drive to take over the Indian trade from the French, Beauharnois held them responsible for ". . .the different war parties of the Foxes against the Illinois, in which there have been many French killed" (ibid. pp. 163-4, 161).

168

The decision was made in favor of a major effort against the Fox (idem). In late summer of 1728 DeLignery, with ". . .about a thousand Indians and five hundred French. . ." came by way of Michilimackinac to Green Bay and went up the Fox River to the Fox village, which was empty except for three women and an old man. Deliette, coming by way of Chicago from Fort Chartres, was to meet him ". . .with five hundred Illinois warriors and twenty Frenchmen" (Parkman, 1892, 1:327).

The expedition was a failure, having succeeded only in burning the village and destroying the crops. But as a result of this action the Kickapoo and Mascouten allies of the Fox withdrew to the Mississippi in a village which may have been located on the Skunk River of Iowa (WHC 17:38). Boucherville who, with his party, had abandoned Fort Beauharnois at Lake Pepin on the Mississippi, and on their way down the river had been taken captive in this village, was told by the Kickapoo: "After the flight of the Renards, the burning of their cabins, and the ravaging of their fields, we were warned to withdraw to the banks of the Mississipi because our father Ononthio is angry with us, and because all the nations that winter in our neighborhood will soon fall upon us" (ibid. p. 42).

The warning to withdraw was probably in the form of combined French and Illinois action against the Kickapoo and Mascouten after the unsuccessful drive against the Fox. For Ouiskouba, a Kickapoo in whose cabin the Frenchmen were lodged when they were brought to the village on October 16, referred to ". . .the loss of my wife and children when the French, acting with the Illinois, have just taken from me" (ibid. p. 40). Subsequently, in response to peace overtures from the Kickapoo and Mascouten in January, 1729, in which they requested the return of captives taken by the Illinois, Deliette replied: ". . .I will speak to the Illinois who will give you back your kinsmen whom they have had since last summer; for they have no others from an earlier time" (ibid. p. 51; italics - JJ). From these statements the inference may be drawn that Deliette and his army of French and Illinois had engaged the Kickapoo and Mascouten in place of the Fox.

169

Because of the failure of DeLignery's expedition Boucherville, who was in command of the garrison at Fort Beauharnois, concluded that his position had become untenable. Shortly after his departure he became involved in an enforced, but nevertheless friendly, stay with the Kickapoo while on his journey to Montreal via the Illinois country. The Kickapoo and Mascouten village was situated 7 or 8 miles up the Skunk (?) River (ibid. p. 38). But it was moved to a neighboring island on the Mississippi after the arrival, on November 2, of ten Fox who expressed their displeasure over the amicable relations between the French and their hosts. There resulted disagreement among the Kickapoo, while the Fox sent a force of 100 warriors to take at least some of the French, and threatened to send another 600 Fox and Winnebago. After an angry exchange between Fox and Kickapoo, the former, on their way home, met and killed a Kickapoo and a Mascouten who were hunting, thus creating further tension between the two allies (ibid. pp. 43-48). The distress of the Kickapoo elders was epitomized in this statement to Boucherville: "We are between two fires; the Renard has killed us, the Illinois has killed us, the Frenchman is angry with us. What are we to do?" (ibid. p. 48).

It would appear that the difficulties between the Fox and the Kickapoo-Mascouten were not merely the result of the present circumstances. They apparently had a falling out in 1727, for the two groups are referred to in a letter of Beauharnois as "former allies" (ibid. p. 58).

Boucherville prevailed upon the Kickapoo to permit his departure for the Illinois area for the purpose of making an effort to create peace all around. Accompanied by ". . . .a Kikapou and a Mascoutin, born of Illinois mothers,. . . ." he left on December 27, 1728 and nine days later arrived ". . . .amongst the Péoaria on the river of the Illinois, twenty leagues [50 miles] from the Mississippi. Several tribes were gathered together in this village, keeping always on the watch and anxious for news of the Kikapous" (ibid. p. 48). This location appears to be somewhat more than half the distance from Lake Peoria to the mouth of the Illinois. From what Boucherville says it seems likely that although the main group here was composed of Peoria there were also members of other Illinois groups present. In view of what Boucherville says later in his account (ibid. p. 55) this was probably a fairly large winter encampment only, not a permanent establishment.

It was from this place that the Kickapoo and Mascouten sent their request for peace to Deliette at Fort Chartres. When the commandant's friendly reply came, with assurance that the French and Illinois were preparing

170

to take vengeance against the Fox, "The Illinois had already begun to chant their war-song with all their hearts; two hundred young warriors had already prepared their arrows" (ibid. p. 51). When Boucherville, with an Illinois emissary, returned to the Kickapoo-Mascouten village they were welcomed with enthusiasm. Boucherville induced two war chiefs to send out two war parties against the Fox, one of which learned that a Fox war party "will soon go amongst the Illinois" (ibid. pp. 52-3).

Thereafter thirty Illinois arrived at the Kickapoo-Mascouten village to return captives and to invite the Kickapoo ". . .to go, in the Spring, to the Illinois who were well disposed to receive them." Boucherville urged the Kickapoo to ". . .go to the Illinois and conclude a lasting peace with them, so that the Illinois may no longer doubt your sincerity; you must offer them the scalps of the Renards." To this they assented. He was delighted at the prospect ". . .for the French and Illinois had no more dangerous foes than the Kikapous and Mascoutins, who killed their people up to the very doors of their village" (ibid. p. 54). There was every indication ". . .that the Kikapous really wished for the peace so greatly desired by the Illinois." A delegation of Kickapoo and Mascouten chiefs accompanied the French to Fort Chartres, where they were given ". . .presents to induce them to maintain peace and union." The chiefs were then escorted back to their village by a detachment of twenty French (ibid. p. 55).

171

By the middle of May, 1729 Beauharnois was to write that he was about to offer presents to the Kickapoo and Mascouten ". . .to confirm them in the resolution that they have taken to wage war against the Renards." He seemed to think that this break with the Fox would result in the Kickapoo and Mascouten becoming ". . .a strong barrier between the Ilinois country and that of the Renards." (ibid. p. 61).

The ability of Boucherville to extricate himself from what was, to say the least, an extremely delicate situation was in no small measure a tribute not so much to his diplomatic skill as to the largesse which he was able to dispense. He was well stocked with goods; and when he first reached the village he was asked to stay and trade before he was compelled to remain for the winter (ibid. pp. 38-9). During the course of his captivity, however, he was able to maintain for himself a delicate balance between the Kickapoo and Fox by means of the presents he distributed on suitable occasions. One instance reveals the attitude of the Kickapoo-Mascouten towards the Illinois before the scales were tipped in favor of peace. Boucherville's memorandum (ibid. pp. 82-86) on the items he gave away contains the following note: "During the winter a large party was got together for the purpose of attacking The Illinois and I did All I could by words and presents to stop It, which I succeeded in doing. . ." (ibid. p. 85).

172

There are three final items of interest in Boucherville's account:

1) "It is estimated that there are about 200 men amongst the Kikapous and 600 men in the three illinois villages. There are two French settlements of very considerable size, containing nearly 200 French some of whom are married to Illinois women and others to French women from New Orleans. They sell flour and pork on the sea coast, and bring back goods from there" (ibid. p. 55).

Although not mentioned by Boucherville the fur trade was still part of the business enterprise here, for a report from New Orleans on April 22, 1729 to the Company of the Indies states that: "The beaver pelts are beginning to come down from this [Illinois] post" (MPA 2:644). The three villages must be those at Cahokia, Kaskaskia and the Michigamea. The "village" of the Peorias at which he stayed was, therefore, probably only a wintering site on the

Illinois River.

For approximately a quarter of a century the French and their European-
izing influence had been established among the Illinois. This factor, rather
than becoming a source of strength to the Illinois, was probably the historical root of their weakness. As in all similar situations where peoples serve
instrumental purposes they were means, not ends, subordinate to the objectives
of the dominant cultural influence. The concern of the French in the area was
the development of production and trade, the role of the Illinois becoming
increasingly that of a "proletariat".

2) When in May, 1729, Boucherville learned from Father Boulanger
". . .the missionary among the Mixik-Illinois [Michigamea and Kaskaskia]
. . .that ten of his people were going by land to the Ouyas [Wea]" he decided
to join them for part of his journey to Canada (WHC 17:55). The probable
reason for the Illinois visit to the Wea was trade.

173

3) It may well be that before reaching the Wea, Boucherville and the
party of Illinois visited the Piankashaw, for he writes: "The distance from
the Illinois to the Peanguichias is about 120 leagues [300 miles] and 15
leagues [37.5 miles] from the Peanguichias to the Ouyas; 60 leagues from the
Ouyas to the Miamis;. . ." (ibid. p. 56).

In the course of the captivity of Boucherville's party the brothers
Montbrun made their escape down the Mississippi. One of them reached Quebec
in March, 1729, ". . .but left his brother ill among the Tamaroids [Cahokia
village]. . ." (ibid. p. 59). Among the captive French was a Jesuit, Father
Guignas. "Seven or eight months after this peace was concluded, the Maskoutins
and the Kikapous returned again to the Illinois country, and took away Father
Guignas to spend the winter with them,. . ." (JR 68:209). This friendly
interaction was to continue, as subsequent events proved.

In July, 1729 Beauharnois reported with enthusiasm the arrival of delegations from a number of tribes who wished to know what the French plans were with reference to the Fox. Among them were the Sac and Potawatomi of St. Joseph River; the Hurons, Potawatomi and Ottawa of Detroit; the Miami and Wea. He said also that virtually all the tribes in the Green Bay and Lakes region were antagonistic to the Fox ". . .who have attacked the Quicapoux, Mascoutins, folles avoines [Menominee], and sauteux. . ." (WHC 17:63).

VII - 1730-1750

It is certainly clear from the events of 1730 that not only had the Kickapoo and Mascouten become enemies of the Fox, but that they, together with the Illinois, Potawatomi and others, inflicted a devastating defeat upon the Fox while the latter were en route to the Iroquois. A tremendous battle which must have contributed significantly to the decimation of the Fox is described or alluded to in four documents which, although they differ in detail and are somewhat obscure on some points, are reasonably clear on the essentials (WHC 17:100-102; 109-113; 113-118; 129-130).

It seems that the Mascouten and Kickapoo, when they learned that the Fox were planning to seek refuge among the Iroquois, notified the French that the Fox were to make their journey via the Wea on the Wabash (ibid. p. 110). Early in the summer of 1730 the Fox were traversing the upper Illinois area where, at that time, the Illinois were apparently occupying a village at Starved Rock. Two of the sources refer to the "Illinois of le Rocher" (ibid. pp. 110, 113, 114).

175

In July, 1730, St. Ange, commandant at Fort Chartres, was informed by the Cahokia "...that the Renards had taken some of their people prisoners and had Burned the son of their great Chief near le Rocher on the River of the Illinois." (ibid. p. 110). It is not clear, however, whether the Illinois in this action were Cahokia or those from Starved Rock. Presumably, this encounter took place while the Fox were on their way to the Iroquois (ibid. pp. 110, 114). They had established two camps on the prairie (ibid. p. 117), where, on August 12, a scout counted one hundred eleven of their cabins (ibid. p. 110).

St. Ange assembled about 100 French and 400 Indians, including Cahokia, Peoria, and Missouri, and set out on August 10 (ibid. pp. 110, 115).

In the meantime, about 200 Potawatomi, Mascouten and Kickapoo, learning that the Fox and Illinois were embattled in the prairies between Starved Rock and the Wea, had joined the Illinois and blocked the Fox on the northeast (pp. 100-101, 110, 111, 114, 115). According to one account, when the Potawatomi, Mascouten and Kickapoo attacked the Fox on one side, the Illinois on the other took flight; but they subsequently rejoined the battle (ibid. p. 101). Two Mascouten messengers were sent for aid to de Villiers at the St. Joseph River post where they arrived August 6; and he, in turn, notified de Noyelle at the Miami post (ibid. pp. 100, 114).

St. Ange arrived on the scene of battle on August 17 and was soon joined by de Villiers, whose forces consisted of Potawatomi, Sac, and Miami in addition to Kickapoo and Mascouten. Apparently the latter two were settled among the Sac on the St. Joseph River (ibid. pp. 114-115, 111, 101). The Fox were palisaded in a grove of trees on the west bank of a small river (pp. 111, 114, 115), and St. Ange blockaded them on the opposite bank to prevent their access to water (ibid. pp. 111, 112, 115). On the same day that de Villiers arrived so did the Wea and Piankashaw in response to a message sent to the Ouiatanon post by the Potawatomi. De Villiers had been summoned by two Mascouten at the same time that a request for help was sent to Cahokia (ibid. p. 114). The Fox also sent to the Wea asking for aid and for permission to pass through to the Iroquois (ibid. p. 115). In addition, both the Wea and the Sac attempted by ruses, albeit unsuccessfully, to alleviate the desperate situation of the Fox (ibid. pp. 111-112, 115-116).

de Noyelle, who arrived on the field September 1, brought an order from the Governor of Canada barring any peace with the Fox; and at a general council of the allies it was decided unanimously to destroy the enemy (ibid. p. 112).

On September 7, after both sides had been suffering from hunger, 200 or 300 Illinois (Cahokia ?) (p. 117) deserted while 100 of their allies were hunting for food (ibid. pp. 112, 117).

Ultimately, after holding out for 23 days (ibid. p. 117) against the combined French and Indian forces of St. Ange, de Noyelle, and de Villiers, totaling about 1400 men (ibid. p. 115; see also p. 130), the Fox attempted to escape on the night of September 8 in an extremely severe rainstorm. They were pursued by the besiegers who, it seems, killed and captured anywhere from 800 to 1,000 individuals, men, women and children (ibid. pp. 113, 117, 130). According to one account the prisoners were given to the Cahokia (ibid. p. 117), while another states that they were distributed among all the allies participating in the action (ibid. p. 130). The latter source located the battle "...in a Plain situated between the River Wabache and the River of the illinois, About 60 leagues [150 miles] to the south of The Extremity or foot of Lake Michigan, to The East South East of le Rocher in the Illinois Country." (ibid. p. 129).

177

In 1730, therefore, part of the Illinois are on the upper Illinois River as well as in their villages located on the Mississippi. In October, 1730 Beauharnois and Hocquart stated in a letter that they granted "...permission to some Frenchmen to escort missionaries to the Tamaroa..." on the Mississippi (Krauskopf, 1955, p. 179; MPHC 34:71). Some Kickapoo and Mascouten are located among the Sac on the St. Joseph River of Michigan, on which there were also Potawatomi established. This information on these tribes is supported by a government memorandum (by DeNoyan) on the "State of Canada in 1730" which refers to the "...Saquis, Maskoutens, Kikapous and the greater part of the Poutouatamis, all of the St. Joseph River,..." (MPHC 34:74); and the author expresses considerable annoyance with these groups for supplying the Fox with "...corn and stores..." (ibid. pp. 74, 82). In a discussion of Detroit it is mentioned that there are two Potawatomi villages there containing at least 150 people (ibid. p. 76).

In July, 1730 Father le Petit, in a letter from the Jesuit mission at New Orleans, wrote fairly extensively about a visit made there in June by several Illinois. Among the visitors was the Chief Chikagou who "...was at the head of the Mitchigamias..." Another was "...Mamantouensa at the head of the Kaskaskias" (JR 68:203). Having heard that the French were at war with the Natchez and the Yazoo they had come to New Orleans to offer their services and also their condolences for the dead. But they stated quite explicitly that although they were prepared "...to offer our Warriors to strike those hostile Nations whom you may wish to designate", they wanted to insure for themselves the allegiance and protection of the French. At the same time they emphasized their devotion to Christianity. This was certain to strike a responsive chord in the hearts of the French and their missionaries. Mamantouensa may be cited as exemplifying the sentiments of both chiefs in his address to Governor Perier of Louisiana: "All that I ask of you is your heart and your protection. I am much more desirous of that than of all the merchandise of the world, and when I ask this of you, it is solely for the Prayer" (ibid. p. 205). The need for security seems to have superseded the desire for material gain.

Although the chiefs may have been "using" Christianity to strengthen their plea, the sincerity of their devotion to the faith is not to be doubted. When the Illinois professed "...That they were almost all 'of the prayer' (that is, according to their manner of expression, that they are Christians);..." it was probably a reasonably fair statement of the situation among them (ibid. p. 203). By this time two generations of Illinois

178

had been brought up under missionary influence, and the amount of intermarriage with the French had increased steadily. According to le Petit
they also maintained "...That they are inviolably attached to the French,
by the alliances which many of that Nation had contracted with them, in
espousing their daughters" (idem).

Early in 1732 the King's instructions to Bienville, who was replacing
Perier as Governor of Louisiana, stated that a letter from Perier, dated
May 14, 1731 "...has rendered an account to the effect that Mtachimé, a
chief of the Peoria Indians, one of the Illinois Indians, had a request made
to him to grant him some Frenchmen to go and settle with his people at
Pimitoui from which they had been driven by the Foxes" (MPA 3:555-6; also
MPA 1:201). It is interesting to note that Perier intended to grant the
request because if troops were to be stationed there "...this settlement
will facilitate communication between Canada and the Illinois..." (ibid.
p. 556). He also expresses the view "...that it is to be wished that the
other Illinois villages should decide to withdraw from the settlements of
the French in order to avoid disputes, that it might be harmful for them to
be too near and that it would be better that they be two or three days'
journey distant because they respect the French more when they are completely
separated from them" (idem). This discordant note in Louisiana soon becomes
louder, as will be seen below.

After the defeat inflicted upon the Fox, Boishébert, the commandant
at Detroit, informed Governor Beauharnois that the Illinois, acting alone,
made an attack upon the Fox, probably during the first half of 1731 (WHC
17:142, 148). It is likely that the latter were sought out by their enemy
"...in the country where the Fox Indians have retreated;..." which may have
been southern Wisconsin (MPHC 34:83). For in the late fall or early winter

179

of 1731 a party of Huron, Iroquois, and a few Ottawa almost annihilated the principal Fox village on the Wisconsin River, not far above its confluence with the Mississippi (WHC 17:150-1).

En route to their attack upon the Fox the Huron (from Detroit) and the Iroquois (from the Montreal vicinity), after leaving Chicago "...Continued their Route as far as the Kicapous..." after which they "...pushed on to the Mascoutins..." At this point they "...found themselves at a distance of more than 250 Leagues from home and almost In the Enemy's country,..." to which they were guided by the Mascouten (ibid. p. 149). A number of days after the departure of their guides, the attacking party reached the Fox village (ibid. pp. 149-150).

It would appear from the data here adduced that the Kickapoo and Mascouten were probably wintering in separate villages in southern Wisconsin or northern Illinois. Here they were south or southeast or, conceivably, east of the Fox.

Following the devastation of their village the remaining Fox sought refuge among several groups, including the Kickapoo and Mascouten who refused to receive any of them for fear of further trouble (ibid. pp. 167-168) In fact those two tribes were trying to enhance their security. In company with the Illinois they went to see the Governor in 1732 in an effort to insure the same consideration for themselves as he was accustomed to show his other "children". Although there is much truth in the Illinois speech made on the occasion of this visit, it may be read also in the light of customary figures of speech employed in oratory: "You know that we were The first to attack the Renards who killed us, which reduces us to a pitiable condition" (ibid. p. 170). But the hopeful note that was sounded was friendship between the Illinois on the one side and the Kickapoo and

180

Mascouten on the other.

With the threat from the Fox under control, if not eliminated, the Illinois, in an apparent change of mind became involved briefly in hostilities with the Chickasaw. This was reported by St. Ange to Beauharnois who wrote that "...the Illinois, about the month of September [1732], began to attack the Chicachas; that they brought him [St. Ange] a scalp from that tribe and two others of the Natchez,..." (MPHC 34:110). It is not clear whether this action preceded or followed a Chickasaw attack "this autumn" against the French on the Wabash. On that occasion the Chickasaw killed three and captured three (ibid. p. 108; see also Dunn, 1902, p. 306). The Chickasaw followed up by sending one of the prisoners "...the man Le Breton to the Illinois with a calumet of peace which they had formerly received from them..." (MPHC 34:108), hoping perhaps, that the Illinois would intercede in their behalf.

181

As regards the Natchez, Illinois hostilities against them were undoubtedly prompted by the French, just as they had instigated the lakes tribes against the Chickasaw (idem; MPA 3:666). It will be remembered that in June, 1730 two Illinois chiefs went to New Orleans and offered their help in the French difficulties with the Natchez and the Yazoo. Those hostilities were still in process (MPHC 34:110).

From the viewpoint of the Louisiana government, however, the state of affairs regarding the Illinois appeared to have a darker hue. For the Illinois became incensed when, in October, 1731, Governor Perier had three Chickasaws burned to death (MPA 1:200). The Chickasaw had solicited the help of the Illinois against the Louisiana French (MPA 3:552). After Perier's action the Illinois were not disposed to join the French against the Chickasaw, and grudgingly gave their help against "our enemies" (idem). Manifesting

their discontent, "the Illinois" "...claimed that there was due them the
payment for the lands that they had given up and for the mines that the lands
contained" (idem). The French feared that "The revolt of this nation might
be regarded as a mortal blow to the colony and it is to prevent it that..."
it was decided to place Pierre d'Artaguette in command at Fort Chartres
(ibid. pp. 200-201; MPA 3:614-616). This is a distinctly different view from
that of the Canadians with whom the Illinois gave every indication of being
cooperative. When they went against the Chickasaw it was in response to the
desire of Canada which sent out several "tribes" against the same objective
(Dunn, 1902, pp. 306-7; MPHC 34:108-9).

It is after the move against the Chickasaw that the Illinois of
Starved Rock are mentioned as being engaged in an action against the Fox by
Boishébert in a dispatch dated November 7, 1732. He writes: "After our
warriors [Huron, Ottawa, and Potawatomi of Detroit] had marched for 22 days,
they found the Fox Indians on the shore of Lake Marameek in fort..."
(MPHC 34:104). The reference is obscure; but the exact location of this
geographical feature is of no particular importance for the present purpose.
It may be connected with the Meramec River of Missouri or, possibly, with
the lake at the head of the Fox River of Illinois. With the latter an
association may have been made, in turn, with the "Maramech" of Franquelin's
map of 1684, denoted on the west bank of the Fox River of Illinois, in either
northeastern Illinois or southeastern Wisconsin (see Steward, 1903, pp. 25,
27, but the suggestion is mine, JJ).

The Huron and a few Ottawa came upon the Fox three days before the
rest of the party. "The Outaouacs and Poutouatamis, who had gone past the
Mascoutins, arrived next day with the Illinois from Le Rocher;..." (MPHC
34:105). Late in 1731 the Mascouten were in southern Wisconsin or northern

182

Illinois. If the Ottawa and Potawatomi, unlike the Huron, went past the Mascouten in the area where the latter were last reported as wintering, it is possible that the war party went west to the Mississippi and then downstream to the Maramec. On the other hand, if they picked up the Illinois at Starved Rock, they would reach the Mississippi and the Meramec via the Illinois River. In that case, how would they go "past the Mascoutins"? They might do so only if the Mascouten were then much farther to the south; or if the war party had first gone to seek the Fox in Wisconsin, and not finding them there, set a new course, which took them past the Mascouten.

If the Fox fort were in northeastern Illinois or in southeastern Wisconsin, there would be not much problem picking up the Illinois en route; but then it would seem to place the Mascouten either in the northeastern region of Illinois or somewhere in northern Indiana.

A 22 day march might suggest that the Fox fort was at the more distant of the alternative locations. But the duration of such a "march" could depend upon any of a number of possible factors. The chief point of concern, however, is that Illinois were in the vicinity of Starved Rock at this time, a place where they were also situated in 1730.

Having weighed the possible alternatives with regard to their location, it may be suggested that the likelihood is greater that the Fox fort was west of the Mississippi in 1732. For de Noyelle and his party of French and Indians, on a punitive expedition against the Fox, found them early in 1735 on the Des Moines River (see below). In view of the antagonism, not only of the French but also of other tribal groups, the Fox probably continued to range over that region after 1732 until the encounter in 1735.

Writing in May, 1733 Bienville, who replaced Perier as Governor of Louisiana, recognized that the attitude of the Illinois towards the French

183

of Canada was friendly in contrast to the hostility with which they regarded the government at New Orleans (MPA 1:205-206). He also wrote to Paris that "...St. Ange testifies that he is little assured of the fidelity of the Illinois, who often give him alarm, and make pretense of fear of our resentment for their past faults to have a pretext for agitation" (Dunn, 1902, p. 301; also MPA 1:206). Additional testimony of this nature was received from Vincennes, who built a fort eighty leagues (200 miles) up the Wabash. According to him (March 7, 1733) "The Indians, Illinois as well as Miamis and others, are more insolent than they have ever been, and that since the Foxes have been overthrown" (Dunn, 1902, p. 304; also p. 303). He also stated "...that the Ouabache nation is composed of five tribes, which include four villages [the Miami speaking groups],..." In addition Bienville reported information received from Vincennes "...that the Piankeshaws, who are established near our fort, wish to draw to them a village of the same tribe which is located sixty leagues [150 miles] higher up" (ibid. p. 308).

184

In the spring and summer of 1733 a smallpox epidemic which apparently originated in Montreal soon spread to the Wabash country causing havoc among the Miami, Wea, and Piankashaw (WHC 17:175; MPHC 34:109). Early in June of the same year, the Illinois at Starved Rock were in a state of anxiety because thirty of their warriors, on their way to the Sioux, had fallen upon a group of families consisting of Chippewa, Menominee, Sac, and Nipissing, killing seven and taking two captives. Four Illinois chiefs returned the captives through the commandant of the St. Joseph post and begged the Governor to intercede against retribution (WHC 17:183-4).

During the year following (1734), the relationship between the Illinois and their Miami-speaking neighbors was apparently more than passively amicable. The strength of the ties among them is brought out in the annual

report to Paris of the state of affairs in Canada (NYCD 9:1048-1051; WHC
17:242-244) for the year 1736. In that document the governor and intendant
discuss a drunken fray between a Wea and a Frenchman at the Wea post and the
resultant pillaging of the French (WHC 17:211-212, 243-244). The affair was
finally settled as d'Arnaud, the commandant at the Miami post, was about to
leave for the Wea with a strong detachment. The report states that "...there
is no doubt, had Sieur d'Arnaud continued his march, but these Indians would
have been advised thereof by the Miamis, their allies, and have retired to
the Peanguichias or Islinois, who are equally their allies, so that, besides
being unable to wreak vengeance on the Ouiatanous, it would be declaring war
against the other nations, among whom they would certainly have found an
asylum, and stopping the path to the Mississippy on ourselves" (ibid. p. 243;
italics-JJ). This excerpt is, perhaps, not so much interesting for its
information with respect to the strong ties between the Illinois and these
eastern neighbors, as it is for its revelation of the precariousness of the
French position, a condition of which they were only too keenly aware, both
in Canada and in Louisiana. The English threat was ever present on the
periphery of these provinces, and the blandishments of their trade was an
enduring temptation to the susceptible Miami and Wea.

During the winter of 1734-5 two Illinois war parties captured thirty-
six Chickasaw, and it was also anticipated "...that the three villages [of
Illinois] are going to march en masse this autumn [1735],..." (MPA 1:265).
But it later developed "...that the Illinois have not executed at all the
plan that they had made to go this autumn en masse against the Chickasaws"
(ibid. p. 293), although they ultimately did participate in a disastrous
French campaign against that tribe in the spring of 1736 (ibid. pp. 311-313).
The "three villages" referred to are the Kaskaskia, Cahokia-Tamaroa, and

185

the Michigamea, who joined the French in the assault upon the Chickasaw in
1736 (ibid. p. 311). On that occasion the Illinois as well as the Miami,
who were also participants, both being considered "the strongest part of
[d'Artaguette's] little army", took flight when they saw themselves out-
numbered (ibid. p. 313).

Before the campaign against the Chickasaw, however, the French of
Canada undertook to put an end to Fox warfare which had flared up again in
September 1733 when the Fox, assisted by the Sac, made a strike at Green Bay
(post?) (WHC 17:206). An expedition under the command of de Noyelle, which
was not at all successful, set out in August 1734 with French and Iroquois
via Detroit and the Wabash, being joined along the way by additional French
and Indians (ibid. pp. 207-210, 231; MPHC 34:130).

In his report (WHC 17:221-229; MPHC 34:122-128) de Noyelle writes that
"When I arrived among the Ouyatanons [on the Wabash], I went to see several
Kikapous who were Six Leagues [15 miles] from there, and asked them where
the Renards might be found. They replied, laying a red calumet at my feet:
'they are in that direction' (turning round); That if I wished to obtain
more positive Information about them I had only to go to Masanne; that I
would find their principal village there and their people would know where
the Renards dwelt. When I went to them they told me that the Renards were
not far away and that they would take me to them" (WHC 17:222; see also
translation in MPHC 34:122). The question of interest here is the location
of the Kickapoo village at "Masanne". This is an area referred to by La Salle
in 1684 when he wrote: "Following the river of Teatiki [Kankakee, descending]
from the confluence with the Checagou [Des Plaines River], one finds the
most beautiful country in the world, for about nine leagues [22.5 miles].
The Indians call it Massane because of the large quantity of hemp that is

186

there" (Margry 2:174, translation - JJ).

In effect then, in the winter of 1734-1735 (de Noyelle left the Wea on January 2, 1735), the main Kickapoo village was situated on the upper Illinois River at some point which was probably between the Des Plaines and Starved Rock. In connection with the foregoing quotation from La Salle it may be noted that he also wrote that the Mascouten, because of Iroquois depredations around the Great Lakes, were not far from the Chicago River. As he put it "The Portage of Checagou is about eight leagues [twenty miles] from the village of the Maskoutens toward the North-West" (idem). This raises again the possibility that in 1732, when a party of Indians from Detroit journeyed to attack the Fox Indians, they passed the Mascouten in northeastern Illinois (see above, esp. MPHC 34:105).

Although forty Kickapoo joined de Noyelle and, presumably were to show him the way (WHC 17:224), it was five Sac who were captured by de Noyelle's troops that ultimately led the way to where the Fox, including some Sac, were situated on the Des Moines River west of the Mississippi (ibid. p. 223). There were also Sac settled on the St. Joseph River (idem. MPHC 34:132).

187

On the basis of a letter from Governor Bienville of Louisiana, written June 21, 1737, it would appear that some time in 1735, after de Noyelle's visit at the Kickapoo village which was then probably situated in northeastern Illinois, the Kickapoo, together with the Mascouten, joined either the Miami at Fort Wayne or the Wea near Lafayette. The question is whether Bienville uses the term "Miami" narrowly, or broadly, to include the Wea and possibly others also. He wrote: "It so happens today that the Kickapoo and Mascouten who came to make their village with the Miami two years ago [1735] do not get along with them, and M.de la Buissoniere [commandant at Fort Chartres] assures me that if only one would invite them they would come to settle there [Illinois]... All that I fear is that the Sieur de Linquetot, the Canadian officer who is commanding at the Miami and Ouiatanon, is opposed to letting the Kickapoo and Mascouten go because these two nations are of his department..." (Krauskopf, 1955, p. 185). Apparently there were efforts to attract the Kickapoo and Mascouten to the Illinois area from Indiana; and if the commandant at Fort Chartres was right, those groups might have been interested in such a proposition.

Subsequent to the defeat, in spring 1736 (WHC 17:259, fn 1) of D'Artaguette and his contingents of Illinois and Miami, a party of Kickapoo and Mascouten engaged in an encounter on the Wabash with some Natchez (MPA 1:327). In October of the same year a census of Indian tribes, compiled by an unidentified source at Michilimackinac from information obtained "from the Voyageurs whom I questioned", estimates eighty men (meaning warriors) for the Kickapoo and sixty for the Mascouten. (NYCD 9:1055, 1058; WHC 17:249,252). In this listing they are included under the heading of "Fox River", following a reference to the Fox Indians who are said to be "now migratory" and former allies of the Kickapoo and Mascouten (idem).

As for the "Indians comprehended under the name of Illinois" the following information is included: the Michigamea with 250 men are situated at Fort Chartres while the Kaskaskia "six leagues [15 miles] below, have a village of one hundred warriors..." The Peoria are again said to be at Starved Rock with fifty men, and "The Kaokias, or Tamarois, can furnish two hundred men..." (NYCD 9:1057; WHC 17:250-251).

It is this anonymous document which apparently provided the information that Chauvignerie used in his official report to the government of Canada in 1736 (Schoolcraft 3:553-556). The original compiler of the census associates the Mascouten and Kickapoo with the Fox River area by implication

188

only, whereas Chauvignerie's report is quite explicit in stating that they
are "Of Fox River..." (ibid. p. 554). But as we have already observed,
de Noyelle found the Kickapoo in northeastern Illinois in the winter of 1734-5,
while Bienville wrote that they, together with the Mascouten, established
"their village with the Miami" in Indiana some time during 1735. It would
appear, therefore, that by 1734 the Kickapoo and Mascouten had begun the
process of a more or less permanent shift from Wisconsin.

Writing to the French Minister on October 17, 1736 Beauharnois referred
to a letter he received the previous July from DeLusignan, the commandant of
the St. Joseph River post, in which the latter reported that the Sac, starving
and naked, came to him to sue for peace, "...Followed by the Chiefs and elders
of the Poutouatamis, Illinois, Miamis, And Outavois who had Gone to meet Them
and take them Food, because one of their People had come to tell them that
they had none". Having accepted their offer DeLusignan added "...that they
have Established themselves at the Place that he pointed out to them, Between
the Poutouatamis, Miamis and Illinois Villages,..." (WHC 17:259-260). The
Illinois here referred to are undoubtedly the Peoria at Starved Rock, mentioned in the preceding enumerations. The area in which the Sac established
themselves was probably somewhere in northwestern Indiana or possibly northeastern Illinois south of Chicago. Such an inference would seem to be
warranted on the basis that the Potawatomi were those on the St. Joseph River;
the Miami were at Fort Wayne and on the upper Wabash if the Wea are included;
and the Illinois were those at Starved Rock.

189

The peace which the French managed to establish with the Chickasaw in
April, 1740 was short-lived; soon thereafter the French were again urging
their Indian allies against this foe. An unsigned document which may have
been written by Beaucourt, the governor of Montreal, in 1741 indicates that

the Illinois were in no position to be of much help to the French in this
renewal of warfare, because they were forced to contend with attacks of the
Fox, who were assisted by their Sioux allies.

At the end of April 1741 Bienville received information "...that the
Foxes have killed two Illinois and that the latter have sent a party against
the Foxes to get vengeance" (MPA 3:748). In May following, one hundred Sioux
and Fox engaged in an offensive against the Illinois at Lake Peoria. But
this was a fruitless effort because the Sac had forewarned those Illinois
in gratitude for their return of captives taken in an attack by the Cahokia
(WHC 17:336-7, 362, 365). Not long thereafter, in the summer of 1741, sixty
Peoria set out against the Sioux, but instead attacked the Fox at the mouth
of the Wisconsin, killing four and wounding one (ibid. p. 365). On their
way back down the Mississippi the Peoria were mistakenly attacked by the Sac,
who killed nine of them and took five prisoners. As a result of this
unintentional assault, it was reported, "...nearly all the Sakis were to go
to le Rocher, and to send to Pimitéouy to parley, and to say to the Illinois
that they had no share in the affair which Had occurred, and that they wished
to live in peace with them" (ibid.pp. 365-6). It is apparent from this
passage that the Illinois in 1741 were situated in their historically authenti-
cated locations at Starved Rock and Lake Peoria.

The existence of Fox-Illinois hostilities in 1740-1741 is confirmed
in the Abstract of Despatchs from Canada...1741 which reveals "...that the
Foxes had sent out some war parties against the Ilinois, whereby several
Frenchmen have been killed,..." (NYCD 9:1086). Additional minor Sioux
attacks and successful retaliation by the Illinois in 1739 and 1740 were also
commented upon by Bienville (MPA 3:736-7). And Beauharnois learned that the
Illinois return of five fox captives had led to an uncertain peace between

190

those two tribes (WHC 17:363).

At the same time the Mascouten were also in fear of the Fox who were reported by Beaucourt to be with the Sioux on the Wisconsin. As a result "On April 26 (1741) eight cabins of Mascouten arrived at the Ouiatanon to settle there with a chief who was there;..." (Krauskopf, 1955, p. 191; WHC 17:336).

The growing importance of the French settlements in the Illinois area along the Mississippi is indicated by another letter from the governor of Louisiana in September 1741. He reports the arrival at New Orleans, in July, of a convoy with 125,000 pounds of flour and "...a rather large quantity of peltries which have been helpful to commerce" (ibid p. 750). A part of the furs was apparently obtained from the Missouri and other Indians west of the Mississippi (ibid. p. 751).

In the same month a report by Beauharnois from Quebec indicates that he was instrumental in getting the Kickapoo and Mascouten to settle near the Wea on the Wabash in an effort to maintain some control over the latter whom he regarded as "one of the most turbulent tribes" (MPHC 34:208). With the same end in view he also tried to convince the Shawnee to move there from the war route of the Ohio, although "...they desired to go and light their (camp) fire at the Maskoutins' prairie, 20 leagues [50 miles] from the foot [fort ?] of the Peauguichias,..." (ibid.pp. 207-8). Although the Piankashaw are definitely established on the Vermillion River, according to a document of 1746, they probably had already been there before this time (Krauskopf, 1955, p. 197). The following year, July 1742, at Montreal in a conference with Beauharnois, attended also by the Mascouten, Wea, and Pepikokia, the Kickapoo also expressed a desire to settle in the Mascouten prairie, stating that they wished to leave the Wea for this purpose (WHC 17:382). This

191

decision seems to have been related to the Shawnee desire to move to the same place, as revealed by a Kickapoo chief (ibid. p. 383). Beauharnois gave them both his permission; but it was not until October, 1743 that he reported the Shawnee "...have set out with that design" (NYCD 9:1098). And in 1745 he wrote that "the emigration of the [Shawnee to the Mascouten Prairie] has at length taken place" (NYCD 10:20). At the 1742 conference the governor requested the four tribes to continue their attacks upon the Chickasaw (WHC 17:387).

The location of the Mascouten Prairie, where the Kickapoo and the Shawnee were to settle, was subsequently further identified by Beauharnois in another communication in which he placed it "near the Ouyatanons", whose village was on the Wabash below Lafayette (ibid. p. 417; see also WHC 18:4 and fn 9). This Indian settlement was near the French post of Ouiatanon (Grand Ouyas or Great Weas) which a memoir of 1746 places 60 leagues [150 miles] above the Vincennes post (Petits Ouyas or Little Weas) which is, in turn, 70 leagues [175 miles] above the mouth of the Wabash (Krauskopf, 1955, p. 194; Dunn, 1902, p. 327).

From September 1746 to May 1747 at the Ouiatanon post, where the trade was said to be "very considerable", the commandant ordered supplies to be distributed to the Wea, Piankashaw, Kickapoo and Mascouten. He did this in order to maintain their loyalty in the face of temptations offered by the Iroquois and English, and also to reward them for their efforts against the Chickasaw (Krauskopf, 1955, pp. 195-205). Although in the distribution lists of this document the Kickapoo and Mascouten are at times referred to together, and at other times separately, in one instance mention is made of "the chief of the Kickapoo and Mascouten" (ibid. p. 203). Reference is also made to "the Mascouten at Terre Haute", on the Wabash below the Vermillion River (ibid. p. 198).

With regard to the phrase "chief of the Kickapoo and Mascouten", the developing unity of these two groups is quite clear from a communication of 1748 by Vaudreuil who, of course, was writing from New Orleans. Referring to plans for the building of a fort on the Wabash, where the Kickapoo and Mascouten had promised to move and settle, Vaudreuil states: "A tribe like that will be sufficient to cover us at that point" (IHC 29:71-72). The original French is quite explicit in use of the singular number of the word translated here by the editors as "tribe" (une Nation). Its antecedent in the sentence immediately preceding is "Kickapoos and Mascoutens".

During 1747 the French were much exercised by disaffections among such groups as the Hurons and Miamis who tried to enlist support among the lakes tribes against the French. The Potawatomi on the St. Joseph were apparently determinedly loyal to the French of Canada. But at the same time Bertel, the commandant at Kaskaskia, was trying to lure them to the interests of Louisiana. Not only was Detroit threatened with destruction, but it appeared as if there were a plot afoot "to seize all the French posts, beginning with the Illinois country;..." The Illinois themselves finally decided to back off from this growing disaffection, presumably fostered by the English through the Iroquois. The French forces without essential supplies were in these circumstances, concentrated at Kaskaskia while awaiting the arrival from Detroit of requested aid, by means of which they hoped "...to ward off the storm that threatens the Illinois country,..." The French were so uncertain about Illinois intentions that they sent three of their principal chiefs to visit New Orleans thereby hoping to gain time to ascertain the disposition of the Illinois (WHC 17:479-489).

It would appear that as early as 1746 the changing Illinois attitude was manifested in part by a lack of cooperation in the execution of French

193

purposes, particularly as regards the war against the Chickasaw. Vaudreuil, Governor of Louisiana, expressed his displeasure over Illinois behavior by threatening "...to cut off their presents if they continue to remain inactive and to give us as sole proofs of their friendship, mere promises to behave better to us in the future" (IHC 29:9-10). It is very probable that the Illinois had a genuine feeling of loyalty to, and friendship for the French, especially the Canadians whom their women had married. But their ambivalence must have been a product of their reluctance to continue fighting the Chickasaw on behalf of these European allies and relatives upon whom they depended for the satisfaction of new needs. The French, however, often found it difficult to supply them (ibid. p. 15), in addition to which their prices were far higher than those of the English, whose goods seemed to be abundantly available, but at a distance. The Illinois might have been tempted by Iroquois, Huron or Miami offers, but they must have felt for several possible reasons that their destiny was tied to the French. When, therefore, Bertet, the commandant at Fort Chartres, asked the Illinois in 1746 to carry out raids against the English toward Philadelphia, they seemed to take a long time deciding; but the Cahokia and Peoria finally agreed to do so in 1747 (ibid. p. 12). The St. Joseph Potawatomi, however, continued to display a firm attachment to the French (IHC 29:121,123).

In May, 1748 Vaudreuil reported that the Illinois and the Piankashaw were engaged in hostilities with the Shawnee who had recently settled on the Wabash. Not only was it difficult for the French to keep the Shawnee supplied, but their proximity "...will give much umbrage to the Illinois and Wabash tribes who have neglected nothing with M.deBertet to make him suspicious of them" (ibid. pp. 68-70). It is probable that the Shawnee in that area were regarded by the Illinois and the Wabash tribes as not merely

194

a competitive nuisance, but as a threat to their trade position.

By 1748 questions were arising as to the value of maintaining the French posts in the Illinois region (WHC 17:499-501). Not only were they difficult to hold and to supply from New Orleans, but their economic advantage to Louisiana seemed to be dubious; for the quality and production of the mines proved to be a disillusionment, while the fur trade passed mainly to Canada (WHC 18:14-15). This was a view propounded by Galissonière, the new Governor of Canada, who, in a consideration of whether it was worth holding on to the area at all, suggested that "...the Fur trade carried on there is one of the least advantageous in Canada,..." although he was not certain of this. He felt it should be held as a barrier to English ambitions, however, and that "...bread, meat, and other produce will attract Savages there whose alliance and trade will be of use to us;..." He suggested forcefully that the way to establish a strong French hold on the Illinois country was to settle it, for it was exceedingly fertile and easy to clear and cultivate. He indicated that the foundations for such an enterprise had already been laid, for "A fairly large number of French families are already there,..." in addition to a considerable number of coureurs de bois, although the troublesome behavior of the latter was hardly an asset (WHC 17:493-497). His view was confirmed, in part, by the fact that with favorable transportation conditions the Illinois region could send a considerable quantity of flour to New Orleans (IHC 29:67,73).

195

In the summer of 1749 LaDemoiselle, the pro-English Miami chief who, in 1747, had settled his band on the Miami River in the vicinity of Piqua, Ohio continued his efforts to rouse the tribes of the Wabash and Illinois areas against the French. In February, 1750 the commandant at Fort Chartres wrote that the Cahokia had apparently expressed their willingness to listen to LaDemoiselle, while the Peoria had not yet replied to his proposal. The temptation was great, for the Miami chief's strongest talking point was the low price of English goods (IHC 29:163-165). Although this price differential between English and French merchandise had ever been so, over the years it had become increasingly difficult, on this account alone, to remain loyal to the French.

The instigation and example of others had undoubtedly been forcing upon the Illinois an "agonizing reappraisal" of their economic position in their relationship with the French. The latter had never been unaware of the problem they presented in this respect; and it was restated by the commandant of the Miami post who, in September, 1749, wrote: "the excessive price of French goods in this post, the great bargains which the English give, as well as the large presents which they make to the tribes, have entirely disposed those tribes in their favor and induce them to go off to the English" (IHC 29:105; see also WHC 18:70-73).

196

In May, 1750 the same writer expressed admirably the economic problem of the Indian in the light of the hopelessly impossible French prices under the competitive onslaught of the English (IHC 29:214-216). Even French merchants, traders, and voyageurs grew rich by trading illicitly with the English (WHC 18:70-73). In effect, French economic policy created a psychological climate in which a chaotic superstructure of dilemma, ambivalence, impatience, and exasperation was piled upon a rotting foundation compounded of Indian economic necessity and deprivation.

It is difficult to see how anyone could resist the attractiveness of English prices and goods, yet at this time the Kickapoo and Mascouten (reported to have 300 men) appeared to do so; for they refused to entertain the disaffection radiating from the Miami focus throughout the Wabash and

into the Illinois area (IHC 29:209-213; Krauskopf, 1955, p. 214).   French
civilians were leaving the Miami post out of fear of the growing hostility
(IHC 29:204-206; see also pp. 197-198), and LaDemoiselle, the Miami chief,
was trying to draw into his anti-French plans not only the Illinois at Fort
Chartres, but also tribes on the Missouri (ibid. p. 241).

In 1750, Benoist, commandant at Fort Chartres, tried to arrange peace
between the Shawnee and Illinois but hostilities continued nevertheless
(ibid. p. 371).   He also reported that the Illinois "...had attacked some
Potawatomi of St. Joseph River..." (IHC 29:240, 242) a statement subsequently
elaborated by la Jonquiere almost one year later, in September,1751.   While
a party of St. Joseph Potawatomi were "passing the Peoria village" on their
way home from the Illinois one of them was killed by a Peoria.   In spite of
French efforts to settle this affair, because "...the matter was of great
importance for the safety of the voyageurs of the Illinois", retaliation
followed in the next spring (1751) when "...a party of Potawatomi, Mascoutens,
Menominee, and Chippewa went to attack the Peoria."   The latter captured
three Potawatomi and one Mascouten whom they sent back with a message of
peace which said,in part: "We have had some of our people who have been
killed in your villages and who were married there, but we have never taken
up arms to avenge them" (ibid. pp. 359-360).

In that same year (1750) the English governor sent George Croghan to
the Miami "to renew the chain of friendship," and during his stay at the
village, in November, 1750 "...there came several of the chiefs of the [Wea]
and (Piankashaw) Nations, living on the Wabash, and requested to be admitted
into the chain of friendship between the English and the Six Nations and
their allies;..." (Krauskopf pp. 215-216).   The Wea and Piankashaw also
responded to an invitation from Christopher Gist, representing the governor

197

of Virginia, and entered into a treaty of peace and alliance with the English (ibid. pp. 216-217).

During 1750 Father Vivier, Jesuit Missionary, wrote two letters from Cahokia, one in September and another in November. The increasing extent of French settlement in this Illinois area along the Mississippi is indicated in this passage from the September letter: "There are 5 French Villages and 3 Villages of Savages within a distance of 21 leagues, between the Mississippi and another river called the Kaskaskias. In the five French Villages there may be eleven hundred white people, three hundred black, and about sixty red slaves, otherwise Savages" (JR 69:145). In November, stating that all these villages are "...within a distance of twenty-two leagues [55 miles]..." he also adds that "they are situated upon a long prairie bounded on the East by a chain of mountains and the river of the Tamarouas, and on the West by the Mississippi. The five French villages contain in all about one hundred and forty families" (ibid. p. 221). The extent of French domestic livestock and cultivation of wheat and maize is fairly considerable (ibid. pp. 145-7); and although there are difficulties (ibid. p. 219), quantities of flour and pork are shipped to New Orleans (ibid. pp. 147, 213, 229). Vivier states, in fact, that parts of Canada, in addition to lower Louisiana, find the provisions they receive from this Illinois area "a great resource to them" (ibid. p. 229). He dwells upon both the strategic and productive importance of the region with considerable emphasis (idem). In addition the French supplement their foods with produce of the hunt, enabling them, as Vivier says "to live very comfortably".

As for the Illinois, he expresses considerable regard for them, except for their addiction to brandy, for which he justifiably holds the French among them responsible. In each of their cabins, he writes,

198

"...there are generally from 15 to 20 persons." Their hunting is done "From the beginning of October to the middle of March,...at a distance of forty or fifty leagues [100-125 miles] from their Village; and, in the middle of March, they return to their Village" (ibid. p. 147). In this connection he writes in November that "Nowhere is game more abundant; from mid-October to the end of March the people live almost entirely on game, especially on the wild ox and deer" (ibid. p. 219). As for the number of villages, after first mentioning the three in the area of the Mississippi, he writes at the end of his September letter: "...in addition to these three villages which I have mentioned there is a fourth one of the same Nation, eighty leagues [200 miles] from here, almost as large as the three others" (ibid. p. 149). This is probably the Peoria mission, under Father Meurin, which in November, he places 175 miles from Cahokia [Kaskaskia?] (ibid. p. 203).

Vivier, in his letters, also gives some population estimates of the Illinois. In September he states, at first, that "the three Illinois Villages do not contain more than eight hundred Savages, of all ages" (ibid. p. 145). At the end of this letter, however, he writes, after pointing out that the first missionaries reported an Illinois population of 5,000: "To-day we count but two thousand" (ibid. p. 149). But now he is including the Peoria, for he follows with the sentence quoted above in which he adds the fourth village, located 200 miles away. There is no definite indication that he has visited the latter.

In his November communication Father Vivier revises somewhat his estimate of the number of Indians in the Illinois mission on the Mississippi, for he now says it "...is composed of over six hundred Illinois,..." almost 200 less than his September estimate (ibid. p. 201). He also adds: "the three villages of Savages may furnish three hundred men capable of bearing arms" (ibid. p. 221).

VIII - 1750-1763

By 1751 it is clear that French plans for the economic development and military and civilian occupation of the Illinois area are taking shape (IHC 29:293-319). Governor Vaudreuil, discussing his proposal for making Kaskaskia rather than Fort Chartres the chief military base, names and locates the five French villages alluded to by Father Vivier. Beginning with Kaskaskia, which is the southernmost, the villages stretch northward along the Mississippi, to Du Rocher; then to The Settlement associated with Fort Chartres; St. Philippe; and, lastly, Cahokia. According to Vaudreuil, Kaskaskia has as many, or almost as many, inhabitants as the other four combined. Its role as something of an entrepôt and convergence point of a number of activities is suggested by Vaudreuil in the following statement: "It is the place of resort of our convoys, of the voyageurs of Canada, of the couriers from the posts of Detroit, and of the greatest part of the Indian tribes especially those of the Wabash, which are the most numerous, and those which are most often seen there on account of the frequent war parties which go against the Chickasaw and others" (ibid. pp. 262-264).

201

The character of the forces operating are indicated more specifically by Vaudreuil in his order of command for the newly appointed commandant of the Illinois country, Major Macarty, on August 8, 1751. Pointing out that "the government of the Indians is the most extensive, the most difficult, and the most essential part of the command at the Illinois," he informs Macarty that ". . .the Indians of these regions are somewhat turbulent from the nearness of the English, but not warlike, especially those called the Illinois whom our small force up to now has rendered insolent" (ibid. p. 300). It seems that the English ". . .have already tried several times, to form some settlements in the neighborhood of the Illinois,. . .on the Ohio or the Tennessee River. . ."

(ibid. p. 303). The Illinois, like other tribes, have begun to trade with the English on the Miami River; and they also incurred the resentment of the French by killing their cattle and engaging in frequent quarrels with them (ibid. pp. 301, 310). But Vaudreuil reveals a point on which the Illinois were probably most sensitive when he states: "As the Illinois Indians have often complained that the French traders carry their best goods to the Missouri tribes, and as this discrimination is one of their chief grievances against us, M. deMacarty will take care to have them given satisfaction so far as he can without however hampering too much the trade of the French" (ibid. p. 313). Although Illinois feelings of resentment are understandable, he feels constrained to complain to them of ". . .the small fidelity which they manifest for the French,. . ." and to threaten ". . .to cut off the presents of those who do not endeavor henceforth to give proofs of their attachment and fidelity" (idem).

202

In the face of such problems Macarty is expected to induce the Illinois, as well as the Piankashaw, Wea, and others, to send out war parties against the Chickasaw (ibid. p. 309). But, as it happens, the exact state of affairs into which Macarty was to run head-on, was embedded in a report by la Jonquière in Canada where ". . .he had just learned that a meeting of the Illinois, Ouyas, Pianguichas, Miamis, Delawares, Chaouanons and the Five Iroquois Nations was to be had this year at La Demoiselle's [Miami River], and that the whole tends, in his opinion, to a general revolt" (WHC 18:112). This was remarkably close to the mark.

As was revealed in Father Vivier's letters, Vaudreuil also indicates that the Peoria are established on the Illinois River where a Canadian trader ". . .built a fort there in the last few years". He writes that "The Peoria, an Illinois tribe, has several times begged us to establish an officer among them with a little garrison to control the voyageurs from Canada" (IHC 29:317).

While the Peoria were established on Lake Peoria, it was undoubtedly they who were also continuing to make use of the Starved Rock area on the upper Illinois. In September,1751 the Governor of Canada reported that a party of Chippewa killed a Frenchman at Starved Rock where they ". . .discovered four cabins of the Illinois and determined to attack them at dawn" (WHC 18:82). According to la Jonquière the Chippewa ". . .went to attack the Illinois at the request of the Poutetouatamis probably from the river of Chikagou, for those of the river St. Joseph did not leave their village" (ibid. p. 81). This action was taken in retaliation for the killing of a Potawatomi by the Illinois, in 1750, discussed above.

Earlier that same month (September, 1751) Vaudreuil, writing to Macarty, who was en route to his Illinois command, expressed his concern over the refractory behavior of the Illinois and the sentiments of the Wabash tribes towards the French. As regards the former, he wrote: "It indeed seems that the Illinois have been the carriers of English messages and belts among all the Missouri tribes, and others on the upper Mississippi. . ." And he told Macarty to ". . .bid them declare what their sentiments are with respect to us, whether they are French or English" (IHC 29:334; see also ibid. p. 402). As for "The Wabash tribes", he expressed his uncertainty in this sentence: "I am assured that the Piankashaw, Kickapoo, Mascoutens and a village of Miami have not yet gone to the Great Miami River" where La Demoiselle's Miami band and others were established in trade with the English (ibid. p. 333). He also adds that "the same applies to the Vermilion Indians [Piankashaw],. . . (idem. and p. 415) to whom the English sent a message which was rejected by their chief, Le Maringouin, who emphatically declared his loyalty to the French (ibid. p. 365).

203

It was quite otherwise with the Indians on the Wabash, however, for on September 25, 1751 the Governor of New France wrote: "the English have won the confidence of the Wabash tribes", adding information received from the commandant at Fort Chartres that the English ". . .are attempting to penetrate in the territory of his post, [which] may happen sooner than we think" (ibid. p. 367; also pp. 375-6). The Governor also stated in connection with the information from the commandant at Fort Chartres that "the Peoria have reported to him that La Peau Blanche [a Wea?] had been last winter with them to induce them to go to the English. There are also some of these people who want to go in search of La Mouche Noire [chief of the Wea]. This is what they ordinairly say when they return in the spring from their winter quarters" (ibid p. 366). The commandant also reported to La Jonquière that "La Mouche Noire has two of his brothers who are chiefs of the domiciled Kaskaskia of Fort Chartres. He has seduced the older who has gone to Great Miami River to take back three English prisoners. On his return he counts on bringing the English in the neighborhood of [the commandant] but to what place is not known" (ibid. pp. 366-7). La Mouche Noire also told his people that he would bring the English to their village and would then ask the Illinois to choose between the French and the English (ibid. p. 366).

204

It was stated above that Vaudreuil had written Macarty that the Kickapoo and Mascouten were among tribes who had not yet left for the Miami River. In this connection La Jonquière also had something to report: "M. de Vaudreuil has written me that the Mascoutens intended to withdraw from the neighborhood of the Wea and that it would be very easy to establish that tribe near Vincennes where it can be useful, and as they are almost resolved to go there he begs me to induce them to take that course, with all the more reason since they were on the point of withdrawing among the Foxes, their allies, where we would be less assured of their fidelity" (ibid. pp. 376-7). La Jonquière opposed this move because ". . .it is of infinite consequence to leave the Kickapoo and Mascoutens in their village near the Wea, less for the harm which their absence would do to the trade of that post than because those two nations being closely attached to the French, it behooves us to keep them in that place, especially under present circumstances" (idem).

In contrast to these supposed sentiments of the Kickapoo and Mascouten the bands of other tribes from the Wabash area which had gone to the Miami River declared themselves unequivocally on the side of the English and their Indian allies, virtually rejecting the French out of hand (ibid. pp. 403-4). Consequently, La Jonquière, in the fall of 1751, tried to gather a force ". . .for the destruction of La Demoiselle and other rebel Miami who have withdrawn to Great Miami River," but this effort had to be delayed (ibid. p. 414). DeLignery, commandant at the Ouiatanon post, wrote Vaudreuil: "The Wea and Piankashaw, who are effectually of the same tribe with the Miami, appear for the most part ill-intentioned, and I doubt not that they will soon take the side of the English, in case we defer seizing the posts these last occupy on the Ohio River." And he went on to state that "the Piankashaw who are at the Vermilion River appear entirely in the English interest" (ibid. p. 415). DeLignery stopped at the Piankashaw village while on his way ". . . to Terre Haute to seek the Kickapoo," but the young men of the Piankashaw tried to stop him by stealing the goods and supplies in his pirogues. The chiefs had his possessions restored, claiming the deed was instigated by the Wea (ibid. p. 416).

From the foregoing statements it is apparent that the settlements of the Kickapoo and Mascouten in 1751 are concentrated chiefly on the upper Wabash; but part of the Kickapoo are also situated at Terre Haute. It was

205

the intention of DeLignery, in which he seems to have succeeded, to induce
the latter to join their kinsmen near the Wea post. At the same time St. Ange
was trying to convince them to move southward to his post at Vincennes (ibid.
pp. 485, 534; see also p. 731).

When Macarty and his troops arrived at Kaskaskia on December 8, 1751 a
party of Indians from the Wabash, mainly Piankashaw made a raid upon the
French settlements in the area (ibid. pp. 432-435; 478-9). Possibly
La Demoiselle hoped that if this affair took a favorable turn the Illinois
would be motivated to join in. In fact "Charetagoue, an Illinois of the
Kaskaskia, said that two deputies of La Demoiselle had come to their winter
camp at Prairie de l'Orme,. . ." to urge them to join the English and their
Indian allies in a planned attack upon the French. La Demoiselle threatened
to begin on the Illinois if they did not take action directly in moving
against the French (ibid. p. 436). The same Kaskaskia Indian said that
Le Loup, the Piankashaw chief who was captured in the attack ". . .had
appeared with his party at the Illinois winter camps;. . ." (ibid. p. 437).

Some Illinois had, however, become involved (ibid. pp. 458-9), and
Macarty sent for the Kaskaskia chief as a result of this affair. On "December
31 Thomas and Papechingouya came to hear my words with nineteen Illinois and
some Cahokia". They admitted receiving the message from the English at their
winter camps, but insisted they had "French hearts". They also confessed to
having gone in the spring of 1751, to trade with the English ". . .because it
was said that goods were cheap there" (ibid. pp. 448-9; 479-80). But Macarty
accused them of efforts to lead the Quapaw to the English, and also of killing
the cattle of the French. At the end of the conference, early in January
1752, he ". . .made them a present of powder and ball to finish their hunt,
sending them back to their posts until the month of March, wishing them to

assemble all their chiefs" (ibid. pp. 450-452). A few days later Patissier, another Illinois chief who apparently was involved in the Piankashaw attack, told Macarty that he rebuffed another Piankashaw proposal to resume hostilities against the French (ibid. pp. 452-3).

The chiefs of the Cahokia and Michigamea came to Macarty professing loyalty to the French. But a Cahokia warned him against the hostile attitude of the Kaskaskia, seven of whose leaders had been with La Demoiselle in the spring of 1751. Three of the most important of the latter had summoned, ". . .the night before they went to winter camps at Prairie à l'heurt, the chiefs and chiefmen of the Cahokia. . ." and tried to win them over to the English, having ". . .already won over the Great Osage of two villages, the Missouri, and Kansa" (ibid. pp. 446-448).

The lengthy report by Macarty to Vaudreuil (ibid. pp. 432-469), dated January 20, 1752, from which the foregoing information was extracted, contains a number of references to the winter camps of the Illinois, two of which are mentioned by name. Just where they were located is not apparent from the text, but it is likely that the distance inland from the Mississippi was not very great. For one thing, two of these winter camp areas, as already indicated, are identified by name and were places familiar to the French. Secondly, at different times individuals seemed to be travelling between Kaskaskia and these camps.

In another document Macarty refers to a third prairie as "the Prairie of the Tamaroa". This is mentioned in connection with a visit of some Illinois who were telling Macarty that the Piankashaw were on the offensive, adding that "They thought there were some war parties in our vicinity now, having heard several gunshots in the prairie of the Tamaroa" (ibid. pp. 523-524). This prairie may have been passed by the Illinois while en route to

207

Kaskaskia, and, with the lapse of time, the war parties could be in the vicinity "now". The statement does not necessarily mean that the prairie was in the vicinity of Kaskaskia.

Judging from another report by Macarty some of the Illinois, during this winter of 1751-1752, were encamped to the east of Kaskaskia, across the state, near the Wabash and/or Ohio. He writes that a Frenchman, Moreau, arrived at Kaskaskia with two Illinois, who were from a group who gave him succor after he and his party had been attacked by some Chickasaw. Moreau had been hunting on the Ohio, and on ". . .the fourth of that month [February 1752] having been held up by the ice for almost six weeks three leagues below the river in the Wabash, he was attacked in the morning". In the course of the encounter "Moreau took to the bluffs and happened on the place where the Illinois were" (ibid. pp. 515-516). The only problem here is the precise meaning of the phrase "three leagues below the river in the Wabash". This is cleared up in a letter from Kaskaskia, written on September 10, by Father Guyenne. "Before taking winter quarters, our Illinois brought to M. Macarty three Frenchmen whose pirogues had been lost in the ice of the Ohio, and then Moreau, who thought himself the sole survivor of his defeat on the same river" (ibid. p. 713). It is more likely, though, that the Illinois were in winter quarters at the time of the rescue.

It appears to be quite plain that most of the Illinois being either "domiciled" among the French settlements, or with their villages in proximity to the latter, were a key factor in any anti-French enterprise in the Illinois country. They could, with considerable justification, be said to be between Scylla and Charybdis. With the French on one side, the importunate Miami-speaking English "allies" on the other, the ambivalent Illinois found themselves in a distressing situation indeed. Macarty was even prompted to express the hope that ". . .we can retain the four domiciled Illinois villages", which are the Peoria, Cahokia, Michigamea, and Kaskaskia. He adds the opinion that the Peoria are loyal to the French, but states that the Kaskaskia are ". . .the most ill-behaved village of these regions" (ibid. p. 462; see also p. 480).

From both the English and Indian points of view, if the French were to be dislodged from the Illinois country, or placed in an untenable situation, the time seemed to be fast approaching. Macarty, as did others mentioned above (passim), wrote to France: "To establish this country we have need of tranquility and many inhabitants. . .how easy it is to settle a country which will sustain not only its inhabitants but all the lower part of the colony . . .we have, counting inhabitants and slaves, sixteen hundred souls who form six villages large and small. This is all the population of the country" (ibid. pp. 480-481).

209

At the beginning of February, 1752 Macarty added this warning: ". . .it is very important that the king's storehouse should be furnished under present circumstances with much merchandise for trade in order to draw the tribes to us and make them active against our enemies" (ibid. p. 482). And at the end of February St. Ange, writing from the Vincennes post, said: "The English traders steadily encroach on our lands, to give greater opportunity to our tribes to bring them their furs. M. deLigneris [at the Wea post] has just informed me that he had learned that they were on White River not far from his post" (ibid. p. 486).

Towards the middle of January, 1752, writes Macarty, ". . .twenty-one Peoria, all chiefs or children of chiefs according to Descaris [their trader], who accompanied them from their villages, came to give me marks of their attachment to our nation, apparently very sincere." They begged him ". . .to

send a French chief to our village" (ibid. pp. 453-4). Macarty told them
that in March he wished ". . .to see all you Illinois chiefs and our allies",
but they replied that ". . .they feared the Foxes and the Sioux this spring"
(ibid. p. 461). But if they told Macarty that it was because they had killed
seven Fox and Sioux he made no mention of it until September 2, 1752 (ibid.
pp. 654-5). In an effort to prevent such an attack Macarty promised to write
to Marin, the commandant at Green Bay. In spite of the fact that ultimately
the Illinois received retribution on June 1, 1752, an undated memoir of
Marin's son states that "In 1752. . .I made peace between the Fox, Sac,
Winnebago, Sioux of the Lakes, Sioux of the Prairies and Menominee with the
Illinois. This peace was absolutely essential, for, if these nations were
not conciliated, the French of the colony, settled at Cahokia, at Forts
Chartres and Kaskaskia would have been obliged to abandon their settlements"
(Margry 6:653-4; translation - JJ; Transl. also WHC 18:158).

210

The involvement of at least part of the Illinois with Piankashaw and
Miami efforts to subvert them is developed further in Macarty's reports in
March, 1752. At the same time the Illinois were trying to counter the accu-
sations of Macarty against those two groups. On January 31, an Illinois
chief named La Puce told Macarty that the Miami, who were a day and a half
distant from his "band" came "three times to enlist them in their party",
claiming they belonged to neither French nor English (IHC 29:510). Then on
the 27th of February La Puce returned again, this time with seven Illinois,
and ". . .said that at his return from his winter camp the Miami had left
them to go and seek the French and that they were all to return to the
Vermilion. Some Illinois from Kaskaskia who had been among the Miami for some
time had come to seek them at their winter camp, but the Piankashaw had
induced several to go back with them and had told them that the English were

at Ouiatanon." In addition these Illinois said that the Piankashaw had won
over the Kickapoo (ibid. pp. 519-520).

One of the Illinois with La Puce ". . .said that the Cahokia who were
with them in their winter camp had gone to ask a refuge among the Peoria
which Descaris [the French trader] had refused,. . ." (ibid. p. 519). Then
on March 2 a Cahokia came to inform Macarty that ". . .Descaris and a Peoria
chief. . .invited them to come there to make a village with them at Peoria"
(ibid. p. 527). Under questioning, the Cahokia said that ". . .the various
parties of Miami who had passed their winter villages. . .had separated from
the Illinois after the attack that had been made on the Miami here;. . ."
(idem). Macarty added the information that "The Illinois of Kaskaskia had
spoken to the Cahokia. . .before wintering to engage them to follow" (ibid.
p. 528). The Peoria, however, demonstrated their good faith by sending ". . .
a party to the Miami in the hope of striking them treacherously" (ibid. p. 535). 211

St. Ange, at the end of February 1752, reported to Governor Vaudreuil
that the influence of the Indians with La Demoiselle was steadily undermining
the French position on the Wabash. He writes: "those who have openly joined
them are the Piankashaw of the Vermilion, part of the Illinois, and those
near us" (ibid. p. 484). The Illinois referred to are probably the Kaskaskia
whose antipathy Macarty had already reported. In the same report he also
states the following: "The Piankashaw that we had near us, who have become
our enemies, have joined those of the Vermilion; these last are said to be in
the plains between the Wabash and the Illinois, but I do not think their plans
are to remain there, unless they feel sure of being supported by other tribes."
And, finally, he ventures the opinion that "The Kickapoo and the Mascoutens
still seem a little attached to us" (ibid. pp. 486, 535).

According to this report of St. Ange, then, the Piankashaw would be south of the Vermilion River between the Wabash on the east and, on the west, probably the dividing ridge between the waters of the Wabash and those of the Illinois Rivers.

In his communication of March 18, 1752 Macarty makes two puzzling statements toward the end, the significance and interpretation of which, might bear directly on the questions at issue. One paragraph follows in its entirety: "March 15 three Illinois reported to me that La Puce, on returning from his winter camp, had found La Biche, the Piankashaw chief, with a French flag, coming from the Miamis [Fort Wayne] with the letters of the commandant for this place and had gone with him to Ouiatanon, whence he should be here in some days" (ibid. pp. 535-536). The question is: Where did this meeting occur? La Biche was undoubtedly coming down the Wabash from the Miamis post. Did he meet La Puce before he reached Ouiatanon? On the face of it, it does not seem reasonable that the encounter took place so far north in Indiana unless these were renegade Illinois mentioned by Macarty (p. 520). Or did the meeting take place on or near the Wabash some distance below Ouiatanon to which, for some reason they returned?

In his second statement which also presents difficulty of interpretation Macarty writes: "I judge that the Illinois who are on the lower river are delaying that all the four villages may come together, along with the Peoria and the Kaskaskia (ibid. p. 536). Macarty probably has in mind the meeting with the Illinois groups that he arranged for March. But what river does he refer to? There are several possibilities, but it is difficult to draw a correct inference.

Another communication of Macarty, in late March, is again exasperatingly lacking in specificity with regard to the location of La Puce's "band" of Illinois. The latter brought Macarty a letter from St. Ange of Vincennes

212

in which that commandant stated that ". . .LaPuce, while he was on his way [to Kaskaskia] to ask favor for his son who is a prisoner here, met six Piankashaw going with a flag to Vincennes. These six Piankashaw assured him that LaMouche Noire, L'Enfant, and Le Maringouin,. . .had retired with their band to the Little Wabash,. . .These six men had remained four days with the Illinois,. . ." (ibid. p. 537).

On March 22 the Peoria, Cahokia, Michigamea, and Kaskaskia arrived for the conference with Macarty (ibid. pp. 538-548). The next day a Mascouten came to assure the commandant of the loyalty of his tribesmen and to say that they rejected a Fox request to join in an attack upon the French. This Mascouten also said ". . .that the Peoria had been won over by the Miami as well as the other villages, and they came here the better to deceive me" (ibid. pp. 538-539).

Macarty tried to convince the Illinois of their folly ". . .when you ally yourself with the Miami," adding these remarks: "You are small, and your tribe few in number. . .The Foxes, Sauk, Potawatomi, Sioux, and many others [?] ask to eat you up... . The Michigamea, the Cahokia, the Peoria stay quiet; you alone, you Kaskaskia, you lose your wits,. . .that is what comes of your trade with the English" (ibid. pp. 541-2; see also p. 507 and Margry, 6:653-4). He later elaborated his remarks on the Kaskaskia: ". . .I am convinced that our greatest enemies are the mutineers of the Kaskaskia village who have been the cause of all our troubles in this region by the journeys which they have made to La Demoiselle's village, whence they have merchandise for no price at all; and where they have allied themselves with the Miamis" (IHC 29:555).

In this connection some remarks of the Vicar-General of Canada and the Mississippi, concerning the "Tamaroa Mission" at Cahokia may be cited. He

213

writes that "...that mission has almost fallen, consisting of little more than a small French settlement,. . .all the Indian tribes being departed to go to the English. . .on all sides it is surrounded by Indian tribes, and every one that we lose is gained by the English. . ." (ibid. pp. 567-568). From these comments and Macarty's reports at this time it is apparent that whatever influence the French may have upon the Illinois is, at best, tenuous, while the Wabash tribes have almost all identified their interests with the English. Vaudreuil "directed" Macarty that the Illinois and Piankashaw could make amends only ". . .by going to commit acts of hostility on those of our enemies who have incited them to attack us". At the same time he told St. Ange he recognized that ". . .the greater part of the tribes of your river appear to me but little in our interest,. . ." (ibid. p. 612).

214

Vaudreuil, in a letter to the French Minister on April 8, 1752, summarizes the situation of plot and disaffection among the Illinois and Wabash tribes which greeted Macarty's arrival at Kaskaskia at the end of 1751 (ibid. pp. 572-576), and also discusses la Jonquière's new plan for contending with La Demoiselle's "republican" forces which were composed of elements from various tribes gathered on the Miami River. He expresses doubts about the proposed harrassment of this enclave ". . .by means of all the tribes which are on our side, paying them for the scalps and the prisoners which they take". He points out that ". . .there are few of those tribes who have not relatives by blood or marriage among these refugees [on the Miami]. As a result they will with difficulty be induced to strike, especially today when they are more than ever persuaded that we are in no situation to undertake anything against them" (ibid. p. 578). Furthermore, la Jonquière, ". . .by taking this course. . .alienates from us in the Illinois country the tribes of the Wabash allied by blood and marriage with these refugees. These tribes will certainly seek to revenge them and will make their resentment fall upon us; thus they will cut our communication between here and the Illinois" (ibid. p. 579). Vaudreuil also includes Macarty's observation ". . .with regard to the hostilities which are to be undertaken against the rebels of Great Miami River that their resentment will infallibly be visited on the Illinois country. . ." (ibid. p. 582).

Similar views came from Canada, where the commandant of the St. Joseph post reported to the Governor on January 15, 1752 ". . .that all the Nations appear to take sides against us, that he would not be responsible for the good dispositions these Indians seem to entertain, inasmuch as the Miamis are their near relatives" (WHC 18:108-9). And the Governor himself, under date of April 21, wrote that ". . .not only have our rebels of the Beautiful river [Ohio] not experienced any ill treatment from the Nations that the late Mr. de la Jonquière had excited against them, but. . .at heart they preserve the same feelings of attachment for those rebels to whom they are connected by blood" (ibid. p. 109).

215

While the foregoing statements indicate briefly the network of inter-relationships, social, biological, political, among various tribes extending from Ohio through Illinois, even some of the French may be included by virtue of intermarriage. Because of these relationships Macarty refused to believe the professions of loyalty on the part of "our domiciled Indians" in the Illinois country. He would "always be suspicious of them until they have made some attacks on our enemies with whom they are too closely allied by blood" (IHC 29:641-2).

In Vaudreuil's opinion the plan for harassment would only serve to draw to the English ". . .one tribe after another as a result of the advan-tages which they afford them, and which the Indians cannot expect of us" (ibid. p. 579). And referring to the fact that in the previous year's shipments from France trade guns and bullets were omitted, he makes the point that these ". . .are the most essential articles for presents to the Indians who have been supplied with bad arms which I have bought from the traders. . ." (ibid. p. 582). It was only too well known that the English were offering better quality and more presents. What hindered the French, as Macarty later summarized it, was that ". . .the tribes on that ["rebel"] side are too much allied by blood even to our domiciles for it to be expected that they should attack each other; moreover there is the profusion and good quality of the merchandise which the English give them, so to speak" (ibid. p. 687).

On June 1, 1752 Macarty conveyed the essence of France's problem with the Indians in one succinct sentence: "the difference in the price of merchandise between the English and us has caused these troubles" (ibid. p. 641). The solution he proposed can also be stated in a single sentence: "The best remedy that could be applied would be to make a settlement at the Falls of the Ohio River [Cincinnati] and there supply them with merchandise at the same price as the English" (idem).

216

When the Peoria came to Kaskaskia the preceding January to confer with Macarty, who asked them to return in March for a conference which all the Illinois were to attend, they told him that they feared an attack in the spring by the Fox and Sioux (ibid. p. 461). On the night of June 1, 1752 an attack was made ". . .on the Michigamea and Cahokia who had sowed their fields together in the fear of being attacked by the Foxes in reprisal for the seven they had killed last year. The attacking party, composed of Foxes, Sioux, Sauk, Potawatomi, Winnebago, and Menominee, killed or captured seventy people, men, women, and children, burned ten or twelve cabins, and scattered about the limbs of the dead" (ibid. p. 654). The attackers, consisting of about four or five hundred men, also "told the voyageurs to be on their guard as there were Sioux war parties out this summer to revenge the great chiefs whom they lost in the former affair" (ibid. p. 655). Presumably these latter were among the seven, including Fox, that had been killed by the Illinois in 1751. And the participation of the Potawatomi is undoubtedly attributable to the fact that they had some old scores to settle dating back to 1750 (ibid. pp. 240, 359-360, 507). It may be recalled that in an undated memoir of 1752 the son of Marin, commandant at Green Bay, claimed to have made peace between the Illinois and the Fox, Sac, Winnebago, Sioux, and Menominee (see above Margry 6:653-4).

As a result of this disastrous episode part of the Cahokia went to join the Peoria (IHC 29:687), most of whom ". . .bewailed their relatives whom they had lost in the attack on the Michigamea" (ibid. p. 663). Macarty locates ". . .the village of the Michigamea. . .near The Settlement,. . ." which was in proximity to Fort Chartres (ibid. pp. 658, 262). One week later, because of a false report that the Fox were returning for another attack, "All the men, women, and children of the three Illinois villages reached here early in the morning, having walked all night in a continual rain,. . ." (ibid. p. 657). This reference is made to three villages of Illinois because the fourth was near French Kaskaskia, to which these terrorized Illinois had come.

217

According to Father Guyenne, who wrote to Vaudreuil from Kaskaskia on September 10, "The Cahokia and Michigamea, after their reverse of June 1, went off to the settlement at Fort de Chartres" (ibid. p. 720). While Macarty related that afterwards part of the Cahokia left for the Peoria, Guyenne states that "several cabins. . .have withdrawn from the two villages [Cahokia and Michigamea] to the Peoria and to the Piakashaw" (ibid. p. 718).

Guyenne also writes that, in the flight of the Illinois to Kaskaskia as a consequence of the false alarm over an impending second Fox attack, there were "four to five hundred people" (ibid. p. 721).

Apparently Macarty was obdurate in his harsh treatment of the Illinois because of doubts concerning their loyalty; and it is this which accounts for the departure of Cahokia and Michigamea. They sought help elsewhere. As stated by the priest: "After the Foxes' attack the Michigamea, whose cabins had been burned, were without food, furniture, clothing or arms, but they were no way helped although intercession was made for them on all sides" (ibid. p. 724). Furthermore, apart from the corn given them by Guyenne the Illinois who fled to Kaskaskia were refused succor. "These wretched people seeing them selves despised resolved to cross the little river [Kaskaskia] and go off into the prairies. . .but despite all pleading, food was refused them" (ibid. p. 722). The missionary and some of the inhabitants, however, saw that they were lodged and fed.

During the summer hunt seven cabins of Illinois and their chief, Le Petit Plat Côtee left "to go to the rebels"; but they later came back with protestations of loyalty to the French. Whereupon St. Ange, commandant at Vincennes "made them take up their winter quarters on the lower Wabash" (ibid. P. 761).

Early in September Macarty reported that in addition to those Cahokia who joined the Peoria there were other families of Illinois who wished to do likewise; while still others wanted to go to the Osage (ibid. p. 687). The chiefs of the Great Osage had come to Kaskaskia on August 23, conferred with Macarty, and, ". . .were that same day to sing the calument with the Kaskaskia and the Michigamea, to whom they gave much in horses and peltry" (ibid. p. 680). This was an annual feature of the relations between the Illinois and the Osage dating back at least to the time of Deliette in the latter part of the seventeenth century. According to Macarty the Illinois, at this time, "have wished to induce the Osage to come closer to us in order to sustain them against their enemies." He also thought "that the Illinois are trying to renew their alliances with the tribes, being always in fear of some surprise from us" (ibid. p. 680). But after stating that "The hostile bands have gone in the direction of the Piankashaw" he seemed to think that "few are left who are not attached to the French by necessity and habit" (ibid. p. 687). Macarty, therefore, seemed to consider the western region of Illinois a safer area for the French than the east in the vicinity of the Wabash and Indiana. Consequently, in sending dispatches to Detroit, "For greater security I had the couriers go by the Peoria and by St. Joseph, whence they will go to Detroit;. . ." (ibid. pp. 685–686).

Macarty's communication of September 2, 1752 is quite specific in its references to hunting by the Peoria in the area of Starved Rock on the upper Illinois. He wrote that after the June 1 attack the Sac returned some prisoners to the Peoria. The latter, therefore, "renewed their alliance [and] gave some horses to the Sac" who, with the "other Sauk who have thirteen prisoners. . .were to join them in their summer hunt toward Starved Rock. . ." (ibid. pp. 664–5). On July 26 a Michigamea prisoner released by the Sac came to Kaskaskia and reported "that the Sauk were to come near Starved Rock as soon as they had, by means of presents, got the rest of the slaves from the hands of the Foxes" (ibid. p. 672). On August 15 Macarty received a letter from Adamville, his representative at Peoria, containing the information "that the Peoria stayed on their hunt only a very short time, the Sauk having warned them that the Chippewa were coming upon them five hundred in number; this leaves them dying of hunger; moreover as a result of the great drought

219

they have little hope for the corn" (ibid. pp. 676-7). Finally, it was learned, indirectly from a Peoria that "the Sauk had not kept their word given to the Peoria to meet them at the hunting grounds and give back their prisoners;. . ." (ibid. p. 678).

It seems to be quite clear from the preceding quotations that in the summer of 1752 the Peoria were hunting in a region which was documented as Illinois before the last quarter of the seventeenth century.

The warning received by the Peoria against a Chippewa attack is related to the fact that the Peoria had attacked the Chippewa in 1751. The Chippewa had already, on June 6, "killed two Peoria a half-league from their village in reprisal. . ." (ibid. p. 664). Macarty also learned that "a number of Potawatomi and Mascoutens are going to the Peoria to sing the calument in order to try and learn their sentiments as to the attack made on the Michigamea by the Foxes and Sauk; they fear the Peoria will in reprisal make attacks on them" (ibid. p. 678). The Mascouten are probably only lending their good offices here for, of the two, only the Potawatomi were among the attackers.

In his September 2 report to Vaudreuil Macarty also refers to other matters pertaining to various tribes. In spite of Piankashaw efforts, the Kickapoo and Mascouten remain loyal to the French (ibid. pp. 662, 691). On July 15 the Sac chief, called Le Chat Blanc, "being on a hunt above the [Vincennes] post, met four young men of the rebel Piankashaw,. . ." (ibid. p. 674). They told the Sac chief that their people "were two short days' journeys from the post of M. de Ligneris [Ouiatanon]. . .A great part of the Wea were with them on White River" (ibid. pp. 676, 717, 731). And the loyalty of those Piankashaw at St. Ange's post (Vincennes) was highly dubious (ibid. pp. 669, 676).

Father Guyenne wrote Vaudreuil one week later that the Illinois tried

220

to win over the Piankashaw, unsuccessfully. The latter, on the other hand "spared neither lies nor threats to gain the Illinois, and in last summer's hunt a man from Vincennes used the brandy he had of M. the commandant to seduce seven or eight families whom he carried off to White River, where the Piankashaw and the Wea who followed them are still encamped" (ibid. pp 716-17). Apparently there was considerable intermarriage between the Piankashaw and Illinois (the Kaskaskia, at least). It was, therefore, considered unlikely that the Illinois "could be constrained to make war on the Piankashaw, many of whose women and children they have in this village [Kaskaskia], and among whom many of their men have married" (ibid. p. 714). The missionary also refers to the eldest brother of the Kaskaskia chief, Rouensa, who was "brought up among the Miami, [and] is with the Piankashaw" (ibid. p. 719).

There are three additional items in Father Guyenne's letter to which attention may be drawn. He refers to "the greater part" of an Illinois village that "had wintered on the Mississippi", a practice which, as previously indicated, goes back to the end of the 17th and early 18th century (ibid. p. 713). In a reference to the Kickapoo he states that the commandant at the Ouiatanon post, "M. deLigneris. . .has but this one village in his region that has not declared against us,. . ." (ibid. p. 715). And finally, with regard to the Illinois, the following statement is made: "On their return from the winter hunt our people according to custom carried dried meat and grease to the commandant and asked for guns." Macarty, who already had been depriving them of their needs in this respect, put them off until the arrival of the next convoy. As a result, the priest wrote that "These petty annoyances make me uneasy and fearful lest these people take some evil course" (ibid. p. 724).

Captain D'Orgon, writing to Governor Vaudreuil from Natchez on October

221

7, 1752, conveys news he has received from the Illinois region. He reports that the Piankashaw and Miami have attacked the Kickapoo, and that half the Wea "who had taken sides with the Piankashaw had abandoned them,. . ." (ibid. p. 736). As for the Illinois, they "continue to be used by the English to seduce the Great Osage, the Little Osage, and the Missouri to come to them" (ibid. p. 738). According to the information received by D'Orgon concerning the Illinois "that tribe is quiet and. . .the distrust shown them for some-time has already caused several to desert. Eight families have gone to the English; several others are ready to follow." The captain seems to have been told that the Illinois "are men who think, and very sensitive to distrust" (ibid. pp. 738-739).

On October 10, 1752 the Illinois left "to go to their winter camp at Pierre à la Fleche in the Illinois River" (ibid. pp. 747-8). On October 25 Macarty received a message from Green Bay, together with five Illinois prisoners returned by the Sac and Fox, stating that if they wished their remaining prisoners the Illinois should remain at peace. Macarty passed the word on to the Illinois, who accepted this condition. "As they had not yet gone to their winter villages they sent word to me that they were going on to look for their brothers the Peoria" (ibid. pp. 752-3). Later on in this communication Macarty states that "There is every appearance that we shall arrange peace between the Illinois, Foxes and Sauk since they remain quiet" (ibid. p. 769).

In the midst of the unrest, anxiety, suspicion and distrust between the French and Indians in the Illinois country, agricultural production for European needs was proceeding, limited only by the available labor supply and the number of European farmers. Macarty, to the extent feasible, was sending supplies of food to Ouiatanon, Vincennes and Detroit (ibid. pp. 748-750, 814).

222

While there were undoubtedly salutary features in this peaceful type of Europeanization of the area, the influence of the voyageurs and coureurs de bois, who made their base at Cahokia, about 40 miles from Kaskaskia, was anything but salutary. For it was through them that an uncontrolled trade in brandy with the Indians took place (ibid. pp. 770-771). It was in this area of the Mississippi that the European impact on the Illinois was most direct. At the same time Macarty, with presents of brandy and trade goods, continued his efforts to incite the Illinois to attack the Chickasaw (ibid. pp. 762-3, 770). The Kickapoo, Mascouten, and others also were sent against the Chickasaw (ibid. pp. 815, 816).

At the end of October 1753 Duquesne, the new Governor of Canada, wrote to France that, after an attack by the Chickasaw, who killed several Frenchmen about 30 miles from Kaskaskia, "The Kickapoo and Mascoutens of the post of Ouiatanon of their own accord have been to avenge these deaths. . ." (ibid. pp. 844-5). There were, however, more serious developments taking place in the Illinois area. These were a reflection of the disintegration of the Europeans and their increasingly deleterious influence upon the Indians. It appears that there was a great increase in drunkeness among the Europeans as well as the Indians, so much so that Duquesne said the Europeans "completely neglect their farms, and there is reason to fear that that place which formerly was a great resource for foodstuffs may not henceforth be able to supply itself,. . ." (ibid. pp. 846-7). Duquesne expressed the essence of the situation in a phrase: "the frightful disorder which reigns in the Illinois." (ibid. p. 847).

One year later in October 1754, another report submitted by Duquesne revealed that "The Poutwatamis, Kickapoux, Maskoutins and Scioux of the prairies, have assembled together to go and destroy the Peorias, who, for a long time, regard with insolence the other Indians;. . ." (NYCD 10:263; WHC 18:141). This characterization of the Illinois, together with other disparaging comments, by one without personal knowledge cannot be taken very seiously. Just why these tribes cooperated against the Illinois is not clear. While the Potawatomi and the Sioux might consider they had grievances stemming from the recent past, the same is not apparent in the case of the Kickapoo and Mascouten.

In the annual summary of the Journal of Occurrences in Canada an entry for the year 1756 states: "A letter, written from the country of the Wiatanons, states that the Illinois have attacked the Kickapaux and Miamis of St. Joseph, on the River of the Iroquois; they have killed two women and taken five children prisoners" (NYCD 10:401). Considering the course of this river up to its confluence with the Kankakee in Illinois, this incident occurred either in northwestern Indiana or in Illinois. The Kickapoo having a settlement in the vicinity of Lafayette, Indiana, the encounter could, conceivably, have occurred while they were on a hunt, since women and children were present.

In August, 1756 Vaudreuil, who replaced Duquesne as governor of Canada, wrote that peace was "concluded between the Illinois, the Nations of the Bay, the Saulteux and Pouteouatamis". This peace was arranged by the French who also effected a reconciliation of the Illinois with the Shawnee (ibid. p. 437).

In 1757 Captain Bougainville prepared a lengthy memoir on the posts of the French containing data on the Indian trade and other relevant information (WHC 18:167-195). The Potawatomi, who "are of all the savages the most attached to our interests" trade at Detroit and at the St. Joseph River post in Michigan, where "a few Myamis" also come to trade. In connection with the St. Joseph trade the Potawatomi are said to have "about four hundred men" (ibid. pp. 174, 185). Most of the Miami, however, deal with the "Post of the

224

Miamis", the later Fort Wayne location (ibid. p. 175). To the post of
Ouiatanon, on the right bank of the Wabash, the Kickapoo, Mascouten, Wea, and
Piankashaw bring their trade. These groups "can furnish three hundred and
sixty warriors" (ibid. pp. 175-6). But the Kickapoo and Mascouten are also
included among the tribes who trade at Green Bay, where the Menominee, Sac,
Fox, Winnebago and Sioux also come for the same purpose (ibid. p. 184). At
Vincennes only the trade of the Piankashaw is mentioned (ibid. p. 176).

At this point it seems appropriate to introduce for comparison an
excerpted document in Krauskopf's compilation (Krauskopf, 1955, pp. 220-221).
According to the editor, this is from "an incomplete, undated memoir, written
after the founding of Fort Duquesne but before 1758" (ibid. p. 220, fn. 105).
The resemblances in wording and data between this excerpt and Bougainville's
memoir concerning the posts of Ouiatanon, Vincennes, and Miami are sufficiently close to warrant the inference that one or the other was the original
source for the information in both; or they derive from one author.

225

Although there are slight variations (or revisions) in the data, the
following examples will make the point.

1) Ouiatanon

   a) Bougainville:

      "The savages who come to trade there are the Ouyatanons, the
      Kickapous, the Maskoutins, the Peanguichias, they can furnish
      three hundred and sixty warriors. "There comes from this post
      and those dependent upon it, in ordinary years, four hundred to
      four hundred and fifty packages" (WHC 18:176).

   b) Krauskopf's excerpt:

      ". . .the savages which trade there are the Ouiatanon, the
      Kickapoo, the Mascouten, and the tribes of the Vermilion. They

can furnish three hundred warriors. From this post and its
dependencies are shipped from three hundred to four hundred
packages" (Krauskopf, 1955, pp. 220-221).

2) Vincennes

a) Bougainville:

"Vincennes. - The post of Vincennes is a pretty village dependent upon New-Orleans which sends there the commandant. It has
three horse mills, and about seventy-five inhabitants who till
the soil and harvest grain.

"The Penguichias trade there. They must produce about eighty
packages" (WHC 18:176).

b) Krauskopf's excerpt:

"Post Vincennes, a pretty village also situated on the Wabash,
a dependency of New Orleans, whose governor sends a commandant
there. It may have eighty habitants who till the soil and
harvest wheat. The Piankashaw trade there; perhaps eighty
packages are made there" (Krauskopf, op. cit., p. 221)

226

3) Miami

a) Bougainville:

". . .; the savages who most commonly come to trade there are
the Miamis and the Tepicomeaux [Tepicon, Tippecanoe]. They
can furnish a hundred and fifty warriors. In an ordinary year
there issues from this post two hundred and fifty to three hundred packages;. . . (WHC 18:175).

b) Krauskopf's excerpt:

"The savages who come to trade are the Miami and the Teppi-
soineaux. The former can furnish 150 warriors. In an ordinary

year from 250 to 300 packages leave this post"

Bougainville's discussion under the heading of "Post of the Illinois"
includes two posts - one on the Mississippi, where "the principal entrepot is
Fort Chartres", and the other at Peoria on the Illinois River (WHC 18:176–
177). In passing, he also refers to "the missionaries of the Tamarous," at
Cahokia where the priests of the Seminary of Foreign Missions were posted.

With regard to the Illinois in the Mississippi River area Bougainville
writes as follows:

> "These are the divisions of the Illinois: the Cahos [Cahokia] on the
> borders of the Mississippi, at the left of the Metchi [Michigamea], at
> six leagues the Kas [Kaskaskia], a little village inhabited by the
> French. The Cahos and the Metchi are no more than a village of about
> four hundred warriors. There are about four hundred warriors at the
> Kas [the Kaskaskia]. These three nations are comprised under the name
> of Illinois, and furnish in ordinary years a hundred packages in
> beaver, deer, cats, lynx, foxes, otters, stags and bucks" (ibid. p.
> 177).

227

According to this source the Cahokia (including Tamaroa), Michigamea,
and Kaskaskia in the environs of the Mississippi can muster a total of eight
hundred warriors.

In referring to the second post Bouganville writes that "the commandant
resides in a fort named Pimiteoui; the nations who trade there are the Peorias;
seven hundred men furnish two hundred and fifty packages, of the same quality
of peltries, with less beaver and more cats than the preceding post" (idem).

Two years later, a British officer, Col. Henry Bouquet, writing in
1759 at Pittsburgh, stated that "The Illionois. . .live on the Mississippi
above the Mouth of the Ohio;. . .they consist of about 400 fighting men"

(Bouquet, 1943, pp. 85, 88). This is about half the number of Bougainville's total estimate. There is no indication that either of these men had first hand information. Bouquet, however, makes the following statement at the head of a list of tribes and the number of warriors in each: "Number of the fighting men belonging to the Indian Nations living to the Westward of Ohio, known to the English as computed by themselves" (ibid. p. 88). It is not immediately apparent whether the computations come from the English or the tribes. The English certainly know about these tribes, and many came to Pittsburgh or elsewhere to counsel with them. Miami and Potawatomi, for example, are listed among those present on November 5, 1759; while at a conference which took place the preceding July the Wyandots purportedly repre-sented, among others, the Potawatomi, Miami, Kickapoo, and Sac (ibid. p. 84).

Of the Kickapoo, Bouquet says that they are "a Nation which live about 80 miles on the other side of Fort D'Troit, have three Towns, about Six hundred fighting men" (ibid. pp. 87, 88). He also states that the Wea, on the Wabash, have two "towns and 200 warriors; the Piankashaw," on the heads of the Wabash possess 300 warriors and two villages; while the Miami, with 300 warriors, live "on the Miame River" (ibid. pp. 86, 88). These same figures were used by George Croghan in a list he submitted to General Stanwix in 1759 (Jefferson, 1955, pp. 102, 105-6). These numbers were probably obtained by Bouquet from Croghan in the first instance.

With the English penetrating the Illinois area in the closing years of the French and Indian War, Vaudreuil, in a letter of June 24, 1760, wrote that the English "have invited the Illinois Nations to go to trade at The Rock [Starved Rock]" (WHC 18:217 and fn. 75; NYCD 10:1092). Macarty's garrison was still at Fort Chartres, and this accounted for the circumvention of the Mississippi area at this time by the English traders. Vaudreuil went on to

228

state that "M. de Macarty having no traders, fears that those Nations, not-withstanding their good disposition, will repair to the English and introduce messages into all their villages" (WHC 18:217).

Whether it was in response to the promise of English trade, as suggested by Vaudreuil, is not apparent, but in the winter of 1760-1761 there was what must have been a fairly sizable population of Illinois, probably Peoria, wintering in the environs of Starved Rock on the upper Illinois River. They were found there by Captain Passerat de la Chapelle and his contingent of royal troops and militia in the course of their retreat from Detroit to New Orleans to avoid capture by the English (Kellogg, 1935, pp. 64-78). The Indians lent assistance for the building of a fort and wooden huts on the right bank of the Illinois river below the Fox River affluent of the Illinois River, almost opposite Starved Rock (ibid. p. 67). A chief presented la Chapelle "with a roll of skin" containing a statement by La Salle, declaring in the name of the king of France a "perpetual alliance with the Nation of the Illinois", signed by La Salle. La Chapelle then stated that "This chief declared that his ancestors had always respected this alliance and that his nation would continue it, if I consented to confirm it by the offering of several presents to his chiefs" (ibid. p. 68). The presence of a sizable population of Illinois may be inferred from that fact that when la Chapelle, before his departure, asked for guides, "They sent me fifty, twelve sledges, and ten dogs to draw them" (ibid. p. 77). They helped him obtain food, sold him skins and furs, in addition to which he purchased dressed bison skins from a coureur de bois, Sieur Billiet, "who had bought of the Indians considerable amounts of dressed buffalo skins" (ibid. pp. 67, 68, 72).

La Chapelle ran into some difficulty with Beaujeau, another French officer who was in charge of a party on Rock River. After a journey to

229

Beaujeau la Chapelle was compelled to proceed to Fort Chartres. On his way
back to Starved Rock, he met a party of Beaujeau's men on the right bank of
"the Illinois River north of Peoria". They told him they were "sent by M.
de Beaujeu to Peoria" (ibid. p. 72). It is thus apparent also that the post
and village of Peoria were functioning at this time. The Illinois are the
only ones referred to in the region of the Illinois River down to the
Mississippi.

In the spring of 1762 Thomas Hutchins left Fort Pitt for a series of
meetings with Indian tribes formerly under French dominion. On August 7th
he met with the Potawatomi on the St. Joseph River; and on the 20th he
delivered his instructions at the post of Ouiatanon on the Wabash to the Wea,
Kickapoo, Mascouten, and Piankashaw (Bouquet, 1943, p. 171; JP 10:526). On
September 28, four days after Hutchins returned to Fort Pitt from this tour,
George Croghan prepared an intelligence report in which he made reference to
the Miami, Wea, Kickapoo, Piankashaw "and other Tribes Settled on the Wabash"
(JP 10:534). On October 5, 1762 Croghan sent to General Amherst a copy of
Hutchins' Journal of his trip among the Indians, and included with it was a
list of Indian groups prepared by Hutchins (ibid. 10:544-546). This was
entitled "A List of the Number of fighting Men of the Different Indian Nations
thr'o which I passed residing at and near the Several Posts as nigh as I could
Asscertain", which seems to be an eminently reasonable and cautious statement
(Italics - JJ). According to this document there were at "Fort St. Josephs"
200 Potawatomi and 150 Ottawa warriors. In a total of 570 men that Hutchins
places within the orbit of the post of Ouiatanon, he lists 200 Wea, 180
Kickapoo, 90 Mascouten, and 100 Piankashaw (see also Krauskopf, 1955, p. 222).

In an enumeration of Indians under the jurisdiction of Sir William
Johnson, superintendent of the Northern Department, dated November 18, 1763,

the same figures are given for the last four tribes mentioned in the preceding paragraph. As for their location, it is stated: "These Nations reside in the neighbourhood of the Fort at Wawiaghta, and about the Wabache River -" (NYCD 7:583). The 200 Potawatomi men "in the neighbourhood of St. Joseph" are situated "A little below the Fort.-" There were also 150 Potawatomi warriors "in the neighborhood of Detroit". Originally they "Resided about a mile below the Fort, but abandoned their village on the commencement of hostilities." As for the 150 Ottawa men, also mentioned by Hutchins, "in the neighbourhood of Fort St. Joseph," they "Resided at a small distance, after the reduction of the Fort probably joined the rest." Here Johnson means the rest of the Ottawa, located at both Detroit and at Michilimackinac (idem).

Johnson also includes the "Illinois number uncertain." He does not give the number of men for this group but says that they "Reside about the Illinois River and hence to the Mississippi-". In his remarks on them he adds these sentences: "We have hitherto had nothing to do with these people, who are numerous, and variously computed. The Six Nations claim their Country, but their Right of Conquest thereto does not appear so clear as to the rest, as represented in the letter herewith." This purported "claim" of the Iroquois seems to date back to the seventeenth century, at which time also it was more a profession of faith than a reality despite their incursions into the Illinois area.

In correspondence concerning preparations for transfer of power to the English in 1763 the French commandant at Fort Chartres wrote in December that another officer, Debeaujeu, "decided to winter sixty leagues away, on the Illinois river [probably at Peoria], with a party of the Poutéouatamis. . ." (WHC 18:259). In this same communication the commandant, Neyon de Villiers, stated: "I have recalled from the Peorias the Sieur Toulon, as well as his

231

garrison" (ibid. p. 260). The use of the term "Peorias" may be either a geographical or tribal designation. As for the reference to the "party" of Potawatomi this is the first indication of the presence of that group in the Illinois River area.

A document to which is attributed a date of 1763, and which is entitled "Minutes of Mr. Hamburgh's Journel," contains additional data on the Potawatomi for this period (Mereness, pp. 359-364). The original journal was apparently a record of travel "from Detroit to Chicago and the Mississippi River by way of Lakes Huron and Michigan and the Illinois River,. . ." (ibid. p. 359). This source states that the fort of St. Joseph is twenty leagues (50 miles) up the river of that name on the east bank; and on the opposite shore "the Chief of the Pottowany tribe Resides." There are three small Potawatomi villages located along the land route between Detroit and Fort St. Joseph. It is six miles farther up from the fort to the Kankakee portage. "About 120 Miles Down this [Kankakee] River Lies an Indian town Consisting of about 20 Families of the Mascotain Tribe and about 60 Miles further falls In the Chykacoo [Desplaines] River and is Called afterwards Ilinois River. The Chief Hunting ground of the Battowaymes is along this River for about 200 Miles Down to a Place Called Le Rocher-" (ibid. pp. 362-363).

The river along which the Potawatomi are said to hunt for two hundred miles down to Starved Rock includes the entire length of the Kankakee plus that section of the Illinois river from the confluence of the Kankakee to Starved Rock. The Mascouten village was probably situated on some part of the Kankakee west of the Illinois-Indiana border. The country along the Kankakee and the entire length of the Illinois River into the prairie is described as filled with game, especially bison and deer.

This document continues with the information that Cahokia, sixty miles

below the mouth of the Illinois River has "A small fort and about 70 or 80
Families." Forty-five miles farther on down the Mississippi is Fort Chartres
with "about 100 french families Living near it". About one-half mile from
here "There is Two Indian [villages]. . .Close upon the Missippi, Called
Beory [Peoria] and The other Metschy Containing Both of them About 300
Warriors" (ibid. pp. 363-4).

mitchigamia

This is the first reference to the Peoria being resident on the
Mississippi; and while the Cahokia are not mentioned they are probably dwelling at the Michigamea village. The Kaskaskia are said to live near a settlement called Aveas (Kaskaskia) on the Kaskaskia River, eighteen miles below
Fort Chartres. Presumably all or most of the Illinois have their villages at
this time along the Mississippi between Cahokia and Kaskaskia. Hamburgh
suggests that "The Hole Settlement is called the Ilenois On Account of the
Indians who Have Settled themselves Here after they Had Been Driven away from
the River Illenois By other nations;. . ." (ibid. p. 364).

233

Caution must be exercised in evaluating the last quotation in the preceding paragraph; for, on the basis of the evidence already adduced it cannot
be accepted as literal truth. The Illinois were not simply "driven" to the
Mississippi by other tribes; they were also drawn there by opportunities and
advantages to be derived from the presence of French settlements. In fact,
Hamburgh himself provides part of the answer by implication, in the following
statement: "This settlement produces Plenty of Wheat Barley, Tobacco and some
Cotton, and it Has Extensive Indian trade;. . ." (ibid. p. 364; italics - JJ).
If the Peoria have moved their village to the Mississippi, the reason may be
that the French abandoned the post at Peoria on the Illinois River (WHC 18:260).
There is no indication at this time that the Illinois were compelled to with-
draw southward, leaving a vacuum which other tribes filled, although the

commandant of Fort Chartres stated that Beaujeau wintered on the Illinois River with a "party" of Potawatomi (IHC 10:50-51). It was essential for the Peoria to be situated at a convenient distance from a source of trade goods. Without a post on the Illinois River they could not conveniently fulfill important needs.

Sir William Johnson, in the same year 1763, reported that the Illinois "Reside about the Illinois River and hence to the Mississippi". Before that, la Chapelle noted that they were wintering at Starved Rock in 1760-1761; while Bougainville located the Peoria on the Illinois River in 1757. The position of the Illinois, albeit not in strength, as far north as the upper Illinois River is well established before 1763. What seems to have taken place in the course of the eighteenth century was a southward shifting of settlements stimulated at least in part, by the attraction of French trade and protection.

234

The territorial range of exploitation by the Illinois had extended to the Mississippi anyway. But whereas earlier their permanent settlements were located in the northerly portion of this region, they were later concentrated in the south. In spite of this settlement shift the Illinois seem to have continued the use of the same lands for the hunting which provided subsistence and commodities for trade. They shifted their focus of settlement within the same total context of land use. No one else is as yet reported to be settled on or hunting on those lands. And until 1763 the Peoria continued the northward exploitation, while those Illinois along the Mississippi appear to have hunted northward, and also eastward of the Mississippi and Illinois Rivers.

At this point perhaps, it might be well for purposes of perspective, to introduce certain considerations relevant to the evaluation of statements in the documents concerning changes in location of settlements and the reasons given for them.

Both Indians and Europeans were living in a world of conflict. Indians apart, the French and British had been engaged in warfare intermittently since the seventeenth century as part of the Hundred Years' War. European observation and recording of events was, interpretively, influenced to a considerable extent by military and imperial values, in addition to those of a mercantile and religious nature. The Europeans unquestionably stimulated or exacerbated intertribal conflict, either directly by using Indians as pawns in their own rivalry or indirectly because of competition for the advantages of European trade. This, again, was related to commercial competition among the Europeans themselves.

But while warfare among the tribes was an important factor in the dynamics of change and movement, one does not underestimate its role with the claim that it was not the only factor. Nevertheless, perhaps because of the European Weltanschauung of the time, the tendency seems to have been to interpret much of the geographical change and movement as resultants of the exercise of direct physical force. To put the matter simply, when a group moves in order to be near a source of supply of trade goods, it is a force of quite another kind that is responsible -- attraction rather than repulsion. But because the group is also engaged (or has been so occupied over a period of time) in warfare, the move may be viewed as a direct consequence of the hostilities.

This problem of interpretation is implied in a statement by General Gage in a letter he wrote on April 14, 1766 to Major Farmar at Fort Chartres: "I understood, those Indians [the Illinois] were drove away from their former Possessions, and Settled along the Mississippi at the desire of the French; . . ." (A-380). Neither half of this statement can stand alone as an exemplar

235

of truth; but there is a _measure_ of truth in both, with the additional qual-
ification that what the French desired was not so much Indian settlement as
Indian trade to be drawn to _their_ settlements.

An account of the Illinois country was written by Aubry apparently in
1763 although, it seems, he was last there in 1759. He writes that the
Kaskaskia, who have one hundred warriors, reside a little over a mile from
the French village of Kaskaskia, which is situated on the right bank of the
Kaskaskia River about five miles above its mouth. Near Fort Chartres, about
fifteen miles farther up the Mississippi are the Michigamea among whom there
are "about Forty Warriors" (IHC 10:4). Northward of this point, about 37 or
38 miles, is the French village of Cahokia; nearby are the Cahokia Indians,
where there are about sixty fighting men (ibid. p. 5).

Thus Aubry, whose information on the Illinois we can assume dates back
as of 1759, mentions three groups, as does Hamburgh. Both include the
Kaskaskia and Michigamea. But whereas in Aubry the third one is Cahokia, in
Hamburgh it is Peoria. On the basis of the foregoing data it would appear
that in 1763 that the permanent villages of most, if not all, of the population
of the Illinois Indians concentrated on the left bank of the Mississippi
River between its Illinois and Kaskaskia affluents.

236

IX - 1763-1777

On March 8, 1764 the British quartermaster general for America, Lieu-
tenant Colonel Robertson, prepared a report containing information on the
Illinois country which he obtained from the French, especially Aubry. The
Piankashaw, near the post of Vincennes, he wrote "have about Sixty warriors."
What he has to say about the Michigamea, Cahokia and Kaskaskia is identical
with Aubry's account except for the additional fact that the last mentioned
Illinois are situated on the left bank of the Kaskaskia River somewhat over
a mile from the French fort opposite the village of Kaskaskia (ibid. p. 218).
The data on the Indians in these documents was concentrated in one sentence
by D'Abbadie, Governor of Louisiana, on January 10, 1764: "The savages of
the different posts of the Illinois are reduced today to a very small number;
war and tafia have almost destroyed them" (ibid. p. 210).

De Villiers, writing to the Governor from Fort Chartres in March 1764,
said that he no longer obtains any information from the Indians.   "Those
who come here are on their way from their winter quarters and come only to
have their arms repaired and to demand assistance".   At the time, a band
of Wea and a band of Piankashaw were at the fort (ibid. p. 224). There is
no indication as to where these bands had spent the winter. St. Ange, the
new commandant at Fort Chartres, reported later that towards the end of
June "the chiefs of the Miami, Kickapoo, Mascoutens, Wea, and Piankashaw
arrived here with their band" (ibid. p. 289).   The obvious reason for the
visits of these tribes was hatred for the English whose attitude toward them
and treatment of them, in spite of the efforts of such men as Sir William
Johnson and George Croghan (ibid. pp. 258,307), made the period of French
dominion seem like halcyon days. The Indians were in dire straits, and they
looked to the French, who were waiting only to turn power over to the British

237

for help.   Towards the middle of April Pontiac came to Fort Chartres, and
when he left at the beginning of June he had roused the Illinois against the
English in spite of all French efforts to maintain calm.

At the end of July a chief of the St. Joseph Potawatomi told St. Ange
that he and the Peoria had gone to a band of Iowa on the Mississippi and
forced them to return horses and slaves that they had stolen from the French
inhabitants. But the commandant also reported that "The Peoria and the
Cahokia who are in a village near this fort always continue their insults to
the French and commit considerable harm by the stealing of horses which they
do very often.   A month ago [July] they set out for the summer chase and
brought away a great number of horses of which several are dead.   They have
just arrived and demanded to speak to me" (ibid. pp. 293-295).

St. Ange's comment that the Peoria and Cahokia are in a village near
the fort brings to mind Hamburgh's statement of the year before (1763) that
about a half mile from this fort were two villages, Peoria and Michigamea,
containing a total complement of three hundred warriors (Hamburgh, 1961,
pp. 363-4).

Colonel Bouquet, in the course of his expedition against the Indians
down the Ohio in 1764, obtained from a French trader of Detroit an estimate
of the number of warriors in various tribes (Bouquet, 1868, pp.153-155).
According to this list the Kaskaskia, "or Illinois in general, on the Illinois
river" numbered 600 warriors, while the Peoria had 800.   The Kickapoo, Wea,
and Piankashaw, located on the Wabash, had among them 300, 400, and 250
warriors respectively.   The Mascouten, who are said to be situated south of
Green Bay, are assigned 500 warriors; while the Potawatomi, "near St. Joseph's
and Detroit" possess 350 (see also Krauskopf, 1955, p. 222).   Thomas Hutchins,
who was with Bouquet, gives exactly the same information (Schoolcraft, 3:554-5).

238

At a court of inquiry conducted at Detroit in February 1765 Maisonville and Godefroi testified that they had been sent by Colonel Bradstreet on a mission "from Detroit to the Illinois Country" to invite "nine nations" to come to Detroit for a conference towards the end of July (A-130). From the testimony it is obvious that the nine "nations" were: Cahokia, Kaskaskia, Peoria, Michigamea, Piankashaw of Vincennes, Piankashaw of the Vermillion River, Wea, Kickapoo and Mascouten. The journey (late 1764?) was apparently made via the Illinois River, for the Cahokia "which were the farthest off" were visited first. The chiefs of the Cahokia "Vilages" accepted the invitation tentatively pending a final decision which would be made in the spring after consultation with the war chiefs who were then absent. The two emissaries then "proceeded to the Chiefs of the Cashcashkie Nation" who replied in the same manner. The latter were requested to convey the same message to the Peoria and the Michigamea "the remote situation of these people not permitting the Informants themselves to deliver them".

When the emissaries reached Vincennes the Piankashaw were hunting on the Ohio and were not expected to return until spring. The two representatives of the English then proceeded up the Wabash "to the large Vilage of the Piankishaws", presumably on the Vermillion River, where the chief Black Fly accepted the invitation. There, or in the vicinity of the Vermillion, "They after spoke to Washion Chief of the Maskouteng's". When they came to Fort Ouiatanon they "were informed the Kikapoos were hunting One hundred and fifty Leagues from thence", but the direction is not indicated. From the fort they went to the Wea, who also promised to attend the conference.

After the French and Indian War Lt. Ross was sent by the British from Mobile to Fort Chartres to take over the command of that post from St. Ange. He arrived on February 18, 1765 and found the Indians every bit as hostile to the take-over as had been represented (IHC 10:442-3). This is somewhat different from the friendly inclinations reported by Maisonville and Godefroi. Some days later both Ross and St. Ange met with the Illinois at Kaskaskia in an effort to effect a peaceful transition to British dominion (ibid. p. 468).

About that time an Illinois chief had left for New Orleans where he joined a Shawnee chief and, possibly, another Illinois (pp. 443, 444, 477) in council with the governor for the purpose of enlisting French help against the English (ibid. pp. 458-460). In particular, they rejected the English contention that the lands had been ceded to them by the French, and the Shawnee reminded the governor that "our fathers have always told us that the land was ours, that we were free there, that the French came to settle there only to protect us and defend us as a good father protects and defends his children" (ibid. p. 445). Levacher, the Illinois chief, expressed surprise "that the great emperor of the French has given away our land; my arm belongs to me; there belongs to the emperor only what lies across the great lake... I do not take hold of the Frenchman's hand but of his arm as do all the Indian nations who are in the country of the Illinois" (ibid. pp. 450-451).

240

When the Illinois returned from their winter quarters early in the spring of 1765 they conferred with Ross and St. Ange, and "came accompanied by the principal chiefs of the Osage and Missouri" (ibid. p. 468). In addressing the Illinois St. Ange referred specifically to the Kaskaskia, Peoria, Cahokia, and Michigamea (ibid. p. 472). The reply was made "by one called Tamarois, a chief of the Kaskaskia, in the name of all the Illinois nation" (ibid. p. 476); and in addressing Lt. Ross he said "that these lands are ours and no one claims them, not even other red men" (ibid p. 478). The chiefs of the Osage and Missouri added that "we Osage and Missouri think as do our elder brothers, the Illinois...for we shall always aid our brothers in preserving their lands" (ibid. p. 479).

In addition to his problem of trying to win the assent of the Illinois and others to the English presence, St. Ange was worried about the virtually total depletion of his food supply. As he put it: "the Illinois, the Osage, the Missouri and some Potawatomi have received almost the last of the supplies which I had" (ibid. p. 471).

Hugh Crawford, a trader who had accompanied Lt. Ross, apparently as interpreter, subsequently gave his version of events during the period of their stay in the Illinois area. According to this account, a few days after they arrived at Fort Chartres parties of various Indians began coming in to confer with the commandant and to express vehemently their resentment at the presence of the English. Among these were Chippewa chiefs (ibid. p. 483). Crawford also stated "That part of the Chippewas, and the Pouteatamies left Fort St. Josephs, in order to Settle about the Illinois" (ibid. p. 484). Both Ross and Crawford seemed to think they might have made headway with the Illinois if parties of other Indians hadn't kept coming in with hostile expressions against the English (ibid. pp. 481-2, 484).

241

Following the departure of Ross, Lt. Fraser arrived from Fort Pitt after the middle of April, while Pontiac and his men were still present. Writing from Kaskaskia the middle of May Fraser said: "I found Pondiack here on my Arrival accompanied by a Number of his Nation and some Chiefs of the Pottowattamies and Chippawas arrived some time afterwards" (ibid. p. 493). Crawford, who left the Illinois country April 7, said that part of the Potawatomi and Chippewa of the St. Joseph River came to "settle". Fraser who arrived later that same month then told of the subsequent arrival of Potawatomi and Chippewa chiefs (A-207). This situation bears all the earmarks of a temporary sojourn probably related to the state of unrest in the Detroit area, which was the center of Pontiac's abortive uprising in 1763, and to the murder by the Potawatomi of some English soldiers in November 1764 (IHC 10: 487-489, 500, 520). In addition, as Croghan reported the following May from the Ohio, "the Ottawas, and Pouteatamies, residing near St. Josephs, and the Twightwees Seem Discontented, and look on themselves as Neglected by the English..." (IHC 11:22). All may have been drawn there, in the last analysis, by the presence of Pontiac, who had been accompanied by his Ottawa kinsmen. Apparently there was a considerable amount of intertribal activity and movement stimulated by antipathy to the English and by Pontiac's movements. Such factors may have been behind Bouquet's reference in June, 1765, to "the Numerous Tribes of Indians resorting to that Post [Fort Chartres and Kaskaskia], who in a manner influence all the Western Nations" (IHC 10:517). There is one final consideration which must not be overlooked in connection with the presence at this time of various Indian groups in the vicinity of Kaskaskia – the convoys of goods which the French were still sending up from New Orleans during a period when the English had not yet organized themselves for the establishment of trade. Fraser wrote from Kaskaskia about "vast Quantities of Goods that are come up here within these three weeks past" (ibid. p. 495).

242

In a statement about "the Number of Men able to bear Arms in this Colony [Illinois]" Lt. Fraser lists 650 Indians without specifying their identity (ibid. p. 492; IHC 11:228). However, in his report of May 4, 1766 he states: "the Illinois Indians are about six hundred and fifty able to bear arms" (Dunn, 1894, p. 411; IHC 11:228).

Goerge Croghan left Fort Pitt on May 15, 1765 on a journey down the Ohio for the purpose of conciliating the Illinois and Wabash tribes prior to the formal entry of British authority into the region. In a journal containing an account of his preparations for this expedition he makes a reference to "Nine Nations living on the Ouabache & in the Illinois Country" without identifying any by name (IHC 11:5; see A-130 above).

In the course of his voyage down the Ohio, while encamped six miles below the mouth of the Wabash at Shawneetown, Illinois, his party was attacked on the morning of June 8 by eighty Kickapoo and Mascouten, who killed five of Croghan's party, plundered their supplies and took the rest prisoner to Ouiatanon (ibid. pp. 30, 39-40; also A-171, 253, 131).   On their way up the Wabash they stopped at Vincennes where "I found a Village of about 80 or 90 French Families settled on the East Side of this River" and where "There is likewise an Indian Village of the Pyankeshaws" (IHC 11: 31-2, 40). According to Croghan "Post Vincent is a place of great consequence for Trade being a fine hunting Country all along the Cuabache and too far for the Indians which reside hereabouts to go either to the Iillionois or elsewhere to fetch their Necessaries" (ibid p. 32).

On the day of their departure from Vincennes, June 17, they travelled eighteen miles; and in the next two days "we traveled thro a prodigious large Meadow called the Pyankeshas hunting ground...the Land was well watered and full of Buffuloes Deer Bears and all Kind of Wild Game."   During the following two days "We passed thro some very large Meadows part of which belong to the Pyankeshaws on Vermillion River...The Game very plenty..." The next day, after they "passed thro' a part of the same Meadows... [they] arrived at Vermillion River...About halfe a Mile from the place where we crossed...there is a Village of Pyankashaws distinguished by the Addition of the name of the River:..."   On June 23 they "came into a very large Bottom on the Cuabache within 6 miles of Ouiatanon.   Here I met several Chiefs to the Kicapoos and Musquatimes who...returned to their Village and delivered us all to their Chiefs" (ibid. p. 33).   Here stood the French fort, containing fourteen French families "on the North Side of the River: The Kicapoos

243

& Musquatimes...live nigh the Fort on the Same Side of the River where they have two Villages and the Cauatanons [Wea] have a Village on the South Side of the River;..." (ibid pp. 33-34; 58).

Although Vincennes was on the east side of the Wabash the journey to Ouiatanon, which was made by land, apparently took place on the west side of the river; for they crossed the Vermillion at a point not far from the Piankashaw Vermillion village. The Piankashaw hunting grounds through which they travelled were thus on the west side of the Wabash beginning about two days north of Vincennes and extending up to the Vermillion River.

In remarks about the French fort Croghan writes: "This post has always been a very conciderable Trading Place" and had the benefit of "a very advantageous Trade..." (ibid. p. 34). Seven days after his arrival, on June 30 "The several Chiefs belonging to those villages at Ouiatanon [Kickapoo, Mascouten, Wea] arrived from the Ilinois [where they had gone to meet Croghan], & there were with them the Chiefs of several other Nations [including Piankashaw] who came to see me..." (ibid. p. 40).

Between July 4 and 8 Croghan conferred several times with the Wea, Piankashaw, Kickapoo and Mascouten who gave "their Consent and Approbation to take Possession of any Posts in their Country which the French formerly possessed..." (ibid. p. 41). On the 13th he met with the Wea, Kickapoo, Mascouten, and Ottawa who sought his aid in making peace with the Shawnee, Delaware and Iroquois because of the killing of three Shawnee in the attack at the mouth of the Wabash. Apparently the Piankashaw and Miami were also petitioners in this situation, undoubtedly fearing that they too would become victims if reprisals were taken by the aggrieved parties (A-172).

On the 18th, on his way to Kashaskia Croghan met Pontiac, "delegations" of Iroquois, Shawnee, Delaware, and "also Deputies with Speeches from the four Nations living in the Illinois Country," by which, presumably, was meant the Kaskaskia , Peoria, Cahokia, and Michigamea. They all returned to Ouiatanon where Croghan "settled all matters with the Illinois Indians – Pontiac & they Agreeing to every thing the other Nations had done,...(IHC 11: 42). In the conferences with Croghan at Ouiatanon, and later at Detroit, all the tribes reiterated the basic point of concern to every one of them (ibid. pp.42-48). Before leaving Detroit, where they had gone to meet again with Croghan in August, the Chiefs of the Wabash tribes made the following very clear to Sir William Johnson's deputy: "That no difference may happen hereafter, we tell you now the French never Conquered [us] neither did they purchase a foot of our Country, nor have [they a right] to give it to you, we gave them liberty to settle for which they always rewarded us & treated us with great Civility while they had it in their power...if you expect to keep those posts, we will expect to have proper returns from you" (ibid. pp. 47-48; see also pp. 53-4 and A-374).

245

Throughout the "Official" journal, in Croghan's discussions of the several meetings he had with the tribes, both at Ouiatanon and then at Detroit, it is unmistakably clear that those from the Wabash agreed only "to your taking possession of the Posts in our Country: (IHC 11: 47). On only one occasion, in connection with a Detroit meeting, is there any indication that there might have been an acceptance of British sovereignty by Wea, Miami, Piankashaw, Kickapoo and Mascouten. Croghan writes that they "farther acknowledged that they had at Ouiatanon before they came there given up the Sovereignty of their Country to me for His Majesty..." (ibid. p. 44). But Croghan, in the summary of a subsequent meeting with the same groups, was apparently more careful in reporting the views expressed, as quoted in the preceding paragraph (see also ibid. pp. 61, 86, 88).

Croghan's list of Indians attending his conference at Detroit in August, 1765 does not include the Illinois. The Ottawa, under Pontiac, had the largest delegation of chiefs and warriors, all of whom came "from their Several Villages on the Miamies River" (ibid. p. 56; see also p. 46). The Chippewa representation came from villages situated b tween Detroit and "St. Josephs". There were also ottawa and Chippewa bands at Saginaw and at Chicago (ibid. p. 57, fn. 1, and p. 49, fn. 1). Among the others present there were, as previously stated, Potawatami, Miami, Wea, Piankashaw, Kickapoo and Mascouten delegations (ibid pp. 56-7). In a letter written from Ouiatanon on July 12 Croghan employs the phrase: "...the five Nations settled on this River..." (ibid p. 59), by which it might be thought he had in mind the Wea, Kickapoo, Mascouten, Vermillion Piankashaw, and their kins- men at Vincennes. Lt. Fraser, in May 1766, makes specific reference to these five groups on the Wabash in the account of his 1765 journey (ibid. p. 227; see also Dunn, 1894, p. 410). But on July 13 Croghan referred to the five as Wea, Piankashaw, Kickapoo, Mascouten and "Twightwees" [Miami] (A-171).

246

Sir William Johnson in a report to the Lords of Trade written in August 1765 discusses the difficulties Croghan had had, before arriving at an agreement with the western Indians, because of French instigation of the latter. Johnson refers to the combined opposition of the tribes against the English as a "league" or an "association" of eighteen created by the French. In one communication on September 28 he wrote: "On Mr. Croghan's arrival at Detroit he had a Treaty with all the Western League...& dissolved the League lately formed by the French with Eighteen Nations...(IHC 11:88-89). The following November, in referring to "the Conduct of the French at N. Orleans and the Ilinois" he mentions "the Artful Suggestions they made use of to Create an Opposition in the Indians to our taking Post in the last mentioned [Illinois] Country, for which purpose they had formed an Association of 18 Indian Nations..." (ibid. p. 118). Croghan's list contains only eleven names, but if the Illinois are counted as four, this addition together with subdivisions of a few others could create the number Johnson uses. But it seems that Croghan, in a letter he wrote in July, had already expressed the idea of the existence of an <u>organized</u> intertribal effort against the English when he stated that the French had "been this three years with great pains & Expense, endeavoring to make a Confederacy of those Nations to Oppose the English, and if Possible prevent their taking Possession of this Country, last fall they Effected it, and had got 18 Nations agreed to oppose our, either coming down or up the River;..." (ibid. p. 58). Croghan is obviously the source for Johnson's statements on the same point.

Johnson also touches upon another interesting and important point. 247 This concerns the reason for the difference in the Indian attitude towards the French and towards the English, which causes them to prefer to trade with the former despite their higher prices - a situation which contrasts with the earlier preferences for the cheaper goods of the English. The psychological factors responsible are simple enough, in that they are at the heart of the human desire to be treated with a modicum of dignity and equality, and to enter into relationships of mutual respect and consideration. Sir William puts the problem this way:"...if these Indians are properly Treated I have good hopes they will be weaned from their Dependence upon and Friendship for the French Inhabitants of that Illinois Country which is at present so great that the latter engross not only all the Trade in that Quarter but also draw away the greater part of the Furr Trade from the Lakes to the Ilinois and are constantly sending very large Cargoes up the Missisipi, the better to maintain

their influence" (ibid. p. 117; see also IHC 10:495). He then puts forward
this interesting contrast:

"I have frequently observed to Your Lordships that His Majesties
Subjects in this Country seem very ill Calculated to Cultivate a good understanding with the Indians, and this is a Notorious proof of it, for notwith-
standing the Expence of transporting Goods from New Orleans to the Ilinois
is greater than by the Lakes, and Consequently French Goods are in general
dearer than ours, yet such is the Conduct of all persons under the Crown of
France whether Officers, Agents, or Traders that the Indians will go much
farther to buy their goods and pay a much higher price for them. This all
Persons acquainted with the Nature of the Commerce to the Westward can fully
Evidence.

"Now altho' there is little reason to Expect that our People in general
will ever treat the Indians with the like kindness and Civility, yet I don't
at all despair of Weakning the Influence of the French Inhabitants & Traders
..." (IHC 11: 117-118).

Once again, as in the case of the eighteen nations joined in a "league"
or "confederacy", Croghan is the ultimate fountainhead of Johnson's knowledge
of affairs in the Illinois-Wabash region. In this case Croghan had probably
written to Johnson shortly before the latter communicated the information to
the Lords of Trade in November, 1765. According to Croghan, despite the
fact that Pontiac and the other Indians eventually became convinced that the
French were instrumental in generating and fostering their hostility towards
the English "...yet it has not changed the Indians Affections to them, they
have been bred up together like Children in that Country, & the French have
always adopted the Indians Customs & manners, Treated them Civily & supplyed
their wants generously, by which means they gained the Hearts of the Indians

& commanded their Services, & injoyed the Benefit of a very large Furr Trade, as they well knew if they had not taken this measure they could not enjoy any of those Advantages" (ibid pp. 53-54).

French attitudes, which led to intermarriage and to the acceptance of Indian culture, behavior, and values with a minimum of invidious distinctions, created problems for the English. But beyond these the French were responsible for an English dilemma with respect to the monetary considerations relating to the size of profits. Croghan pointed out, and Johnson followed him in this, that "The french sold them Goods much dearer than the English Traders do at present,..., but they made that up in large presents to them for their Services, which they wanted to Support their Interest in the Country, & tho' we want none of their Services yet they will expect favours, & if refused look on it in a bad light, & very likely think its done to distress them for some particular Advantages we want to gain over them." Croghan could not have come closer to the mark. Not only was he an intelligent observer who knew how to gather information, he also knew how to interpret it. For he goes on to say: "...the French have learned them for their own Advantage a bad Custom, for by all I could learn, they seldom made them any general presents, but as it were fed them with Necessaries Just as they wanted them Tribe by Tribe, & never sent them away empty, which will make it difficult & troublesome to the Gentlemen that are to command in their Country for some time." But in a final burst compounded of high dudgeon and imperial ethnocentrism he writes: "...they are a rash inconsiderate People and don't look on themselves under any Obligations to us, but rather think we are obliged to them for letting us reside in their Country." His concluding words on this facet of Indian effrontery are these: "As far as I can Judge of their Sentiments by the several Conversations I have had

249

with them, they will expect some Satisfaction made them by Us, for any Posts that should be Established in their Country for Trade" (IHC 11:54).

Early in October ,1765 Captain Stirling arrived to take over command for the English at Fort Chartres.   On December 15, in a letter to General Gage, he wrote: "I have not been able to find, that the French King had any Possessions in this Country, Except the Ground the Forts stands on, as no Lands were ever bought from the Indians, who Claim the whole as their property. He then goes on to state that "...the Caskaskias Indians, who live within half a League of that Village [French Kaskaskia] are about a Hundred & Fifty Warriors; The Metchis & Peory as live one Mile from this Fort [Chartres], The former have Forty, the latter about Two Hundred & Fifty Warriors; The Caho's are about Forty, likewise; These Indians I am informed, intend all going to the other side to live;...the French Emissarys have spared no pains to debauch the Indians & Inhabitants to leave us;..."   (ibid. pp. 126-7).

250

At the beginning of December Major Farmar arrived, after a voyage up the Mississippi, to take permanent command from Stirling. At the Arkansas River he met a party of Illinois to whom he gave presents and who notified their kinsmen of their pleasure over this circumstance (ibid. p. 128).   Lt. Fraser, who accompanied Farmar, wrote to Gage that "The Indians have also left our Side [of the Mississippi], and gone to the Spanish Side;..." With reference to the expedition's meeting with the Illinois he added the following information: "The great Chief of the Ilinois met us on his way to New Orleans with no good Intention I believe, but the Threats of the Chickasawes brought him back after he had refused Major Farmar, He has Since prevailed on a few of the Caskaskias, to come to receive presents from Major Farmar, but none of the other tribes of the Ilinois has come in yet" (ibid p. 131).

John Jennings of the Philadelphia firm of Baynton, Wharton and Morgan came down the Ohio to Kaskaskia, arriving on April 5, 1766 with a large cargo of trade goods. His journal records that the Indian village of Kaskaskia, whose "Head Cheif" was Tomera [Tamarois?] was situated about four miles from Kaskaskia on the road to Fort Chartres (ibid. p. 177).

William Franklin, Governor of New Jersey, prepared a document in 1766 consisting of "Reasons for establishing a British Colony at the Illinois..." (ibid. pp. 248-257). In it he suggests that "the Crown purchase of the Indians all their Right to that Tract of Country lying on the East Side of the River Mississippi, between the Illinois River & the River Ohio, and Fifty Miles back from the said River Mississippi." Appended to this document are a series of "remarks" which were probably made by Sir William Johnson. In connection with the foregoing statement of Franklin he writes: "This Tract includes Fort Chartres, Cahoki, & Kaskasquias (three considerable French Settlements) and it is said, from good Authority, that the Indians have expressed an Inclination to part with it to the English on very moderate Terms, and that they might very easily be persuaded to sell all the Lands as far back as the Heads of the several small Rivers which empty themselves in the Mississippi between the Illinois & the Ohio: - They having a greater Quantity of fine Hunting Country than they can ever have any use for" (ibid. p. 252).

251

Although the Indians who might be inclined to sell the area described are not mentioned by name it is reasonable to assume that "the Lands as far back as the Heads of the several small Rivers" are territory within the traditional domain of exploitation by the Illinois. The data adduced thus far do not reveal the continued presence of any other groups up to this time.

On June 18, 1766 Captain Harry Gordon was accompanied by Croghan and Thomas Hutchins down the Ohio to the Illinois country, arriving at Kaskaskia August 19. Like Jennings before him, Gordon's journal records that from

Kaskaskia "The Road to Fort Chartres...passes thro' the Village of the Kaskaskia Indians of 15 Cabbins..." (ibid. p. 297). He also includes the information that at Cahokia "There is likewise 20 Cabbins of Peioria Indians left here. The Rest and best Part are moved to the French Side [across the Mississippi] 2 Miles below Pain Court" (ibid. p. 299). He locates the latter village on the west side of the Mississippi, three miles above Cahokia.

In a reference to the expense and inconvenience of "supporting" the newly acquired Illinois region Gordon writes: "The French carry on the Trade all round us by Land & by Water; 1st Up the Mississipi, & to the Lakes by the Ouiascoasin, Foxes, Chicagou, and the Illinois Rivers; 2ndly Up the Ohio to the Wabash Indians, & even the small Quantity of Skins or Furs that the Kaskaskias and Peiorias (who are on our side) get by hunting is carried under our Nose to Misere and Pain Court" (ibid. p. 301). As regards the small quantity of furs produced by the Kaskaskia and Peoria this may have been due to the relatively fewer number of those groups remaining on the east side of the river; for he states earlier that most of them had crossed to the west bank to a situation two miles below Pain Court.

252

Croghan who, as mentioned previously, was on the expedition with Gordon provides other data. In a letter to Johnson from Fort Chartres on September 10, 1766 he wrote: "...I found the Several Nations of Indians residing in this Country was Collected together at the Kaskaskias a large Indian Village near [blank in MS.] a French Town" (ibid. p. 373). This "French Town" may have been Kaskaskia or Prairie du Rocher. Gordon places the latter three miles from Fort Chartres. Jennings says that three miles beyond the French Kaskaskia village en route to Fort Chartres is the Indian village of Kaskaskia. Both Jennings and Gordon agree that Indian Kaskaskia is between French Kaskaskia and Prairie du Rocher. Stirling seems to locate

Indian Kaskaskia within a half league of French Kaskaskia. However, Gordon's village of 15 cabins hardly seems to accord with Croghan's "large Indian Village of Kaskaskia".

In addition to this information on village location there are also some data on where the Kaskaskia were situated while carrying on their winter hunt in 1766-67. This is supplied by George Morgan in his journal of a voyage down the Mississippi. He left Kaskaskia on November 21, 1766, and the next day "...(about 16 Leagues below the Kaskaskias River) I pass'd the Kaskaskias Tribe of Indians who were encamp'd on the English Shore to hunt for the Winter Season --" (ibid. p. 439). This was at a point between the Kaskaskia River and the Ohio, which Morgan reached late the following morning.

In a letter to Sir William Johnson in September, Croghan wrote that his general conference with the Indians, which lasted two days, was begun on August 25, 1766 at Fort Chartres "where was Assembled the Chiefs & principle Warriors of Eight Nations, divided into Twentytwo tribes or bands" (idem). The Indian population gathered here for this occasion was quite considerable for, as Croghan wrote, "...here has been above One Thousand Indian Men, besides Women & Children, & there was an absolute necessaty of Convincing them at this time, that the English were as able to Support them as the French [i.e. with hospitality and presents]..." (ibid. p. 374). At the conclusion of this meeting "a General Peace & Reconciliation was then declared in Public between...the Northern Nations, & all those Western Nations..." According to Croghan this result was due, in part, to the fact that "those Nations in this Country stand in great Awe of the Northern Nations" (ibid. pp. 373-4).

In a report on this trip which Croghan sent to General Gage in January, 1767, his earlier references concerning this enterprise become a little clearer (ibid. pp. 487-495). The "Western Nations" of his letter to Johnson are now

253

referred to as "The Western Confederacy", and their names, appended to the report, are as follows: Kaskaskia, Peoria, Michigamea, Cahokia, Piankashaw, Wea, Kickapoo, Mascouten, Miami, Potawatomi, Sac, Fox. Representatives of all these groups attended the conference at Kaskaskia. Croghan states that "The above mentioned twelve Nations of Indians composed the Western Confederacy, in the Illinois Country..." He says further that "The French During the late War, divided them into Twenty six Tribes & appointed a Chief, to each Tribe, so that now they consider themselves, as so many distinct Nations Which makes it more difficult, to Transact business with them. Since that time, many of the Tribes, have divided from the rest, left their Old Settlements, and have Settled in other parts of the Country" (ibid. pp. 494-495).

Croghan also employs the phrase "Northern Confederacy" (ibid. p. 493) in which he obviously includes at least the Iroquois, Delaware, Shawnee, and
254   Huron, deputations of which accompanied him and participated in the conference at Fort Chartres (ibid. pp. 494, 488-9). The following September (1767) Johnson uses "confederacy" in still another context when he writes: "The Illinois Confederacy Consisting of the Piankashaws, Kickapoos, Kuskeiskees, etc are on good terms with the rest..." (IHC 16:46). The last two words in this excerpt, "the rest", refers to the so-called "Northern confederacy". But this seems to be the first use of "Illinois confederacy", which probably includes the subdivision of the Illinois together with the Wabash tribes. Used in this way "Illinois" is a general reference to a geographical region more or less synonymous with the widely used phrase "Illinois Country". Nevertheless, it may be that what Johnson has in mind is the "western confederacy" composed of the twelve groups listed by Croghan in his report to Johnson in January of the same year.

One of the items of business at the Fort Chartres conference in the latter part of August, 1766 was "...an Adjustment, of the Difference, between

the Western & Northern Confederacys; occasioned by the Warriors of the former
[Kickapoo and Mascouten], Striking and Plundering me, and the Deputies of the
latter, the last year, at the Mouth of the Wabash. And in Order, that a safe
Communication, Might be kept up, from Fort Pitt, Detroit, and other Northern
Posts, with the Illinois, and an extensive Commerce, might be carried on, with
the numerous nations" (IHC 11:489).

The importance of the Illinois area on this score was quite apparent,
for as Croghan put it: "That Country, is the Frontier of all our Canadian
Conquests - is a place of a most extensive Trade, whereby the French are able
to rival us, in the Furr business,..." (ibid. p. 493; see also p. 301). In
addition, the Illinois country was becoming the entrepôt of the developing
Missouri River trade, which the French saw as _their_ new frontier (ibid. pp.
146-7). At the same time men like Croghan and Captain Gordon were not unaware
of this new field of opportunity for British enterprise. Gordon reported the
recent (1764) establishment of Laclede at St. Louis. This trader, he wrote,
"...takes so good Measures, that the whole Trade of the Missouri, That of the
Mississipi Northwards, and that of the Nations near la Baye, Lake Michigan,
and St. Josephs, by the Illinois River, is entirely brought to Him" (ibid.
p. 300; see also p. 491).

But Croghan took immediate action with an eye on the future prospects
of the trans-Mississippi trade. He writes: "Finding, when I was at the
Illinois, That a Strong Connection subsisted between the several Indian
Nations, who resided on His Majesty's side of the Missisipi and the Missouri,
and Arkansa, Nations, who dwelt on the other, I Judged it for the good of the
Service, to send a Deputation, from the Kaskaskeys, to inform them... that a
free Trade, would be allowed to them,...at Fort Chartres or at any other Posts,
possessed by His Majestie's Troops, in the Illinois Country and on the River
Missisipi" (ibid. p. 493).

255

In addition Croghan recommended the establishment of two posts for the trade. One proposal was to erect "...a Fort immediately, at the Mouth of the Illinois River, whereby [the French] could be Hindered, from going into the Indian Country, and the British Traders, would enjoy a very Valuable Trafick, from the numerous Indians, who would come down, to our Posts, from Lake Michigan and the great Tract of Country, lying between it, and the Missisippi" (ibid. p. 492). As in the days of the French the Illinois area was envisioned as a focus of concentration into which the trade of the surrounding regions would be drawn.

Croghan's second suggestion was "...that a Post should be Erected on the Wabash, from thence the five Nations, who are settled on that River, may be Safely supplied with British Goods" (idem). This reference to five nations on the Wabash reiterates a statement he made in the summer of 1765 (ibid. p. 59) and a similar one by Lt. Fraser (ibid. p. 227). When, in March, 1767 Father Meurin was at Kaskaskia in preparation for Easter services there he wrote a letter to Quebec in which he makes reference, in passing, to "the Miami Piankashaw" at Vincennes (ibid. p. 526), one of the five groups on the Wabash.

An urgent recommendation for a post on the Wabash was again made in April, 1768 by the Indian agent at Fort Chartres, who wrote to Sir William Johnson: "I think there is an absolute necessity of Establishing a Post, at Post Vincennt [Vincennes],...it being the great path throw which all the northward Indians pass, and a Great place of Trade" (ibid. p. 255).

256

Croghan was concerned to insure peace not only for the transaction of trade in the Illinois area, but also for settlement there. On the question of land, he claimed to have obtained information which would, presumably, open the way for cessions from the Indians for which they would expect to receive compensation (ibid. pp. 490-491 and fn 1). This plan, together with visions of trade, placed the Illinois Indians in the center of a dynamic complex of external forces whose impact upon them was bound to be more highly destructive than upon other groups peripheral to their situation on the Mississippi. It should be added, however, that General Gage was rather skeptical of the optimistic view of Croghan with regard to the promise of trade in the Illinois country (ibid. pp. 498 ff). He was among those who regarded the expense as too great and who believed that the British traders would send their furs either down the St. Lawrence or down the Mississippi to the French at New Orleans (ibid. pp. 500-503; IHC 16:317-18).

257

Croghan's "private journal" covering the period May 15, 1765- December 13, 1766 includes a list of tribes with data on fighting strength, "dwelling ground","hunting ground", and "with whom connected" (A-170). It is of interest that whereas in a letter of July, 1765 (A-171) Croghan included the "Twightwees" among the five tribes of the Wabash he now places them on the "Miammie [Maumee] River near Fort Miamis"; and their hunting ground is "Where they reside." He gives the number of their warriors at 250. He places the "dwelling ground" of the Wea, Piankashaw, and the Sac (?) [Shoghkeys] "On the branches of the Ouabache near Fort Ouiatanon. With 300, 300, and 200 warriors, respectively, they hunt "Between Ouiatanon & the Miammies [Maumee? or the Miami Indians?]" They are all, he states, "Connected with the Twightwees".

It is by no means apparent why the Sac (if they are actually the group Croghan had in mind) are placed in Wabash country among other tribes historically associated with the area. In view of Croghan's knowledge of that region the inclusion of the Sac is puzzling. At the same time he also groups them ("Shockeys") with Chippewa and Menominee, forming a total comple-ment of 500 warriors. All of these are situated near Green Bay on Lake Michigan and do their hunting "thereabouts".

One is also struck by Croghan's failure to group the Kickapoo and Mascouten with the Wea and the Piankashaw, particularly in view of his earlier clear statements associating the Kickapoo with the Ouiatanon area of the Wabash. The Kickapoo and Mascouten are listed among others in the following manner: "Kickapoos Outtagamies Musquatans Miscothins Outtasacks Musquakeys 4000." This collection of peoples is located "On Lake Michigan and between it and the Mississippi," engaging in hunting "where they respective reside." One might infer that the phrase "between it and the Mississippi" was meant to apply more specifically to the Kickapoo and Mascouten.

The Kaskaskia are listed separately from the "Illinois", each of them with 300 warriors. The dwelling ground of both, however, is "Near the French settlements in the Illinois Country"; but there is no mention whatever of their hunting grounds.

Edward Cole, who was in charge of Indian trade at Fort Chartres, wrote to Croghan early in July, 1767 that "The Indians About here, seem well disposed as also those from the Messourie, that have been with me". As to the latter, he seems to think that "Many more would have been here before this had not the war between these nations, the Sakies and Reynards prevented, but I am told they are now on the way from an Imense distance up the Messourie" (IHC 11:581). It is not entirely clear whether the Illinois alone are involved in these hostilities, or whether allies from the Missouri River

258

have joined with them against their old enemies. It is also possible that
some Missouri tribes only were embroiled in this warfare.

In the same letter Cole also reveals an interesting sidelight on his
relations with the Illinois, although he does not mention them by name in
this particular context. He writes: "The nation assembled before me in order
to have another chief - Young Dequoney [Ducoigne] being the next heir, he
was Unamimously pitched on if agreeable to me" (idem). Cole not only found
the candidate acceptable, but also possessed of qualities which "makes me
think he will become one of the Greatest Chiefs in this country -" (idem).
In view of their consultation with Cole in this matter it would seem that the
Illinois were anxious to insure good relations with the British. This friendly
disposition was, in fact, reported to Croghan a month or two before in a letter
from Maisonville, a resident of Ouiatanon. According to this source not only
the Illinois and Wabash Indians but also more distant tribes were beginning
to trade with the English (Johnson Papers 5:561-2). In addition a Huron,
sent by the British on an intelligence mission to the Illinois area found
"the Chiefs, and principal Warriors of the different Tribes...well pleased
with English;...They seem inclined to peace,..." (A-95, p. 37). All these
things seemed to be borne out in fact by a letter to Gage from Detroit,
dated May 29, 1767 in which George Turnbull stated: "Pontiac and a Large
Band of the Kicapous are here just now they have brought better than a
Hundred Packs of Peltry, and the Traders Declare there has not been so much
Trade at Detroit for Severall year's--" (A-326).

On August 24, 1767 General Gage reported the information that the
Michigamea "...who had left their Habitations on the Arrival of the English
in that Country, and settled with the French on the opposite Side of the
River, had returned again to their old Town:..." (IHC 11:596). On the Wabash,

259

Croghan, in October, again makes mention of "the five Tribes of Indians which Reside on that River" in connection with their dissatisfaction over the failure of the British to establish a trading post in their region as was done at Fort Chartres and Detroit (IHC 16:88). The French traders were filling this gap in the western country by going directly to the hunting grounds of the Indians (idem). The British traders at Detroit, although forbidden, wanted to do like-wise. In a communication to Jehu Hay, Indian agent at Detroit, in September, they stated "...that the French traders from the South side of the Mississipe bring goods all the way up to St. Vincent [Vincennes], the Highlands [Terre Haute], Vermillion [River], Ouya [Ouiatanon], river languille [Eel River], Le Cour de Serf, & the Miamie [Ft. Wayne]..." (ibid. pp. 4; 44-5; 84-5; 130-1). And in the spring of 1768 General Gage reported that in addition to trading with the Indians up the Illinois, Ohio, and Wabash Rivers the French were also hunting on their lands (ibid. p. 267).

260

Not only were the French depriving the British of a very substantial amount of trade, but their hunters were contributing to the depletion of the bison on the Ohio and shipping the meat to New Orleans. George Morgan, who made this point in a letter to his partners in December also added that "...it will in a short Time be a difficult Matter to supply even Fort Chartres with Meat from thence" (ibid. pp. 132; 499). Presumably this hunting by the French took place in the Kentucky area of the Ohio (ibid. p. 132, fn 1). The hunting parties sent out by the firm of Baynton, Wharton and Morgan did their work on the Ohio in the vicinity of the Wabash (ibid p. 376); and they also exploited Western Kentucky to provide bison meat not only for local consumption by the military and civilians, but also for shipment to the colonies. This part of the firm's efforts was occasionally referred to by Morgan as "our Buffalo Adventure" (ibid. pp. 67, 129, 131, 142-3, 161), and was the subject of elaborate planning by Morgan at Kaskaskia (ibid. pp. 222-224). On one occasion, at the end of the summer of 1767, a party of this company's hunters on the Ohio River "...killed upwards of seven hundred Buffaloe & renderd their Tallow. Besides which there were twenty large Perriogues employd in the same Trade on the Ohio from New Orleans" (ibid. p. 223; see also p. 354). With hunters coming in from the east and south, the attack on the game resources in the region of the Ohio and Mississippi Rivers was a virtual pincers movement in the historical process of ultimate extermination (ibid. pp. 499, 634).

Farther to the east on the Ohio the Indians were increasingly aroused by murders and settler encroachment from Pennsylvania and Virginia (A-174). As a result messages were passing from the Shawnee, Delaware, and Iroquois to the Great Lakes and Illinois areas (IHC 16: 38-48; 71-77; 85; 89; 92-3). Although Cole, the agent at Fort Chartres, reported in October that "the Indians here Seem to be as well attached to the English, as any I ever saw" he was, at the same time, "Informed by the Chiefs of the Kaskaskias Village, that there is a belt which came from the Irequois, Shawanese & Deleweres passing through the nations Inhabiting the Lakes up to the [Menominee] on the Missisipi...and to the northward among nations unknown to those here,..." (ibid.p. 96). The Illinois promised to reveal the contents of the message to Cole as soon as they became known in the spring of 1768. But Croghan had already written to Johnson a week earlier that the anger of the Indians on the Upper Ohio bore promise of trouble to come (ibid. p. 89; see also pp. 156-8, 209). In November and December Croghan was informed of anti-British plans of the Indians to unite as one people (Peckham, 1939, pp. 41, 46). And in the spring of 1768 Morgan, writing to his partners from Kaskaskia, said that "There are also reports here, of the Sacks, Renards etc being badly disposed & it is said that the Wiotonans, Piankashaws & other Tribes on the Wabash have Evil Designs" (IHC 16: 225-6).

261

Events shortly began to reveal the substance in these reports. Early in May, 1768 John Jennings recorded in his journal the receipt of a letter at Fort Chartres from Cahokia indicating "that several Tribes of Indians, consisting of Sotie's or Chippewa's, Otawas, Poutewatimies, & Cecapous, had been at Paincourt" (ibid. p. 275). A party of Peoria, while on their hunt, met sixty Potawatomi who told them of their plan to attack the English. The Peoria passed this information on to a frenchman at Cahokia who notified the English at Fort Chartres (idem). The Kaskaskia, at the request of Cole, the Indian agent, went in pursuit of the Potawatomi who had captured a British soldier and his wife, but they failed to make contact (ibid. pp. 276-7). As soon as the capture became known, the Michigamea, whose village was three quarters of a mile from Fort Chartres, set out after the Potawatomi but returned empty handed (idem).

262 Additional hostilities of a similar nature were described by George Morgan. He wrote in July that a party of Indians from Vincennes had attacked his firm's hunters who had been out on the "Shawana River". These Indians, according to Morgan, "are a Mixture of Potawatomies, Piankishaws, Wiotonans Kickapous Miamis & Virmillion Tribes - but whether the Party that did the Mischief were of all or but One of those Nations - I cannot yet learn" (ibid. pp. 354, 363). What is of particular interest in Morgan's account is that he refers to all of these as "Post St. Vincent Indians". The following October (1768) General Gage, in a letter to Johnson, reports on the same event and states: "The Indians of the Ouabache, Miamis, Pouteatamies, and some Tribes of the Chippewas, which last killed the Boats crew [on the Shawnee River] last year, are those who are principaly concerned in committing Hostilities upon the Ohio" (ibid. p. 417).

With the exception of the Potawatomi and the Chippewa the Indians

mentioned by Morgan and Gage were from the Wabash and its tributaries. As
for their being from Vincennes, as stated by Morgan, this could only have been
temporary. All these groups probably participated in the attack upon the boat
in which the hunters from Fort Chartres were travelling. But their association
with Vincennes may derive from the fact that Captain Forbes, commandant at
Fort Chartres "received a Letter from One of my Correspondents at St. Vincent,
in which he says that the Indians of the Village were just arrived with Nine
English Scalps, and Eight Horses Loaded with Peltry etc etc They Attacked a
Hunting Party upon the Shawanese River that left that Place in April last,..."
(ibid. pp. 367, 415, 418). Apart from the previous statements there are no
indications that other than Piankashaw were at Vincennes.

An account of Baynton, Wharton and Morgan, certified by Commissary
Edward Cole and Captain Gordon Forbes at Fort Chartres on September 13, 1768,
reveals the distribution of presents to various tribes who came there
(ibid. pp. 405-408). Only the Kaskaskia and Peona are recorded in the account
of Baynton, Wharton and Morgan as receiving goods, although Forbes in a letter
to Gage the previous July (?), makes reference to the "four Tribes in this
District" which it can be assumed were Kaskaskia, Cahokia, Peoria and
Michigamea. On one occasion "Black Dog a Chief of the Piorias and sundry
Parties of his Nat [ion]...came here on their Return from Their Winters Hunt"
(ibid. p. 406). Later, the same chief "with a great Part of his Nation came
to acquaint us that they were going out on their summe[r] Hunt on the Grand
Prairies to Provide Meat for their Old Men,..." (ibid. p. 407). The Grand
Prairie extended north or northeast of Prairie du Rocher into Illinois (ibid.
p. 519). It seems that Baynton, Wharton and Morgan bought a "plantation"
which was "Situate in the Grand Prairie on the road between Fort Chartres &
Kaskaskias..." (Mason, 1890, p. 423).

263

It can be assumed that these Peoria were settled and hunting in English territory on the east side of the Mississippi, for a third mention of this group refers to "the Piorias at Pain Court, who had returned from their Hunt..." (IHC 16:406). In this case, however, the question may be raised as to whether they were hunting east or west of the Mississippi.

The Kaskaskia are recorded as receiving presents twice, from B., W. & M. Unfortunately the manuscript is burned in one crucial place: "Kaskaskias and other Indians living at and around [MS burned]..." What follows can be interpreted to mean that they were at this time on the west side of the Mississippi: "They begged, that as they had brought a Considerable Share of their Trade to this Side, they might receive Sincere Marks of our Friendship for them" (idem).

Other tribes who came to Fort Chartres in friendship were the Vermillion Piankashaw; "a Chief and Tribe of the Missouris, who returned from their Win [ter] Hunt"; "the Chief of the Osages with a large Party of warriors who came to Trade"; "Seven Chiefs of the Putowatamies, with with their Par [MS burned] bring back the two prisoners named Stewart (& his Wife) taken...from this place April last"; "a Chief of the Arcanzas and one of his Warriors, who...demanded to know, whether they may hereafter come and Trade with Us on the Same Terms with the rest of their Brethren"; "Pondiac and his Attendants...He had Wintered on the Wabash..." ; "The Grand Chief of the Osages..."; "Sundry Chiefs and Partys of Ottaways and Chippaways..." (ibid.).

According to the B.W. & M. account, therefore, the aforementioned tribes from both east and west of the Mississippi came to Fort Chartres during 1768 to extend the hand of friendship and to arrange for trade. It seems to bear out a report by Captain Forbes with reference to "the State of Commerce in the Ilinois Country" in which he indicated the desire of tribes on the

264

Missouri to trade with the English. In this connection he recommended the establishment of "Fort Dupice upon the Ilinois River, where the Traders may carry on a very extensive Trade with the Indians living upon the Missouri, they having frequently expressed a Desire of an open Trade with the English" (ibid. p. 382). The fort mentioned is probably an allusion to Peoria (idem fn 1) where Missouri River tribes began coming to trade as early as the latter part of the seventeenth century.

On September 30, 1768 Sir William Johnson conveyed to General Gage information he received from a Delaware Indian who had come from the Illinois-Wabash area. From the Kaskaskia chiefs "and other tribes of Indians who live in that Country" he learned of their anti-British feelings and their identification with the French and Spanish interests. A well-informed Shawnee there told the Delaware that all the Indians throughout the region "had engaged to Assist the French and Spaniards as far as St. Joseph's, and were ready to strike the English as soon as the French and Spaniards let them know they were Ready." Johnson's informant also learned that among the Wabash Indians only the Miami (Twightwees) and the Wea were friendly to the English "and while he was at Weoughtanon a Party of the Kicapos past by there with two English scalps which they had taken at Fort Chartres after he left it" (JP 12:601-3).

265

Nevertheless, trade and distribution of presents went on at Fort Chartres where, the journal of Col. Wilkins indicates, the Kaskaskia chief "Tomeroy" and his party were given presents on December 23, 1768. Twice in January, 1769 the Kickapoo came to trade and receive presents. In one case Wilkin's statement was "a large party of Kickapoes from the Wabash" A-344 These transactions were taking place at the very time (Jan. 21, 1769) that Johnson was referring to the following members of the "Western Confederacy" as malcontents who had broken the peace; Wea, Kickapoo, Piankashaw, Miami, Ottawa, and Illinois (JP 12:689-690).

Thomas Hutchins, who was based at Fort Chartres from November,1768 to October,1770 (Hutchins, 1904, p. 18), wrote in a letter dated November 15, 1768, that the Wea, Kickapoo, Piankashaw, and Mascouten reside on the Wabash (Dunn, 1894a,p. 420). These same groups, plus the Miami, are listed as tribes of the Wabash district in a Spanish document dated May 2, 1769 (Houck, 1909, 1:44-45; WHC 18:299-301). They, in addition to many other tribes, were accustomed to receiving presents from the French and Spanish authorities at St. Louis. In this report, certified by both the French commandant and his storekeeper, the tribes in question are grouped by geography. Those of the Illinois are Kaskaskia, Cahokia, Peoria, Michigamea. Apart from the ones already mentioned the only other grouping of particular interest for present purposes includes the Potawatomi, Chippewa, and Ottawa who are associated in part with the Illinois River. The geographical designation for these groups is: "Of the river San Joseph and that of Ylinneses."

266

On October 31, 1769 Don Pedro Piernas, appointed Spanish commandant at St. Louis, wrote a memorandum on his first stay in the Illinois country. He had moved to St. Louis from the Spanish fort at the mouth of the Missouri River. He writes: "In the short time of my residence in that post there came to bold discussions the tribes of the Osages, Ayoua, Kikapu, Masasten [Mascouten] Pou, Putatami [Potawatomi], Utoa [Ottawa], Putchicagu [Potawatomi of Chicago?], Renad [Fox], and others of the vicinity..." (Houck, 1909, 1:74; WHC 18:306). Piernas says further that to this Spanish fort came "the near and distant Indian tribes, both those of the Misisipi River, and those of the Misouri and its branches, whose names are contained in the enclosed report... The season of their greatest gathering is during the months of May and June.

At that time they descend the rivers in numerous parties with their traders to declare their furs. That is their first object..." (Houck, 1909, 1:73-74; WHC 18:305; the report to which Piernas refers was alluded to above in Houck 1:44-5). This statement appears to lend support, in part, to the contentions of Colonel Wilkins and others that "the French still carry away all the Trade..." (IHC 16:632,382,498). Additional information from Wilkins tends to substantiate this claim.

In December 1769 Colonel Wilkins, in a report from Fort Chartres, made a comparison of the commercial potentialities of the upper Mississippi with the Illinois River in which he concluded that the latter "is less considerable from the few Nations which inhabit it" (ibid. p. 633); but who they were was not indicated. It is apparent, however, that he did not include the Illinois (Peoria) among them. In listing the number of packs of peltry that might be obtained from certain tribes at proposed establishments he distinguishes the Peoria, Kaskaskia and Cahokia from groups on the Illinois River. At one point he states that the Peoria, Kaskaskia and Cahokia "might furnish 3 or 400 packs P [er] Annum" (idem); then he changes this grouping to "Peorias, Kaskaskias, and Wabash" who might provide 400 packs (ibid. p. 364). The Illinois River, he suggests, might produce 500 packs. He also thinks that "a Post at the Illinois" would attract trade from the Missouri River tribes in the amount of 1,000 packs, while the Wabash area would bring in 900 (idem).

267

Wilkins' Journal of his transactions with the Indians (A-344) reveals that throughout 1769 at Fort Chartres he dealt almost exclusively with the four groups of Illinois who came regularly to trade and receive presents. Nevertheless, there were occasional visits from others, east and west of the Mississippi; and once in August, the Arkansas came to trade. From the west the Osage and the Missouri each came to trade on two occasions. But from east of the Mississippi only the Kickapoo "from the Wabash" appeared three times for a fairly large trade.

Of the Illinois, the Peoria and the Michigamea are most often mentioned, especially during the fall and winter months, as coming in from the hunt to trade. The implication is that their hunting took place in an area not too far off, judging from the frequency with which parties of Michigamea and Peoria appeared at the fort. Once, on February 2, when Black Dog, "The Chief of the Peories" came in with a party for trade he indicated that the rest were "at their hunting ground which as he said was within Sight of the Smoak of this Fort,..." At this time the Peoria, or at least part of them, were at Cahokia (March 10 entry). More than a year later, on May 11, 1771 Wilkins again made reference to the arrival at Fort Chartres of "the Black dogg & party of the Peorias from Kahokie." But after the murder of Pontiac at Cahokia in April, 1769 by one of their number, the Peoria told Wilkins "that they intended to leave their village & come here under the protection of this Fort fearing Pondiacks followers...". Although Wilkins requested them "to keep their ground", on May 2 "The Peories arrived in 30 Canoes by water & a large party by land..." On May 10 Wilkins told "The 4 Chiefs and warriors of the Peorias" that they would be under his protection, but five days later five Illinois were scalped. This latter incident may be the one referred to by Cole in a letter written in June in which the Sac and Fox were said to have scalped six Kaskaskia Indians between Fort Chartres and their village (IHC 16:548). According to a letter written by General Gage on October 7, 1769 Wilkins wrote to him on June 30 that "there was great Danger to be expected from a number of Missouri Indians and nineteen Canoes of Sakis and Reynards" (IHC 16:630). But there is no mention of this by Wilkins in his journal.

Not only the Peoria came from Cahokia to settle with or near the Michigamea in the vicinity of the fort, but also another group of Illinois came from there. For on July 7 Wilkins recorded: "Came to trade and visit the Peyes [?] that lately (with their Chiefs) left their Village of Kehakie to Settle here with the Peories & Mitches..." All three groups joined together in a fortified village "on a rising Ground in full Sight (& within Cannon Shot) of the Fort..." This action was taken because news kept coming in of the hositle intent of other tribes, especially against the Peoria. When Black Dog and his party came to trade at Fort Chartres on February 2 he also asked "what news etc, as reports are Spread about that Several Nations from the Wabash are determin'd to Cut off the peories etc,...". On the 15th "A party of the Nation of the Mitches visited to know what news from the many reports of the other Nations..." Then on March 29 "The Chief and warriors of the Kaskaskias came to demand powder and lead to prepare their nation to defend themselves against Pondiac daily expected with some nations in 150 Canoes who have long since threaten'd to Cutt off the nations of the Illinois..."

269

But it was not until the murder of Pontiac that the Illinois were filled with the trepidation and anxiety that led them to band together near Fort Chartres. They were further induced to take measures for the common defence because of what they learned early in July. At that time three Peoria warriors "return'd from Visiting the Kickapoos on the Wabash above Post Vincent where a party of the Patawamies took from them a Peorie Indian (that went with those three men now return'd) & bound the man & told them they would keep him prisoner in their nation & would with Several other Nations go and Strike the English and Peories when the Indian Corn is ripe..." It was on the receipt of this news that the Peoria, Michigamea and "Payes" "join'd together and Fortified their Village with a kind of Stockade..." Wilkins estimated that

"there is near 500 in the Village," and they also had "near 100 large
Canoes..."

On July 31, 1769 Wilkins wrote in his journal that once again three
Peoria "had just arrived from the Wabash Indians who had declar'd that they
were going with belts to 10 nations demanding of them to go with them to
Strike the Peories, but that they would prevent the Stroke if possible, &
if oblig'd to go to the Peories had but little to apprehend there from..."
This news seemed to qualify the danger, and since their scouting parties
found no sign of the enemy the Illinois began to feel more secure. For the
remainder of 1769 there are no entries in the journal to indicate any hostile
intentions against the Illinois.

It was stated above that the Peoria and Michigamea were the most frequent visitors at Fort Chartres. While they did not come quite as often, the
270 Kaskaskia were also active in trade and receipt of presents. Wilkins records
that they came in on September 29, 1769 before "going to hunt on the Ohio."
There is a statement by Wilkins which seems to indicate that part of the
Kaskaskia or the Illinois were at St. Genevieve on the west side of the
Mississippi opposite Kaskaskia village. This is revealed in connection with
a Kaskaskia request to Wilkins that he appoint a new wearer of the King's
medal in place of the "fool fellow" who returned it. Wilkins writes that
the latter "had displeas'd all his nation by this Step & others since at
Kaskaskie & Misere [St. Genevieve] etc..." It is difficult to discern the
exact meaning. Is Wilkins referring to other Kaskaskia, or to other Illinois?
The same problem arises in the entry for September 20, 1770 where in relation
to the Kaskaskia he mentions "a Tribe of their Nation on the Spanish Side...".
Unfortunately, here, as in documents by others, the use of the term nation
is quite indiscriminate. In one context it may refer to the Illinois generally;

and in another, to one of the subdivisions. Still another statement of the
same type occurs in the Wilkins journal on April 17, 1771: "Baptist & Petagauge
& another Chief of the Kaskaskies & miser [St. Genevieve] Indians & party..."

All throughout that winter (1769-70) parties of Illinois kept coming
in from their hunt to trade. Rarely are the Cahokia mentioned--in fact, only
twice. The first occasion was in connection with a conference the four groups
of Illinois had with Wilkins on March 22. The second time was when, on
October 20, 1769, "A party of Kahokie warriors [came] to trade & Visited with
professions of Friendship etc,..."

At the end of 1769 or early in 1770, it seems, about half the Peoria
went up the Missouri River where they sojourned for approximately eighteen
months. This information comes from an entry Wilkins made in his journal on
June 1, 1771. On that date Black Dog, the Peoria chief came in and "brought
with him the other Chief and half the nation of Peorias that both been
absent for 1 1/2 year up the Missoury, they made heavy demands for
everything..."

271

At the outset of the year 1770 goods were delivered to the Spanish
commandant at St. Louis for distribution as presents to twelve tribes.
Although the Sac, Fox and Chippewa [Santeux?] were among them, none of the
tribes from the tribes from the Wabash are on the list. Of the Illinois,
only the Kaskaskia are mentioned (Kinnaird, 1946, 2:155). This may explain
the references cited above which, presumably, indicated the presence of
Kaskaskia or other Illinois at St. Genevieve, below St. Louis.

During the first three months of 1770 the Peoria, Kaskaskia, and
Michigamea appeared regularly at Fort Chartres to trade. In addition Wilkins
records that on March 20 a "Party of Kickapoes to trade & enquire for News,
told me much of belts flying about from other Nations to Strike the English

etc etc.--". The next day marked the first of several entries by Wilkins in 1770 concerning the possibility of hostilities against the Peoria or the Illinois generally. This was reminiscent of a similar state of affairs during the year preceding. Thus, on March 21 "Black Dogg Chief of the Peories & part of that Nation return'd from their winter hunt to trade & Visit & report the Combination of Nations Against the Illinois..." Then, three days later the journal records that "A Chief and another party of the Peorias just return'd from hunting & to trade Visit etc talk'd much of their Apprehensions of many Nations coming to cut them off this Summer & demanded Strongly to be permitted to build their Village close to this Fort,..." Wilkins then states that he "persuaded them to return to their old village about 14 hundred yards from the Fort..." In view of impending hostilities against them the Peoria "demanded to have a war dance in the Fort..."

272   If the Sac and Fox were among those planning further action against the Illinois, as was the case the year before, then the "friendly speech" they sent to Wilkins suggested otherwise. Wilkins refers to the Sac and Fox on April 6 and May 7. On the latter date he reports having received a message from St. Ange, at St. Louis, "who declar'd that he had done his best to prevent 7 nations coming Against the Illinois Indians for Pondiacks death..." It seems that the murder of Pontiac kept haunting the Illinois.

Apart from the Kickapoo trading party of March 20 there are again, as in 1769, few references to the Wabash tribes during 1770. On March 29 a war party of Kickapoo came through to receive provisions on their homeward journey. On May 19 there is a reference to a party of Mascouten having been killed by Cherokee near Vincennes, "The Muskato Chief" being the sole survivor. On July 17 and on August 9 and 10 Wilkins reports having conferred with Piankashaw chiefs.

After October 15 and 20, 1770 Wilkins states that there were few visits by any of the Illinois, "The nations having been far off to hunt..." On those dates only parties of Michigamea came in "from hunting" for powder, ball, and other supplies. Subsequent to these visits the first entry in Wilkins' journal refers to a party of Kaskaskia who came in "from hunting" on February 12, 1771.

If in the late fall of 1770 and in the winter of 1770-1771 the Illinois were hunting at too great a distance from Fort Chartres to make trading visits, there is, nevertheless, evidence of where the Kaskaskia were hunting during the early summer of 1770. This information comes from the record of the proceedings of a court of inquiry which was convened at Fort Chartres on September 20 of that year. Included in the testimony is a statement that "in the Month of June or July last [1770],...the Kaskaskia Indians... [were] out upon a Prairie a Hunting about one hundred Miles from the Village of Kaskaskia" (Mason, 1890, pp. 437-438). From the context this area is obviously east of the Mississippi. 273

The spring of 1771 saw the Illinois area on the Mississippi aroused by intermittent alarms of impending enemy attacks. Reports of strange Indians skulking about sent parties of Illinois out on scouting forays with little success. Apparently enemy probes succeeded in killing a Michigamea woman and in capturing an English soldier from the garrison, but no battle contact was effected. Wilkins suspected that the Potawatomi and Kickapoo were involved. On the basis of letters received from Wilkins in May, 1771, Gage later wrote that the Kickapoo were responsible for "killing three or four people at the Illinois" (Gage, 1931, 1:307-8). The Kickapoo were also reported to be engaged in other depredations against the English (ibid. p. 310); and Maisonville "heard" that they went against the Illinois and took four scalps (JP, 8:225).

The writer of a letter from Kaskaskia told that in July, 1771 he was captured
by eight Kickapoo and taken to their village at Ouiatanon. He was subsequently ransomed by French traders from Detroit. Other information in this
letter contributed to the general picture of Kickapoo depredations which
occurred since the arrival of the English in the Illinois country. But when
two Kickapoo came to report that the Piankashaw chief Black Fly at Vincennes
was in great need Wilkins sent him some supplies. Subsequently, he gave
assistance to an old Piankashaw chief and his party from Vincennes. There
was also a visit by "The Musqueta Chief and warriors from the Wabash..." In
spite of such distress, according to Gage the Wabash tribes refused to permit
English traders among them, presumably because "The French Traders have
instigated those Nations, against the English" (idem). Because the St.
Joseph Potawatomi had also been engaged in depredations against the English
(ibid. p. 310; A-344, p. 22), Gage felt constrained to find "Means to reduce
the Pouteatamies and Ouabache Indians to Peace, by forceable Measures;..."
(Gage, 1931, 1:311).

274

On May 11, 1771 there came to Fort Chartres "the Black dogg & party
of the Peorias from Kahokie with the greatest Apprehensions of that nation
being soon to be Struck by many other Nations,..." This visit was followed
by another from "the Black dog with thundering reports of nations coming to
Strike in this Country,..." But despite all these alarms there seem to have
been no hostilities in the area against the Illinois other than the forays
of the Kickapoo, which were directed chiefly against the British (A-379).

Twenty Chicakasaw warriors who had intended making a strike on the
Wabash came to Fort Chartres instead; and Wilkins took the opportunity to
arrange a council of peace which included the Illinois, Chickasaw, and
Shawnee. Later in the year, on November 20, the Kaskaskia chief came to

Fort Chartres from the hunt and "reported that a party of Chickasaws in great friendship had past the hunting time with himself and party..."

As regards trade, Wilkins reports the occasional visits of parties of Illinois for this purpose during 1771. The only other group mentioned in this connection is the Missouri who came on three occasions.

Wilkins considers the Michigamea "a weak & a poor Nation yet their being near this Fort are to be encouraged, as they bring useful Intellegence of Sculking partys of the Enemy etc,..."

Early in October, 1771 Sir William Johnson sent Maisonville on a good will mission to the Indians on the Wabash (JP 12:930-1). In his report of this journey Maisonville included the following data: Wea and Kickapoo villages were situated opposite each other at Ouiatanon and had a combined total of six hundred warriors. At the Vermillion River there were "about sixty [Piankashaw] men --", while at Vincennes there were only ten warriors because the rest of the Piankashaw had left out of fear of the Cherokee (ibid. p. 931). Maisonville also included in his report the statement that "the Illinois are often at War with the foxes & Sacs --" (ibid. p. 932; see also pp. 945, 946, 949).

275

According to Johnson, Maisonville was "my Resident at Ouiaghtonon", who wrote that in December, 1771 a war party of eleven Kickapoo captured two Englishmen at the mouth of the Wabash and took the "prisoners to their wintering place about 120 miles from Ouiaghtonon." Maisonville also reported the ransom of an Englishman in August, 1771 "who had been taken last Spring at the Illinois by the Kickapous..." (JP 8:453).

The conclusion of the Journal of Transactions which Wilkins kept at Fort Chartres covers a brief period of 1772. Apart from mentioning that some Michigamea, who came to trade early in the year, told him that the Spanish commandant was trying to win their favor with presents, the only important item is the disaffection of the Wabash tribes. As a result Wilkins proposed "to see the Chiefs of the Kickapoes, Muskutains, Piankishas, Wiatanons & Potawatamis if mett with." In addition, the Kaskaskia chief reported that he had met two Indians from the Maumee who said that "part of their nation" was on the warpath against the town of Prairie Du Rocher for the killing of one of their number (A-344 pp. 30-31).

This last piece of news fits into a pattern of harrassment from the Wabash area which persisted in 1772. In the spring "The Pouteatamies killed a soldier near to Fort Chartres...and it was Said that hostile Partys of Kikapous and other Indians of the Ouabache were lurking in the Woods,..." (JP 8:551). Not long after, Major Hamilton and his troops, on the way from Fort Pitt to Fort Chartres, met about forty Kickapoo without incident (idem). After destroying Fort Chartres in accordance with a British plan Hamilton left Captain Lord in command at Kaskaskia (Gage, 1931, 1:332). During the summer of 1772 there were a number of Indians from the Ohio at that post. And according to a letter of General Gage, "They were of some use to Captain Lord in bringing the Kikapous to Kaskaskies, a Tribe from the Ouabache who at times have killed and captivated People at the Ilinois, with whom the Captain hoped to make a Peace, that would render the Communication with that Country more secure" (ibid. p. 343). This lack of security on the lines of communication was implicit in a memorial of the French settlers at Vincennes to General Gage on September 18, 1772 in which they referred to "...the center between Detroit, Fort Pitt, and the Illinois country [as] the thorough-fare of the nations..." (IMH 34:211).

In addition to the depredations of the Kickapoo, the Potawatomi of St. Joseph had over the past three years killed and plundered English traders

276

in the vicinity. The British suspected that the French traders were instigating those Indians in order to obtain the advantage over their rivals
(Gage, 1931, 1:348).

On July 23, 1773 Patrick Kennedy set out from Kaskaskia with several
traders on an expedition up the Illinois River to explore for copper mines.
On August 1 they "stopped at the Piorias wintering ground" which was "About
a quarter of a mile from the river, on the eastern side of it..." Kennedy
describes it as "...a meadow of many miles long, and five or six miles broad,"
dotted with numerous inter-connecting small lakes. This general area of the
Illinois River was forty eight miles from its confluence with the Mississippi,
and contained "great plenty of buffalo and deer" (Kennedy, 1797, p. 507).
On August 7 Kennedy's party arrived at "...The old Pioria fort and village
on the western shore of the river, and at the southern end of a lake called
the Illinois [Peoria] lake;..." Although the houses were still standing
the fort had been destroyed by fire. The entire place seems to have been
vacant. At this point they were 210 miles up from the Mississippi (ibid.
p. 509). The lake contained "great plenty of fish" and the land an "abundance of cherry, plum, and other fruit trees" (idem). Although they eventually met some French traders above the Fox River they did not encounter
any Indians.

277

Such a report of direct observation along the course of the Illinois
River is an unusual event for this general period, especially by comparison
with reports coming from the Wabash. The obvious explanation is that the
posts on the Wabash, Vincennes and Ouiatanon, were continuously occupied
since their establishment by the French. And even in this period Sir William
Johnson employed a Frenchman, Maisonville, to supply him with information.
The resident tribes on the Wabash are thus relatively well known; but

on-the-spot observations of tribal events and movements on the Illinois River have been rare or non-existent since at least 1763. Kennedy's location of the Peoria wintering area is the first specific reference that far north since that group, or a part of it, took up residence on the Mississippi.

However, July 5, 1773 William Murray, representing the Illinois Land Company,"negotiated for the purchase of two large tracts, one lying between the Ohio and the Mississippi rivers, and the other on the Illinois river" (Alvord, 1920, p. 302; see also ASP-PL 2:88-89 and 96-98). According to Murray in June, 1773 "I held several public conferences with several tribes of the Illinois Nations of Indians, at Kaskaskia village;..." (Alvord, op.cit. p. 301). The Indian participants and signatories in this transaction were chiefs of the Kaskaskia, Peoria, and Cahokia (ASP-PL 2:97).

A partially burned memorandum from Maisonville to Johnson written in late September,1773 apparently refers to the Indians (Piankashaw) at Vincennes and on the Vermillion River as the same tribe. Among the former are 110 warriors, and the latter, 125. The Kickapoo village near Ouiatanon, on the north side of the Wabash has 250 warriors; the Wea on the other (south) side of the river are said to have about 270 (JP 8:894-896).

Early that same month Captain Lord, in command at Kaskaskia, had written to General Haldimand who then conveyed to General Gage the information "that two French citizens have (after the manner of Mr. Murray) bought all the land belonging to one of the tribes of the Illinois, who were formerly very numerous and who are now reduced to a dozen warriors" (Dunn, 1894, p. 434). In this document there is no indication whatever as to which Illinois are meant or where the lands were situated.

In 1773 Sir William Johnson had sent a Seneca chief as an emissary with peace messages to "the Hurons, and Ottawas at Detroit, Twightweis, Miamies,

278

and other Western Nations living on the Branches of Mississippi,..." Early
in January,1774 this chief and representatives of some of the Indians he had
visited met with Johnson to deliver the replies (JP 8:1044-61). The answer
of the Hurons referred to the "Twightwees [Miami] who are the head of a
Confederacy of Nine Nations living upon the Wabache, as far as Fort
Chartres..." (ibid. pp. 1044-5). The reply of the Twightwees was in the
following vein: "...we the Twightwees who are the principal Nation from this
to Fort Chartre have determined in Council to take all your Belts, and
Messages, and communicate them truly, and honestly to the whole Confederacy,
with our Advice and Direction to receive them, and make them known to their
Young People, and for the future to drop all Hostilities against the White
People,..." (ibid. p. 1046).

Present at this conference was also a Shawnee chief who had delivered
messages from the Iroquois "to the Nations living about Fort Chartres..."
In addition to the friendly reply which the Shawnee chief delivered, he also
brought "a Message from the three Illenois Indian Nations called the
Kaskaskeys by which they acquaint the Six Nations that they cou'd not comply
with their desire to come to their Country, on account of the nations about
them being in continual war with some Nation, or other who they must always
be in dread of being struck by, and therefore cou'd not leave their Families
exposed to them. but if one general Peace was brought about with the Indians
in that Country, they wou'd with Pleasure receive their Call, and attend"
(ibid. p. 1049).

The circumstances mentioned in this reply are sufficiently vague so
that there are a few possibilities as to what the Kaskaskia or Illinois,
generally, had in mind. They could have meant the Kickapoo or Potawatomi
incursions to which reference was made above. There were also the Chickasaw

forays against the Wabash Indians. On the other hand, the kind of thing implied may have been contained in an Iroquois accusation against the Ottawa at this conference, in which it was stated that Ottawa "young men had gone to War against the Fort Chartre or Kaskaskey Indians, and killed, and scalped two of them last Spring..." (ibid. p. 1050). Since this act was committed without the knowledge of the Ottawa people their chief, who was present, asked Croghan, McKee, "...and the Senecas to intercede for them, and accomodate the Breach with the Kaskaskeys" (ibid. p. 1051). It is possible, however, that the Ottawa war party originally had had quite another objective.

Attributed to the year 1774 is a table of distances from Detroit to the Illinois country via Fort Wayne, Ouiatanon and Vincennes (MPHS 10:247-248; also Dunn, 1894, pp. 435-438). Remarks in this document by an anonymous author offer the following information:

280

1) There are "a few" Potawatomi near Fort St. Joseph.

2) At the confluence of the Kankakee and Iroquois Rivers "is a village of 14 large cabans of Mascontains".

3) At the juncture of the Des Plaines and Kankakee Rivers "is a village of Puttawatamees of 12 large Cabans."

4) The Wea are on the left bank of the Wabash opposite Fort Ouiatanon "and the Reccapories [Kickapoo] are round the Fort, in both villages are about 1000 men able to bear arms".

5) A Piankashaw village "of upwards of 150 men" is situated a mile above the mouth of the Vermillion River.

A manuscript which is essentially a bill of sale reveals that the Piankashaw in council at Vincennes on October 18, 1775 purported to sell to a French merchant, Louis Viviat, representing the Wabash Land Company, several extensive tracts of land along the Wabash. The total area described was

seventy leagues (175 miles) in width along both sides of the Wabash and
ninety-three leagues (232 miles) in length, extending from Cat River, 130
miles above Vincennes, to the mouth of the Wabash (Alvord, 1915, pp. 1-6; A-5;
IHC 1:222).

The following June (1776) a petition to the Virginia Convention from
the committee of West Fincastle on the Kentucky River stated that the Delaware
"are now settled near the mouth of the Waubash..." The chiefs of this Indian
community sent a message to the committee that the English were to confer with
the Kickapoo at Vincennes and that the latter might attack the Americans
(IHC 8:15).

In April 1777 Gabriel Cerré, a trader, made a sworn statement before
Rocheblave, British commandant at Kaskaskia, that after "having been among
the peorias on the River of the Illinois," he spent the winter of 1776-7
"with the Kickapoos and Mascoutens at a place called the bad land..." While
he was with these Indians, who inhabited "the Village of the Raven on the
River of the Illinois," two Kickapoo arrived with a message for the chief
"fair weather" from Rocheblave (Mason, 1890, pp. 389-390). Although it was
apparently named and was referred to as a "village" by Cerré there is no
indication as to whether this was actually a settlement or a winter camp.
Thus, while Kickapoo and Mascouten spent the winter on the Illinois river at
the bad land or "La Mauvaise Terre" (Kinnaird, 1946, 2:415), Peoria were
elsewhere on the same stream at about the same time.

At the beginning of 1781 a small Spanish detachment of militia under
the command of Mayet (Malliet) had been stationed by Cruzat at or near the
site of the Kickapoo-Mascouten "village" where Cerré had wintered in 1776-7.
Whether or not Mayet actually was in such a village at the time, he wrote to
Lieutenant Governor Cruzat from "La Mauvaise Terre on the Illinois River" on

281

January 9, 1781 (idem). But the point to be made at the moment is that Mayet had been on the Illinois at least as early as 1777; for in the winter of 1777-8 (January 26) the inhabitants, or traders, of Peoria sent a communication to Rocheblave, British commander at Kaskaskia, in which they affirmed "the arrival of your letter to F. Maillet and of your word to be carried by him to the Mascoutin chiefs..." (Mason, 1890, pp. 397-8).

This reference to Mayet and the Mascouten could mean that the Spaniards were based in the vicinity of the Kickapoo-Mascouten village or camp at the time (January 1778). It would indicate, also, that those Indians were favorably disposed to the Spanish. Elsewhere in the same document it is revealed that they have "prejudices and objections" against the British, a state of mind which Rocheblave had already reported on May 8, 1777 (ibid. p. 391). On that date, in a reference to the "Canadians" on the Illinois River (at Peoria; see MPHC 9:389) Rocheblave wrote that the Indians "so far will not permit the native English to penetrate there, which is an injury to commerce" (Mason, 1890, p. 391).

282

In this same letter, which he wrote to Lieutenant Governor Hamilton of Detroit, Rocheblave said that some time in the spring of 1777 the Illinois had experienced a foray by the Sac and Fox. This may have some connection with a remark made the following month (June 1777) by DePeyster, British commandant at Michilimackinac, that "the savages of La Baye and those of the Illinois Country are constantly at War, with one another" (MPHC 10:273). The use of the word "constantly" seems to be an exaggeration.

Another letter by Rocheblave, written June 1, 1777, mentions Potawatomi on the Illinois River, but gives no indication of location (Mason, 1890, p. 393). Included with the reference to the Potawatomi are other groups: "I have here a party of Delawares, and a collection of Kickapoos, Mascoutens and Pottawatomies from the River of the Illinois" (idem). Rocheblave, incidentally, blames the Spanish for the hostility of the last three against the British. Although Spanish responsibility was alluded to by the letter of the Peoria traders to Rocheblave at the beginning of 1778, it did not prevent Rocheblave from seeking Mayet's assistance in an effort to overcome the "coolness on the part of the savages..." (ibid. pp. 397-8). At any rate, Rocheblave's letter of June 1 seems to associate Kickapoo, Mascouten and Potawatomi with the Illinois River.

In his report of November 15, 1777 Cruzat also included the Potawatomi among the tribes receiving presents at St. Louis. He locates them, with 150 warriors, on the St. Joseph River and states that not only are they "somewhat in revolt" but they also "commit many thefts in this district" (Houck 1:147). Four months later, March 1778, George Morgan in a letter from Fort Pitt included a list of tribes and the number of men among them. The Potawatomi situated at Detroit and Lake Michigan have 400 men. He groups together the following tribes "on Ouabache" with a combined total of 800 men: Piankashaw, Kickapoo, Mascouten, "Vermillions" (Piankashaw), and the Wea (A-275).

283

Morgan's data on the Wabash tribes differs considerably from the information in a letter by Edward Abbott the British Lieutenant Governor and Superintendent at Vincennes. Having been recently appointed and arrived at this post he wrote to Governor Carleton on May 26, 1777 stating that along the Wabash River "are several Indian Towns" among which "the most considerable is the Ouija [Wea], where it is said there are 1,000 men capable to bear arms, I found them so numerous and needy, I could not pass without great expense..." (Dunn, 1894a, p. 440). The disparity between the figures given by Morgan and Abbott may be diminished significantly if we accept the latter's attribution of 1,000 men to the Wea as actually including all the Wabash tribes. In this way there is a net difference of 200 between the two estimates (see Hutchins, 1904, p. 136).

At this juncture it might be well to introduce data from one of the appendices (No. 3) in Hutchins' "Topographical Description" (ibid. pp. 135-7). The appendix consists of a list of tribes, and information on each, which clearly derives from the same source as that in Croghan's "private journal" of 1765-6 discussed earlier (A-170). Some of the data in both are identical, but there are some significant differences. One point should be made at the outset, however. The numeral given by Croghan after the name of each tribe pertains to "the number of their fighting Men" in the Hutchins table. That the same meaning is attached to Croghan's figures is evident from his statement on the Sioux.

284 Hutchins' work was originally published in 1778 in London where he had arrived before the outbreak of war with the colonies. The information on which both his map and "Topographical Description" are based was acquired during the war with France and subsequently until 1775 (Hutchins, 1904, pp. 22-3). Croghan's "private journal", on the other hand, covers the period from May 15, 1765 until December 13, 1766.

As stated above, comparison of these two sources reveals some revisions and at least one significant error made by Hutchins. According to Croghan there were 400 (warriors) among the Chippewa living "near the entrance of Lake Superior & not far from Fort St. Mary" whose hunting grounds were situated "Thereabouts". He adds that "There are several villages of Chipawaes settled along the Banks of Lake Superior, but as I have no knowledge of that Country cannot ascertain their number".

In Hutchins the Chippewa become Kickapoo, and their hunting grounds, instead of "Thereabouts", become "About Lake Superior". This may be a concise

form of Croghan's added sentence. It is quite obvious, on the basis of the
information available on both these groups, that the geographical locale of
dwelling and hunting grounds applies to the Chippewa, not to the Kickapoo.
Since Croghan's statement about the Chippewa villages along the shores of
Lake Superior is written in the first person it would appear that he obtained
and recorded the information originally and that he was the source of Hutchins'
table. Comparison of the information on the Sioux may also be used to support
the theory that Hutchins used Croghan as the basis for his table of tribes.

Whereas Croghan mentions the Kickapoo only once, in the following
context: "Kickapoos Outtagamies Musquatans Miscothins Outtasacks Musquakeys
4000," Hutchins also includes them in the same grouping with the same number
of warriors. The dwelling and hunting grounds are also stated in identical
fashion by both men. To quote from Hutchins, these groups dwell "On Lake
Michigan and between it, and the Missisippi" while their hunting grounds are
"Where they respectively reside" (ibid. p. 136).

285

The Kickapoo appear a third time in Hutchins' list together with the
Piankashaw, Mascouten and Wea. With a total of 1000 warriors among them,
these tribes are situated "On the Wabash and its branches," and they occupy
hunting grounds "Between the mouth of the Wabash and the Miami Rivers". But
in place of these four Wabash tribes Croghan lists in one group the Wea - 300
(warriors); Piankashaw - 300 (warriors); "Shoghkeys" (Sac?) - 200 (warriors).
This grouping of tribes lives, according to Croghan, "On the branches of the
Ouabache near Fort Ouiatanon", which is not quite the same as Hutchins' "On
the Wabash and its branches". The hunting grounds of Croghan's grouping,
"Between Ouiatanon & the Miammies [Maumee]" is significantly different from
the location of those occupied by Hutchins' Wabash tribes, "Between the mouth
of the Wabash and the Miami Rivers". On the face of it the statement by

Hutchins seems to imply that these hunting grounds are east of the Wabash, although the same is not necessarily true of their "dwelling grounds".

In connection with a statement on the "fort" of Ouiatanon in the "Topographical Description" Hutchins writes: "The neighbouring Indians are the Kickapoos, Musquitons, Piankashaws, and a principal part of the Ouiatanons. The whole of these tribes consists, it is supposed, of about 1,000 warriors" (Imlay, 1797, p. 497).

Hutchins reduces by one half the total number of Illinois as listed by Croghan. The latter states that there are 300 Kaskaskia and an equal number of Illinois. But the figure of 300 warriors in Hutchins, is the combined total of the Kaskaskia, Peoria, and Michigamea. The dwelling grounds are identically described in both sources, except that Croghan refers to the settlements as French. Hutchins says only that the Illinois live "Near the settlements in the Illinois country". While Croghan is silent on the question of hunting grounds, Hutchins places them "In the Illinois country."

In the "Topographical Description" Hutchins, after locating the European village of Kaskaskia five and one-half miles up the river of the same name, writes: "three miles northerly of Kaskaskias, is a village of Illinois Indians (of the Kaskaskias tribe), containing about 210 persons and 60 warriors. They were formerly brave and warlike, but are degenerated into a drunken and debauched tribe, and so indolent, as scarcely to procure a sufficiency of skins and furs to barter for clothing" (ibid. pp. 500-501). This reference to the Kaskaskia is followed by another pertaining to the rest of the members of that tribe: "One mile higher up the Mississippi than fort Chartres, is a village settled by 170 warriors of the Piorias and Mitchigamias (two other tribes of the Illinois Indians)" (ibid. p. 501).

286

Croghan and Hutchins both agree that living near Detroit and hunting about Lake Erie are 150 Potawatomi warriors in addition to 250 Wyandot and 400 Ottawa. There is also agreement that there are Potawatomi and Ottawa living near St. Joseph. Croghan, however, states that each of the last two has 150 warriors while Hutchins allots that number to the Ottawa but claims 200 for the Potawatomi. As for the hunting grounds of these two groups Croghan places them "Therabouts" to St. Joseph; but Hutchins states that they hunt in "The country between Lake Michigan and the Miami Fort [site of Fort Wayne]". This description seems to place their hunting area in southern Michigan and northern Indiana.

Both sources state that the "Twightwees" (Miami) have 250 fighting men, dwell near Fort Miami, and hunt "where they reside". This area, then, would be contiguous with that of the St. Joseph tribes.

According to Hutchins the only groups dwelling and hunting in the "Illinois Country" are the Kaskaskia, Peoria, and Michigamea. His map of 1778, published with the "Topographical Description", labels this area distinctly between the Mississippi and Illinois Rivers on the west and the Wabash on the east; the northern periphery is the Illinois Kankakee, while the Ohio forms the southern boundary (see also Imlay, p. 499).

287

Comparison of Hutchins with Croghan, and inference that may be drawn from the comparison, suggests the following conclusion. The basic information as recorded by Croghan was obtained in 1766. In that year both men accompanied Captain Harry Gordon's expedition from Fort Pitt down the Ohio and up the Mississippi to Fort Chartres. It is Croghan alone who probably sought such information and recorded it. Hutchins could have made a copy which he later revised, in part, before publication in 1778. It is reasonable to assume that Croghan was the one responsible for this information in view of the fact that he was a Deputy Superintendent of Indian Affairs in

the Northern District under Sir William Johnson. His inclusion of the Sac
(?) with the Wea and Piankashaw on the Wabash is confusing. Although Hutchins
improved on this, he, at the same time, committed a glaring error by replacing Chippewa with Kickapoo on Lake Superior.

It would be well to bear in mind that the terminal date of Hutchins'
direct knowledge and observations can be no later than 1775. The possibility
that he also incorporated information which he might have obtained from
other sources subsequent to that date can not be excluded.

X - 1777-1795

The activity of the Wabash tribes is referred to in a letter of George Rogers Clark written in the summer or fall of 1777 in which he wrote that Rocheblave had "by large presents engaged the Waubash Indians to invade the frontiers of Kentucky..." and was also employing the same methods to stimulate the western Indians to war against the Americans (IHC 8:31).

Early in the summer of 1778, Clark led an American invasion of the Illinois country. He took Kaskaskia and Cahokia from the English and followed this with the capture of Vincennes and Ouiatanon. He later wrote that the Kaskaskia, Peoria, and Michigamea "immediately treated for peace". He then sent Captain Helm "to the Chief of the Kickebues & Peankeshaws residing at Post St. Vincents desireing them to lay down their Tomahawk..." (IHC 8:124).

The previous November (1777) Cruzat had located the Kickapoo and Mascouten near Vincennes (Houck, 1909, 1:146-7). But he had made no mention of the Piankashaw, presumably because they were not receiving presents from him at St. Louis.

According to Clark the message he sent with Helm to the Kickapoo and Piankashaw not only won over those two tribes, but it also had an influence on others as much as 500 miles away. At Cahokia there soon gathered large numbers of Indians among whom were Chippewa, Ottawa, Potawatomi, Miami, Sac, Fox, Winnebago and others east of the Mississippi (IHC 8:125).

Despite Clark's view of the favorable disposition of the Indians the British had reason to believe that affairs were quite otherwise. In late June and early July 1778 chiefs of the Wea and Kickapoo, the latter also representing the Mascouten, met with Lieutenant Governor Hamilton at Detroit and affirmed their tie to the British cause (MPHC 9:452-458; IHC 1:319-328). The behavior of these groups was not only a reflection of prevailing Indian

289

reaction to the westward movement of American settlers. More specifically it was probably a result of the Piankashaw sale of lands along the Wabash in October 1775 to the Wabash Land Company (MPHC 9:475,476,480).

The following September Hamilton held a similar conference with the Ottawa, Chippewa and Potawatomi (ibid. pp. 482-483). And on October 5 he received a report that Ducoigne, the Illinois chief, came to Ouiatanon and informed the British commandant there of the contents of a message from Clark to the Wabash Indians (ibid. p. 486). Nevertheless, as late as November Patrick Henry, Governor of Virginia, wrote, on the basis of information from Captain Helm at Vincennes, that "the Wabash and Upper Indians, consisting of the Piankashaws, Tawaws [Ottawa?], Peorias, Delawares, Pekakishaws [Kickapoo?], Masketans, and some of the Shawnese chiefs, had...pledged their fidelity to the United States" (IHC 8:73; A-241,242,243).

290   DeLeyba, Spanish commander at St. Louis offered another view of the Indian position in July 1778 in a report to the Spanish Governor-General. After mentioning the Kickapoo and Mascouten among the tribes who came to welcome him, he wrote: "The war with the English is causing a great number of Indian tribes to go from one side to the other without knowing which side to take;..." (Kinnaird, 1946, 2:298).

Early in October 1778 Hamilton set out from Detroit with a force of militia and about seventy Indians (MPHC 9:484-5, 487) in an unsuccessful effort to retake the Illinois-Wabash area from Clark. He subsequently wrote from Ouiatanon on December 4, that along the way he was joined by two hundred Indians of several tribes, including the St. Joseph Potawatomi, Eel River Miami, Wea, Kickapoo, and the Potawatomi of Tippecanoe River (IHC 1:220). By the time he arrived at Vincennes the number of Indians may have risen to as many as 400, or even 800 (IHC 8:266-7).

On October 24 Hamilton reached the Miami villages at the head of the
Maumee River. There he held council with the chiefs of the Ottawa of Detroit
and Au Glaize River, Miami, Chippewa, Wyandot, and Shawnee; and he smoked
the pipes which had been given him by the Kickapoo, Mascouten, Wea, Shawnee,
and Cherokee (Hamilton, 1951, pp. 114-115). He also conferred with the St.
Joseph Potawatomi who came to the Miami village. The Piankashaw chief,
Grande Couette, "declared he should act in conformity with his elder Brothers,
meaning the [Kickapoo and Wea]" (ibid. p. 116).

Descending the Wabash, Hamilton and his forces camped above the mouth
of the Eel River from November 18 to 24. A messenger from the Eel River
Miami came to tell Hamilton that they were eagerly awaiting his arrival as
were the Wea at Ouiatanon. On the 19th he "met" the Eel River Miami and
Tippecanoe Potawatomi, the latter declaring their neutrality. But Hamilton's
interpreter told him that "several of the Miamis and Pouteouattamies of this
district meant to accompany us." On the 29th he visited the Miami village
and received their support (ibid. pp. 124-125).

On November 25, between the Eel and Tippecanoe Rivers, Hamilton
received a visit from some leading men of the Wea, and again on the 27th near
the mouth of the Tippecanoe. The next day Hamilton camped about a mile above
the Wea village which, he estimates, had a population of about 900. He went
to the cabin of one of the chiefs, White Head, who expressed his pleasure on
seeing Hamilton and told him "that the Chiefs who were out at their hunting
ground were not very distant and could readyly be summoned..." Hamilton
records that "The few Indians at this wintering ground had killed an amazing
quantity of game -." White Head also told him of the displeasure of "all
the Indians" over the sale of the Wabash lands by Old Tobacco, the Piankashaw
chief (ibid. pp. 131-134).

291

It is apparent that at the time of Hamilton's visit, or perhaps because of it, the Wea were hunting in an area not too far distant from their village. They not only had brought in "an amazing quantity of game" but "the six pounder was fired frequently to draw in the Indians from their hunting" (ibid. p. 133).

On December 2 a French trader from the post on the west side of the Wabash went for "some of the Chiefs in the Neighbourhood" and reported that two of the Kickapoo chiefs, although reluctant at first, were persuaded to come. Another chief returned "from his hunting ground 25 leagues distant..." Hamilton met with "all the Chiefs", whom he pleased "by smoaking out of the Calumets presented me by the Shawanoes and Quiquaboes at Detroit..." The Kickapoo chief who spoke at the council assured Hamilton that in the spring they would begin hostilities against the Americans. According to Hamilton the Kickapoo population in this village was approximately 960 of which at least 192, and possibly 320, were warriors (ibid. pp. 135-137).

292

Resuming his journey down river on December 5, Hamilton camped on the 7th about two leagues below the Vermillion, noting that the village on that river was unoccupied then because the inhabitants were out on the winter hunt (ibid. p. 139). On December 10 camp was made in the vicinity of Terre Haute, and the next afternoon Hamilton's forces arrived at the Piankashaw wintering ground and camped "a little below their Village". Hamilton conferred with the chief Black Fly who "rejoyced at our arrival" and said he had been waiting expectantly for two months. They smoked the Kickapoo calumet and Hamilton reassured Black Fly that he had nothing to fear from the tribes accompanying him (ibid. pp. 140-143); see also IHC 8:181 re Piankashaw at Vincennes).

It thus appears that Hamilton secured the alliance of virtually all the tribes along the Wabash. Before arriving at Vincennes Hamilton recorded passing "the Quarry", a Piankashaw wintering ground (Hamilton, 1951, p. 147).

While Hamilton was at Vincennes, and before it was recaptured by Clark's forces, he met with chiefs of the following tribes on January 26, 1779: Shawnee, Delaware, Wyandot, Ottawa, Chippewa, Miami, Wea, Piankashaw (ibid. p. 168; also IHC 1:394-397). A few days later "A Chief of the Peoria nation arrived with six of his followers, spoke highly in favor of the English,..." The next day this chief "declared his intention to act in concert with his brethren being sensible the English alone were able to provide for the Indians,..."

After Clark had sent Hamilton, his officers, and some of his men prisoners to Williamsburg he called "together the Neighbouring Nations, Peankeshaws, Kickepoes, & others..." According to Clark, after reassuring them that he was not after their lands, they were won over despite the fact that Hamilton, as he put it, "was almost Deified among them" (IHC 8:146-148). In the journal of Major Bowman, one of Clark's officers, it is stated that on March 15 "A Party of Piankishaws, Peaurians [Peoria] and Miami Indians wait on Col. Clark and Assure him of fidelity etc. to the Americans and beg their Protection" (IHC 8:163). The following April, in a letter to Patrick Henry, written at Kaskaskia, Clark made this statement: "Those nations who have treated with me, have behaved since very well; to wit, the Peankishaws, Kiccapoos, Orcaottenans [Wea] of the Wabash river, the Kaskias, Perrians [Peoria], Mechigamies, Foxes, Socks, Opays [Wilkins' "Peyes"?], Illinois and Poues [Potawatomi], nations of the Mississippi and Illinois rivers" (ibid. p. 172).

A document (A-198) dated 1779 (?), prepared or copied by Richard McCarty, an English trader of Cahokia at the time of Clark's conquest of the

293

Illinois country, contains some brief information with regard to tribal locations. According to this source there were Potawatomi situated at St. Joseph,
at Chicago (see also IHC 8:311-312 and MPHC 20:133), and on the Illinois
River. This last location brings up again the problem raised by the same
geographical association made by Rocheblave in his letter of June 1, 1777.

Mascouten are said to be "At the Forks", which may mean the junction
of the Kankakee and Des Plaines, but more probably refers to the confluence
of the Iroquois River and the Kankakee in northeastern Illinois. Reference
is made to Kickapoo in this fashion: "At the Pass [Pé? Peoria?] Kicapoos &
Others mixed". Piankashaw are situated on the Wabash at Vincennes and also
at the Vermillion River, while there are Wea and Kickapoo at Ouiatanon. As
for the Kaskaskia, Peoria, and Michigamea, they are written into the manuscript by a different hand, and are quite erroneously listed as "$5,000
fighting men on a Meridian of Fort deTroit, to the Westward in Alliance with
us —".

294

In March 1780 DePeyster, British commandant at Detroit conferred with
"The principal Chiefs of the Hurons, Pottawatomies, Chippawas, Ottawas,
Ouiattanons, Miamis, Ouiats and the Piorias, with the Keekapoos..." They
all made their services available to the British; and the "Wabash Indians"
consented to participate in an attack upon Clark at Louisville (MPHC 10:379).
By June 1 DePeyster could write that "There are now about 2,000 Warriors
fitted out from this place to reconnoitre the Ohio and Wabash" (ibid. p. 398).
A letter from Ainse, interpreter at St. Joseph, dated June 30, stated that
the two parties of Potawatomi, on their way to attack Chatre (Chartres) had
been repulsed by the Miami (ibid. p. 406). A third party, which had gone
against Vincennes (idem) returned because of a false report that overwhelming
American forces were there (MPHC 19:519). Still another war party went

towards Louisville (MPHC 10:424). For these services the Potawatomi, as did others, flocked to Detroit to receive their reward (idem, and ibid. p. 434).

Early in 1780 Patrick Sinclair, Lieutenant Governor of Michilimackinac planned and then executed in May an attack upon St. Louis and Cahokia. The Menominee, Sac, Fox, Winnebago and Sioux came down the Mississippi (WHC 11:147-8), while another group proceeded via the Illinois River (ibid. p. 151). Apart from the toll in lives, capture of prisoners, and destruction of property, the objective was not achieved and the forces withdrew (ibid. pp. 154-7).

Later that year the Kickapoo and Wea came to St. Louis requesting aid. These tribes had sent messages to Cruzat, the commandant, by a Frenchman from Vincennes, who was intercepted by the Americans at Kaskaskia on December 5, 1780 (Kinnaird, 1946, 2:403-4). Two weeks later Cruzat referred to the deplorable straits of the Indians: "Lacking all the most indispensable things for their sustenance and defence, they find themselves obliged to come continually to this town of St. Louis" (ibid. p. 411).

295

In January, 1781 a combined Spanish and American Expedition, including sixty Potawatomi, Ottawa, and Chippewa who joined the undertaking "on the bank of the Illinois" set out for an attack upon St. Joseph. Journeying up the Illinois River to Peoria they then continued by land to their objective. They captured the post of St. Joseph on February 12, distributed the booty among the Indians, and withdrew twenty-four hours later (ibid. pp. 431-4; WHC 11:163).

On January 25 DePeyster had written that some Illinois traders established themselves at Chicago and at the "forks" of the Kankakee (MPHC 10:547). Although DePeyster refers to "the Indians in that neighbourhood" there is no mention of any specific groups, though it is probable they were Potawatomi or Mascouten.

Towards the end of the year, on November 3, 1781, Lieutenant Dalton, stationed at Vincennes, wrote Clark that he had received assurances of fidelity from the Ottawa, Piankashaw, Peoria and some of the Wea, at the same time stating that "there are upwards of Five hundred Warriors Piankishaws etc now hunting near the mouth of Wabache..."   (A383a)

On February 25, 1782 DePeyster conferred with chiefs and warriors of the Kickapoo and Mascouten (ibid. pp. 550-2). The latter said that some of their people "were now at war against the Rebels towards the Falls of the Ohio", and expressed their friendly feelings toward the British. Later that year, complying with DePeyster's demand for a demonstration of their sincerity, they ranged the Wabash and brought in Dalton, the commandant at Vincennes (MPHC 20:54-55).

296   In April (1782) DePeyster met with the Wea and the Eel River Miami who tried to convince him of their loyalty by bringing him two prisoners (MPHC 10:567-9). Then, on June 14, the British commandant treated with about fifty chiefs and warriors of the Kickapoo, Mascouten, Wea, Piankashaw, Miami, and Peoria (ibid. pp. 587-591). It was apparent that the Indians were vitally concerned with trade for the fulfillment of their needs (see IHC 5:163-5), while DePeyster was equally concerned with employing them as allies. At this time Wabash Indians were going to Michilimackinac in large numbers to trade (MPHC 10:594-5).

Cruzat, at St. Louis, was at the same time successfully employing some of these Indians for his own ends. In 1782 he sent some Peoria and Kaskaskia down the Mississippi to the Chickasaw in an effort to obtain their neutrality, if not their allegiance; and subsequently he sent the Kickapoo and Mascouten to make war upon the Chickasaw (Kinnaird, 1946, 3:49-54).

Ultimately the Kickapoo, Kaskaskia, and Wea, in addition to the Shawnee and Abenaki, visited the Chickasaw to make peace and to persuade them to the Spanish side (ibid. p. 57).

But in March, 1783 it was reported that the Kickapoo "are tired of the promises of the Spaniards, for their men are without breeches and their women are without petticoats" (ibid. p. 72). The following June the Kickapoo were with the Wea attending a council at Detroit with DePeyster. As an earnest of good faith the Wea gave the commandant a prisoner, at the same time stating: "...we yet hope that you'll supply our wants our women and children who are almost naked" (MPHC 11:370). The Kickapoo speaker said the following: "Father! I have now to recommend to your care the warriours, in short our whole village who did what I told them, which was no more than your order, they therefore expect to receive your bounty, as they were prevented from hunting and have not wherewith to procure for themselves necessaries - " (ibid. p. 371). The Kaskaskia, on the other hand, went down to the Arkansas River later that year "to buy horses for their winter hunt" from the Spaniards (Kinnaird, 1946, 3:90). But just before the coming of spring (1783), about the middle of March, the Potawatomi of Chicago made a foray on the Kaskaskia River, taking three Kaskaskia scalps and three prisoners (MPHC 37:516-517).

In 1785 Kickapoo, according to Cruzat, were "constantly" coming to St. Louis. They were also engaged in hostilities with the Chickasaw whose friendship the commandant was still trying to secure in order to render the Mississippi safe for travel (Kinnaird, 1946, 3:133-135). The Kaskaskia, in a Spanish Memorandum of December 12, 1785, are the only group of the Illinois-Wabash area mentioned as receiving annual presents at St. Louis (ibid. p. 160).

297

Early in 1786 the Indians on the Wabash were up in arms against the Americans (MPHC 24:29-31). The French inhabitants and British policy were being held responsible for this state of affairs (IMH 34:456-467; MPHC 11:482). According to General Clark there were "upwards of 1500 Warriors" among the Wabash Indians participating in the mounting hostilities (Palmer, 1884, 4:122; ibid. pp. 156-7). The expressed intentions of the Indians was "to revenge themselves for the insults that the Americans were continually heaping upon them" (Kinnaird, 1946, 3:178). As if to confirm the truth of the Indian contention a band of Piankashaw from Vincennes and a band of Miami were attacked by Americans, who hacked and mutilated the bodies of the dead (ibid. pp. 179-181; also A-221).

As the flow of the American tide began moving beyond the Ohio, and submerging Indian lands, the Wabash Indians made efforts to stem it by hostile reaction (Smith, 1882, 2:18-22; IHSP 19:9-10). In November and December, 1786 the "Wabash confederates" Miami, Potawatomi, Ottawa, Chippewa, in addition to Iroquois, Huron, Delaware, Shawnee and Cherokee met at Detroit and addressed themselves to the Congress of the United States in an effort to achieve a modus vivendi with the Americans. The "United Indian Nations" pleaded with the United States to "prevent your surveyors and other people from coming upon our side the Ohio River" (ASP-IA 1:9). Americans who came to Vincennes and squatted on public lands antagonized by their outrageous behavior both the Indians and the French. In the summer of 1787 Lt. Col. Harmar was sent to Vincennes to dispossess the lawless Americans and to establish a garrison commanded by Major Hamtramck (Thornbrough, 1957, p. 7). Having arrived on July 17 he received a visit on the 28th by eight Piankashaw "from the Terre haut up the Wabash". With these Indians Harmar sent a message "to all the chiefs of the different tribes on the Wabash, inviting them to

298

assemble here & hear what I had to say to them" (ibid. p. 37; see also
MHSP, 7:307).

Harmar visited Kaskaskia on August 17 (1787) and received a calumet
from "Baptiste de Coigne, the chief of the Kaskaskias Indians" (Thornbrough,
1957, p. 47). He also met "some of the Pioria Indians". His letter to the
Secretary at War, on November 24, 1787 included the following statement:
"The Kaskaskias, Piorias, Cahokias, and Mitchi tribes compose the Illinois
Indians. They are almost extinct at present, not exceeding forty or fifty
total" (ibid. p. 48). Harmar had arrived back at Vincennes on September 3
accompanied by "the Kaskaskias chief with his tribe (about 10 in number),..."
(ibid. p. 51). Two days later "the Piankishaw and Wea Indians arrived at
the Post from up the Wabash, to the number of about 120" (idem; also Hildreth,
1848, pp. 156-7, and MHSP 7:307-11). After expressions of peace and friendship on both sides "the chief part of them left the post for their different
villages up the Wabash" (Thornbrough, 1957, p. 52).

299

Hamtramck, left in command after Harmar's departure, wrote on January
1, 1788 that he was convinced of the sincerity of the Wabash tribes "but
they are menaced by the upper Indians who have ordered them to cease all
communication whit us" (ibid. pp. 60-61). Another letter from Hamtramck to
Harmar on April 13, 1788 informed the newly promoted general that "Last
winter [1787-1788] a party of the Kikapoo who lieves on St. Joseph River
made an excursion in the Ilinois, killed four and tooke prisoner 12 men"
(ibid. p. 71). That same winter (December, 1787) a war party of Mascouten
under Tanclel, "the principal chief" attacked "the Illinois and Kaskaskia"
killing or taking prisoner nineteen persons (Kinnaird 3:244-5). The following
month Hamtramck notified Harmar that his "intelligence from the Weyah
villages" indicated that Wea depredations were daily producing more scalps.

After suggesting that the Wea villages could be taken if he had four or five hundred men, he told Harmar that "About 80 of the Weyas are out at war on the Ohio" (Thornbrough, 1957, pp. 76-7).

In this same letter, which he wrote from Vincennes on May 21, 1788 Hamtramck stated (ibid. p. 78): "I have made out to ascertain the number of wariors on the Wabash and those of the Miami, a return of which I send you". The enclosure, entitled "Return of the number of fiting men in different villages on the Wabash and at the Mawmee and distance from the post [Vincennes]" (ibid. p. 80) follows:

	Miles	Men	
"Highlands [Terre Haute]	120	30	
Vermillion	60	200	
Wyahtinaws [Wea, Ouiatanon]	60	300	
Kickapoos opposite the Wyah		100	
The Isle River [Eel River]	60	150	
Mawmee	120	350	
Grand Elks hart	60	100	) those leaves [lives] on
			) the two rivers that
Little Elks hart	15	60	) forks at the Maumee
		1290	"

300

Data on Kickapoo camps and villages in 1788 are contained in an account of his captivity by William Biggs, who was taken on March 28 while en route from Bellefontaine to Cahokia (Biggs, 1922). With his Kickapoo captors, with whom there was also a Potawatomi, he walked 255 miles overland to "an Indian hunting camp, where they made sugar that spring... The Indians that lived there...gave us plenty of everything they had to eat [meat, hominy, grease, and sugar]" (ibid. p. 17). After having left this camp they travelled another ten or twelve miles until they arrived at "a new town, on the west bank of the Wabash river, where those warriors resided..." (ibid. p. 19). From there he was taken ten miles farther up river by three other Indians on horseback to their "sugar camp, where they had made sugar that spring, on the west bank of the Wabash, about ten miles below the old Kickapoos' trading town, opposite to the Weawes town" (ibid. p. 21). This village was thus near the Ouiatanon post, an identification established on numerous occasions in the past. From this sugar camp, while Biggs, accompanied by an Indian, went by land, the family to whom he had been given took "a large perouge and moved by water up the Wabash river to the old Kickapoo trading town, about ten miles from their sugar camp..." (ibid. p. 24).

Apparently this was the northernmost point of Biggs' travels, for his next move was to the village where his Kickapoo family resided, which seems to have been about six miles to the west. As Biggs put it: "These Indians lived about six miles west of the old Kickapoo trading town, on the west side of the Wabash river. They had no traders in their town" (ibid. p. 29).

301

It would appear, therefore, that the Kickapoo camps and villages visited by Biggs were within a thirty to forty mile radius west and south of Ouiatanon.

In August (1788) Hamtramck again reported on the continued scalpings by the Wea who claimed that they were unable to control their young men (Thornbrough, 1957, p. 108). In addition, the Vincennes garrison's supply boats were being plundered constantly (ibid. pp. 105-107). On the 31st of that month Hamtramck wrote Harmar: "The Indians who have destroy'd our boats at the mouth of the Wabash are the Kickapoos who lieves near the Illinois River. Their is about 300 men of them" (ibid. pp. 119 and 109-110).

Apparently the plea of the Wyandot chief to the Kickapoo chiefs in council at the mouth of the Detroit River the previous July was ineffective in securing peace with the Americans (A-395).

General St. Clair, who had been appointed Governor of the Northwest
Territory, wrote in September from Fort Harmar that the distance from
Vincennes to Terre Haute "where the Piankishaw reside" is the same as from
the latter "to the settlements of the Kickapoos", presumably at Ouiatanon
(Smith, 1882, 2:89).

Early in October (1788) Hamtramck received an offer of allegiance
from the St. Joseph Potawatomi who, he said, "consist of about 200 wariors".
They were prepared to "war against the Wabash Indians" apparently because
"Some years ago the Weeyas killed a Petowatomie chief" (Thornbrough, 1957,
p. 122). These Potawatomi later sent a war party "headed by one of their
Chief La Grande Couete" into Kentucky where they suffered casualties (ibid.
p. 159).

302   Towards the end of November Hamtramck wrote to Harmar from Vincennes:
"The Peankichas who were in the village have gone to make a setlement near
Kaskaskias in consequence of Major Brown expedition. They are joined by the
greatest part of the Vermillion Indians and some other nation" (ibid. p. 139).
The Major Brown referred to was Patrick Brown, who on August 18 last had
appeared at Vincennes with a contingent of about sixty men from Kentucky.
The object of their expedition was to kill Indians indiscriminately in
reprisal for hostilities against Kentuckians (ibid. pp. 114-117). They did,
in fact, kill nine friendly Indians near Vincennes (ibid. p. 150), the result
of which was retaliation by the Indians against innocent victims (ibid. p.
139); see also ASP-IA 1:13).

Apparently the Piankashaw from Vincennes and from the Vermillion River
thought it would, under the circumstances, be safer elsewhere and, at the
same time, might also avoid intensification of hostilities. However, on

October 28, 1789 John Edgar, a citizen of Kaskaskia, referred to the Piankashaw as living on the Spanish side of the Mississippi from where they came
to depredate and steal horses, presumably under the instigation of some
renegade Americans (ibid. pp. 198-9). Edgar also wrote in his letter: "These
Indians have hatred enough to the Americans without being pushed on by white
men, for this reason I am fearful of Ducoigne's [Kaskaskia chief] life this
winter, as the Piankashaws threaten hard because he is a friend to America"
(Thornbrough, 1957, pp. 199, 202-3).

In the spring of 1789 a Frenchman from Ouiatanon informed Hamtramck
that all the Wabash Indians, with the exception of those who were on the hunt,
had gone on war expeditions against Kentucky (ibid. p. 166). According to
Hamtramck the Indians were receiving war supplies from the British at Detroit.
On May 27 he reported that "they have killed a number of people" on the
Wabash. The Eel River Miami and the Wea were implicated in some of the
murders (ibid. pp. 169-170). Hamtramck then sent "two Illinois Indians" on
an embassy to the Wabash Indians threatening action if they did not cease
their depredations (ibid. p. 176). But in defiance of the authority of the
American government Kentuckians continued to engage in hostile expeditions
against the Wabash Indians (ibid. pp. 182-3, 195).

On June 15 Secretary of War Knox, in a report to the President, made
the following statement relative to the Indians on the Wabash: "By the best
and latest information, it appears that, on the Wabash and its communications,
there are from 1500 to 2000 warriors" (ASP-IA 1:13). In another passage in
the same document Knox estimates "The whole number of Indian warriors...to
the northward of the Ohio and to the southward of the lakes, at about 5,000"
(idem).

At the beginning of November (1789) Hamtramck wrote Harmar that as a

303

result of efforts he initiated the preceding summer "a tribe of about eighty
[Wea] warriors have come under the protection of the United States and
delivered me two white prisoners taken some time ago in Kentukey" (Thornbrough, 1957, p. 205). He also stated that the Kaskaskia came to him again
"with new protestations of their fidelity" (idem).

In the winter of 1789-1790 Governor St. Clair went down the Ohio to
the Illinois-Wabash area in an effort to conciliate the tribes on the Wabash.
He sent to Hamtramck "a speech to the Indians of the Wabash and those of the
Miami village" to be forwarded to them by an agent who would translate it
into French (Smith, 1882, 2:130). After one messenger had been turned back
in March, 1790 by "the Vermilion Indians", Hamtramck sent another, Antoine
Gamelin, on April 5 (ibid. p. 135; also Thornbrough, 1957, pp. 223-4).

Proceeding up the Wabash from Vincennes, Gamelin came to the first
304   village, Kikapouguoi, whose chief "is called Les Jambes Croches" (ASP-IA
1:93). The village was probably located in the vicinity of Terre Haute,
although neither geographical nor tribal identification is indicated. The
second village to which he came was Piankashaw, at the Vermillion River.
Having left there he met a war party of 13 Kickapoo on April 10, who told
him they were going against the Chickasaw. The following day Gamelin
"reached a tribe of Kickapoos" who told him they could not reply to the
message "having some warriors absent, and without consulting the Ouiatanons,
being the owners of their lands." The location of the village is not given,
but it could have been near Ouiatanon, the name of which does not appear in
Gamelin's "Journal". Of significance here is the acknowledgement by the
Kickapoo that they were situated on Wea land.

The Kickapoo told Gamelin "to stop at Quitepiconnae [Tippecanoe],
that they would have the chiefs and warriors of Ouiatanons, and those of

their nation, assembled there, and would receive a proper answer;..."
According to a letter of Governor St. Clair, written from Cahokia on May 1,
1790 "...Quetepiconnuais...is about fifteen miles higher than Quiatenon..."
(Smith, 1882, 2:136).

That there were also Kickapoo to the west of the Wabash, in the
interior of Illinois, is implied in Gamelin's statement that the Kickapoo
"promised me to keep their young men from stealing, and to send speeches to
their nations in the prairies to do the same" (idem). This assumption is
supported by evidence that the following June (1790) captives taken in a
Kickapoo raid into Kentucky were brought back to a village on Salt Creek,
an affluent of the Sangamon River, in Logan County, Illinois (Hair, 1866,
pp. 274-277). Although the newspaper account concerning the circumstances
of this event is not quite accurate, there seems no reason to question the
general location at least, of the Kickapoo village. This location not only
ties in with Gamelin's statement, but also with other data adduced below.

305

The actual facts concerning these captives would appear to be more
in line with statements made by the husband and father of this family in a
letter which he wrote to General Putnam in September, 1792 (A-210). According
to this document the Piankashaw made the capture in May, 1791 and took the
family to a village, probably on the Embarras River, situated about two and
one-half days from Vincennes. The captives were then sold to the chief of a
Kickapoo village, the location of which was not indicated.

Gamelin met the Wea and Kickapoo in council on April 14 at the
Tippecanoe River and was told, among other things, that they could not reply
to St. Clair's message until they heard "the answer of their eldest brethren",
the Miami, at the head of the Maumee River (ASP-IA 1:93). He reached the
Eel River Miami on April 18 and arrived at the Miami village on the 23rd,

where he also found Shawnee and Delaware assembled. Gamelin was told by Le Gris, the Miami chief, that before replying to the message he brought "we must send your speeches to all our neighbors and the Lake nations" in addition to consulting with the British commandant at Detroit. Le Gris said that it was necessary to communicate with "all their confederates" because they had "resolved among them not to do anything without an unanimous consent" (ibid. p. 94).

Journeying back down the Wabash to Vincennes, Gamelin again visited the Eel River village on May 2. The following day he reached the Wea, and on May 4 was at the Kickapoo village where he was told by the chief that "we cannot stop our young men from going to war" even though the elders were interested in peace. Arriving at the Piankashaw village on the Vermillion on May 5, Gamelin found that with the exception of two chiefs all the people were out hunting (idem).

306

Writing on March 17, 1790 to Harmar about the first attempt to bring St. Clair's message to the Wabash tribes, Hamtramck enclosed a statement of "distances of the Wabash". This information he obtained "from people who have often been in that countrey" (Thornbrough, 1957, p. 222). There seem to be only three references pertaining specifically to Indian locations. First, it is twenty leagues up the Wabash from the Vermillion River "to the Weeha" (ibid. p. 225). This is followed by the statement that "From the Weeha to the River and town Teopicanoes north side six leagues" (idem). Thirdly, he refers to the Miami village on the St. Joseph, which joins the Maumee at its head (ibid. p. 227).

At the end of the month (March 31) an incursion by a strong party of Kickapoo on the Kaskaskia River, about twenty-seven miles above the village of Kaskaskia, led to an attack upon four Frenchmen. Governor St. Clair, who

was in the Illinois country at the time, wished to send a message to the
Kickapoo "towns" about this affair. He "sent the message in French because
it was necessary to intrust it to a Mr. May [Mayet, Malliet?], who resided
at a small village on the Illinois River, commonly called Au Pè, the place
where the Peoria Fort stood, where there are five or six French families"
(Smith, 1882, 2:138). As St. Clair went on to say, May or Mayet, who had
earlier (1776 or 1777) been in command of a small detachment of Spanish
militia on the Illinois River, "had been appointed Commandant of that place
[Peoria] by General Clarke, and...is a person of influence among the
savages..." (idem).

St. Clair made these statements in a letter which he wrote to the
Secretary of War from Cahokia on May 1, 1790 a few days before the return
of Gamelin from his inconclusive mission. He said, further, that his reason
for asking the Kickapoo to meet with him at Cahokia rather than at Vincennes
where the other Wabash tribes were requested to come by Gamelin, was the
following: "...that a part of that nation [Kickapoo] living at no great
distance from hence [Cahokia], and far from the rest, and hunting constantly
in this country, it appeared of consequence to conciliate them if it could
be done, and thereby procure safety for the people in the mean time"
(ibid. p. 139).

307

This statement, together with the reference in Gamelin's report of
Kickapoo in the prairies west of the Wabash, when added to the story of
Kickapoo captives taken to a village on Salt Creek in Logan County, Illinois,
tends to place the Kickapoo in central Illinois.

St. Clair alludes briefly to the Kaskaskia whose chief, Ducoigne,
lives in Kaskaskia. He writes: "The nation is very inconsiderable, and I
do not think it necessary to trouble you with them at present" (idem).

With reference to the Piankashaw, St. Clair says: "In the country below the Kaskaskia [tribe? river?] there are a great many Piankeshaws,...They wanted much to visit me at Kaskaskia..." (idem). In spite of St. Clair's refusal of their request they practically all came "...and since I left that place there have been many more, in consequence of one of their parties being attacked upon the Saline River, which empties into the Ohio below the Wabash, by the Chickasaws" (ibid. pp. 138-9).

Several years later (1796) in referring to the time (1789-1790) at which he was in the Illinois country investigating "the claims of the Indians to lands and to extinguish them" St. Clair wrote the following: "The Cahokia nation, reduced to four or five families, had abandoned the country entirely. The Peorias, amounting to about one hundred [individuals? or families?], had likewise abandoned it, and the Kaskaskia tribe, of about twenty families, laid claim to nothing but the site of an old village near Kaskaskia, and about four thousand acres of land, which was confirmed to them by an act of Congress. In all the country from Kaskaskia to the mouth of the Ohio and across to the Wabash, not one Indian resided, though the Miamies, the Kickapoos, and the Oiatanon, and, perhaps, some others, occasionally hunted in it;..." (ibid. pp. 400-401).

There are two points in the foregoing statement upon which clarification would be helpful. The first is: What did St. Clair mean when he said that certain of the Illinois had "abandoned" their areas? Obviously, the remaining Illinois Indians were still settled on the Mississippi. It is also apparent that the Kickapoo and Potawatomi were ranging the northern half of Illinois, on the Illinois River and the Sangamon.

The second point concerns St. Clair's use of the word "residence". He appears to have thought of residence in terms of the European mode of

308

occupancy of agricultural lands. This would imply, from his viewpoint, residence or settlement in the midst of cleared lands being exploited agriculturally. This is how use and occupancy becomes visible to the naked eye for any and all to see. With this kind of culturally conditioned perspective and meaning, lands exploited for hunting only, or mainly, are observed and conceived of as "empty" lands, devoid of residence or settlement. St. Clair distinguished "residence" from use of the land by Indians for hunting, and he was under the impression that hunting was only occasional in this area. The General's knowledge of Indian culture and relationship to the land probably left something to be desired, and his observations would therefore be vague and superficial.

In his 1796 report, from which the preceding quotation was taken, St. Clair went on to say that the area which he described as being "occasionally hunted in" "is now [1796] a good deal frequented by the Shawanese and Delawares from the Spanish side" (ibid. p. 401). He adds, however, that "the country was the Peorias" without any indication of the basis on which this statement was made (idem).

309

On April 19 and 20 (1790) Hamtramck wrote letters expressing the belief that continuing depredations on the Ohio, while Gamelin was on his Wabash journey, were the work of the Miami (Thornbrough, 1957, p. 231; Smith, 1882, 2:135,144). Ottawa and Chippewa from Lake Superior, in addition to Winnebago and Potawatomi, were also sending war parties out (ASP-IA 1:94; Thornbrough, 1957, p. 233). But it was Gamelin's report that led St. Clair to the conclusion that force was the only remaining alternative in dealing with the Wabash tribes (Thornbrough, 1957, p. 224, fn. 6; ibid. pp. 236-7; TP 3:311-312).

In the meantime, early in 1790, Lt. Armstrong had been sent on a mission to ascertain the possibilities for exploring the Missouri River (Storm, 1944, pp. 48-55). On June 2, 1790 he sent a report to Harmar with information he obtained at St. Louis. Attached to the report was a map of the Illinois River together with explanatory remarks by the person who was Armstrong's source. At eight circles in the fork of the Des Plaines and Kankakee Rivers is the notation "Indian Villages of Different Nations" (ibid. map opp. p. 52; see also p. 53).

On June 1 Governor St. Clair issued instructions to "Captain John Baptiste Mayet" in which it was stated: "The Command of the Settlement at the Pioria Village upon the Illinois River is again committed to you, & you will do, (as you have heretofore done) your best, to keep the Indians of your River in Peace --". All persons were forbidden to trade without a license or to travel along the river without a pass from the Governor (TP 3:309-310).

310   In July, subsequent to St. Clair's decision to plan hostilities against the Indians, Winthrop Sargent, his Territorial Secretary, learned that the Miami invited the Wabash tribes and the Sac, Fox, Ottawa and Potawatomi to assemble at their village in force (ibid. pp. 320-321; Thornbrough, 1957, p. 242). A few days later, on July 20, 1790 Hamtramck wrote a letter to Sargent listing the number of warriors in each of the villages on the Wabash up to the Miami. His table follows:

"Chipikokii [Pepikokia (?) Piankashaw] or Vincennes	35 warriors
High Lands [Terre Haute]	30
Vermillien [Vermillion Piankashaw]	200
Owia [Wea]	300
Kickapoo	100
Ell [Eel] river	150
Miamie	350
Grand Elks hart	100
Little Elks hart	60
	1325"

In a despatch to Harmar on August 7 Hamtramck used, in part, substantially the same figures in a comparison which revealed the superiority of the total Wabash Indian forces over his. He wrote: "...I am apprehensive that I should not come off so safe, for the Indians of the Vermillion who are 200 warriors, the Ouia 330, the Keecapoes (opposite the Ouia) 100 and those of Ell River 150, all whom are close to each other can assemble them selfs in to one body, amounting to 750 men, which force would then be more than mine and perhaps make a too powerful obstruction to my return" (Thornbrough, 1957, p. 246). Two weeks later, in another communication to Harmar he stated that "...two Potawatomies and some Weeya Indians have come to the garrison to make peace. Those Potawatomies are of a band who lives near the Weeya (they are about 100 warriors)" (ibid. p. 247).

The figures in both these documents are identical with those last used by Hamtramck two years earlier, in 1788 (ibid. p. 80). With the exception of one change they were again recorded in a document dated December 20, 1791 which, apparently, a Judge Turner gave to James Madison (A-336). The notable difference from Hamtramck's letter of July 20, 1790 is the number of warriors attributed to the "Vermillion". The original number was 200; but on the basis of "information obtained at Vincennes" Turner lists 100 warriors for this group.

311

In September,1790 Harmar's campaign against the Miami village on the Maumee was actively undertaken. Hamtramck engaged in an unsuccessful movement up the Wabash on a diversionary effort in the course of which he met no Indians. His letter to Harmar of November 28 is of particular interest for its passing reference to "the Kickapoos, from the prairies", again indicating the distribution of Kickapoo westward from Ouiatanon on the Wabash (Thornbrough, 1957, p. 266).

Following the destruction of the Miami villages near the confluence of
the St. Joseph and St. Mary's rivers the Indians were engaged by Harmar in
battle, with losses on both sides. Harmar's force withdrew to Fort Washington
by November 3. With the failure of the expedition, renewed efforts for a
peaceful resolution with the Indians were again unsuccessful. Consequently,
in the spring of 1791, a military solution was sought once more (MPHC 24:180-
198; ASP-IA 1:129-130).

On May 23, 1791 General Scott's forces began their march to the Wabash
from the banks of the Ohio River opposite the mouth of the Kentucky River.
Their objective, according to Scott's instructions from the Secretary of War,
was "the Wea, or Ouiatanon towns of Indians" (ASP-IA 1:130). On June 1,
after a march of 155 miles they approached the Wabash from the east in the
vicinity of the Wea village. Scott's account of the action which followed
reports the destruction of the Wea village on the east bank of the Wabash,
the Kickapoo village opposite on the west bank, and three smaller villages
below the Wea. In addition, Scott sent Colonel Wilkinson with three hundred
and sixty men "to destroy the important town of Kethtipecanunk, at the mouth
of Eel River, eighteen miles from my camp, and on the west side of the
Wabash..." (ibid. : 132-2). On June 4, after addressing a plea for peace
"to the various Tribes of Picankieskaws and the nations of the Red People
living on the waters of the Wabash River" (MPHC 24:244-6; ASP-IA 1:132-3),
Scott started back to Fort Washington "after having burned the towns and
adjacent villages, and destroyed the growing corn and pulse,..." (idem). A
British version of General Scott's attack was set down in letters by Colonel
McKee (MPHC 24:261-2, 273).

On July 31, 1791 General St. Clair "authorized a second expedition
against the Indians of the Wabash,..." (Smith, 1882, 2:227-9). The

312

instructions he sent to Wilkinson stated that "The principal object of the expedition will be the Indian village, sometimes known by the name of Kikiah, situated near the junction of the L'Anguile or Eel River with the Wabash, about three miles up the L'Anguile,..." After an assault upon this village Wilkinson was to "proceed to such other Indian towns or villages upon the Wabash or in the prairies, to the destruction of which you shall judge your force adequate. Of these there are several higher up the river, and none of them considerable. The first is at the Calumet River, about ten or twelve miles distant from Kikiah, and on the south side; after that is the Mississinewa,--miles further up. Formerly it contained a considerable population, but at present it is believed is much reduced. Some miles further up are the forks of the Wabash. In going to the Miami village, the north fork is used, and at the junction of those branches there was formerly an inconsiderable village, but whether it is now inhabited or not is not known. From thence it is from twenty-four to thirty-six miles to the Miami carrying place, which is about ten miles over, and you are at the Miami towns. To the westward and northward of L'Anguile lies the Kickapoo town, on the prairie, distant about sixty miles" (ibid. pp. 227-8, italics - JJ).

313

The distance from Eel River given by St. Clair for the location of the Kickapoo village would place it in the vicinity of the Illinois-Indiana state line, possibly on the Kankakee or Iroquois rivers. The instructions later go on to express the hope that Wilkinson will find it possible to attack another "Kickapoo town, situated in the prairie not far from the Sangamon River, which empties itself into the Illinois. By information, that town is not distant from L'Anguile more than three easy days' marches. A visit at that place will be totally unexpected,...; neither will it be hazardous, for the men, at this season, are generally out hunting beyond the line of the Illinois country" (ibid. p. 228; italics - JJ).

This village is most likely the one discussed above as being on the
Salt Creek affluent of the Sangamon. It should also be added in this connection that St. Clair's instructions to Wilkinson contain this statement:
"Between L'Anguile and the Kickapoo town you would meet with two or three
branches of the Sangamon,...; there are three, certainly, between that place
and Ouiatannon" (ibid. p. 229). St. Clair's reference to the Kickapoo
"hunting beyond the line of the Illinois country" would imply the area beyond
the Illinois River, meaning generally west, which might also be taken to mean
north of the upper part of the river. The latter includes country which the
Kickapoo ranged before they established themselves near Ouiatanon during the
first half of the century. It will be recalled, however, that the year
before, when he was in the Illinois country, St. Clair wrote from Cahokia on
May 1, 1790 that those Kickapoo, situated "at no great distance from" Cahokia
were "far from the rest, and hunting constantly in this country" (ibid. p. 139,
italics - JJ). While, on its face, this statement is contradictory to the
one in his instructions to Wilkinson where he says the Kickapoo hunt beyond
the Illinois, when one is at Cahokia both sides of the Illinois River may be
part of the same country. But from a distance, and under other circumstances,
the "line" of the Illinois country which was probably the Illinois River, may
become significantly relevant under conditions where greater precision is
required.

At this point it may be said that in 1791 the Kickapoo are established
in central Illinois (Logan County) northeastern Illinois or northwestern
Indiana, and on the Wabash in villages, at and in the vicinity of Ouiatanon.
From their village near the Sangamon, they may range westward on the hunt to
exploit both sides of the Illinois River.

314

On August 1, 1791 Wilkinson marched his force north and northwest from Fort Washington with the immediate objective of reducing the village at Eel River. By his northward course the first 3 or 4 days he "thereby avoided the hunting ground of the enemy, and the paths which lead direct from White river to the Wabash, leaving the headwaters of the first to my left; I then being about 70 miles advanced of Fort Washington, turned northwest;..." (ASP-IA 1:133). On August 7 he reached the Wabash about five miles above the mouth of Eel River. Crossing the Wabash he proceeded westward to the Eel River where the village was situated on the opposite bank. Wilkinson writes that he "found this town scattered along Eel river for full three miles". After burning the village, destroying the crops, and taking prisoners, Wilkinson "commenced my march for the Kickapoo town in the prairie" (ibid. p. 134). At the Eel River village he was "not more than one and a half days' march from the Pattawatamies, Shawanese, and Delawares". Moving down the Wabash "by the road leading to Tippecanoe" the entire company, including prisoners, "encamped, that evening, about six miles from Kenapacomaqua, the Indian name of the town I had destroyed". From there they marched west and northwest and "launched into the boundless prairies of the West, with the intention to pursue that course until I could strike a road, which leads from the Pattawatamies of lake Michigan, immediately to the town I sought..." Forced to return to the Tippecanoe road by swampy country, they proceeded instead to the village near the mouth of that river. "After the destruction of this town, in June last, the enemy had returned, and cultivated their corn and pulse, which I found in high perfection, and in much greater quantity than at l'Anguille [Eel River]." Here Wilkinson refreshed his horses and destroyed the corn. The next day, en route to Ouiatanon, he intended to reach "the Kickapoo town, on the prairie, by the road which leads from

315

Ouiatanon to that place," but he abandoned the project because of insufficient provisions and the dissatisfaction of his men. Instead, he "marched forward to a town of the same nation, situate about three leagues west of Ouiatanon... I destroyed this town, consisting of thirty houses, with a considerable quantity of corn in the milk, and on the same day I moved on to Ouiatanon, where I forded the Wabash, and proceeded to the site of the villages, on the margin of the prairie, where I encamped, at 7 o'clock. At this town, and the villages destroyed by General Scott, in June, we found the corn had been replanted, and was now in high cultivation, several fields being well ploughed, all which was destroyed" (ibid. p. 135).

Wilkinson summarized the achievements of his enterprise in this manner: "I have destroyed the chief town of the Ouiatanon nation, and made prisoners of the sons and sisters of the king. I have burnt a respectable Kickapoo village, and cut down at least 430 acres of corn, chiefly in the milk. The Ouiatanons, left without houses, home, or provision, must cease to war, and will find active employ to subsist their squaws and children during the impending winter" (idem).

316

When, in the fall of 1791, St. Clair attempted to establish an American position in the Miami villages by force of arms his disastrous and humiliating defeat by the Indians did not result in annihilation only because the enemy failed to take advantage of such an opportunity (Smith, 1882, 2:251-267).

The Wea and Eel River chiefs, however, did not view this victory too optimistically. If they felt their hand was in any way strengthened, as a consequence, they apparently sought only to insure peace for themselves and security of their lands. These two factors were included as stipulations in articles of agreement they entered into with Major Hamtramck at Vincennes on March 14, 1792. This document was "signed" by seven chiefs of the Wea and by two of the Eel River. But the item of particular interest is the "provisional article" which states: "As the <u>Kickapoos of the Weya have left that Country and gone on the Illinois River,</u> and are not represented with us in council We the Chiefs of the Eel River and Weya Indians farther agree that in case the said Kickapoos should return on the Wabash we shall use our endeavours to bring them to the above mentioned measures or otherwise to drive them out of the Country" (TP 2:374-5, italics - JJ).

The same month Governor Trudeau of Spanish Illinois wrote from St. Louis that two hundred Sac, Fox, Kickapoo, Mascouten, and Potawatomi "were assembled, either from those who were in the town or others who had to be called from the immediate vicinity." These attempted to kill some Little Osages in the town (Nasatir, 1952, 1:167-8).

At the end of the month Hamtramck informed the Secretary of War that these articles were "the only ones I could find to be consonant with their wishes." He was also optimistic that the Piankashaw, "the only nation remaining on the Wabash, who have not yet been with me" would enter the same agreement (TP 2:380), which they did on April 20, 1792 (A-223).

317

In the same dispatch Hamtramck told the Secretary that he learned that Michilimackinac traders "were in the prairies towards the Illinois River trading with the Indians." In addition he expressed grave concern over the clandestine sale of liquor to the Indians by unscrupulous traders at Vincennes. Selling their furs for this commodity the Indians, says Hamtramck, "will find themselves and families naked in the spring and having no means to procure ammunition or other necessaries will go to war for plunder - " (TP 2:381).

In April the Spanish commandant at St. Louis made the first reference to the Mascouten in some years when he sent a dispatch to the Governor stating that they and the Kickapoo were among those refusing to unite against the

Americans at the instigation of groups on the upper Mississippi (Kinnaird, 1946, 4:35). Then, in September following, two Mascouten participated in the signing of a short-lived treaty at Vincennes negotiated by General Putnam with the Illinois and Wabash tribes (see below).

In June Hamtramck reported that eleven tribes had met in council at the confluence of the Kankakee and Des Plaines rivers to consider again peace proposals made by the Americans (A-223). The "Kiccapoos of the prairie" approached him separately to declare their inclination for peace, but that they "were every day threatened by the Indians of the Lakes for not joining them against the Americans..." The Indian who conveyed this message to Hamtramck also told him "that the Indians would have no objection to a garrison at the Pioria Town..." a place now within the area of the prairie Kickapoo. He also wrote that for some unexplained reason, perhaps "occasioned by some sudden fright," "a great number of the Weya and Pyankeshaws have retired towards the Illionois..." (idem).

Shortly before Putnam came to Vincennes to negotiate a treaty with the Wabash and Illinois tribes, the Kaskaskia chief, Ducoigne, wrote to Zenon Trudeau, Governor of Spanish Illinois at St. Louis, asking for a loan occasioned by the expense of sending his son to school (Kinnaird, 1946, 4:77-78). Putnam, on July 24 in a message addressed "To the Kaskaskia and Peoria Indians, and to All the Other Nations of the Red People in the Illinois Country" had requested them to meet him at Vincennes on September 20 "to establish a durable peace and friendship..." (ibid. p. 78).

Putnam's treaty with the Indians at Vincennes was concluded on September 27, 1792 (A-225; ASP-IA 1:319, esp., p.338), and his list of (31) signers comprises representatives of the following tribes: Eel River, Wea, Potawatomi, Mascouten, Ottawa, "Kickapoos of the Wabash", Piankashaw,

318

Kaskaskia, Peoria (A-313). Another document in the Putnam papers gives the total number of Indians in attendance at Vincennes in connection with this treaty as 686, of which 247 were men and 439 were women and children. By far the greater number came from the Eel River Miami, Wea, and Piankashaw, and it was believed that more of the latter might have been present except for the numbers of the other groups (A-310). The difference in numbers is also revealed by the amount of goods given the different groups by Putnam (A-123).

Secretary of War Knox's communication to the Senate on November 8, 1792 concerning conclusion of this treaty omits mention of the Ottawa and refers to the Potawatomi as "of the Illinois river..." (ASP-IA 1:319). The Journal of the proceedings of the council connected with the treaty (Buell, 1903, pp. 335-362) reveals that an Ottawa was present, apparently as an observer, who said he would report to his "nation" (ibid. p. 345). It was Ducoigne of the Kaskaskia who, as the best speaker, was delegated by all the Indian groups present to address General Putnam in their behalf (ibid. p. 341). In essence the Indians were concerned with two fundamental points: to retain the lands they still possessed, and to have traders to supply their needs.

At Vincennes, when this treaty was signed, was Captain Joseph E. Collins, who in July had set out upon a spying mission under instructions from General Wilkinson (A-406). On September 28, after the treaty was signed, he went to the "Illinois settlements" (Kaskaskia) where he learned from the Indians (Kaskaskia and Peoria) who came back from Vincennes that they intended to abide by the terms of the treaty.

Proceeding up the Illinois River late in October (1792) "he landed often at the Indian towns & villages passing for a British trader--". Presumably it was along the Illinois River and the area up the Des Plaines

319

to Chicago that he was "at the principal towns of the Potawatimes—& Kickapoos—" where he was told that the Indians who signed the Treaty with General
Putnam at Vincennes were not chiefs, and "in fact they were nothing but
common men or rather blackgards—" (ibid.).

In connection with Collins' reference to Potawatomi towns and villages
on the Illinois River as far as Chicago, it is relevant to introduce a
Spanish document of Zenon Trudeau at St. Louis, dated May 18, 1793 (Nasatir,
1952, 1:180). In a list of tribes who brought "canoes" of furs to St. Louis
from various geographical locations, Trudeau indicates four places from which
the Potawatomi came: St. Joseph, "Grande Colomi" (Grand Calumet River?),
Chicago, Illinois River and Peoria (Rivierre des Yllinois y los Pés). With
this last geographical reference are also associated the Kickapoo and
Mascouten. The Illinois, Peoria, and Kaskaskia are mentioned as separate
entities associated with the American Illinois area in one of two sentences
appended at the end of the list, cited in the original Spanish by the editor.
Freely translated it states: 30 canoes from the Illinois area in American
territory with the Sac and Fox, Kickapoo, "Loups" (Delaware), Shawnee,
Mascouten, Winnebago, Illinois, Peoria, Kaskaskia, and other nations (idem).

320

Captain Collins left Chicago on November 16, 1792 and journeyed along
the south end of Lake Michigan to the St. Joseph River, meeting up "with
numbers of hunting camps of the Potawatimes—". He went up the river to the
old St. Joseph post where, according to Collins "there is about 220 Warriors
of the Potoewatimais - those Indians appeared to be disposed for war & had
about 30 — American prisoners - " (A-406).

Because his life was endangered Captain Collins abandoned his objective of reaching the Miami villages. Early in 1793 he arrived at Legionville
where he made his deposition on February 16 before Anthony Wayne with the

following conclusion: "Upon the Whole from every thing he cou'd learn In
case the Ohio was not agreed to as a boundary - there was a determination
among the Indians to form a General confedracy against the Americans & that
it wou'd in all probability be a general war..." (ibid.).

About this time (February 1, 1793) a deputation of chiefs from the
Kaskaskia, Piankashaw, Potawatomi, Kickapoo, and Wea had arrived in Philadelphia where they conferred with Thomas Jefferson, then Secretary of State.
They complained of the destructive inroads of the Americans from Kentucky
upon their lands and requested that Captain Prior, to whom they were greatly
attached, be permitted to remain among them as the government representative.
Ducoigne was the chief speaker on behalf of the others present "and all of
the Indians of the Mississippi and Wabash", including, in addition to those
already mentioned, the Peoria and "Mosquitoes" (Mascouten?). In addition to
the depredations of the Kentuckians he also pointed out "that the Shawanese
and Delawares came from the Spanish side of the river, destroyed our corn,
and killed our cattle. We cannot live if things go so." Among the remarks
made by the other chiefs was this from Little Doe, a Kickapoo: "I am a
Kickapou, and drink of the waters of the Wabash and Mississippi". This was
a metaphor to convey the idea of the range of Kickapoo groups from the Wabash
to the Mississippi (Bergh, 1907, pp. 377-389).

321

Again in the summer of 1793 the effort was made to treat with the
Indians at Sandusky. They were adamant in their insistence upon the Ohio
River as the boundary between their lands and the United States. In view of
the failure to reach agreement hostilities were resumed (ASP-IA 1:349-357).

Jacob Lindley was one of three Quakers who journeyed to Detroit for
the purpose of attending the councils held between the three treaty commissioners and the Indians. In his account he included information which he

copied from "a Quebec Calendar, wherein was inserted the names, situation, and supposed number, of such Indian nations as have hitherto been discovered in North America - ..." (MPHC 17:586-588). The date to which the information pertains is, unfortunately, not given, nor is the original source. Lindley states that the figures for each group refer to "the number of men fit for bearing arms; to which add about one-third that number old and superanuated - the amount of which number multiplied by six, is estimated to be the whole number of men, women and children, of the native Indians now discovered" (ibid. p. 588).

There are clear indications that at least some of the information is outdated to a considerable extent; and it certainly does not reflect the situation as of 1793. For example, a group called the "Piantias" (probably the Peoria) are stated to be "a wandering tribe, on both sides the Mississippi," and the number of their warriors is given as 800. This obviously does not reflect the current state of affairs in that tribe - assuming that the Peoria are meant. This group is followed immediately on the list by "The Kasqueasquias, or Illinois - in general on the Illinois river, and between the Wabash and the Mississippi." The number of warriors among them is listed as 600 - again a thing of the past, as is their association with the Illinois river "in general".

The next three groups on the list are the Piankashaw, Wea, and Kickapoo in that order, all situated on the Wabash, and possessing fighting men to the number of 250, 400 and 300 respectively. The Mascouten on this list are attributed to Green Bay, while the Potawatomi are situated "near St. Joseph's river and Detroit", with a combined total of 350 warriors.

On September 21, 1793 Thomas Pasteur, who in May had replaced Hamtramck in command at Vincennes, wrote to Anthony Wayne that "On the 13th Inst. a

322

Chief from the Potowatomie Towns, & St. Josephs, came to this place..." with messages "from four other Chiefs..." (A-287). They were anxious for peace to be established, but with the condition that "...all white people...move over the Ohio, that they [the Indians] may not be disturbed in their hunting which might be the cause of War again,..." (idem).

When Pasteur wrote to Wayne again the following December he reported that he was unable to discern any warlike activity among the Wabash tribes and that his information "from the Illinois" was "that the Indians in that quarter seem to wish to remain in peace.--" (A408)

Towards the end of January, 1794 two Piankashaw told Pasteur that the Spaniards had informed the Kickapoo and others of an American plan to come down to the mouth of the Ohio and from there "to go through the Prairies by way of the Keckipoo Towns to destroy the Indians of that, & the Wabash..." (A-288). Pasteur also learned from other sources that rather than joining the Spaniards the Indians were more apt to respond to Miami invitations for hostilities against the Americans in the spring of 1794. It was nevertheless true that the Spanish called the Peoria, Piankashaw, Miami, Shawnee, Delaware, and Ottawa to the west side of the Mississippi offering them an opportunity to settle in Spanish territory (Houck, 1909, 2:60-70). Although the Spanish seemed to think the Peoria receptive, the same did not appear to be true of the Kaskaskia under Ducoigne (Kinnaird, 1946, 4:250-251).

In this connection it is relevant to refer to a message addressed to Lieutenant Governor Trudeau at St. Louis by Delaware, Miami, Ottawa, Potawatomi, Peoria, and Shawnee at the end of 1792 or the beginning of 1793 (ibid. pp. 110-111). They said that earlier, at the invitation of Cruzat, they had hunted peacefully in Spanish territory, but when he was replaced by Perez (1788) "we were assaulted on all sides by the Osages who murdered us,

323

stole our horses,..." They therefore addressed this appeal to Trudeau to restrain the Osage "and prevent them from killing our horses which are our sole resource [sic] for the maintenance of our families" (ibid. p. 111).

Acting on the basis of the information he received, Pasteur "sent for the Chief of the Keckipoo's and Weiyos..." They arrived on February 19, 1794 "with two other chiefs of their nation, & thirty three of their young men, accompanied by four chiefs of the Potawatomy Indians that live on Tippicanooe, & fifty two of their young men, exclusive of Women & children,..." (A-288). According to William Clark the entire company of Potawatomi, Wea and Kickapoo arrived in twenty canoes (A-135, pp. 11,12). Apparently satisfied with Pasteur's explanations and treatment, the Indians left at the beginning of March and presumably notified the Chippewa, Ottawa, Sac "and others" to remain in peace.

324

The following June 20 Pasteur did, in fact, meet in council with some chiefs and warriors of the Sac, Fox, and Kaskaskia. "Several" Piankashaw and Wea were also present; and the Kaskaskia chief, Ducoigne was the principal speaker because of his great fluency (A-289). Then on July 17 the Kaskaskia, Sac and Fox came once again, this time to listen to Pasteur who was explicit in stating that unless the Indians agreed to live in peace with the Americans they would "experience the force of...Gen. Wayne who is now advancing to destroy all the Towns and Cornfields of the hostile Indians and to put to death all such as dare oppose his progress..." (Kinnaird, 1946, 4:323).

Four months earlier (March 10, 1794) Captain Prior, Pasteur's deputy for Indian affairs, had received a letter in French addressed to him on behalf of Ducoigne who "signed" as "chief of the Illinois" (AHR 4:108). Ducoigne requested aid because "we are being continually tormented by the

Kis [?] and the Kickapoo" and also because "The Chickasaw and Choctaw are coming to war against the Illinois and against the Peoria" (translation - JJ). The latter quotation might possibly mean - against the Illinois country and against the village of Peoria - although this is doubtful, particularly in view of the fact that Ducoigne signed as chief of the Illinois. It seems, however, that "Illinois" was used on occasion interchangeably with "Kaskaskia". It should also be observed that the salutation of this letter might be translated in either of two ways: "To Mr. Prior from the Kaskaskias [Indians]"; or, "...from Kaskaskia [village]".

At the same time another letter came to Prior from a Francois Duquetil (?) who seems to have been a trader among the Potawatomi and the Mascouten and Kickapoo on the Illinois River (ibid. pp. 109-110). Apparently he had brought a message from Prior to those Indians concerning the establishment of peace; and with his own letter Duquetil (?) enclosed the reply he had written for them. The heading of this document, in translation (mine - JJ) · reads: "Reply of the Indian chiefs on the Illinois River on the speech I made to them" (ibid. pp. 110-111). The one who dictated the reply was a Potawatomi, Turkey Foot, who concluded as follows: "I am not a chief, my father, but I speak to you with their approval and in their presence. These are my chiefs who have asked that I speak for them, with whom I join in extending our hand [all together]" (ibid. p. 111). At the end of the document, in addition to Turkey Foot as the "speaker", there are the names of three "chiefs". The first of these is simply listed as "Coudgiache". The second name is that of "Michikitenon, brother of lagesse". An asterisk at this name refers to a footnote at the end of the reply which states: "Michikitenon is the brother of lagesse who died in the colonies".

Lagesse, in the summer of 1792, made a speech to Hamtramck at Vincennes

325

in which he referred to himself as "the first and great chief of the
Pattawatamies" (ASP-IA 1:241). One of the statements he made in that speech
clearly implies that Potawatomi were on the Illinois River or, at least, in
the Illinois country: "It would be very necessary that you should have a
garrison at Kahokia: It would be a convenient place for all the Indians of
this country to speak at. A Father should be near his children, and it
would give terror to the bad Indians" (idem). This was said in connection
with the fact that "We are every day threatened by the other Indians, that if
we do not take a part with them against the Americans, they will destroy our
villages". The reference here may have been to the Miami, for Lagesse also
said that "I am deaf to everything that comes from the Miami. Every day we
receive messengers from those people, but we have been deaf to them, and will
remain so" (idem).

326   To return to the reply of Turkey Foot in behalf of his chiefs, the
last name appended to the list of chiefs was that of "L'Étourneau, chief of
the small fort West of lake michigan". This individual was obviously not
from the Illinois River, although the geographical reference may be to Chicago.

One of the statements made in the reply to Prior's message concerned
the fact that the Mascouten and Kickapoo were pleased with the whiskey that
had been given them. This would imply that they, too, were in the Illinois
area then, a fact already established in previous documentation.

According to the chiefs, Prior seemed to think that their people were
few, but they assured him that "we are many" (AHR, 4:110).

By July, 1794 the state of affairs among the Indians northwest of
the Ohio was such that none of Wayne's efforts for a peaceful resolution were
of any avail. In anticipation of such an eventuality of irreconcilable
differences Wayne had since 1793 established a chain of forts north from

Cincinnati to the headwaters of the Wabash at the site of St. Clair's defeat
of November 4, 1791. Whereas on April 14 the Kickapoo and Wea seemed
"inclined to join" the anti-American confederation of tribes which included
Shawnee, Delaware, Miami, Mingoes and others, such as Potawatomi and Wyandot
(MPHC 24:656), on July 14 delegations from the Kickapoo, Wea and Piankashaw
attended a general council at the Maumee Rapids "at which they expressed
their sorrow for having listened to the big Knives and beg of the Confederacy
to take Pity on them and receive them again among them as Brothers" (ibid.
p. 697). They were readmitted on condition that they immediately assemble
their warriors at the Au Glaize River near the Maumee. In the meantime,
parties of Ottawa, Chippewa, Potawatomi, Wyandot, and Delaware were moving
out to harrass Wayne by interference with his lines of communication (ibid.
p. 696).

Subsequent to the defeat inflicted by Wayne's forces upon the Indian
alliance at Fallen Timbers on August 20, 1794, (ASP-IA 1:490-1) the General
wrote to the Secretary of War early in 1795 concerning "the strong & pleasing
prospect of a General Peace between the United States and all the late
hostile tribes of Indians North West of the Ohio;..." In this communication
Wayne "enclosed copies of speeches & agreements that lately took place
between The Wyondots, Chepawas, Ottawas, Putawatimes, Saukey's Miamis &
myself;..." (Knopf, 1959, pp. 379-380; ASP-IA 1:559-560). Then on February
12, 1795 he informed the Secretary that the Shawnee and Delaware also came
to him at Greenville on the 7th to sue for peace (Knopf, 1959, p. 384). With
this letter he sent a "Summary of their speeches & a Copy of the Preliminary
Articles entered into with those Nations in behalf of themselves & the Miamis
lately inhabiting the banks of the Miamis & Au Glaize Rivers -" (idem).
Wayne went on to say that actually "The whole of the late Hostile tribes

327

have now come forward with overtures of peace,..." (idem).

On March 8, 1795 Wayne wrote the new Secretary of War, Timothy Pickering, with regard to the impending treaty to be held at Greenville that: "The Chiefs and Warriors belonging to the Wyondots Chepawas Ottawas, Putawatimes Saukey's Shawanoes Delawares & Miamis with whom I have already entered into Preliminary Articles of peace amount to at least Four thousand fighting men - the greater proportion of which were actually in the Action of the 20th of August last: if to those shou'd be added the Wabash & Illinois & Michigan tribes of Indians, which is more than probable will be the case, the Assemblage of Chiefs & warriors will be Numerous indeed!" (ibid. p. 389). In an earlier communication (September 20, 1794) Wayne said he was "most certain that a considerable Number of" Wabash Indians had not only been in the battle at Fallen Timbers but also in a previous action on June 30 near Fort Recovery (ibid. p. 357).

One month later Pickering sent Wayne an extensive set of instructions with regard to the conduct of negotiations with the Indians at the forth-coming treaty council to be held at Greenville. In this connection Knox's comments of the year before in anticipation of the possibility of peace negotiations are also pertinent, and will be dealt with first.

On April 4, 1794 the Secretary of War, Henry Knox, had sent to Anthony Wayne a set of instructions "relatively to a proposed treaty with the Indians North West of the Ohio" (M-34, p. 1). According to this document it was to be "one of the first objects of the proposed treaty to ascertain from the Indians what tribes are the allowed proprietors of the Country lying to the Northward of the Ohio and Southward of the lakes" (ibid. p. 3).

Knox also called Wayne's attention to the fact that although the treaty made by Putnam with the Wabash tribes in 1792 did not define

328

boundaries, Putnam said "that he understood the Eastern boundary claimed by the said Wabash Indians would be described by a line drawn from the Miami Village [site of Fort Wayne] to the Creek a few miles above the falls of the Ohio [Cincinnati]" (ibid. p. 6). It was important, therefore, to establish clear-cut boundaries, in case of a treaty, in order to avoid future problems. In view of the fact that the Senate failed to ratify Putnam's treaty because of the vagueness of the boundaries "it will be necessary that the said Wabash Indians should be parties either to the general treaty or that a particular treaty should be formed with them hereafter" (ibid. p. 7).

A final point that may be mentioned in the instructions to Wayne is the following: "While at the treaty you must endeavor to ascertain as accurately as may be the names and numbers of the respective Indian tribes within the limits of the United States North of the Ohio - and also the names of the influential Chiefs - their divisions of lands and all other matters relatively to trade and intercourse with them" (ibid. p. 8).

329

One year later, in April, 1795, Timothy Pickering, Knox's successor as Secretary of War, once again sent instructions to Wayne before the treaty of Greenville (Knopf, 1955). These were a reiteration and elaboration, with some revision, of the basic instructions Wayne received the year before. In order to forestall the problems and complaints deriving from the earlier "Treaties of Fort McIntosh, Miami and Fort Harmar" Pickering told Wayne to "use every practicable means to obtain a full representation of all the nations claiming property in the lands in question. And to obviate future doubts it may be expedient to get lists of all the principal and other Chiefs of each nation, to ascertain who are absent, and whether those present may be fairly considered as an adequate representation of their nation. The explanations and declarations of the Chiefs on this point may be noted, and subscribed by them upon each list" (ibid. p. 24).

The instructions from Knox had made reference to the fact "that the Chippewas and five nations have had the project of inducing the four hostile tribes to accede to a peace upon the terms specified in their messages" (Def. Ex. No. 45, p. 9). Pickering also made a similar reference in the following context: "Besides the four most hostile tribes have, I am persuaded, not the smallest pretensions to the Country about Lake Michigan and the Illinois, and," he goes on to say, "to make peace with those four tribes is really the great object of the treaty" (Knopf, 1955, p. 34).

What is of particular interest here is the reference to "pretensions" of the four supposedly "most hostile tribes" to the Illinois country. These tribes are not mentioned by name, but they may be inferred from the four which appear most often, and which lead the names of others, in the councils held with the "western Indians" or those "North West of the Ohio." They would appear to be the Delaware, Shawnee, Wyandot and Miami (ASP-IA 1:319 et passim).

It is also interesting to note that after attaching the greatest importance to peace with the four tribes, Pickering continues with the following observation: "The other tribes generally seem to me rather to be auxiliaries than principals in the war, and consequently may not attend in such numbers as to constitute an adequate representation of their tribes" (Knopf, 1955, pp. 34-35). Wayne's response to Pickering on May 15, 1795 included the statement that the Indians "with their distant auxiliaries (numbers of whom joined them in the campaign) are far more powerful & Numerous than has been generally calculated upon: however this fact will be well ascertained during the pending treaty, in the interim I take the liberty to enclose a list of the Nations & computed Number of Warriors - from whom I have received Visits or Messages" (ibid. pp. 49-50). This list was not attached

330

to Wayne's letter as published. But when he wrote to Pickering on June 17
next, the day after the Greenville treaty negotiations began, he said that
"A Considerable Number of Chiefs belonging to the Chepawas, Ottawas -
Putawatimes & Pyankeshaws are already arrived - the Wyandotts Shawanoes
Miamies & Hurons are said to be on their way from the big rock [near the
mouth of Detroit River] - under the Conduct of Blue Jacket. & some of the
Michigan and Wabash Indians have reached Fort Wayne on their way in But I
can not as yet form any just estimate of the Numbers that may eventually
assemble--" (Knopf, 1955, p. 427).

While Wayne was preparing for the meeting of the tribes at Greenville
to effect a peace treaty, difficulties were being created by parties of
Kentuckians who were crossing the Ohio and making attacks upon the Indians.
Writing to Governor St. Clair on June 5, 1795 Wayne stated that to the
"aggressions" of the "predatory parties" from Kentucky "may justly be attributed all the recent depredations committed by the savages" (Smith, 1882,
2:374-5). He specifically alluded to "certain acts of hostilities committed
by a Mr. Whitesides and his gang of marauders upon the Indians in the Illinois
country,..." involving the murder of two Indian prisoners (idem). Subsequently, in a "Report of Official Proceedings in the Illinois Country"
Governor St. Clair wrote about "some confusion in the western countries of
this Territory (Illinois)..." This was, in part, a reference to "information
from General Wayne that, after the armistice had taken place (before the
Greenville Treaty), a number of Indians peaceably following their occupation
of hunting had been killed in that country, and, about the same time, I was
informed of two Pottawatamies, in the custody of the sheriff, having been
murdered there" (ibid. p. 396). This latter is apparently an allusion to
Wayne's report of the murder of two Indian prisoners in the Illinois country.

331

It is not stated, however, whether the Indians hunting in that country were Potawatomi, although the inference is not without merit because of evidence already adduced that they were on the Illinois River in the Spring of 1794 (AMH 4:110-111).

In addition, a letter written from Cahokia by St. Clair to Wayne on May 12, 1795 refers to "...Several murders that have been Commited here by the potewatimies of the Illinois River..." and also notes that a party of Kickapoo murdered a number of Americans near the mouth of the Ohio (A-412).

During the same month (May, 1795) Captain John Wade, journeying up the Wabash River from Vincennes, met parties of Kickapoo and Potawatomi, and also recorded that "The names of the Potowatamies Chiefs at The Thipecanos are La Masse - and La Blau or Bennac..." (A-411). Then, in June, Thomas Bodley, another officer who went up the Wabash with some families of civilians stated that at Terre Haute "...some of the Wabash Indians are raising Corn this Season -..." Bodley also observed that in the vicinity of the Tippecanoe River "...about 200 acres is now under Cultivation by the Potawatomy & Weyaw Indians,..." And farther up the Wabash, at the Salamine River, he noted, "...part of the Miami Indians are raising Corn up this River - " (A-413). In a letter to Wayne, written at the same time, Bodley stated that at the Tippecanoe "about fifty Potawatomy's & some Wyaws" asked him for provisions and supplies, the chiefs present being the same ones met by Wade (A-414).

332

XI - 1795-1819

After the Treaty of Greenville animosities arose between some of the Potawatomi and other tribes on the Wabash River, including Miami. According to a message sent by "Wabash Indians" in February, 1796 to General Wilkinson at Fort Wayne they were pillaged during the winter by Potawatomi, and they wanted the commandant to avert the outbreak of hostilities (A-418). A chief of the St. Joseph Potawatomi repudiated the hostile behavior of the Potawatomi complained of. In his reply to Wilkinson's message to the Potawatomi this chief stated in March that "I have used every measure to prevent our people from settling on the Wabash - as I expected difficulties and disputes would arise". He went on to say that "last Summer I ordered my people from the Wabash, but they were deaf to me. . .not an Inch of Land of that Country belongs to us, and those obstinate intruders who now hunt there - are dependent upon their Wabash Brethren for permission - . . .Too many of our nation aspire to be chiefs - and when they find they cannot be such in their own Country - they fly to the woods, and impose themselves upon people of other tribes, as Chiefs - intrude upon Lands not belonging to them, and are not only troublesome to us, but to all who meet them.--" He further stated that "These are the sentiments of the Chiefs (Children of the Pottawatamees of the St. Joseph) now living - they have always respected the Miamis, as their best friends - and in consequence of this friendship, a part of our nation has been permitted to live and hunt at, and near the Thopicanos --" (italics - JJ). According to the Chief, he had several days before " . . .sent a Speech to my Wabash Brethren, assuring them of my friendship, and blaming the Conduct of the accused, for the damage done last winter. . ." (A-420).

333

Of the Illinois Indians only the Kaskaskia are listed as participants in the treaty of Greenville, and then, jointly with the Kickapoo as signatories. One year later, in August, 1796, "Ducain Chief of the Kaskaskias Tribe of Indians" acted as spokesman for the Illinois, Sac and Fox, and the Piankashaw in a meeting at Vincennes with Captain Pasteur (G-29). In connection with the first of these tribes Ducoigne's statement was, in part: ". . .I am going to Speake for the Illinois Indians, the Piories the Kaskaskias & Cahokia. . ." And then again: "We beg you will lestin & beleave us three nations. . ." (ibid). Although the chief requested that the Illinois be maintained in peace and security on their lands he did not mention geographical location. But of immediate interest is the fact that only the Kaskaskia, Peoria and Cahokia are mentioned as constituting sub-groups of the Illinois Indians.

On the basis of his visit to North America in 1796 Victor Collot groups the Kaskaskia, Peoria, and "Mitchigamas" together (Cahokia are not listed), attributes 300 warriors to them, and locates them "Near the Illinois, on the American side (Collot 1:304). While the general location is reasonable enough, the number of warriors is considerably dated. Harmar, in the summer of 1787, attributed to the Illinois a maximum population of fifty (Thornbrough, 1957, p. 48). At that time Harmar included the Michigamea with the Kaskaskia, Peoria, and Cahokia. Since then Collot apparently is the only source in which the Michigamea are listed.

As regards other tribes Collot groups together a "Portion of the Kickapoos", Piankashaw, Mascouten, and Wea and places them "On the Wabash, or adjacent branches" with a combined total of 1,000 warriors (Collot 1:303). He also has Potawatomi at Detroit, with 150 warriors and "Near St. Joseph" with 200 warriors (ibid. p. 304). There are 400 Kickapoo warriors on Lake Superior, and others of that tribe "On Lake Michigan, and between the Mississippi," with Mascouten included in the latter location (idem). It is

334

obvious that Collot had no first hand information and that he used earlier sources. He receives support from other sources only as regards location of the Illinois, Potawatomi, and part of the Kickapoo.

In October, 1796 the Kickapoo are reported to have "moved to the Banks of the Mississippi below the mouth of Kaskaskia River. . ." This information was conveyed in a letter to Anthony Wayne written at Fort Wayne by R. J. Meigs, the Commissary at that post, who learned it from Ducoigne, the Kaskaskia chief. The latter told Meigs that on his way to Fort Wayne he had met a small Kickapoo hunting party (A-426). But where the Kickapoo were hunting is not indicated. Information obtained by Captain Zebulon Pike at Fort Massac on the lower Ohio, and confirmed by Captain Pasteur at Vincennes, revealed that the Kickapoo chiefs had determined to make a strike upon the Chickasaw and Cherokee (A-404). It is possible that this decision was related to their movement to the Mississippi; and it may also explain why they had failed to come to Fort Wayne to receive their annuity, as reported by Meigs (A-425, 426, 427).

335

One observer's view of the situation in the Illinois country at the beginning of 1797 is recorded in the journal of Moses Austin who left Virginia to explore lead mines in Missouri (AHR 5:518-542). Having arrived at Vincennes on January 1, 1797 he writes of the Piankashaw that they ". . .had a Town within One Mile of St. Vincennes but its now destroyd and there Number reduced to about 120 men. they have not any Town or fixed place of residence but wander about from place to place always calling Vincinnces ther Home". The sentence immediately following this statement concerns the Wea who ". . .are said to be 150 men and are settled up the Wabash 200 miles from Vincennces" (ibid. p. 530).

Another town visited by Austin was Cahokia where, he notes, there was

formerly under the English, "an Extensive Indian Trade" but that under
American dominion "many of the best families have Crossd the Missisipi and
with them the Indian Trade" (ibid. p. 534). He also crossed the Mississippi
on a visit to St. Louis, and in this connection made the following observations: "The Aborigines which Trade to St. Louis are the Kakapoos Piankishas
Piorias Sioux Shawanees (west of the Missisipe) and Osages on the Missouri.
There is none of the above Indians that confine there Trade to St. Louis
Except the Osages. but St. Louis gets the best part of all as well as many
other Nations both on the Missisipi and Missouri which seldom or ever Visit
the Town of St. Louis, but have goods taken to them by Traders, imploy.d by
the Merchts of St. Louis, who make there returns in the Months of April and
May" (ibid. p. 535). In another reference to the St. Louis trade he said that
it comes "from the Missouri Illinois and upper parts of the Missisipi" (idem);
but Trudeau, the governor of Spanish Illinois, wrote Governor-General Gayoso
de Lemos concerning the Indian trade of the Mississippi above St. Louis that
"now it is in the hands of the Americans" (Nasatir, 1952, 2:528). Austin
suggests that unless the U.S. Government reverses its policy of neglect the
Indian trade will become permanently established on the Spanish side of the
Mississippi River.

336

Finally, in writing of the Illinois Indians, Austin states that the
Kaskaskia "now do not consist of more than 8 or 10 men at most" and then adds:
"the Neighbouring Tribes who called themselves Tamaroicas Mitchigamias, and
Kahokias, are all extinct, or at Least, if they are living they have Joined
other nations, and the Piorias, the remaining Tribe of those Indians who
were Called by the general Name of the Illinois Indians, now live on the
Spanish side of the Missisipi, and do not consist of more than 40 men" (AHR,
5:539). Whether or not the Tamaroa and the Michigamea may be considered

extinct or absorbed, the Cahokia, according to Ducoigne, quoted above, are
still in the picture. As for the Peoria, this is not the first time they
have been reported as residing on the Spanish side of the Mississippi. How
fixed this residence was is, at this point, still an open question. It is
hardly to be doubted that they moved on both sides of the river and that the
attraction of the Spanish lay in the easily accessible trade. They did not
necessarily abandon the traditional exploitation of their lands east of the
Mississippi.

In a letter to an unidentified official, possibly the commandant of
Fort Knox at Vincennes, written in September, 1797 from Kaskaskia Chief
Ducoigne stated, on the one hand, that he "can give no information of" the
Indians on the Spanish side who, he claimed, were "Continuelly exclaiming
against Me, as I am an American and all the Americans, and threten my life
. . ." (A-428). On the other hand, in referring to Delaware, Shawnee and
Miami, he stated that "Now they are running away daily taken protection under
the Sp. [anish] and exclaiming against the Americans to be bad people they
will not be satisfied with what the Spanish gave them, but are continuelly
coming on this Side and killing up our game,. . ." (idem).

337

Since Ducoigne was writing from Kaskaskia "this Side" obviously means
the Illinois country east of the Mississippi. A report from Trudeau, the
Spanish governor at St. Louis, throws a different light on the situation.
Writing on December 20, 1797 Trudeau said: "Small parties of the Chavanones
[Shawnee], Loups, Peorias, Illinois, Miamia, Otave, Mascutin, Kikapoux, and
Pouteatamia nations are scattered over our territory. Many of them, encamped
close to our settlements, carry on commerce or exchange as best pleases them.
Most often they bring their skins to the different villages, and the same is
done with us by the nations of the American side when they find that goods

are sold to them cheaply" (Nasatir, 1952, 2:529; italics - JJ).

From the way Trudeau put it the groups he mentions may have been, for the most part, essentially trading parties of temporary sojourners engaged in economic exchanges. There is no indication or implication of regular, continued residence in Spanish territory. However, as regards the Shawnee and Delaware (Loups), in 1793 Ducoigne told Jefferson that they "came from the Spanish side of the river" to make raids against the Kaskaskia and others (Bergh, 1907, 16:389). In June, 1805 Governor Harrison had occasion to write of part of "the Delawares who reside on the West side of the Mississippi" while others were living on White River in Indiana (TP 7:294). In 1805, Major James Bruff, in a despatch from St. Louis to General Wilkinson, reported that a Potawatomi chief who refused to attend the treaty of Greenville took his party across the Mississippi and "put himself under Spanish protection and had land assigned him & party on the Missouri at the upper edge of the settlements,. . ." (TP 13:102). This same report made reference to "the warriors of the nations up the Mississippi & Illionois who hunted on the Missouri. . ." (idem).

According to a petition submitted on October 1, 1800 to the Government by inhabitants of what is now southern Illinois (Randolph and St. Clair counties of Indiana Territory) "the Kaskaskia Tribe of Indians, who alone can claim the Country in their neighbourhood, do not exceed fifteen in number. . ." (Dunn, 1894, p. 457). The population figure is significantly less than that implied in a letter of July 15, 1801 written to the Secretary of War by the governor of Indiana Territory, William Henry Harrison, who referred to "the remnant of the Kaskaskias which have only fifteen or twenty warriors" (Esarey, 1922, 1:30 and 1:45; italics - JJ). In this same communication Harrison states that the Kickapoo, by contrast, "are a strong and warlike Nation" and then adds

338

that the Prairie Kickapoo are "a large branch of that nation [who]. . .fre-
quently steal Horses. . ." (idem). In view of Indian complaints of encroachment on their lands and the wanton destruction of game by the whites "in
violation of law," Harrison urged that the boundaries between lands of the
U.S. and the Indian tribes be "ascertained and marked" in order to avert the
ultimate outbreak of an Indian War (ibid. pp. 25-31). By the end of the
following December, (1801) Harrison wrote President Jefferson "that the
American name has become almost universally odious to the Tribes upon this
frontier." He recommended that troops be stationed at Kaskaskia and on the
Illinois River in an effort "to put an end to the petty depredations which a
Banditti composed of outcasts from all the Tribes (who have established themselves on the Illinois river) & the Kickapoos of the Prairie are continually
making upon our settlements --". Such troops, Harrison stated, could also
be used to interdict the "valuable" Spanish trade on the Illinois River in
goods smuggled into American territory from Canada via Louisiana territory
(TP 7:42-3).

339

     The Indians in the Illinois and Indiana area under Harrison's juris-
diction, being much concerned about the definition of boundaries under the
terms of the Treaty of Greenville, the Governor wrote to the Secretary of
War on February 26, 1802 recommending that a settlement of this question and
others be reached with the following tribes: Delaware, Potawatomi, Eel River,
Wea, Kickapoo, Sac and Kaskaskia. He also indicated that some of the tribes
were "much irritated against each other" (Esarey, 1922, 1:41-46). Although
it is not clear that it was related to the latter comment of Harrison, the
Secretary of War, Henry Dearborn, writing to the Governor the following July
3, 1802 expressed the hope "that your Agent may succeed in adjusting the
disputes between the Pottawattamas and Kaskaskias" (A-437).

On this same date (July, 1802) another letter, written in France by Louis Vilemont a "former Captain of the Regiment of Louisiana" who had spent several years in the Mississippi River area stated that the Potawatomi possessed 1,000 warriors and were situated 100 leagues (250 miles) north of St. Louis; while the Kickapoo and Mascouten with 700 warriors are given the same location. With respect to the Mississippi River each of these tribes is located on the "Eastern Bank. . ." (Nasatir, 1952, 2:694).

On September 17, 1802, at Fort Wayne, Harrison reached agreement with Potawatomi, Kickapoo, Eel River, Kaskaskia, Wea and Piankashaw chiefs in which "The United States shall relinquish all claim to lands in the neighborhood of Vincennes excepting [the Vincennes Tract]." The names of the signatory chiefs of the aforementioned tribes are part of this document (Esarey, 1922, 1:56-7).

340

In an unofficial letter to Governor Harrison (February 27, 1803) in which he outlined Indian policy and suggested means of acquiring Indian lands both in terms of the future best interests of the aborigines, as he saw them, and in order to consolidate and strengthen the western frontier of the United States, Jefferson thought that there was "a favorable opening" for taking steps to extinguish the title of the few remaining Illinois Indians. The President stated the position thus: "the Cahokias being extinct, we are entitled to their country by our paramount sovereignty. the Piorias we understand have all been driven off from their country, & we might claim it in the same way; but as we understand there is one chief remaining, who would, as the survivor of the tribe, sell the right, it will be better to give him such terms as will make him easy for life, and take a conveyance from him. the Kaskaskies being reduced to a few families, I presume we may purchase their whole country for what would place every individual of them at his ease,

& be a small price to us." After this statement with respect to the Illinois
Jefferson continued: "thus possessed of the rights of these three tribes, we
should proceed to the settling their boundaries with the Poutewatamies &
Kickapoos; claiming all doubtful territory, but paying them a price for the
relinquishment of their concurrent claim, and even prevailing on them if
possible to cede for a price such of their own unquestioned territory as would
give us a convenient Northern boundary" (TP 7:88-92; Esarey, 1:69-73).

In September (1803) the "remnants" of the Illinois Indians were included in "An Account of the Indian Tribes in Louisiana" sent from New Orleans by
Daniel Clark to Secretary of State James Madison in answer to Madison's
request for information on this subject. Clark's information, which is more
specific, lends support to Harrison's general statement above on the Illinois.
According to Clark: "At St. Genèvieve in the Settlement among the Whites are
about 30 Piorias Kaskaskies & Ilinois, who seldom hunt for fear of the other
Indians, they are the remains of a nation which 50 years ago Coud bring into
the field 1200 Warriors --" (TP 9:64). In writing of the situation a little
further south along the Mississippi River, also within the present state of
Missouri, Clark states: "On the River St. Francis, in the neighbourhood of
New Madrid, Cape Gerardeau Reviere a la Pomme, & the environs, are settled a
number of Vagabonds, emigrants from the Delawares, Shawnese, Miamis, Chicasaws,
Cherokees, Piorias and supposed to Consist in all of 500 families,. . .They
. . .seldom remain long in any place,. . ." Crossed out in the original
document is the statement that "they were Attracted to the Country by the
Spaniards some years ago when their views were hostile to our Country--"
(idem).

Consistent with some of the preceding information are some of the
"notes" made by Nicholas Biddle during his visit with William Clark in

341

Virginia. Although written in 1810 (c.April) the data recorded by Biddle probably pertain to 1804 or the years 1804-06. The following statement is made regarding the Peoria: "Near St. Genevieve roving about are the Piories, a band of about 30 men -- the only remnant of a large nation of the same name who formerly lived on the Eastern side of the Mississi" (Jackson, 1962, p. 523; italics - JJ). This is followed by a statement on the Kaskaskia: "Opposite Ste. Genevieve in the town of Kaskaskia, live in a part of the town (now Seat of govt.) by themselves the Kaskaskia tribe of about 15 men the remains of a numerous people of Kaskaskias who lived in the same place" (idem).

Continuing, Biddle's "notes" have this to say about the Potawatomi and Ottawa: "Roving about the settlements sometimes on Missouri sometimes the Gasconnade & the Osage are tribes of Potawatamies & Taways the first from the Illinois near Lake Michigan the 2d from the Illinois river -- sometimes joined and sometimes separate - in the whole not more than 20 men - hunting etc" (idem). The total number from these groups obviously comprised a relatively small band which probably operated independently of the main concentrations in the northerly half of Illinois, southwestern Michigan, and northwestern Indiana.

That some of the Kickapoo were also in the general area of the Mississippi River, south of St. Louis, is evident from information provided by Meriwether Lewis prior to his departure on the expedition with William Clark. Writing to Clark on February 18, 1804 from "Camp at River Dubois" (Wood Creek, opposite the mouth of the Missouri), Lewis said: ". . .my detention has been caused by a visitation on the 13th and 14th insts. from a principal Chief of the Kickapoo nation,. . ." (Jackson, 1962, p. 167). On May 17 next several Kickapoo visited Clark at St. Charles (Thwaites, 1959, 1:19);

342

and the following day Clark recorded that Lewis had sent an emissary "to the
Kickapoo Town on public business,. . ." (ibid. p. 21). On their way up the
Mississippi just before reaching the Missouri the expedition passed a Kickapoo
camp on the east bank (ibid. p. 26). A parenthetical statement refers to the
Kickapoo as "An Indian nation residing on the heads of Kaskaskis & Illinois
river. . .,& hunt occasionally on the Missouri" (idem). Another version of
this is recorded in Nicholas Biddle's "Notes": "The Kickapoos on the heads of
Kaskaskia river also hunt about the Illinois settlements - bands of these
people hunt on the Missouri the whole about 200 men" (Jackson, 1962, p. 523).
It may be that when Major Bruff in his letter to General Wilkinson on March
12, 1805 mentioned that "warriours of the nations up the Mississippi &
Illinois. . .hunted on the Missouri" the Kickapoo were among those he had in
mind (TP 13:102).

The Kaskaskia, having ceded lands under terms of a treaty negotiated   343
by Harrison on August 13, 1803, the Secretary of War wrote the Governor on
April 20, 1804 on the subject of pursuing the matter further. It was not
only necessary "to ascertain the boundaries of the lands ceded by the
Kaskaskias" but also, since "the adjacent Tribes may feel interested in the
boundary from the mouth of the Saline creek northward and from the North-
westerly corner to the mouth of the Illinois it will probably be necessary to
have a conference on that subject. . .I presume [the Piankashaw and Kickapoo]
will feel more immediately interested than any others" (TP 7:190-1).

As regards the possible interest of the Kickapoo in these boundaries it
is relevant to note that Harrison issued to one Michael Brouillette on July
10, 1804 a license "to trade with the said Kickapoes nation, at their towns
on the Vermillion. . ." but not at their hunting camps (Esarey, 1922, 1:102-3).
Subsequently on May 27, 1805 Harrison informed the Secretary of War that

during the spring he had met with "a large deputation from the Kickapoos of the Prairie another from those of the Vermilion River" (ibid. p. 133). In June he wrote Jefferson that in addition to the Piankashaw, Wea and Eel River Miami "the Putawatimies of the Wabash & the Kickapoos of the Vermilion River have lately been with me & am persuaded that they are more warmly attached to us than they have ever been" (TP 7:294). Writing again to Secretary Dearborn on July 10, 1805 he mentioned that "two large parties of the Kickapoos of the Prairie...visited me in the latter part of the Winter..." (A-232).

Harrison wrote to the Secretary of War March 3, 1805 concerning Miami and Potawatomi claims to the tracts ceded by the Delaware and Piankashaw in 1804 (Esarey, 1922, 1:76-84). According to the Governor the Piankashaw had been "in possession of the country on either side of" the Wabash from its mouth up to the Vermilion at, and from, the time the French appeared on that river; and the Wea "have occupied the country above Point Coupee since their Towns at Ouiatenon were destroyed by Generals Scott and Wilkinson in the year 1791" (ibid. p. 77). And as for the Potawatomi, "so far from having any claim on the South East side of the Wabash [they] acknowledge that they have trespassed upon the Miamis by settling on the north bank of that river..." (ibid. p. 80). In support of Harrison's remark concerning Potawatomi trespass on Miami lands on the north side of the Wabash is the statement of the St. Joseph Potawatomi chief in 1796 cited above (A-420). In comments on the Illinois Indians Harrison refers to "the contemptable band which follows Ducoign and a remnant of Peorias who procure a miserable subsistance by begging and stealing from the inhabitants of St. Genevieve,..." (Esarey, 1922, 1:78).

Reference to the Potawatomi on the Illinois River was made by the Kaskaskia chief Ducoigne on March 2, 1805 in a message he sent to the

Potawatomi chief Gomo at Peoria inviting "all the Nations of Wabash, Delaware,
Chawnees, Piankaskas, Miamis, Pouttewatemies, Ottawas, Osakees and Yourself
in the Illinois River" to join in destroying The Osage who "are everyday
killing us, Plundering our Horses, and our furs, where they meet us alone.-"
(TP 13:103-4; and p. 296; italics - JJ). As for the Potawatomi of St. Joseph,
Harrison wrote Jefferson in June, 1805 that they had come under the influence
of the Miami chief Little Turtle and that he (Harrison) had "sent Col. Vigo
to the Miamis & Putawatimies to enquire into the causes of their uneasiness..."
(TP 7:294), which apparently derived from contentions of the Miami over the
cession made by the Delaware and Piankashaw the previous year (A-209, A-234,
A-186). According to Harrison a satisfactory resolution was achieved. Then
on November 29, 1805 Harrison informed Dearborn, Secretary of War, that "I
have sent for the Piankashaw chiefs to negociate for the tract of land between
the Wabash and the Kaskaskias purchase - two or three of them are near me but
one of them whose presence I think necessary is on the Mississippi and it will
take some time to get him Here" (A-235).

   In December Harrison received a report on the Kickapoo in which was
contained the information that it was customary for some of them to gather
persimmons in the vicinity of Goshen, Madison County, Illinois (Esarey, 1922,
1:176-7). This coincides with what some Kickapoo told William Arundell, a
former Indian trader, regarding their intentions of planting corn "a short
day's journey above Goshen" (A-518). This general area is in the southwestern quadrant of Illinois opposite St. Louis. It will be recalled that
Lewis and Clark observed in the Spring of 1804 a Kickapoo camp on the Illinois
side of the Mississippi, referred to a Kickapoo town, and were visited by
several Kickapoo below St. Louis while the expedition was at Camp Dubois.
Arundell also stated that "The principal village of the Kickapoos is East of

345

[Peoria], about two day's journey" and that they "are said to have among them about three hundred warriors, but in my opinion their number is greater (A-518). Arundell also characterizes the relationship between the Kickapoo and Mascouten. He writes: "Several years ago a few of their tribe [Kickapoo] separated from them, and called themselves Mascoutans, or the Indians of the meadows, who have recently settled in the vicinity of St. Charles, or Portage des Sioux, and have probably among them about forty warriors" (idem).

Although not often mentioned in recent years, the Mascouten reappear once again in association with the Kickapoo in a "Commission of Oyer and Terminer" signed by Governor Wilkinson in St. Louis on May 24, 1806 (TP 13:541).

Pierre Chouteau, resident and trader of St. Louis, in a report to General Wilkinson, Governor of Louisiana Territory, noted that "the Nations of the Mississippi and the Illinois river...come to the Missouri to hunt,...";

346 he also stated that, during the Spanish régime, among "the nations which received presents and provisions from the Lieutenant-Governor of Upper Louisiana" were the Peoria and the Kickapoo (Nasatir, 1952, 2:767, 769). This document reveals that the same interpreter functioned for the Peoria, Delaware, Shawnee, and Kickapoo.

In an effort to deal with the increasingly hostile attitude of the Kickapoo Governor Harrison sent to William Prince instructions as an emissary to the Kickapoo village on the Vermilion River. If it should prove safe to do so Prince was then to proceed "to the [Kickapoo] villages on the Prairies". From there, if time and circumstances permitted, he could go on "to the Potawatamie villages on the Wabash,..." (Esarey, 1922, 1:191-3). But these efforts were apparently unavailing, for the following August Harrison wrote that the Kickapoo and Sac were soliciting others "to join in a War against us --" (TP 1:375-6).

In William Clark's table of information on Indian tribes, the data of which were obtained in the course of the Lewis and Clark expedition, a population of 40-60 Kickapoo is recorded "about the mouth of the Missouri". This group hunted up the Missouri as far as Osage Woman River (Thwaites, 1959, 6:112). Captain Pike, on his voyage on the Mississippi in 1805-06, observed that "Immediately on the peninsula formed by the confluence of the rivers Mississippi and Missouri is a small Kickapoo settlement, occupied in summer only" (Pike, 1895, 1:288). Clark also lists the "Piories & Illinois" among whom, he says, there are eighteen warriors in a population estimated at approximately fifty or less. Their residence is in the vicinity of St. Genevieve, below St. Louis (Thwaites, 1959, 6:112).

Another indication of the presence of Potawatomi on the west side of the Mississippi is in a communication to the Secretary of War on January 6, 1807 from Acting Governor Browne of Louisiana Territory who wrote that "an Indian of the Pottawatamy tribe, who resides on the head Waters of the River Merrimac [Meramec], arrived here [St. Louis] on his way to the Pottawatamy Kickapoo, and other Nations of Indians, who inhabit the east side of the Missisippi,..." (TP 14:72).

The American inhabitants of Peoria addressed a memorial to Congress on February 26, 1807. This document again restated the historic importance of the Illinois River and of Peoria. It refers to the fact that the river "has hitherto been the channel of an extensive trade between Canada and Louisiana;" that "Peoria is a deposit of the furr-trade west of the lakes and North of the Illinois river" and is also "the yearly rendevouz of Several Nations of Indians--" (TP 7:431). According to William Arundell, Peoria "is the principal place of rendezvous for the Indians and Traders of the Illinois river in the Spring..." (A-518).

Late in April, 1807 when a Kaskaskia was found murdered seven miles from the village of Kaskaskia a "war sign" on the body implied that the Kickapoo were bent on exterminating the Kaskaskia (Esarey, 1922, 1:211-212). A party of Kickapoo told William Clark at St. Louis that one of their tribe did in fact perpetrate the deed, but they disavowed any hostile intentions against the Kaskaskia (ibid. pp. 222-3). In the meantime Harrison ordered the militia to provide protection for the Kaskaskia and at the same time he "sent a message to the Chiefs of the Illinois Kickapoos through the chief of that Nation who resides on the Vermilion..." (ibid. pp. 213-214).

In reporting to the Secretary of War on his actions with regard to this situation Harrison also took occasion to refer to the developing influence of the Shawnee Prophet, Tenskwatawa, among the tribes (ibid. pp. 223-224). Nevertheless, on August 13, 1807 he wrote to the Secretary: "I pledge myself for the peaceable disposition of the Delawares, Miamis, Weas, Eel River Tribe, Piankeshaws, Kickapoos and the greater part of the Shawanos. Overtures have been made to them both by the British and Spaniards which they have rejected with indignation" (ibid. p. 229). Exactly one week later (August 20), however, Harrison received a communication from William Wells at Fort Wayne which threw an entirely different light on the situation. Wells wrote that although there did not appear to be indications of danger, the Indians from the Mackinac region "have continued to flock to Greenville which increases the fears of our frontiers" (ibid. p. 239). Two Indian informants reported to Wells that the upper lakes Indians "believe in what the Prophet tells them which is that the great spirit will in a few years distroy every white man in america that every Indian has made himself a _war club_..." (idem). Wells went on to say that he had just learned "that upwards of 200 Delawares have gone to meet the other Indians at the Kickapoo town in

348

the prairie where it is expected 13 different nations will be represented" (ibid. p. 240). The purpose of this meeting was being kept from those friendly to the Americans, and Wells felt, therefore, that "the Indians are certainly forming an improper combination one that it is not friendly towards us..." Wells not only noted that "the prophet keeps up a communication with the British at Malden", but he also expressed the opinion that "the British are at the bottom of all this Business and depend on it that if we have war with them that many of the Indian tribes will take an active part against us--" (ibid. p. 242).

When Harrison wrote the Secretary of War on August 29, 1807 he stated the belief that "the stir and commotion which have existed amongst [the neighboring tribes] for some time past" was "stimulated in the present instance by British influence. I am confident however that the ultimate object of the British (which no doubt is that of forming a general confederacy against us) has not yet been communicated either to the Miamis, Weas, Delawares or even to the Kickapoos. The Shawnees are certainly entirely devoted to the British as are a part of the Potawatomies, the Chippeways and Ottawas" (ibid. p. 243). With this letter Harrison enclosed a deposition made by Francois Ducharme in July at Chicago in which the latter expressed the belief that the St. Joseph Potawatomi "are hostile to the United States and meditates an attack on some part of the American settlements or garrisons..." (ibid. p. 245).

In his letter of August 20, referred to above, William Wells had mentioned that three Miami chiefs, Richardville, Pecan [Pacanne], and Owl, had been instrumental "in assembling the Indians at the Kickapoo towns". Then on September 30, in a dispatch to the Secretary of War, after stating that none of the Indians at his agency (Fort Wayne) "have been seen among the large bodies of Indians that have gone to see the Shawnese imposter at green vile--"

349

he mentioned the fact that the Delaware chiefs "have been for some time gone to a great council at the Kickapoo towns --" (A-458).

There is again a reference to the Kickapoo as "Illinois Indians" by Harrison on November 12, 1807 in a communication to Captain Hargrove, in command of Rangers east of the Wabash River (Cockrum, 1907, p. 226; also in Esarey, 1922, 1:273-4). Several days later Harrison again wrote to Hargrove telling him that after "some trouble between the settlers and the [Piankashaw] Indians who had a few wigwams some distance to the east of the Wabash river," the Indians joined "another band of Piankashaw Indians west of the Wabash several miles below the mouth of the White river" (Cockrum, 1907, pp. 227, 229-231). This would place these Piankashaw in southern Illinois some distance north of the Ohio.

In February 1808 Harrison, writing from Vincennes, still had the impression "that the disposition of the Indians in this vicinity is as friendly towards the United States as it ever has been," but he thought quite otherwise of the Potawatomi, Chippewa and Ottawa in the Detroit area. He also reported that a party of Sac "had passed through the Delaware towns on White River" on their way to the Shawnee Prophet to declare their tribe's intention of supporting him (Esarey, 1922, 1:283-4). Then on March 6 William Wells informed the Secretary of War that "The Shawnese Prophet is about to move to the Wabash 120 miles Southwest of this place and has sent for" the Sac, Fox, Iowa, Winnebago, and Menominee to meet him there (TP 7:531-2). When Wells wrote to the Secretary the next month (April 20, 1808) he seemed to think that "the Shawnese Prophet is losing his influence very fast" and reported that the latter "has moved from green vill on to a branch of the Wabash it is yet unknown where the chiefs of this agency [Fort Wayne] will suffer him to settle--" (ibid. p. 557). Other information contained in his

350

report indicated that the Potawatomi "that listened to the prophet last year ware hovering round this place in large numbers in a State of Starvation" and that "Marpack the great Poutawatamy War chief" intended making war on the Osage (idem). A few days later the Potawatomi chief Five Medals told Wells that all the Potawatomi would shortly meet at the St. Joseph Village and that he would try "to put them in the right path again" (ibid. p. 559).

In May, 1808 Harrison reported that the Prophet, who had moved to a village on the Wabash just below the Tippecanoe despite the original opposition of the Miami and Delaware, "has acquired such an ascendency over the minds of the Indians that there can be little doubt of their pursuing any course which he may dictate to them, and that his views are decidedly hostile to the United States is but too evident." In addition, Harrison had learned that "some of the villages of the Potawatimies...are under the Prophet's influence" (Esarey, 1922, 1:290-1).

According to a letter of Abraham Luckenbach, a Moravian who had travelled up the St. Mary's River to Fort Wayne in the latter part of the summer of 1808 there were Miami and Kickapoo "who live at the source of the Wabash and the streams which flow into it..." These groups would meet with Potawatomi from St. Joseph in the hunt (A-519).

Towards the end of December, 1808 Jefferson wrote to Harrison with respect to the country between the Kaskaskia cession of 1803 and the Sac and Fox cession of 1804. It was his "understanding" that this area "belonged to the Peorias, and that that tribe is now extinct." Under these circumstances the United States would "succeed to their title by our being proprietors paramount of the whole country" (Esarey, 1922, 1:322).

"In this case," Jefferson continued, "it is interesting to settle our boundary with our next neighbors, the Kickapoos. Where their western boundary is I know not; but they cannot come lower down the Illinois river than the Illinois lake,...and perhaps not so low. The Kickapoos are bounded to the S.E. I presume, by the ridge between the waters of the Illinois and Wabash, to which the Miamis [Piankashaw? - JJ] claim; and N.E. by the Potawatamies." And he urged Harrison to try to ascertain, as cautiously as possible, "the real location of the S.W. boundary of the Kickapoos, and then endeavor to bring them to an acknowledgment of it..." Jefferson's purpose was to "close our possessions on the hither bank of the Mississippi, from the Ohio to the Ouisconsin, and give us a broad margin to prevent the British from approaching that river," and smuggling themselves and their trade goods into the Louisiana Territory (ibid. pp. 322-3).

Although Jefferson believed the Peoria extinct, except for one individual, evidence cited above shows that he was not quite correct. Furthermore, when Harrison wrote to William Eustis, the new Secretary of War, on April 5, 1809 and referred to Jefferson's directive, quoted above, he phrased it as directing him "to commence a negotiation with the Kickapoo Indians and with the remnant of the Peorias for the settlement of our boundary and eventually for a further extinguishment of the title south of the Illinois river" (Esarey, 1922, 1:336).

Later that same month Harrison informed the Secretary that two Indian traders "who have spent the winter [1808-9] at the towns of the Potawatomies a few leagues below the station of the Prophet [on the Wabash below the Tippecanoe]...positively assert that the Prophet is feared and hated by all the neighbouring tribes, the Kickapoos excepted..." (ibid. p. 342). Harrison added that he had reason to believe in "the fidelity of the Miamis, Delawares, Weas, and Potawatomies of the Wabash..." (idem).

At the same time, however, Governor Clark wrote to the Secretary of

War from St. Louis that the Winnebago and the Prophet were conspiring during the late winter and spring with the Kickapoo, Sac and others on the upper Mississippi "& Illinois River to War against the frontiers of this Country" (TP 14:260).

When Harrison wrote again to Eustis early in July he had occasion to state, in a reference to the Wea, that they live in the country between Vincennes and the Vermilion River (A-481). Exactly one year later (July 11, 1810) in another letter to the Secretary he made mention of "the Wea village of Terre Haute" (Esarey, 1922, 1:444). By the middle of the same month (July, 1809) Ninian Edwards, Governor of the newly created Illinois Territory, reported to the Secretary of State that the Kickapoo had killed a Kaskaskia and stolen thirty horses from the tribe. Ducoigne not only demanded protection but also complained of the sale of liquor to his tribe (TP 16:51-2).

On September 30, 1809 Harrison concluded at Fort Wayne a treaty with the Miami, Eel River, Delaware and Potawatomi. The Miami gave up a claim to lands northwest of the Wabash. The Kickapoo claimed the same lands, and Harrison thought that being under the influence of the Prophet they might possibly refuse to surrender their claims. In writing to the Secretary of War on November 3, 1809 Harrison called the Miami "the real owners of the land" and said that the title of the Kickapoo to the same lands "derived only from present occupancy" (A-536).

When the Kickapoo chiefs came to Fort Wayne early in December they agreed to the cession made by the Miami northwest of the Wabash "and also a further extinguishment of Title as high up as the Vermilion River". Harrison informed the Secretary of War in a letter dated December 10, 1809 that he "was extremely anxious that the cession should have been extended to the river by the Treaty of Fort Wayne, but it was objected to because it would include

353

a Kickapoo Village" (Esarey, 1922, 1:396).

In April of 1810 the presence of Potawatomi near Peoria is evidenced by several depositions of white men concerning the possession by the Potawatomi chief "Main Pock's" wives of European articles which it was thought had been stolen (TP 16:116-117). "Main Pock" himself was accused of having stolen the contents of a canoe on the east bank of the Mississippi opposite the mouth of the Missouri (ibid. p. 116). These seem to be indications only that Potawatomi ranged the Illinois River area. They are not statements of actual residence. However, in a letter written in June (1810) Harrison made reference to "the Marpoe the Putawatimee Chief of the Illinois River..." (A-237).

At this time there was a report by Harrison of information from a trader who was at the Prophet's village on the Wabash. This trader claimed that the Prophet "has at least 1000 Souls under his immediate control (perhaps 350 or 400 men) principally composed of Kickapoos and Winebagos, but with a considerable number of Potawatimies and Shawanees and a few Chippewas and Ottawas", leading Harrison to the conclusion "that the Shawnee Prophet is again exciting the Indians to Hostilities against the United States" (Esarey, 1922, 1:417). Harrison did not doubt that the British were behind the "hostile disposition of the Prophet and his Votaries" and that they provided these Indians with the "considerable supply of ammunition" in their possession. They also seemed to have received an abundance of goods from the British, and this led the Indians to refuse to deal with American traders (ibid. p. 418).

The middle of May Harrison conveyed to the Secretary of War information he had received concerning the adherents of the Prophet. He wrote: "the Prophets force at present consists in the part of his own Tribe which

354

has always been attached to him; nearly all the Kickapoos, a number of the
Winebagoes, some Hurons from Detroit who have lately joined him, a number of
Potawatomies, 20 or 30 Muskoes or Creeks and some straglers from the Ottawas,
Chippeways and other tribes in all perhaps from 6 to 800. If the disaffection
extends to all the Tribes between the Illinois River and Lake Michigan, the
number will be doubled,..." (ibid. pp. 420-421).

By June the Prophet had won the allegiance of the Wyandot. As a result,
according to Harrison "those who were before indifferent or innimical to the
views of the Prophet are now hastening to him from every direction -". After
a visit from the Wyandot, the Miami of Mississinewa River and the Wea decided
to attend the Council to be held at the Prophet's village near Tippecanoe.
Harrison learned from a party of Iowa that they had separated, between
Vincennes and the Illinois River, from eleven Sac, Fox, and Winnebago "all
going to the Prophet and the British". The Potawatomi chief Mainpoc and his
followers were said also to have "taken the same direction..." (A-237; see
also A-238).

Another report received by Harrison from a French trader who was at the
Prophet's village indicated that there were "about 3,000 men within 30 miles
of the Prophets Town, that they are constantly councilling but that they are
very secret in their proceedings -" (A-237). When the boat which Harrison
sent up the Wabash with the salt annuity for the Indians reached the Tippecanoe
village "the Prophet & the Kickapoos who are with him refused to receive" the
consignment.

Finally, in this same document by Harrison there is this comment on
the plight the Indians in his area: "The Indians of this country are in fact
Miserable. the Game which was formerly so abundant is now so scarce as barely
to afford subsistance to the most active hunter - The greater part of each

355

Tribe are half the year in a state of starvation and astonishing as it may
seem these remote Savages have felt their full share of the misfortunes which
the troubles in Europe have brought upon the greater part of the world -"
(ibid).

In another letter Harrison said that not only did the Wea, Miami, and
Piankashaw "consent to attend the Great Council about to be holden at the
Prophets Village" but in addition "the country towards the Illinois River is
filled with Indians Puttawattamies. Iaowas. Sacs. &. & bending their
course to the same spot -" (A-238; see also Esarey, 1922, 1:449). About this
time (June 23, 1810) the editor of the Western Sun, a Vincennes newspaper,
published information he obtained from Harrison in which was included the
statement that "a principal Putawatimie chief arrived, being sent by the
representatives of 16 villages west of the Wabash to inform the governor that
356 they had abandoned the Prophet, and had thrown away the tomahawk which he
had put into their hands." This change seems to have taken place as a result
of representations by the Delaware whom Harrison encouraged and urged on in
these efforts (A-112). Whether or not the Delaware emissaries were present,
it was not only Potawatomi but also Chippewa and Ottawa who withdrew from
the Prophet's side at "the Council held at the Parke à Vache", according to
Harrison (A-484). The information he received from traders acting as his
agents indicated that the Wea, Eel River, and even some Kickapoo were apprehensive of becoming involved in a war with the United States as a result of
the Prophet's efforts. Not only did the latter claim "that the Indians had
been cheated of their lands" but he was insistent "that no sale was good
unless made by all the Tribes" (ibid). His arguments were developed at some
length by his brother Tecumseh before Harrison at Vincennes in August, 1810,
and were supported by representatives of Wyandot, Kickapoo, Potawatomi,

Ottawa and Winnebago (WS-1810; A-444, A-485).

Apparently Potawatomi chiefs friendly to the United States were "actively employed in forming a combination to disperse the banditti, which the Prophet has collected at Tippecanoe. They inform me [Harrison] that the Delawares, Miamis, and part of the Ottawas, Chippewas, and Potawatimis will unite for this purpose. Indeed I am told, by some young Potawatimis...that the Winebagos (who form the Prophet's principal strength) have been already warned to depart and that they agreed to go as soon as their corn is ripe." The Delawares also informed Harrison "that they were determined to put out the Prophet's fire this fall." But apparently Tenskwatawa was as determined and as implacable as ever. Even the Kaskaskia "were invited to the Prophet's congress and were informed that the object was to consult upon the subject of recovering their lands" (Esarey, 1922, 1:449-450).

Harrison was convinced that not only Tenskwatawa but also Matthew Elliott, the Indian Agent of the British, was active in subverting the Indians. Harrison was certain that the latter was responsible for the lavish distribution of British presents to the tribes (ibid. pp. 450-1). And in this he was borne out by William Hull at Detroit, who informed the Secretary of War on July 27, 1810 that "Large bodies of Indians from the westward and southward continue to visit the British post at Amherstburgh, and are supplied with provisions, arms, ammunition, etc. More attention is paid to them than usual" (ibid. p. 453).

357

According to Harrison "the principal part of these presents are given to the Miamis, Delaware, Shawnees, Potawatimies, Kickapoos, Chippewas, Ottawas, and Wyandots, and I calculate that they exceed in value all the Peltries collected by the British Traders from the country inhabited by those Tribes." In this case then, if there was no commercial advantage, British behavior must be motivated by "a desire to retain in their influence the most warlike of the Tribes, as a kind of barrier to Canada." (ibid. p. 451).

Harrison was under no illusions as to the reasons why some of the tribes had second thoughts about supporting the Prophet. As he put it in his letter of July 25 to Eustis: "You may rely upon it, Sir, that it was the fear of being involved in the correction which they saw preparing for the Prophet that has given life to the zeal which some of the tribes now manifest against him. The bustle amongst the Militia here [Vincennes], the Reviews and frequent musters which I caused to be made, the arival of Capt. [Thornton] Posey's company and the report which I had circulated that the Militia of Ohio and Kentucky were also preparing themselves produced a most beneficial effect and supported my representations with the best of all possible arguments which can be used to a savage" (ibid. p. 452).

358   Nevertheless, at the beginning of August, Harrison was reporting depredations against the settlers on the Embarrass fork of White River in Indiana, which he thought were probably committed by Kickapoo, Potawatomi and Shawnee at the instigation of the Prophet (ibid. pp. 453-4). But it developed that those responsible "were principally Creeks & stragglers from other Tribes" (A-485). Actually Harrison learned that the Kickapoo and others at the Prophet's village were "displeased" and "apprehensive over a possible American attack" (ibid.). At the same time Harrison received a petition from settlers in the area between the Wabash and the Little Wabash alerting him to the rumors of an Indian War which were responsible for the departure of about two-thirds of the forty-two families in the region (Esarey, 1922, 1:455).

In July four Americans who lived near the Missouri River about one hundred miles from St. Louis had been murdered by Potawatomi as the four were in pursuit of their stolen horses. Subsequently Governor Clark had a meeting "with Gomo the principal Chief of the Pottawatomies who reside on the Illinois River, with several Village Chiefs and about 40 of his Wariours 'who Came expressly to See and Speak to me, and to assure the white people that the portion of the Pottowatomies under his authority did not Commit the late murder; of the White people' This Chief blames the Pottawatomies under the Prophet influence, with whome he disclaim's any Connection with" (TP 14:413).

Early in November Harrison informed the Secretary of War that Tecumseh had gone to Canada to visit the British. He also wrote that "A party of Kickapoos from the village of the Prairie (the principal Town) headed by several chiefs have been with me" but Harrison refused to give them their annuities "untill all or a majority of the Chiefs shall attend and formally and solemnly renounce the Prophets party and again put themselves under the protection of their father the President -". When the Kickapoo left "pouring execrations upon the Prophet and the British" Harrison entertained few doubts that the entire tribe would return shortly for their annuities" (A-487).

In May, 1811 the Secretary of War received word from both Matthew Irwin in Chicago and William Clark in St. Louis that there were indications of a possible Indian uprising against the United States. From Chicago the intelligence was that "in the early part of the ensuing Summer, an assemblage of Puttawattamis, Shawanese & Kikapoo Chiefs, with their tribes, is to take place at the mouth of the Theakiki river...; and, after the objects of the meeting are developed, are to proceed to the British Garrison at Amherstburgh, which is in Canada, 18 miles from Detroit" (TP 16:159-160). Clark wrote of "the hostile appearance of the Indians towards the [Great] lakes and about the head of the Wabash river..." on the basis of information received from Iowa Indians (Esarey, 1922, 1:510-511). Clark also received word from John Lalime,

359

the Indian Interpreter at Chicago, that horses were stolen by two brothers-in-law of Main Poc, the Potawatomi chief who "is residing at the Peorias, or a little above it, at place they call Prairie du Corbeau [about 20 miles above Peoria]" (ibid. p. 511). A week later, on June 2, Lalime again wrote Clark saying that "A great number of Sakies and Kikapoos are gone to Detroit and the Putowattamies are preparing to go – they say that they are called by their English father –" (A-489). Later that same month (June) Governor Edwards described an incident on the Mississippi involving "five Pottawattimies who resided near Peoria" and added that "A considerable number of Indians from those bands that appear to be most hostile are collecting on our frontier near the Missisippi – They descend the Illinois in Canoes." In this same letter to the Secretary of War Edwards also included this statement: "All the accounts which I have received relative to the Prophet agree that he is embodying a considerable force on the Wabash, that it is daily increasing, and that his object is to strike one grand and decisive stroke as soon as he is prepared" (TP 16:162-3).

360

   Early in July, 1811 Governor Clark, in a long dispatch to the Secretary of War, conveyed evidence of his belief "that the Crisis is fast approaching". The information he received from various sources including not only sub-agents, interpreters, and spies but also some Ottawa and friendly Kickapoo chiefs in part concerned "the _hostile_ disposition of the greater part of the Pottowatomies...perticularly the Bands on the Illinois River, who are joined by the out cast vagabonds of the neighbouring Tribes" (A-490). Clark referred to Potawatomi depredations on "both Sides of the Mississippi" and "on the Northern frontiers of the Illinois Territory". In his discussion he referred to "the Pottowatomies towns on the Illinois River" and also to "those bands of Pottowatomies, & Winnebagoes on the head of the Illinois River and about Milliawaky..." Clark had "no doubts of the hostile disposition of those Bands of Indians on the Illinois River..." (ibid). At the same time Governor Edwards wrote that "...I consider peace totally out of the question. We need never expect it till the Prophets party is dispersed and the bands of Pottowattimies about the Illinois river are cut off" (TP 16:164).

Clark's letter to the Secretary also contained information about some Ottawa and an apparent division of allegiance among the Kickapoo. Concerning the Ottawa he had this to say: "a Small Band of Toways who resided on the Illinois river not far from its mouth, were alarmed at the Conduct of the pottowatomies & others, have moved to this [west] side of the Mississippi for fear (as they say) of the white people killing them in mistake for their enemies.-" (A-490). As for the Kickapoo: "Above half the Kickapoo Nation have left their Towns and joined the prophets party; the remaining part of that nation are well disposed and wish to continue on friendly terms with the white people their neighbours, the principal Chiefs were with me a fiew days ago - the Object of their Visit was to inform me of the disposition and Conduct of the pottowatomies & winnebagoes, and the Situation and disposition of their nation, to effect an arrangement for the Safety of that part of the nation who were deturmaned to live in friendship with the white people - They expressed some desire to move on this side of the Mississippi (from a Situation in the event of War between two fires) as they are Situated between the settlements of the Illinois and the Pottowatomies Towns. They have solicited my assistance to get back that part of their nation, who were then under the influence of the prophet -" (ibid).

361

According to Clark's data Potawatomi were located on the Illinois River from Peoria north; a small group of Ottawa were situated above the mouth of that river; Kickapoo were situated in the general region of central Illinois.

In Ninian Edwards' <u>History of Illinois</u> the Governor discusses the
events of Capt. Levering's commission to the Potawatomi, located in the
vicinity of Peoria, to obtain the murderers of some Americans and to seek
the return of stolen property. This discussion refers to various Potawatomi
villages: "a village on Yellow creek, whose chief is named Mat-cho-quis,
about ninety leagues from Peoria"; the village of "Latourt, or White Pigeon,
on the road leading to Detroit, about twelve leagues from St. Joseph";
another village "twelve or fifteen miles beyond White Pigeon, toward Detroit -
"; the village of Chief Gomo about seven leagues above Peoria." Gomo gave
Captain Levering "the names of the following Pottowottamie chiefs:
"Neng-ke-sapt, or Five Medals, at Elkhart, near Fort Wayne; Topennyboy, on
the River St. Joseph; Mo-quan-go, on the Qui-que-que [Kankakee] River;
Wi-ne-magne, or Cat Fish, on the Wabash River. He said that Marpock and his
principal chiefs had gone to Detroit, and probably would not return until the
fall. The chiefs of the towns on Fox River resided at Milwaukee; Little
Chief, on River Au Sable, or Sand River;..." (Edwards, 1870, p. 39). On
August 6, 1811 Levering's party, having gone "seven leagues up the Illinois
River" from Peoria, the leader and one of his men were taken "about four miles
higher up the river to a creek, from which place they were conducted, through
a moist and thicketty bottom, to Gomo's village,..." (ibid. p. 40).

362

Most of the foregoing data were apparently derived from a letter
written from Peoria by Captain Levering to Governor Edwards on August 12, 1811
(TP 16:175-179, esp. p. 176). In giving his impression that Gomo was somewhat less than candid Levering was constrained to admit: "that he [Gomo] is
under considerable dread of other chiefs, there can be no doubt, He is
unpleasantly situated, he is the nearest to our frontiers except a Band of
Kickapoos of about 40 to the north & east of this [Peoria], on his opposite

quarters, he is surrounded by Tribes that find themselved further removed from our vengeance. And in case they wish to depredate on us, they pass by him making his nation serve as a cover to their retreat" (ibid. p. 176).

Levering makes an interesting observation on the geographical disper- sion of various groups of Potawatomi. He writes: "At present the Putowatomies are so far one Nation, that those of another name and nation aggrieved by any of them revenge themselves on the first Putowatomie they meet, no difference what tribe, or whether situated north of the lakes in Michigan, Indiana, or Illinois Territories - Yet there are different interests, and opposing ambitions and jealousies among the tribes --" (ibid. p. 178). Levering suggested, therefore, that it would be easier to deal with them if they were to be united "closer in one interest" to the extent that they could create" a joint mission from Michigan Indiana, Illinois, and Louisiana, whether one man or more" (idem). This statement gives some idea of the wide geographical spread of the Potawatomi at this time. Again Captain Levering suggests that "The Mission might call their councill at Chicago and have the Chiefs to attend from Green bay and north of it, from Michigan, St. Josephs the Kankikee, Wabash, Illinois, and its waters, and this would be nearly central for the whole" (idem).

363

The speech of Governor Edwards which Levering delivered to the assembled chiefs of the Potawatomi on August 15, 1811 was addressed: "To the Chiefs and Warriors of the tribes of Pottawottamies, residing on the Illinois River and its waters, in the Territory of Illinois" (Edwards, 1870, p. 45). However, when Gomo made his reply the next day he was expressing "The ideas of the Pottawottamies, Ottaways and Chippeways...", as did Little Chief who followed Gomo (ibid. pp. 49-50). The preceding quotation which appears in the published version of Gomo's address was edited somewhat as were other parts of the speech. In the manuscript record the chief said: "The Ideas and sentiments of the Putowatomies, Ottoways and Chipaways belonging to this river [the Illinois]..." (A-491, italics - JJ).

Both Gomo and Little Chief also included the Kickapoo in their expression of friendly and peaceful feelings toward the Americans. Gomo placed the blame for the unruly behavior of the young men on the shoulders of the Shawnee Prophet. The position of the Potawatomi, Ottawa and Chippewa between the Prophet on the one hand and the Americans on the other was put this way by Little Chief: "We are like a bird in a bush beset and not knowing which way to fly for safety, to the right or to the left -". And he added: "Ever since the Shawnee Prophet has been on the Wabash River he has been jealous of the chiefs and warriors of the river [the Illinois]" (A-492; Edwards, 1870, p. 50).

364   Thomas Forsyth was returning from St. Louis late in October when he met a band of Potawatomi on the Illinois River below Peoria, and learned that they were going to spend the winter downstream above the river's mouth. Forsyth's information was sent to Governor Clark November 1, 1811 in this manner: "...on my assending the Illinoise River on my way home I met Shequinebee's band of Potawatimies encamped about 80 miles below this place [Peoria] I stopped a very short time to get some meat from them...This band of Shequinebee's is going to winter at a place called the Grand Pass about 60 miles from [above] the mouth of this River and not more than 30 or 40 Miles over land to the Settlements,..." (A-521).

Forsyth had also informed this band that the army was marching against the Prophet's Town situated on the west side of the Wabash just below the Tippecanoe. At that place on November 7 Harrison's forces defeated those of the Prophet consisting of Indians from the Shawnee, Ottawa, Chippewa,

Potawatomi, Wyandot, Kickapoo, Winnebago and Sac (Cockrum, 1907, p. 269).

Apparently the Kickapoo were those of the Prairie, for on November 27 Governor Harris informed Secretary Eustis that he requested Governors Edwards and Clark "to send speeches to the Kickapoos of the Prairie urging them to withdraw their warriors from the Prophet..." (A-494). According to the agent at Fort Wayne, John Johnston (November 28): "In the action [at Tippecanoe] there was no Delawares no Miamies, no Eel Rivers, few Putawatimies no Shawanoes except those who originally Seperated from the Tribe with the Prophet there was between 3 and 400 Indians in the action there were principally Kickapoos Winebagos some Shawanoese some Putawatimes and a small number of Wyandotts, in short a collection of all the vagabond Indians he could find, there was not in all his party a single ancient respectable chief" (A-495; see also Esarey, 1922, 1:680). Subsequently, on December 24 Harrison stated in a letter to Eustis that the Miami chief Owl came to him and confirmed "the opinion which I had before entertained that all the Potawatamies who reside on the Wabash (excepting the Chief Winenac) were in the action. He says he saw the warriors from both the villages above the Prophets Town going to join him the day before the action and that it was with the greatest difficulty that the young men of his own Tribe could be prevented from joining him also" (Esarey, 1922, 1:684). On May 7, 1812 Benjamin Stickney, then agent at Fort Wayne, referred to Winnemac as "a friendly Putawatamie Chief, who resides on the Wabash, about 6 miles above the Prophets Town;..." (Thornbrough, 1961, pp. 116-117).

365

But on January 14, 1812 Harrison again wrote Eustis contradicting the information from Chief Owl. According to the Governor: "It is agreed by every one that the whole of Winemac's party of the Potawotimies fought against us and it is equally well known that he received a considerable reinforcement of Kickapoos Potowatimies from the Illinois River. a very few days before the action -". Harrison also took issue with Johnston, agent at Fort Wayne, who estimated that there were 300 to 400 Indians in the battle at Tippecanoe. Harrison then cited information which the latter obtained from Indian informants whose estimates of the number "varied from 560 to 732" (A-499; see also Esarey, 1922, 1:680). In an account published in the Vincennes newspaper Western Sun, Captain Snelling, commandant of Fort Harrison, included the Piankashaw in the battle (WS-1812).

Early in December, 1811 two chiefs of the Prairie Kickapoo came to Vincennes and delivered a message "from the Chief of that part of the Kickapoos which had joined the Prophet" saying that the chief would shortly visit Harrison. The messenger chiefs also informed Harrison that Tenskwatawa and his Shawnee were now "at a small Huron village about twelve miles from his former residence on this [east] side of the Wabash,...The Kickapoos are encamped near to the Tippecanoe - the Potawatomees have scattered and gone to different villages of that Tribe - ...The Prophet had sent a messenger to the Kickapoos of the Prairie to request that he might be permitted to retire to their town" (Escarey, 1922, 1:656). As Harrison was reporting these facts in a letter to the Secretary of War on December 4 he added a P.S. stating·· "The chief of the Vermillion Kickapoos has this moment arrived" (ibid. p. 658).

When on April 16, 1812 Governor Edwards held a council at Cahokia with the chiefs of the Potawatomi, Kickapoo, Ottawa and Chippewa, the Kickapoo chief Little Deer took the occasion in his brief remarks to say that "I am of the village of Great Lick" and later referred to it as a "small" village (Edwards, 1870, p. 60). In his response to Edwards chief Gomo said he had considered asking the government "to place a factory in our town of Peoria" and he later added that "I am at the other end of Peoria Lake. It is where we will reside, and remain at peace in hunting to support our families" (ibid.

p. 63). This association of the Potawatomi with the Illinois River in the general vicinity of Peoria was also alluded to by Edwards. In referring to the murderers of Americans whom he was trying to obtain, Edwards said: "My children, you say these bad men are gone to the Prophet. This I know is not true - for one of them you left near Peoria, with a sore foot, and they have lived within three leagues of Peoria for a long time" (ibid. p. 64).

By the end of January, 1812 Harrison was recommending "that half of the Piankashaw and as much of the Kickapoo's annuity be confiscated by the Government in consequence of their having permitted their Warriors to join the Prophet & make War upon us. Considerably more than half of the Kickapoos were with him, and nearly half of the Pianikshaws. The Potawatimies, ought also to be made to suffer for their Conduct - but that tribe is so large that the Annuity which they now receive is not Sufficient for them" (A-239).

On February 10 Governor Edwards wrote Secretary Eustis that he had "sent for the chiefs of the Kickapoos and Pottawottamies of the Illinois River," but they refused to come. According to Edwards, "The Winnebagoes, Kickapoos and Pottawottamies comprise the principal strength of the Prophet's army, and are certainly greatly irritated by their losses," but they were also being influenced by British agents (Edwards, 1870, p. 301; ASP-IA 1:806, 807). Apparently it was the opinion of Edwards and others by March 3, 1812 that "The Prophet is regaining his influence," in addition to which Edwards learned "that the Kickapoos & Pottowattomies lately held a council near Pioria in which it was determined to attack our frontiers" (TP 16:193-4; ASP-IA 1:808). But on this same date a letter from Vincennes by Lt. Bacon reported that a total of about one hundred and fifty Miami, Kickapoo, Piankashaw and Winnebago were visiting Harrison on a mission of peace (A-124). Then on April 24 Edwards also reported on his peace efforts in "a council with the

367

Pottowattomies Kickapoos Ottawas & Chippewas who reside on the Illinois river and near Lake Michagan -," but he had little faith in their sincerity (TP 16:215).

Early in April Captain Helm came to St. Louis with a party of sixty Indians comprising "Sundry Chiefs Warriors Women & Children of the Kickapoos Pottowatomies Chipaways & Ottoways *from the Illinois River*..." (A-525, italics - JJ; same in ASP-IA 1:807).

At the end of May Governor Edwards sent a statement to the Secretary of War giving the location and other data relative to these Indians (Edwards, 1870, pp. 315-318). This information was not obtained by Edwards through direct personal observation. In order to acquaint himself "with the country, the Indian villages and the respective forces of different Indian tribes, Gov. Edwards employed agents to ascertain the different routes of travel to and from the lakes, the location of the villages and the number of warriors belonging to each tribe, and such other information as might be useful during the year". During the spring of 1812 he collected data in the form of notes and "maps on which are designated the rivers, villages and routes from Mackinaw to St. Louis..." (ibid. p. 92; see also pp. 96-98, esp. in relation to quotations below from ibid. pp. 315-318. The sources of Edward's information are given more specifically in ibid. p. 98 and also A-523). In fact, Edwards' only source appears to be a letter of May 31, 1812 from John Hays (A-523).

The following extracts are grouped to show, first, the distribution of the Potawatomi and, secondly, the Kickapoo:

"The Pottawottamies of the Illinois River are divided into three bands, viz: That of Gomo, the principal Chief, consisting of about one hundred and fifty men, who now reside on the Peoria Lake, seven leagues above Peoria [at the north end of Peoria Lake]. Pepper's band, at Sand River, about two leagues below the Quin-que-que, consisting of about two hundred men, of different nations - Pottawottamies, Chippeways and Ottaways. Little Chief was, last year, head of this band. He is now dead, and Pepper has succeeded him. Letourney and Mettetat, brothers, both Ottaways, are war chiefs of this band, under Pepper. Their village is fifty leagues above Peoria and twenty below Lake Michigan. Main-pock's band, consisting of fifty men, residing seven leagues up the Quin-que-que... his number of men is less than either Pepper's or Gomo's..." (Edwards, 1870, p. 316). According to Forsyth Main Poc's village was on Fox River of the upper Illinois (TP 16:251).

"At Little Makina, a river on the south side of Illinois, five leagues below Peoria, is a band, consisting of Kickapoos, Chippeways, Ottaways and Pottawottamies. They are called warriors, and their head man is Lebourse or Sulky. Their number is sixty men,...great plunderers" (idem). In the notes which Edwards used to compose this document it is recorded that the Mackinaw River is "One league below Peoria" and that "the Kickapoos have a village here" (Edwards, 1870, pp. 96-7). Earlier in the notes there is information, as in the preceding quotation, which includes others with the Kickapoo at this location (ibid. p. 96). It may be, however, that there were two villages on this river, one of which consisted only of Kickapoo. If Edwards is not clear on this point neither is his informant, John Hays.

"On Fox River, which empties into the Illinois...about thirty-five leagues above Peoria, there is another band, consisting of Pottawottamies, Chippeways and Ottaways...Their number is not less than thirty...The principal part of the other Pottawottamies reside on the River St. Joseph, that empties into Lake Michigan, and they have on that river three or four villages...

"At Mil-waa-kee, thirty leagues from Chicago, just on the west of Lake

369

Michigan, there are several villages of Pottawottamies and Fulsowines [Menominee]...

"At the carrying place at Chicago, three leagues from the fort [Dearborn], is a village of Pottawottamies and Ottaways, of three hundred men.

"Five leagues from Chicago, on the south side of Lake Michigan, is a river called the Little Calamick [Calumet], on which there is a village, consisting of about one hundred men, of Pottawottamies, Chippeways and Ottaways...

"Thirty leagues from Chicago is the river St. Joseph. Ten leagues up that river is a village of about ten Pottawottamies;...

"At the Terrecoupé [a small affluent of the St. Joseph, ibid. p. 97] is a village of about one hundred Pottawottamies. This village is ten leagues, by land, to the lake. It is also about thirty leagues to Chicago, over fine, open country and good traveling.

"On the St. Joseph, about forty leagues from its mouth, is another small village of Pottawottamies, at the mouth of [Speckled River]...

"On Stag-heart [Elkhart] River, ten leagues from its mouth, is another small village of Pottawottamies...Stag-heart River empties into the St. Joseph. The most of those Indians described as being on the south of Lake Michigan and on the St. Joseph or its waters, are now with the Prophet, on the Wabash" (ibid. pp. 315-317).

The information which Edwards gives on the Kickapoo follows:

"The Kickapoos in the Illinois Territory are divided into three bands. Pam-a-wa-tam [Pemwatome] is the principal chief. His band consists of one hundred and fifty men. They have left their old village [at the Vermilion?] and are now building a village on Peoria Lake, three leagues from Peoria.

"Little Deer has also left the great village [in the Prairie?], and is

370

now building one opposite Gomo's village. His band consists of one hundred and twenty.

"The other Kickapoos are those above described, who live at Little Mackina below Peoria. From these three bands of Kickapoos there are now with the Prophet about one hundred men" (ibid. p. 316).

It should be pointed out that Edwards had some additional Kickapoo information in his notes which he did not incorporate in the present account. This was that there were formerly Kickapoo villages on the branches of the Sangamon (ibid. p. 97). Edwards omitted what was included in his original source, a letter from John Hays, dated May 31, 1812. This was that the villages were "abandoned to come on Lake On the North Side (M-75), which seems to mean on Peoria Lake on the north (west) side of the Illinois River.

Another Kickapoo village is identified by Thomas Forsyth in July, 1812 as being near the Iroquois River, which could mean that it was either in Illinois or Indiana. Forsyth was referring to information he received about Kickapoo who were said to have committed murders the previous spring near Vincennes and in 1810 in Louisiana Territory. "These fellows with all their relations, and others of the same stamp have a Village near the river des Iroquois, that falls into the Teakakee river,..." (TP 16:251).

On the basis of the Edwards account the Kickapoo, by the middle of the year 1812, were continuing or resuming an earlier movement at their settlements westward across Illinois from the region of the Wabash and central Illinois to the vicinity of Peoria on the Illinois River. In this connection Edwards also made the statement that "Those Indians, in the late council I held with them [Kickapoo and Potawatomi], told me they were about to settle themselves together in a large town at or near Peoria" (Edwards, 1870, p. 318). This fact is probably related to a statement which Edwards made later in the

371

same document: "The proximity of the Indians between Lake Michigan and the Mississippi to Peoria, would enable all those bands to unite their forces in a very few days. If the Prophet should be driven from his present ground, or the Illinois Indians become decidedly hostile, he will rally all his forces on the Illinois River, from which he can do more injury to our people, with less danger to himself and his followers, than from his present position" (idem).

In a letter dated May 16 which he wrote before he could have composed the foregoing summary, Edwards, in a reference to the murder of a white family, said that it "was perpetrated by a party of Kickapoos, residing near Peoria" (ibid. p. 321). Four days later he wrote again to say that "All except a small band of the Kickapoos reside in this territory [Illinois], and also a very large portion of the Pottawottomies,...." which coincides with what he wrote above (ibid. p. 322).

Toward the end of the same month at about the time that Governor Edwards was expressing concern over the possible hostile intent of the Indians and the increasing strength of the Prophet (ibid. pp. 323-324), Stickney, the agent at Fort Wayne, reported on "a grand council...on the Wabash, where twelve tribes were represented - consisting of the Wyandots, Chippeways, Ottaways, Putawatamies, Delawares, Miamies, Eel River Miamies Weas, Piankashaws, Shawanose, Kickapoos, and Winnebagoes". The council resulted in "a formal request to [Stickney],...more effectually to suppress the sale of spirituous liquors to Indians in the State of Ohio, Indiana Territory, and other places inhabited by white men." The illegally sold liquor caused the drunkenness which led to the murder of white men and exacerbated Indian problems with the government (Thornbrough, 1961, pp. 130-1). Two weeks later Stickney again wrote, stating that the council, which

372

actually took place on the Mississinewa branch of the Wabash, reached a decision in which the twelve tribes represented "agreed to consider themselves as one Nation for the purpose of making peace" (ibid. p. 139).

By June Edwards' view of the previous month regarding the increasingly hostile disposition of the Indians was proving to be true. The Kickapoo adamantly refused to surrender the murderers of a family of ten as demanded by Edwards. Indians were gathering in large numbers at the northern end of Lake Peoria (Edwards, 1870, p. 326). On June 8 Forsyth estimated "that the number of Indians now at the end of this [Peoria] lake consisting of Putowatomies, Kickapoos, Miamies and Ottoways must exceed six hundred warriors and should they be inclined for war, they can in the course of eight or ten days draw from the Kiankakee river, from the upperparts of this river, from Fox river, and from Roche river at least 600 warriors more which would make an Indian Army of at least 1200 warriors, exclusive of the prophet's band which is now considerable, and I am informed that they are augmenting daily,..." (TP 16:229). On June 23 Edwards estimated that "the number of Indians now embodied near Peoria is not less than seven hundred,..." (Edwards, 1870, p. 328).

373

In the meantime the Governor had mounted riflemen, rangers, and volunteers covering the area "principally between the Illinois and the Kaskaskia rivers, and sometimes between the Kaskaskia and the Wabash -" (ibid. pp. 328-9). While such measures were considered by Edwards as a restraining influence upon the Indians they probably regarded them as provocative especially when, as Colonel Russell reported on July 1, he had "much difficulty in keeping the rangers from falling on the friendly tribes,..." (TP 16:239). Russell appears to have been correct at this time in concentrating his attention upon "those two Strong points viz the Peoria, and the proppets party on the Wabash" (idem). Russell's letter to Eustis on July 22 would appear to confirm the view that the activities of his forces aroused the Indians, for he wrote: "Our trailes through their country is certainly alarming to them. I have Kept a company for some time at fort Harrison, and have Kept a small party every day ranging on boath sides the Wabash, for 16 or 20 miles out, and also Kept a sentinel every Knight on the bank of the river to prevent their passing by water from the Prophets Town to these frontier's. In addition to that I have sent out small parties to the trace leading from the Peoria (on the Illinois) to the Prophets Town,..." (A-332).

On July 19, 1812 Forsyth's June 8 estimate was confirmed by a Frenchman who travelled down the Illinois River on his way to St. Louis from Chicago (A-507). According to General Howard this man "states that there are about 15,00, warriors on the [Illinois] river above Piorias, that they subsist principally on Fish also that they have canoes sufficient to carry the whole of them this collection is not at one place but they are encamped at different points on the river for about one hundred miles,..." (idem).

Forsyth's report of June 8 also stated that "the whole body of Indians now in the vicinity of this place [Peoria] have been counciling for some time past," and that they "are now busy planting their corn, but for want of clear land their fields will be rather small, so you see by this they are fixed to remain this season in this part of the country -" (TP 16:230). This concentration of Indians was further augmented by Miami who "have come to this country from an Island of woods in Praires commonly called White or Lynwood Island, distant from the old Kickapoo towns 25 or 30 miles - They consist of twenty odd lodges and can furnish at least from 120 to 150 warriors. These Miamies are only about half of the whole that were at the above mentioned Island - The other half is gone to the S. Prophet and will make his number greater..." (ibid. p. 229; see also TP 14:570-1). There are no indications that the Miami move into this area was more than temporary.

The Kickapoo refusal to surrender the murderers of the O'Neill family was made in a letter to Governor Edwards by Chief Pemwatome from Peoria on June 8. And although Edwards claimed he reneged on an earlier promise (Edwards, 1870, p. 326), the chief's arguments would, on the face of it, appear to possess considerable merit (TP 14:571-2). An indication of the geographical range of Kickapoo activity is given by the chief who cited several places where Kickapoo were killed by whites without retribution being exacted or punishment meted out by American authorities: a chief on a hunt near the Kaskaskia River; a chief near Cahokia together with a number of Miami; a Kickapoo at Florisant on the Missouri; two Kickapoo at St. Charles on the Missouri; a chief, after he surrendered Kickapoo murderers to General Wilkinson, at St. Louis (idem).

375

Late in June another Kickapoo chief at a council at the Sac village, speaking also in behalf of the Winnebago, Potawatomi, Shawnee, and Miami representatives, tries to enlist Sac, Fox, Iowa, Oto and Sioux in the gathering forces of the Prophet, but he was unsuccessful (TP 14:578-580). And during July the reports received by Governor Edwards from Thomas Forsyth, who had been to Chicago, and from Antoine Le Clair, a trader who had travelled to Chicago and Milwaukee, was that the Indians were preparing for war with help expected from the British (TP 16:250-255, 244-247). Additional details confirming these reports were supplied by Governor Edwards on August 4 and again on August 8 in letters to Eustis (Edwards, 1870, pp. 332-337). That same month Ottawa, Chippewa, Winnebago, Kickapoo, Menominee and Potawatomi to the number of five or six hundred attacked the garrison at Fort Dearborn dealing death and destruction (A-510; TP 16:261-3). On the other hand, General Hull reported from Michigan that as a result of his councils with the Indians in July, Ottawa, Chippewa, Potawatomi, Wyandot, Delaware, Munsee, some Kickapoo, Sac, and Iroquois were "unanimous for remaining neutral," and that "Tecumseh and Marpot [Mainpoc] are the only chiefs of consequence remaining with the British" (MPHC 40:420).

Towards the end of July Thomas Forsyth wrote that an alliance extending from Detroit and the Great Lakes to the Mississippi, made up of four divisions, had been organized by the Indians two months before (A-202). The Sioux and Fox formed the first, while those of the second were "the Potawatimies and Kicapoos of the Illinois and Fox Rive " in addition to "the Sakies of the Mississippi, Winebagoes on Rocky River [Menominee] and what Chipeways and Ottawas that may be in the vicinity of Millwakee and Green Bay..." (idem; italics - JJ). The third division was comprised of the Potawatomi of the Kankakee, St. Joseph, Kalamazoo, and Yellow Rivers, "with all the Indians on the Wabash, as also all the Indians of White River and its vicinity. In the fourth division were included Potawatomi, Chippewa and Ottawa extending from Detroit along Lake Huron to Lake Superior, plus Indians on the Maumee and Lake Erie. Forsyth also stated that "there is now in the different villages near the Peorias between 5 or 600 Warriours of the Potawatimie, Kicapoo and Piankeshaw Nations including some few Chippeways & Ottawas that is living among the Potawatimies" (idem).

In August Edwards wrote that there were approximately 1500 Kickapoo, Miami, Potawatomi, Ottawa and Chippewa on "the Illinois River and its branches" (A-199). Another letter by Forsyth, dated September 7, 1812 made mention of "a Potawatimy Prophet of the Elk's Heart village", the Potawatomi villages of Gomo and Shequenebec on the Illinois River, and the Potawatomi of St. Joseph (TP 16:263). He also referred to the fact that there were Kickapoo "who

376

formerly lived about Portage des Sieux" (ibid. p. 264). A few days earlier, on September 3, a letter by General Harrison mentions his plan to undertake an offensive on the Wabash to include "the villages of the Putawattimes upon it & the headwaters of the Illinois" (A-511).

Government efforts to hold a grand peace council at Piqua, Ohio led to an attendance of approximately "800 Indians (men women and children)...composed of Shawanoes Delawares Wyandots Taw-ways [Ottawa] & Kickapoes" (MPHC 40:457-8). Among them were "about 30 Keckapoes from near pioria," including one chief, who were awaiting the arrival of their other chiefs (ibid. pp. 459-460). But in the Illinois area the military activities of Edwards and those under him were founded on the assumption that war with the Indians was inevitable.

On October 31 Colonel Russell in a letter to Secretary Eustis reported the destruction of a Kickapoo village on the Illinois River which he describ- 377 ed as "a flourishing Town, with an immence deal of Indian plunder in it, togather with a great deal of corn, all of which was committed to the flaime's. I believe no less than Eighty horses fell into our hands belonging to the Enemy" (TP 16:269). This was the village of chief Pemwatome "situated about twenty one miles above Peoria, and immediately at the head of the Peoria, Lake,..." (idem).

According to another published account of this expedition which was said to have been received from Governor Edwards, who accompanied Colonel Russell, three villages on the Illinois River were destroyed. The force left Camp Russell near Edwardsville, Illinois, about twenty miles from St. Louis, and "proceeded to the saline fork of the Sanguemon, where [they] burnt two villages [Kickapoo]. From thence the little army progressed to the head of Peoria lake, 24 miles above the villages; there they found the Kickapoos and a party of the Miamies embodied,...." Pursuing the Indians on foot through a swamp "to the bank of the river, a distance of three miles,...they found and burnt a Pottowatomy village,...." (JISHS 24:342-3). This account went on to state that "At the principal Kickapoo village upwards of 4000 bushels of corn was destroyed, besides a prodigious quantity of beans and dried meat, pumpkin, tallow furs and peltry. Their houses were strong and well built, some large enough to accommodate 50 persons were found well provided with indian effects; all were in a few hours reduced to ashes. Eighty head of horses with their furniture, about 200 brass kettles, a great quantity of a variety of silver and Indian ornaments, guns, bags of gunpowder, flints etc were brought off.

"Immediately after burning the Kickapoo town, a party was detached to Peoria who burnt a village within a half a mile of that place; this last mentioned place was lately erected by the Miamies" (ibid. p. 343; see also TP 16:271).

378

Edwards' own report (Edwards, 1870, pp. 69-72), sent to Secretary Eustis on November 18, communicated the same information, as the following excerpts show: "we burnt two Kickapoo villages, on the saline fork of Sangamon River -"; "a large village at the head of Peoria Lake, inhabited by Kickapoos and Miamies"; "the Town of Chequeneboc, (a Pottawottamie chief, who headed the party that came down to attack us,)...was burnt"; "burnt another village that had been lately built within half a mile of Peoria, by the Miamies" (ibid. pp. 71-2).

At about the same time that Russell and Edwards had been engaging in their expedition General Hopkins, who marched from Kentucky with another force, proceeded "across the Country from Fort Harrison direct for the Grand Kickapoo village in the Prairie" (A-515).

After Edwards' "victory" on the Illinois River in October, 1812, he wrote on January 16, 1813: "The Kickapoos & Miamies that I defeated at the head of Peoria Lake run off to Rock river and are now with the Sacs..." (TP 16:286), and that "The whole of the Kickapoos are among [the Sac] enraged at their defeat & preparing for revenge" (ibid. p. 287). At this time Governor Howard made recommendations for military action against the Indians, among which was a suggestion to "strike a blow at the Indians on the Kantakie [Kankakee]...where there is a large Potowatome Village,...There take a course to the mouth of Sandy Creek fork of the Illinois where there is a large settlement of the Enemy --" (TP 14:617).

Early in February, 1813 the Secretary of War was informed that "the Western shores of lake Michigan were covered with indians" the estimates ranging from twelve or fifteen hundred to three thousand. Among them were "almost all the Pottowatomies, Kickapoos, Miamies, Delawars, Shawonees, Piankyshaws &c.&c. of the Rock, Fox, Illinois and the other rivers which head near the lake,..." (ibid. p. 630). One month later Governor Edwards "received certain information from Fort Madison, that two strong indian parties, consisting of Pottowottomies Kickapoos Miamies Shawanese &c' are now in motion to attack these settlements somewhere'..." (A-201) A report by Robert Dickson, British trader and Indian agent, written from St. Joseph, Michigan on March 16 stated: "I have seen the Poutewatamies of this place [St. Joseph], who are going to join the Shawanies, Kickapous, and Delawares, and with them proceed to Detroit" (MPHC 15:259).

From January to the beginning of April two spies, La Roche and Chevalier, sent by Governor Howard up the Illinois River, gathered information on the Indians which they assembled in a report dated April 4, 1813 (TP 14: 652-654). Leaving St. Louis, they "crossed the Mississippi at Portage de Sioux, we then took the Pirarie toward the Illinois River, seeing many fires

379

ahead of us, and fearfull of falling in with the Kicapoos, we changed our course; and struck the Illinois River at Grand Isle, 60 miles below the Peorias, where we fell in with three Potawatimies,...Those Indians told us that we did right to leave the Piraries and come down to the River, as we would have fallen in with the Kicapoos, who would have certainly killed us,..." (ibid. p. 652).

Apparently the travellers were heading generally northwestward from where they crossed the Mississippi in order to reach the Illinois River. The "fires" which they saw in this direction and which they assumed were Kickapoo, were, therefore, in the vicinity of the southern reaches of the Illinois River. After the two men changed their course and reached the river sixty miles below Peoria, they must have been travelling generally north with a slight bias to the east. Since they were told that they would have encountered the Kickapoo in the prairies if they had not approached the river when they did, the Kickapoo must have been in the region north of the Sangamon. Thus far the report indicates that the Kickapoo were to be found generally east of the Illinois River.

LaRoche and Chevalier were told by three Sacs who learned it from the son of White Pigeon, a Potawatomi, "That it was Kicapoos who killed Young on Kaskaskia River, the party consisted of five or six: and a party headed by Little Deer [Kickapoo chief] killed two men some where on the Kaskaskia River..., that two of the little Deers party remained behind, and killed another man who was making Sugar, near the Saline,..." (ibid. p. 654; A-205 p. 4). From this statement it is apparent that the Kickapoo were then also ranging through the southern reaches of Illinois.

When the two spies met the Potawatomi on the Illinois River they were taken to the Potawatomi "camp on the River de Sheesheequen 30 miles below

380

Peorias...those Indians sent a young [man?] with us as a guide to their Fort or Fortification, that they have built on the River Au Burau [Bureau R.], which falls into the Illinois River 60 miles above Peorias, when we arrived at that place we were asstonished to find such a Fortification built by Indians;...this place was built last winter [1812-13],...At this Fortification all the Indians of the Illinois River are, Kicapoos and Potawatimies, and from the different alarms that they have had all winter, they have not been able to hunt, and are now in a state of starvation" (TP 14:652; also 16:312-13). The two agents were told by Gomo that ten one hundred pound kegs of gunpowder were being sent as presents to the Potawatomi, Kickapoo, Winnebago, Menominee, and the Sac and Fox. Their statement that "The Mainpoque came home to Fox River last fall [1812]..." from Detroit (ibid. p. 653) ties in with Thomas Forsyth's information of the previous July, 1812 (TP 16:251).

On April 3 Maurice Blondeau, Sac and Fox sub-agent, in a report to Governor Howard on his conferences with the Sac and Fox on Iowa River, stated that on March 10 "an express come from the Kikapoux and Potawatomies on the Illinois River telling them to come on to Chicago and get powder and Ball that their father the British was impatient to see them..." (TP 14:659). The Sac and Fox had already told Blondeau "that the British had sent them word to go and get powder at Chicago -" (idem).

On April 10, 1813 Governor Edwards sent to the Secretary of War a summary of the two foregoing reports (TP 16:312-315). The general state of affairs was summarized by Edwards in this comment: "By every other account that has been received for a long time past it appears that all the Indians West of Lake Michigan and on the Illinois and Mississippi rivers (except the Sauks & Foxes) have joined the hostile Confederacy" (ibid. p. 314). A final note by Edwards reveals the rather pathetic situation of the Kaskaskia in the

381

surge of these events: "I have called in the Kaskaskia Indians it being
dangerous both to them & the people of the Ty to permit them to support themselves by hunting and I am consequently compelled to support them at the
public expense" (ibid. p. 315).

Before LaRoche, Chevalier and Blondeau had submitted their reports,
Governor Edwards had written the Secretary of War on March 27: "The Indians
of the Illinois and its waters amount to about fifteen hundred warriors." On
Rock River there were eight hundred Sac, six hundred Fox, and about four
hundred fifty Winnebago. "Besides, there are a great number of bands of
Pottawottamies, Ottaways, Chippeways and Menominies residing between Lake
Michigan and the Mississippi,..." (Edwards, 1870, p. 347).

About the middle of April Thomas Forsyth left St. Louis and ascended
the Illinois River where "On the 24th I fell in with three families of
Potawatimies at Crow Praire 45 miles above the Peorias,...I was informed that
all the Indians were at or on their way up Sandy Creek." Joining this group
he proceeded up the river, met another family the next day, "and we all
encamped together at the mouth of the Vermillion River." Forsyth arrived at
Sand Creek two days later and there he met Mainpoc and Gomo. The latter
imparted considerable information which, in part was: "...that the Shawanoe
Prophet gone to Detroit with all the Shawanoes. That the Winebagoes and
Kickapoos were still at the Prophet's village on the Wabash,...but supposed
they would go on to Detroit - That about 400 Miamies were on their way to
St. Joseph's to make a village--" (TP 16:324-326). Forsyth also stated that:
"A General Council was held by all the Indians of Sandy Creek Kickapoos &
Potawatimies & Gomo himself spoke in the name of the whole" requesting
Forsyth to use his influence to bring back to Peoria the old settlers, stating
"That if any number of families of French would go & live there, the Indians

382

agree that they shall have the same rights of hunting & fishing & the same
use of land & wood as themselves & promise not to disturb any property belonging to them, but to live as if the whole was one family" (ibid. p. 327).
Early in July General Howard reported that "The Pawtawatimies have returned
to the Head of Peoria Lake and are settled in their villages which they left
last Fall..." (ibid. p. 347).

In May Governor Edwards notified the Secretary of War that a force led
by Major Stephenson destroyed the village of the Prairie Kickapoo or, as
Edwards called it, "the old Kickapoo Town on Mink river a fork of the
Sanguemon -", which had been evacuated prior to the arrival of Stephenson's
rangers (ibid. p. 331). The latter marched from Fort Russell, near
Edwardsville, on May 8. Stephenson's report (ibid. pp. 333-335) states: "I
kept my course along the ridge that seperates the waters of Kaskaskia from
those of Illinois and Sanguemon rivers untill I arrived at a point opposite
the celebrated old Kickapoo Village of the Praire - To which I then steered
my course and crossing the Sanguemon arrived at it on the seventh day of my
march being then opposite to and within a little better than one days march
of Crow Praire on the Illinois river forty five miles above Peoria - On
approaching the Town...we arrived too late - none [of the Kickapoo] were to
be found...it was very evident that a party of them had left that place not
more than three or four days previous to our arrival & in its vicinity was an
indian camp containing fourteen lodges of considerable size that had been
recently abandoned which together with the Town - we burnt - in the latter
there were some very large houses built in the first style of indian arche-
tecture and a considerable number of smaller ones --...On my return with Capt.
Shorts company I crossed Mink river about twenty miles below the old Town -
and on the dividing ridge between that river and Sanguemon was found a new

383

Indian Camp in which the lodges were connected for about twenty five yards –
Which must have been very lately and hastely deserted – some of the lodges
not being entirely covered & fresh bark and other materials lying ready for
the erection of others – Much other indian sign was discovered but it appeared to have been made about three or four weeks before and no doubt can exist
that a considerable number of the savages had occupied that quarter and were
driven from it by the terror which was created by the march of the detachment lately commanded by Captain William B. Whiteside --". It was Major
Stephenson's opinion "that our tour must have an important effect in relieving
the frontier from those Sanguinary savages that have so seriously infested it
– Their Villages & Camps burnt – the heart of their own country penetrated --."

On the basis of this account it is evident that the Sangamon River
region continued to be settled and occupied by the Kickapoo. Documents cited
384 above make it clear why, under the circumstances prevailing at this time, the
Kickapoo were not to be found in central Illinois. The following August
Governor Edwards had occasion to mention to the Secretary of State: "I had
caused to be burnt every Kickapoo village except a small one of five or six
lodges – and had penetrated further into the indian country than any force
had gone --" (ibid p. 354).

A summary report prepared by Thomas Forsyth for William Clark on July
20, 1813 includes considerable data on the geographical distribution of
Potawatomi and Kickapoo, and on the depredations committed by those groups
(A-205). According to Forsyth, although the Potawatomi, Kickapoo "and other
tribes on the Illinois river and towards Lake Michigan, may be considered
hostile towards the United States" the Potawatomi chief Gomo, the Kickapoo
chief Pemwatome, and some of their followers have been involved in warfare
against their will. Apparently Mainpoc and Little Deer have considerably

more influence over the Potawatomi and Kickapoo respectively. And since the
followers of the latter two chiefs receive British supplies from time to time,
it keeps "the warriors who are naturally inclined to war, continually in
hopes of obtaining a superiority over the Americans..."

Forsyth goes on to state: "as to the situation [location - JJ] of the
Indians of the Illinois river and towards lake Michigan there is little or no
difference from that of last year." He first discusses Potawatomi locations:
"Shequenebec with his band of Potawatomies resides. at the same place he did
last year at the head of Peoria lake and may furnish one hundred warriors,
Gomos band of Potawatomies is at his last years Village about three miles
higher up from the head of the lake and about a Mile Back, from the river".
Forsyth estimates the number of men with Gomo at fifty on the basis of the
previous year's count. "at Sandy Creek near the forks of Illinois River is
where the Black Patridge and pepper two Potawatomies Chiefs reside, this
Village can furnish at least 200 warriors without some have left it since I
was there in April last.

"The Mainpoc Village of Potowatomies on Fox River is about 30 or 36
Miles from the mouth of said River by water and not more than 18 or 20 miles
across the Peoria [prairies - JJ] from Sandy creek, it is the residence of
Mainpoc with all his relations and friends when in that part of the country
but since May. 1811 he has been mostly at Malden I should suppose when all
this band is at home they will amount to 100 warriors and perhaps more".

Forsyth continues with the statement that "There are several small
Villages up fox river, being a mixture of different nations, by Potawatomies
Ottawas Chipeways and Minnominies which might furnish altogether 150 warriors."
He then goes on to say that "at the Portage of Chicagou on river des Plaine
is Mittitasse Village of Ottawas & Potawatomies and perhaps there may be

385

about 100 warriors at this place,..." Forsyth also writes: "on the head waters of River des Iroquois there is a Potawatomie Village which I am informed is considerable, but I cannot say for a Certainty what their Numbers are but may Calculate them to be at least 100 men capable of taking the field I am not acquainted with their Chief, nor many of themselves as they are principally from the Wabash Country,

"The distances from Sandy creek across the Peorias [prairies - JJ] to the last mentioned Village is not more than 25 or 30 miles". This estimate of the distance appears to be quite inaccurate, for if the location is correct then the village would be in northwestern Indiana and the actual distance would be about seventy-five miles.

Additional Potawatomi locations are revealed in Forsyth's discussion of the murders they committed. In the summer of 1810 Captain Coles and some men were "killed [on Salt Creek in the St. Charles district] by a party of Potawatomies headed by one warrior Catfish [Winnemac?], who resides at some of the small Villages on fox River two of this party formerly resided on the head waters of the Vermillion that falls into the Wabash". After fleeing "...to the Prophet's Town...they left...and have ever since resided on the headwaters of the river des Iroquois." The attack on Fort Dearborn in the summer of 1812 included "near four hundred Indians consisting of all the Potawatomies and ottawa of Sandy Creek Mainpoc Village some Potawatomies from St. Joseph and Wabash all the Calamic [Calumet River?] Indians as also the Indians from Millwakee..."

Forsyth's information on the Kickapoo now follows: "all the Kikapous who resided on Illinois River last year except those that are with the Piankisaus on the Mississippi, are now residing in one Village [on the Kankakee - JJ] about 6 miles above the mouth of River des Iroquois that falls

386

into the Kankeekee about 45 miles from the forks of Illinois river the
Kikapous at this Village can furnish about 200 warriors and should those
Kikapous who live at the Prophets town at this place remove to the village on
the Kinkikee it will be a verry considerable Village, and may be able to turn
out 400 men of the first class as warriors,..." He also refers to the fact
that the party of eight Kickapoo who killed the O'Neill family on August 15,
1812, came "from their winter Camp on Sagamon [River]..."

The previous January (1813) Governor Howard had written that on
September 21, 1812 "between 6 & 700 Indians at once came to our frontier,
with a view to overrun the whole Settlements between Missouri and Mississippi;
..." (TP 14:615). The following April Forsyth wrote that "upwards of four
hundred Indians" came down to Peoria "from the upper parts of the Illinois
River" in an attempt to attack the settlements on the frontiers of Illinois
and Missouri (TP 16:310-311 and 379-380). In the present document (A-205)
which he addressed to Clark, Forsyth identifies the groups who participated
in this foray. He wrote: "In septembr last, a party of about four hundred
Indians consisting of about, Potawatomies, Kikapous Ottawas and Piankasas
headed by Black Patridge and Shequenebec decended the Illinois river in
Canoes to strick on the frontiers of this [Missouri] and Illinois Territory"
(A-205).

387

In the latter part of September (1813) General Howard deployed forces
up the Illinois River but the villages were found to be deserted. Another
detachment which marched against "the old Kickapoos Towns" also failed to
make contact with the Indians there (TP 16:370-373). Then on October 6 a
communication from General McArthur at Detroit stated that "Since Genl
Harrison's departure five nations of Indians, to wit, the Ottaways, Chipaways,
Potawatomies, Miamies and Kickapoos, who were but a few miles back, have come

in for peace,..." (MPHC 40:535-6). On the other hand, William Clark stated several months later, on February 2, 1814 that although "The Indians remain quiet as yet - Those tribes up the Mississippi and towards Lake Michigan i'e the Winnibagoes, Kickapoos, Wild-oats [Menominee], and parts of the Socks & Socs, have not come in, or shewn that disposition for peace as was expected, ..." (TP 14:738). But early in January, 1814 the Potawatomi chief Black Partridge and ten of his men went from Peoria to St. Louis to talk with Clark about peace (A-541).

At the same time Robert Dickson, the British agent at Prairie du Chien, reported that he withheld some supplies for the Sac "so as to assist the Kikapoose and Ioways who are in a miserable situation..." (A-464). These may be the Kickapoo referred to by William Clark when he reported at the beginning of the following June, after the capture of Prairie du Chien: "Several Small Bands of disaffected Socks & Kickapoos Settled on the banks of the river below this [Prairie du Chien] ran off in great Confusion on the approach of the Armed Boats" (TP 14:768-9).

According to another letter written January 11, 1814 by Governor Edwards "neither the Kickapoos nor any that reside west of Lake Michigan nor about Praire de Chien (a few Pottowottomis excepted) have as far as I can learn either come in for peace or manifested any other disposition to sue for it" (TP 16:408). But apparently Black Partridge was sincere as regards his peaceful approach, for as Forsyth wrote Clark at the end of March (A-522) "...Dickson had invited the Potowatimies of Illinois River to go and see him particularly the black Patridge but none had gone nor meant to go to see him Dickson, but meant to remain stedfast friends to the U.States." Forsyth also said that he met the Potawatomi chief Grand Quet some thirty miles above Peoria on the Illinois River. He received valuable information from the

Chief concerning Dixon's activities among the tribes. According to Forsyth:
"...as I understand that Forty odd Lodges of the Kicapoos under Pemwatome are
at or near the mouth of Ricky [Rock] River, Dickson will no doubt furnish
them with goods etc, and our Frontiers will be again drenched with the blood
of our Citizens" (idem).

Shortly after the middle of February, 1814 a report appeared in the
Missouri Gazette on the whereabouts of several Indian groups at that time
(A-541). According to this newspaper's information "The Pottawattamies are
now hunting on the river Mequen [Spoon River], north of Peoria;..." This
area is west (or north) of the Illinois River, possibly around latitude 41°.
As for the Kickapoo, they were hunting "from the head waters of Mequen
[Spoon River] towards the mouth of Rock River:..." (idem).

The following month a party of six or ten warriors who "appeared to
be Kickapoos" attacked Nelson Rector, a surveyor on the north fork of the
Saline River which joins the Ohio below the mouth of the Wabash (TP 16:401;
see also WHC 11:320). The report which Forsyth sent to Clark at the end of
March (A-522), cited above, also contained references to the Kickapoo. At
one point he said that "The little Deer with the greatest half of the
Kicapoos are towards Fort Wayne or perhaps in the State of Ohio." And then
again "the Kicapoos who were said to have come in to Fort Clark and ask Peace
are the Mascotans who formerly lived at Portage des Sioux" on the Mississippi
between the Missouri and Illinois Rivers. This is the first reference to
Mascouten in several years, and apparently they had been apart from the main
body of the Kickapoo for some time.

The last point of interest in Forsyth's statement is that the
Potawatomi chiefs Gomo, Black Partridge, Mittetass, Pepper, and Grand Quet
are "very friendly to the Garrison of Fort Clark" at Peoria (idem).

389

Presumably it was these chiefs, or most of them that Forsyth had in mind when, towards the end of May, he wrote Edwards: "...I sent for Gomo and other chiefs from the head of the [Peoria] lake,﹐" (WHC 11:318). Gomo told Forsyth "that a great number of Indians were to have made [a] village with them at the head of the Lake, but the killing of the Kickapoo sometime since, has dispersed them to different parts of the country" (ibid. p. 319).

At the end of June Clark reported to the Secretary of War that while there were definite indications of diminishing hostility in the upper Mississippi region "The Winnebagoes, Wild-oats [Menominee] a part of the Kickapoos and a parcel of Stragglers towards Lake Michigan, we may expect will Continue hostile while they can be supplied --" by the British (TP 14:776).

Early in June the United States Government issued a call to "the Indian nations of the west and north" to assemble at Greenville for the pur-pose of negotiating a treaty of peace and alliance (ASP-IA 1:829). In this connection John Johnston, agent at Fort Wayne, wrote from Greenville late in June to General Harrison, one of the treaty commissioners, noting which tribes were present or on their way (A-466). About 1600 Indians had already arrived, but, he wrote, "The Putawatimies, Ottawas, Kickapoos & Chippeways are not come, and it is more than probable they will not attend". Johnston went on to say that "The Indians here...find their own safety consists in adhering to us as they are menaced by the hostile party, the Putawatimies & Kickapoos have stolen many horses from the Miamies and Delawares,..." (idem).

In the meantime (June, 1814) the Potawatomi on the Illinois River were engaging in peaceful relations and trade with the inhabitants of Peoria and Fort Clark. According to Forsyth "this post [Fort Clark] has been visited by many Indians from the head of the [Peoria] Lake, and upper parts of this [Illinois] River: indeed, they are here daily, bringing in to trade, Meat,

391

Fish, etc. which is of very great assistance to the garrison of this place.
We see none but Potawatomies" (WHC 11:320). In the same letter (July 6,
1814), which he wrote to Governor Edwards, Forsyth stated that at the beginning of July "Gomo, Black Patridge and several others came to this place
[Fort Clark],...many to go down the [Illinois] river, a hunting, and I have
told them to hunt on the west side and by no means to cross over on the east
side" (ibid. p. 322). It is difficult to infer from this statement on which
side of the river they customarily hunted. From what Forsyth said the west
side, presumably, was safer in that they were less likely to become embroiled
with the American military. At any rate, when Forsyth again wrote Edwards on
July 31 he stated that "On the 26th all the Potawattamies who went down the
river in Canoes a hunting, arrived on the way up to their villages" (ibid.
p. 324). In another reference to this group he revealed that they "were
hunting along the river, .." (ibid. p. 325).

390

Part of the information imparted by Gomo and Black Partridge was that
"a British agent, Chandonet, came to the mouth of St. Joseph's river, to
council with the Indians, and did ask them (the Potawatomies of St. Joseph)
permission to build a Fort at that place,...to furnish the Indians with all
their wants, that their British Father...would build another Fort at Chicago
shortly to supply the Indians also with their wants,..." (ibid. p. 322).
Thus the Potawatomi around the Great Lakes were subjected to British entice-
ment, but by this time those on the Illinois River had accepted American
hegemony. In addition they were Forsyth's chief source of information on
British-Indian relations.

Forsyth's letter to Edwards also conveyed information about the
Kickapoo: "All the Kickapoos that are in the country being the the Saukies
on Rock River, and come over occasionally to the Potawotomies villages [on

the Illinois] to steal horses" (ibid. p. 320). Some of the same Kickapoo were observed in the vicinity of Spoon River, for Gomo told Forsyth "that a Potawatamie Indian was hunting on the Mequon some time ago, who fell in with a party of ten or fifteen Kickapoos, and supposes them to be a war party from Rock River, that the Saukies and Kickapoos have made their brags of having killed Americans thrice since winter..." on the Missouri and on the west side of the Mississippi (ibid. p. 323). Forsyth may also have been referring to the Kickapoo or Potawatomi when he wrote of the "Kankakee Indians who came down to trade" at Peoria (ibid. p. 320). With regard to the Kickapoo who had been observed on Spoon River, probably some time in June, Forsyth subsequently reported that on July 18 "the Little Eagle's son arrived here [Fort Clark] from the mouth of the Mequon and informed me that he had seen five Kickapoos on their return from war,..." (ibid. p. 324).

392   In another report to Edwards at the end of July, 1814 Forsyth stated that he was "informed by Indians [Potawatomi - JJ] who were hunting in this vicinity [Fort Clark], they saw where a party had crossed the Illinois river over to the East side,...and it is generally supposed that it was the Kickapoos who were formerly seen on the Mequon,..." (WHC 11:324, 323). Apparently the latter succeeded in killing some Americans; and when Gomo returned from hunting on July 27 he told Forsyth "that this party of Kickapoos are from the old Pemwatome's band who have their village on one of the branches of Rock River, called Pekeetennoe [Pecatonica River]" (ibid. p. 325).

A letter from Harrison and Cass, the treaty commissioners at Greenville, on July 17, 1814 (A-465) also dealt, in part, with the Potawatomi and Kickapoo. They wrote that "Of the Potawatomies only two chiefs of note have arrived, and but one or two of the secondary class of chiefs of the Kickapoos & Ottawas-". The chiefs of the "friendly tribes" had suggested to Harrison,

when he first arrived on July 3 and found 3,000 Indians assembled, "that the
Potawatamies & Kickapoos residing between the Wabash & Illinois rivers were
prevented from attending the Treaty from an apprehension of danger which had
been infused into their minds by the British emissaries-" (A-465 and ASP-IA
1:828).

On August 8 Forsyth wrote to Edwards: "About the latter end of last
month a Kickapoo Indian from Rock River passed through the village of Sandy
Creek on his way to the Kickapoos who are now with General Harrison, and
there is no doubt but what he is a spy sent on [by?] the British. He told
the Potawattamies of Sandy Creek that the Fort at Prairie du Chien was taken
by the Indians..., and he said that the Kickapoos now with Gen. Harrison
must go to the Rock river, and that he was going to bring them away;..."
(WHC 11:326, 327). Less than two weeks later Forsyth again wrote to say that
he was told by Gomo "that since the affair at Prairie du Chien, the Saukies,
Kickapoos, Foxes and Winnebagoes have received [at Rock River, p. 329] from
the British thirteen kegs of gunpowder of 100 lbs. each, with some goods, and
are expecting many more shortly:..." (ibid. pp. 327-328). Despite this
temptation for the fulfillment of the needs of his followers, Gomo declared
that he "is now happy that he is at peace, although they are in want of
everything and the Indians all about them are plentifully supplied with
clothing, etc" by the Americans and the British (ibid. p. 328).

Forsyth again made reference to the Potawatomi predicament early in
September when he wrote Edwards: "You will please observe, that the Indians
[of Illinois River] are all now busily employed with their corn, and as soon
as that is done, (which will be towards the latter end of the month) they
will remove to their wintering places. I do not see how the Potawatomies of
Illinois river can commence their hunt, as they receive no presents, can get

393

no credit and having nothing to purchase ammunition to commence hunting: and
as they are surrounded by Indians who receive presents from us and the British,
they must and will be obliged to visit the enemy...presents are very tempting
to the Indians, particularly to those who are naked, for I can assure you
that I never saw Indians so much in want of everything, as the Potawatamies
of Illinois river are at present" (ibid. p. 329).

The final note in the preceding document concerned the Kickapoo and
was put thus: "...as for the late Grenville Treaty, it is to be supposed
that the Kickapoos under the Little Deer will make war against Pemwatome's
band of Kickapoos on Rock River? No never, in my opinion" (ibid. pp. 330,
332). At this treaty of peace, which was concluded on July 22, 1814, only
one or two minor Kickapoo chiefs attended according to Harrison (A-465).
Apparently the only Kickapoo chief who spoke at the proceedings was Little
Otter. Pemwatome's band was obviously anti-American. Forsyth's remark seems
to imply that although Little Deer might have joined Harrison he (Forsyth)
would not expect him to participate in American hostilities against Pemwatome.

According to another letter of Forsyth (September 18), in addition to
Kickapoo, Sac, and other groups on Rock River there were also Potawatomi. But
contrary to the hostile and pro-British disposition of the others the
Potawatomi there "have perfectly adhered to the armistice entered into with
Gen. Harrison as relates to being quiet and not visiting the British..."
Nevertheless, with the Potawatomi in dire need of gunpowder and arms for the
winter hunt, Forsyth fully anticipated that the British on Rock River "will
make an offer of presents to them, and common sense will tell us that the
offer will not be refused" (ibid. p. 333). Discussing the possible numbers
of Indian warriors available in the event of some groups joining the British
in an attack upon the frontiers, Forsyth estimated that the "Pottawattamies

394

can furnish 1200 warriors but suppose one-half will not come if asked" (WHC 11:334). As for the Kickapoo, he suggested that "when altogether" there were 400 fighting men (idem).

Because of the failure of the government to fulfill obligations and to provide essential needs, not only friendly Potawatomi, but also the Kaskaskia were tempted to swing their support to the British. On October 18, 1814 Governor Edwards was constrained to write that "The situation of the Kaskaskai Indians is...truly distressing, and the conduct of Govt towards them both...impolitic and unjust..." (TP 17:33). For the past two years they had received only the cash part of their annuity, but not the merchandise which was so necessary. Consequently, as Edwards put it, "They are literally naked and are becoming very much dissatisfied." According to the Governor "they can hunt no where without manifest danger from our people, or from those Indians whose hostility they have provoked by their uniform friendship to us...they are restrained from hunting which is a right stipulated in their favor, & necessary to their support..." Edwards went on to say that "unless something shall be done for them shortly I have no hesitation in believing that they will be compelled to join the hostile confederacy that surrounds us - and although they are few in numbers their intimate knowledge of all our settlements will render them extremely dangerous -" (ibid. p. 34).

During the latter part of October two representatives of a small band of Wea, then encamped on "Little White river" east of Fort Harrison, came to Vincennes and declared their friendship toward the Americans (A-467). Sending this information to Governor Posey of Indiana on October 24 Joseph Barron, interpreter at Vincennes, wrote that the Wea also told him "that there were many other famelies, or large parties equally anxious to come in, could they only have assureance of being well received, among which a camp of Kickapoos

395

of about 20 cabbins residing North of Tippecana." These Kickapoo, according
to Barron's information, "are in two parties, one about 12 miles above
Tippecanoe, & the other about 16 miles farther. And that about 60 miles from
thence, on the road to St. Josephs, on Yellow creek, at a place called the
great cutoff is a band of about 40 Potawatime warriors, under Mainpotle—"
(A-467). The latter, according to the friendly Kickapoo, earlier had made
the forays against Fort Harrison in which men were killed and horses stolen
(idem). Barron then suggested that, since there were enemies to the north,
in order to distinguish friend from foe those who were friendly should "be
placed on our West or South, say Embarras, little Wabash, or White river, near
the mouth, in all which places game is abundant—" (idem).

At approximately the same time representatives of the Potawatomi of
St. Joseph and of a "village near the bottom [mouth?] of the Tiakikee
396 [Kankakee]" were in council with the British at Michilimackinac, requesting
supplies of ammunition and clothing (MPHC 23:453-455). In replying to a
British message which had requested the Kickapoo and Prairie Potawatomi to
assemble in the vicinity of St. Joseph, Bad Sturgeon a Potawatomi, stated:
"It is necessary that they should remain at my village near the bottom of the
Tiakikee to attack the Big Knives, who I understand mean to lay our Country
waste and I want your children the Kickapoos to remain with us, in order to
fight and maintain our independence,..." (ibid. p. 454). Chebainse, a
Potawatomi chief of St. Joseph, said that in accordance with the British
request he had sent word to the Miami, Kickapoo, and Delaware, and that they
had agreed to come to St. Joseph. The last statement in his speech was that
"The Kickapoos will be detained by the Bad Sturgeon on the Teakikee" (ibid.
p. 455). This probably means that those of the Kickapoo who were in the
Kankakee village would remain there to assist Bad Sturgeon if necessary.

Other Kickapoo would join the Miami and Delaware at St. Joseph.

Apparently British help was not immediately forthcoming; and subsequently Chebainse, at his own request, met with the British again on January 29, 1815 at Michilimackinac to reaffirm his people's loyalty and their need for arms, ammunition, and clothing. On that occasion, addressing the commanding officer "in the name of all the Village chiefs of our Nation residing at and near St. Josephs," the Potawatomi chief said that "The Kikapoos have already reached the Teakekee and made their village with the Bad Sturgeon, the other nations Miamies & Delawares are to follow the example of their Brethren by removing" to the village of the St. Joseph Potawatomi (ibid. pp. 469-470).

On November 13, 1814 Benjamin Parke, the acting agent at Vincennes, conveyed to Governor Posey the following information which Captain Andre had obtained from two Miamis: "That there are about two hundred Kickapoos, warriors, & a few Putawatamies on the Vermilion - about three hundred Putawatamies at Tippecanoe - & other Bands of that tribe scattered from them to the Chicago & other posts of the enemy - The Kickapoos, in part, are represented as friendly - & the greater portion of the Putawatamies decidedly, hostile - About the 1st of Octr a number of these Kickapoos & Putawatamies received a considerable present of ammunition & clothing from a British trader near Chicago..." (A-469). Within a week after this letter Parke again wrote to the governor informing him that the Potawatomi had again established themselves on the Wabash and that the Miami believed "it is for the purpose of awing the Miamis into the hostile confederacy..." (A-284). The major portion of this letter was a discussion of why the Indians "detest" the Americans in contrast to their high regard for the French and their friendly disposition towards the British.

397

Having reported on November 13 that there were two hundred Kickapoo on the Vermilion River, Parke subsequently wrote Posey on December 7 that several days ago "the principle chief now with the Vermillion Kickapoos came to [Fort Harrison] with strong professions of Amity & good will toward the U.States-". The chief said "that in a few days a considerable number of his people might be expected at the Fort, all friendly disposed" (A-475). Despite the fact that a ranger murdered the chief's wife, three hundred Kickapoo and Miami men, women, and children came in friendship not long afterwards. Their situation was represented "as extremely necessitous - their arms out of order - with little or no ammunition - and their clothing miserable - They expressed a wish that some arrangement could be made that would enable them to have access to our traders - and above all that they could get their arms repaired -... To hunt they must have their arms in order - to procure clothing and ammunition they must have an opportunity of sending their skins and furs - as these people have made a peace with the United States they consider that they have some claim to the priviledge that they ask - and it is very certain that if they do not obtain it from us they will seek it else where - they will go to the British,..." (A-477; also A-479).

It is quite obvious from the foregoing and from what has been said of the Potawatomi on Illinois River that those Indians who either grudgingly or from conviction were prepared to ally themselves with the Americans were severely strained to follow through on their investment when there was so little return for it. It is, however, probable that the real reason the Kickapoo, at least, made this approach to the Americans was the difficulty of obtaining supplies from the British at this time. On February 18, 1815 Colonel McDonall, British Commandant at Michilimickinac, wrote of the "inadequacy of the Indian supplies" which resulted in large measure from the fact

398

that Robert Dickson had appropriated more than a proportionate share for the
Indians in the Mississippi region (MPHC 23:475-479). In his letter to
Captain Bulger the colonel stated that "I had scarcely any thing to spare for
the numerous tribes at Sagana, St. Joseph River, Grand River, & to such of
the Kikapoos, Pottewattamies Sacs as are still inclined to our side, & which
doubtless has compelled some of them to apply for that help to the Americans,
which I was unable to give" (ibid. p. 476; also Askins' statement p. 479).

On November 15, 1814 Thomas Forsyth had sent a report to the Secretary
of War on what he had learned during a recent visit to the Indians in the
area of Fort Clark (A-470). Concerning the Kickapoo Forsyth wrote: "That
last summer a runner was sent from the Kicapoos residing on Rocky River, to
the Kicapoos then in council at Greenville [July], inviting them to break up
that council, and join thier friends on Rocky River,...that a few Lodges of
Kicapoos went straight from the council to Rocky River, ten Lodges of some
Indians (Kicapoos) are to pass the ensuing winter on River des Iroquois, and
to proceed on to Rocky River...next spring, that the remainder of the
Kicapoos that were at the Council at Greenville were about a month ago at the
Prophet's old town on the Wabash,..." and they too will probably join the
others on Rock River (ibid).

399

Some Potawatomi from Gomo's village, located about twenty miles above
Fort Clark, had gone to Rock River in October seeking the return of stolen
horses. While there they learned that all the Indians of Rock River, with
the exception of the Winnebago, "were encamped on the West Side of the
Mississippi; near the mouth of Polecat River..." waiting for presents from
the British. They all "intended to hunt the ensuing winter, on the Polecat
river and its head waters, and between that and the Missouri River,..." (ibid).

As regards the Potawatomi on the Illinois River, it was clear to

Forsyth that in spite of all temptation and dire need they were still loyal
to the Americans, "bringing in [to Fort Clark] to trade, large quantities of
wild meat and fowl, which has been of very great assistance to the troops of
that place,..." It is ironic that despite the fact that their desperate need
of European goods went unrequited, the Illinois River Potawatomi nevertheless
provided the garrison at Fort Clark with food. As Forsyth put it they "are
much in want of everything."

On his trip up the Illinois River Forsyth "found near thirty Lodges
about twenty miles below Fort Clark all Potawatimies, and under the following
Chiefs, Gomo, Blackpatridge and Pepper." Both Forsyth and the commander of
the garrison "advised them to cross over from the East side of Illinois
where I found them, to the West side, where they would be out of the way to
hunt the ensuing Season,..." (ibid). It will be remembered that when Forsyth
was at Fort Clark the previous July he urged the Potawatomi, who were about
to set out on the hunt down the Illinois River, to confine their activities
west rather than east of the river (WHC 11:322).

A letter of Easton and Stephenson to James Monroe on December 17, 1814
includes an estimate of the number of warriors in various tribes (A-476).
This information would appear to be based mainly on Forsyth's letter of
September 18 to Easton (WHC 11:331ff), cited above. According to the present
document the Potawatomi "who are scattered over a great extent of Territory,
from Detroit to the Sakie villages--" have 1200 warriors, and of these 600
are known to be hostile. As for the "Kickapoos, of the Illinois," they have
400 warriors, all of whom are considered hostile (A-476).

The Kickapoo of Rock River were referred to in a letter from Forsyth
to Clark on April 13, 1815, largely on the basis of information obtained from
the successor of the late Gomo, his brother Petchaho, who was mentioned as

one of "the two principal chiefs residing near the Illinois river", the other
being Black Partridge (A-554; WHC 11:336-7). The latter had been to Rock
River in March, and there he saw Sac and Kickapoo receiving "great quantities
of Gunpowder" from the British. In addition a party of Kickapoo from Rock
River were participants in murders which took place at Vincennes (A-554). By
the end of April it was reported that the Kickapoo on Rock River "have abandoned the British, & demand peace agreeable to the treaty" to be made with
the Indians (A-545). According to Forsyth "The Kickapoo said they were glad
to hear of the Peace, and would withdraw from that quarter [Rock River],..."
(WHC 11:338).

After receiving instructions on May 16, 1815 to gather the Indians for
a treaty council at Portage des Sioux, Thomas Forsyth went to Fort Clark to
enlist the aid of "Petchaho, the chief of the Potawatamies living at the head
of Peoria lake who I made acquainted with my mission to that country,..."
(ibid. pp. 338-9). Through Petchaho speeches were sent "to the Kickapoos and
Saukies residing on Rock River,..." and to other groups elsewhere. "As the
Potawattamies are living over a very extensive country, he [Petchaho] will
deliver the speech to that nation in two parts, one part to be sent to St.
Joseph, Elksheart and Eel river, the other part to be sent to Milwaukee..."
(ibid. p. 339). In this communication a passing reference was also made to
"the Kickapoos on the Vermillion that falls into the Wabash" (ibid. p. 340).
Another letter written by Forsyth on August 20 mentioned "the old Kickapoo
chief Pemwatome" in a statement concerning "the Mississippi Indians" (ibid.
pp. 341-2).

On July 15 John Kinzie stated in a letter to Governor Cass of Michigan
Territory that "the most determinedly hostile are the Chippeway, Potawatomies,
Ottawa, of L'Arbre Croche, and the Winnebago Tribes, who inhabit the country

401

between the Southern extremity of Lake Michigan, and Michillimackinac, and whose chief residence is upon Grand and Muskeegon rivers,...." The interesting point about these groups, however, is that they, "from the want of a proper supply of game, are compelled to emigrate at certain seasons to the waters of Chicago, Illenois and Fox Rivers" (TP 17:201).

The following day the treaty commissioners wrote from Portage des Sioux to the Secretary of War that whereas "With the Pattawatamies of Illinois river, and the small band of Piankeshaws who are prisoners of war, we shall probably conclude a treaty in a day or two...neither the Winnebagoes, Sacs, Foxes, Ioways, Kickapoos, or any others residing upon Rock river, have sent forward competent deputations of chiefs to treat with us" (ASP-IA 2:8; A-136). By July 22 a treaty had been concluded with the Illinois River Potawatomi and the Piankashaw; a separate treaty was signed with the Kickapoo and others in September (ASP-IA 2:9).

402

On September 1 Black Partridge, the Potawatomi chief on the Illinois River, sent a message to the President stating that while at Portage des Sioux he learned that the Sac in 1804 "without our knowledge, sold to the Americans all the lands or chiefly all lying on this [Illinois] River the Principal Hunting ground of our Nation..." He went on to say that "we wish you now to understand that no Part of this River does or ever did belong to the Sacks that whatever Sale they may have made was wholly unauthorised...we think you will see us righted, and not deprived of the principal hunting ground relied on for the Subsistance of ourselves our Women and Children-". Black Partridge also included in his message the following statement: "At Present we are not numerous on this River being few more in Number than those whose wishes were to Support a Neutrality during the late war, but we shortly expect our Settlement will give from five to seven Hundred families-"

(TP 17:227-8; see also ASP-IA 2:10).

In forwarding this message to the Secretary of War on October 9, Governor Edwards apparently supported the Potawatomi claim, stating: "I have long anticipated that they would assert a claim to the land mentioned in their address & which they have for years past occupied as their principal hunting ground - and nothing but the indelicacy of interfering or seeming to interfere with the duties of others, has restrained me from suggesting my apprehensions on that subject-" (TP 17:226).

Assertion of this claim by the Potawatomi obviously involves lands on the west side of the river. On October 15, the treaty commissioners, Clark, Edwards, and Auguste Chouteau informed the Secretary of War that "The Pottawatomies now occupy & assert a right to the land on the Illinois river which is contained in the cession made by the Sacs & Foxes in 1804..." (A-137).

The following November 10 a letter from the War Department expressed the following view to William Clark, Governor of Missouri Territory: "It is believed that the Pattawatamies can have no well-founded claim to the lands..." which were being surveyed for military bounty (ASP-IA 2:12, 10; A-137). To Governor Edwards the Department had written four days earlier in the following vein: "As a band of the Potawatamie nation have been in the habit of hunting on the lands directed to be laid off, between the Mississippi and Illinois rivers, to satisfy the bounties due to soldiers of the late army, the President of the United States,...has directed me to authorize you, to present to this band of the Potawatamies, two thousand dollars worth of goods, as a compensation for any inconveniences they may experience, by being deprived of any part of the grounds on which they had been accustomed to hunt. Their claim to the lands, in question, must not be recognized: the Sacs and Foxes, in whom the title was, having ceded it to the United States, by the

403

treaty of the 3ᵈ of Novemr 1804" (TP 17:237-8).

In connection with other treaty proceedings, which were to be held at Detroit in August, 1815 runners were sent in July, "one for the Potawatomies residing in the neighbourhood of Chicago & Illinois, one for the Kickapoos & Weeas the other Moran and Manpock,..." (A-633). The Wea and Kickapoo were those on the Wabash; Moran "and other potowatimis Chiefs" were on "the Grand River (that empties into Lake Mishigan) and that County,..." (A-559).

In a list of tribes "computed" as of September 20, 1815, the following data are incorporated (ASP-IA 2:76-77):

a.) The Peoria are located south of St. Louis on the St. Francis River. In a total population of forty there are said to be ten warriors.

b.) The Kaskaskia, situated at the town of Kaskaskia, have fifteen warriors in a population of sixty.

c.) To the Kickapoo is attributed a population of 1,600 among whom are 400 warriors. Their location is "On the heads of Kaskaskia river."

d.) The Potawatomi "On the Illinois river, etc." with a population of 4,800 have 1,200 warriors.

Thus, approximately half the Illinois Indians were in Missouri and the other half in southern Illinois; the Kickapoo were in central Illinois, while the Potawatomi extended from the Illinois River to the lakes area in Michigan and Indiana.

On November 1, 1815 Judge Parke, at Vincennes, wrote Governor Posey of Indiana that, having visited the Wea and the Vermilion Kickapoo, he talked with a Kickapoo chief who attended the treaty negotiated at Portage des Sioux the previous summer. This chief told Parke that his people were on their way to their winter hunt on the Embarrass and the Little Wabash in southeastern Illinois (A-285).

404

Parke, in the same letter, also discussed the Piankashaw of the
Vincennes area. After they had gone for safety in the spring of 1812, to
"the Neighborhood of the Kickapoos," knowledge of Colonel Russell's expedition
subsequently caused them to move across the Mississippi. But now, Parke reported, they "earnestly solicit to return to their old hunting grounds, on
the Embarrass, & little Wabash,...They have I believe a considerable Tract,
of Country between the lands they sold the United States, and the lands of
the Kickapoos, but all in the Illinois Territory" (ibid). Parke also mentions
in passing, "the Prairie Kickapoos."

While Parke had information on the Vermilion and Prairie Kickapoo,
Benjamin Stickney, the agent at Fort Wayne, sent to the Secretary of War at
about the same time (November 12) news of some other Kickapoo, still disaffected, who were with the Shawnee Prophet at Malden, where there were also
some Sac, Potawatomi and Winnebago (A-560). Apparently these die-hards were
still sending out runners through American territory in an effort to solicit
Indians in an anti-American cause (see also A-589, 590, 591). But as far as
Governor Edwards was concerned officially "The Kickapoos all reside in [the
Illinois] Territory..." and they told him they would like to receive their
annuities at Kaskaskia (TP 17:253).

On December 1, 1815 Governor Edwards had occasion to return to a discussion of the Potawatomi claim on the Illinois River where, he wrote "at
least one half" of that "Tribe" reside (idem). At the time of his writing
they were apparently on their winter hunt at the Grand Pass on the lower
Illinois River (ibid. pp. 255 and 260). Reference to this hunt was also made
by Governor Edwards the following March 20, 1816 in a letter to the Secretary
of War in which he said: "Captn Philips who commanded at Ft Clark (Peoria)
informs me that between 6 & 7 hundred [Potawatomi] hunters passed that place

405

in the course of last fall [1815], on their way to their hunting grounds below it, and no doubt some must have gone without his knowledge, and probably in a different direction-". This information led the Governor to the conclusion that "The Pottowottomies of the Illinois are much more numerous than seems to be supposed by Mr. Grahams [Chief Clerk, War Department] letter-" of November 6, 1815 (ibid. p. 319).

In his letter of December 1, 1815 to the Secretary of War, Edwards stated that he would "without delay invite the Pottowottomies to a council for the purpose of adjusting the difficulty with regard to the land they claim, according to the wishes of the President-". According to Edwards the Potawatomi would, in turn, ask the Chippewa and Ottawa to be present at the council "For it is under those Tribes, particularly the latter, that the Pottowottomies set up a claim to the land on the Illinois river-" (ibid. p. 255).

406

With considerable justification he added: "That country originally belonged to the Illinois Nation, which was composed of the Peoria, Cahokia, Michigamia, Kaskaskia, and Tamorwa Tribes-" (idem). The statement which follows immediately, however, is, as it stands, highly dubious. On the basis of facts already adduced it is obvious that the situation is far more complex. This is also apparent from Chouteau's "Notes" (see below). Edwards writes: "The Ottawas who had for their allies, the Chippawas, drove off the Peoria Tribe, and claim the country by right of conquest; and through their courtesy the Pottowottomies intermixed with bands of Chippawas & Ottawas have been permitted to occupy it-" (idem).

At this point it is necessary to introduce an important document prepared by Auguste Chouteau, who was one of three treaty commissioners at Portage des Sioux in the summer of 1815. He had been a merchant in Louisiana

Territory at the time of the Spanish regime; and later, because of his extensive and intimate knowledge of Indian affairs, he made his services available
to the United States.

Late in 1815 he assembled, in a document entitled "Notes", what he
referred to as "extracts from notes which from time to time I have made for
my own satisfaction during a long residence in this Country, and many years
intercourse with the Indians therein mentioned,..." (Chouteau, 1940, p. 122).
The major portion of this document, which Governor Edwards forwarded to the
War Department, centers on a discussion of the territory originally occupied
by the Illinois Indians and also on the question of the validity of the
Potawatomi claim to the Illinois River lands.

If Chouteau's inclusion of the Mascouten and the Miami as part of the
Illinois Indians is omitted, then the territory he attributes to the latter
comprises most of the state of Illinois and an eastern strip of the state of
Missouri down to the mouth of the Ohio River (ibid. pp. 123-4 and fn. 11,
p. 124). According to Chouteau the country on the west side of the
Mississippi River between the Des Moines and Missouri Rivers was used by the
Michigamea (ibid. p. 135). East of the Mississippi the Peoria were at Lake
Peoria; the Michigamea were situated where St. Louis was later established;
the Cahokia were where the town of Cahokia was subsequently settled; the
Kaskaskia were twelve miles up the Kaskaskia River; and the Tamaroa were
thirty miles farther up (ibid. p. 125).

Chouteau's statement is generally correct, if not precise as to some
of the details. Continuing his account, he notes that the Illinois were
assailed on the north by various groups, among whom were, at various times,
Sioux, Chippewa, Iroquois, Ottawa, Potawatomi, Sac and Fox. The Peoria were
forced down to the mouth of the Illinois River, then down the Mississippi

407

River to the area of Fort Chartres. There they joined the Michigamea and
Cahokia in a fortification and stood off the attacks of their enemies.
Chouteau says that at this time there were 3,000 warriors among the Illinois.
But by 1763 the number was reduced to 1000; and when they crossed the
Mississippi to St. Genevieve in 1780 there were no more than 200 warriors
left (ibid. pp. 125-6).

According to Chouteau the Peoria (and Mascouten and Miami) having
"abandoned their residences in the delightful country which they had inhabited,
it remained unoccupied by any particular Tribe till the year 1743, when a
part of the Pottowatimies who resided near Detroit, together with Some bands
of Ottawas and Chippewas removed to it and Settled themselves near Chicago,
and on Some parts of the Illinois river; and have continued in the uninterrupted possession there-of to the present time. This possession is presumed
to have been taken conjointly by those three tribes,...and of having under
that alliance contributed their joint exertions in expelling the Illinois
Indians in that Country which they now claim by right of conquest" (ibid.
pp. 131-2). But Chouteau argues that it was the Sioux in particular who
"contributed more than any other to drive the Illinois Indians off their
land" (ibid. p. 135), and that on this basis the Sioux and others had at
least as good a claim "by right of conquest."

In support of the aboriginal priority of the Illinois Chouteau also
cites the description of the two tracts sold by part of the Illinois to
William Murray's company in 1773 (ibid. pp. 130-131). What Chouteau was
trying to demonstrate here was that the Illinois claim was "much more extensive than it is represented to be in the treaty" of cession signed by the
Kaskaskia on August 13, 1803.

According to Chouteau, then, Potawatomi, Ottawa, and Chippawa had been

408

on the Illinois River since 1743, a time when the country was supposedly "abandoned" by the Illinois.

On March 20, 1816 Edwards wrote that the Potawatomi had not yet responded to an invitation for a council on their claim to the lands on Illinois River. He also stated that according to his information the Indians "are all invited to British Councils, are made to believe that war shortly recommence, and they almost universally appear to be pleased with it - Some Tribes have made direct propositions to others to engage in war against us-" (TP 17:318-319; see also A-594, A-589). A week later Parke, the agent at Vincennes, wrote, probably of other Potawatomi, that "There are strong reasons to believe that many of the Puttawatamies are hostile--and it is probable that two war parties of that nation are now on their march against the Wabash Settlements"(A-597). He could not, however, be certain that his information was accurate. Then on March 28 William Clark wrote from St. Louis: "I must give it as my opinion (founded on the information of Indian agents and traders) that the Indians on the Illinois have been for several months discontented and restless--and as they are much opposed to the surrender of that country which they pretend to claim, the surveyors might have reasonably expected some opposition from those bands" (A-599).

409

Nevertheless, it was quite clear that the attitude of the Kickapoo was unfriendly, the immediate stimulus being the government survey of lands on the northwest side of the Wabash River (A-595, 596, 597, 598). Judge Parke tried "to assemble as many of the Chiefs of the Weas and Vermillion Kickapoos as could be conveniently collected and obtain from them a small guard for the protection of the Surveyors -- Owing to high waters, and Some of the Indians being at distant hunting grounds, I was unable to procure a full meeting, but a respectable deputation from the two Bands met me at

Fort Harrison..." They wanted to wait until "Little Otter of the Prairie
Kickapoos could be present" but Parke objected to the delay this would cause
(A-597). After an angry exchange the chiefs stated "that with respect to the
land on the North West Side of the Wabash, claimed under the Treaty of
December, 1809, they had just learned from me, for the first time, that it
had ever been sold by the Kickapoos--", and towards the end of the meeting
all they would agree to was "that they lent to the United States a Strip of
land on the N.W. side of the river, comprizing the river bottom, as a grazing
ground for the horses and cattle of the white people;..." (ibid). Parke
thought that "This prevaricating, impudent conduct of the Indians" might be
related to the fact that "Some of the young men of the Vermillion Kickapoos
are restless and inclined to war--Some of their friends are with the Prophet--
they are intimately connected with the Prairie Kickapoos and the Sauks--and
410 the Winebagoes, and the British agents and traders are intriguing with all--"
(ibid; also A-606).

Again on April 3, Parke wrote the Secretary of War that a war party of
eight Vermilion Kickapoo had gone against American settlers on the Embarras
River, and that the Potawatomi and Prairie Kickapoo "will probably interpose
a claim to the land between the Illinois and Mississippi-" (A-702, A-604).
Shortly thereafter some Kickapoo did, in fact, accompany the Potawatomi to
St. Louis, where they met with Governors Edwards and Clark and Auguste
Chouteau without, at that time, achieving a mutually satisfactory resolution
of the issue. This became a matter upon which further deliberation was
necessary among the Indians (TP 17:354-5). But on August 24, 1816 a treaty
was finally concluded with a group comprising Ottawa, Chippewa and Potawatomi
(ibid. pp. 387-389).

As regards the lands on the Wabash from which the Vermilion Kickapoo wanted to remove the surveyors, these lands were apparently claimed by the Miami. According to a letter of April 7 by Major Morgan, commandant at Fort Harrison, the Miami "alledge that the land did not belong to the Kikapoos--that it belonged to them, and that therefore, the Kikapoos had no right to sell it" (A-603). Three days later Parke added a statement of his own on this subject: "The Vermillion Kickapoos are intruders; but they have for many years been in the quiet possession of the country they inhabit on the Wabash & Vermillion, & may now be considered as the rightfull occupants" (A-604).

When Forsyth returned from a visit to Fort Clark at the end of March he wrote Edwards that on his "way up I fell in with eight lodges of Kickapoos and Potawattamies at the grand pass,..." which is where some of the Potawatomi had spent the winter on their hunt. And in addition, Forsyth wrote, "At Arrowstone creek I found several lodges of Kickapoos who informed me that there were still twenty lodges of Kickapoos under the old chief Pemwatome on the Mississippi: that they could not return home last year for want of horses, and as yet they do not know where they will build their villages...", and that those Kickapoo who were in Canada with some of the Sac "passed the winter at the Elksheart not far distant from Fort Wayne and are expected home as soon as the season will permit" (WHC 11:345-6).

411

It would thus appear that "home" for the Kickapoo of the Rock River and the Pecatonica was the interior of Illinois east of the Illinois River, where they would be if they were together with the rest of the Kickapoo. Edwards, in requesting an agent especially for the Kickapoo, said that they "all reside in [the Illinois] Territory...;" and, further, that "Edwardsville in the most northern part of our settlements [is] in the vicinity of the hunting grounds of the Kickapoos;..." (TP 17:347-349). Calling the Kickapoo

"much the bravest & most warlike of all the neighboring savages-" he added
that "the country they have long occupied, lies directly between us; and the
northern Tribes above mentioned; none of whom can approach our settlements
without passing through their lands" (ibid. p. 349). The northern tribes to
which Edwards had alluded earlier in this letter to the Secretary of War on
June 3, 1816, are listed in the following statement: "The Indians most
difficult to manage, and the most necessary to be managed judiciously, are
certainly the Kickappos, Pottowottomies, Sacks, Foxes, Winnebagoes, Menomenees,
Chippewas, and Ottawas who reside between Lake Michagan & the Missisippi
river-" (ibid. p. 348).

Still, as late as June 19, 1816, some of the Kickapoo. Ottawa,
Chippewa and Potawatomi joined with the Shawnee, Munsee and Huron in attending
a council with the British at Amherstburgh (MPHC 16:471). There were 151
Kickapoo listed in a statement of August 15 as "Dependent on the Post of
Amherstburg" but, according to the editor, these "had their homes in Michigan"
(ibid. p. 524 and fn. 1).

Although the Mascouten had been rarely mentioned during the early years
of the nineteenth century they were again brought up in connection with the
Kickapoo in a letter of Thomas Forsyth on September 8, 1816. Discussing the
amalgamation of linguistically related Indian groups, he wrote Clark: "...we
see the remnants of Indian Nations continually incorporating themselves with
others whose language is similar, witness the Mascotains now living with the
Kicapoos, also the Missouris, they live with the Ihoways & Kansez. Whenever
an Indian Nation becomes reduced as to numbers, they immediately incorporate
themselves into a nation whose language is similar, and who have been their
allies for many years-" (A-555).

While what Forstyh says is largely so, the process, which is neither

412

inevitable nor immediate, is conditional; and is dependent upon circumstances which conduce to such action.

One of the last references to the Kickapoo for the year 1816 was made by Governor Posey, writing from Vincennes on December 21, when he estimated the population of the Vermillion Kickapoo to be "four hundred and forty persons" (A-299).

At the outset of 1817 (January 4) Stickney, the agent at Fort Wayne, reported that not only Kickapoo, but also Shawnee, Sac, and the Shawnee Prophet's own band had left Canada and reestablished themselves at the Tippecanoe village (A-611). As a consequence, Stickney wrote, "The Miamies and Puttewattemies have come forward in a formal manner, and complained to me, that the Prophets Band had taken possession of their country without their consent,..." (ibid). Later that same month (January 24) Richard Graham, the new agent at Fort Clark, wrote General Smith: "It has just been communicated to me, that the Chippeways, Potawatamies, Kickapoo's, Iowas, Minominies, and some of the Shawnies, have lately held a Council the Object of which was, to form a confederation of all the Indians for the purpose of preventing the settlement of those lands lately ceded to the U.S. lying in the Illinois Territory...They intend to attack Fort Clark in March next,..." (TP 17:473-4). Governor Edwards' information concerning what was probably the same event was that "a great council [had] been held about the beginning of the present winter [1816-1817] by the Ottawas, Chippawas, Pottowottomies, Winnebagoes Sacks Foxes and Kickapoos in which it was agreed to recommence war against the United States, and as the first step towards it, to endeavor to take Fort Clark (Peoria)..." (ibid. pp. 484 & 504).

In an attempt to forestall these impending hostilities Governor Edwards went from St. Louis to Edwardsville in February "for the purpose of holding a

413

council with the Pottowattomies and Kickapoos..." He also learned that
"runners have been sent by the Kickapoos in all directions, to call their
people to a great council, which at this season of the year is extraordinary-"
(ibid. pp. 483-4; see also ibid. p. 504). Additional news of this nature was
sent to Judge Parke at the end of March informing him that at the end of
April "there is to be a large council held at the forks of Chicaugo, Kankikee,
between eleven tribes of Indians the Kickapoo will form one of the tribes at
the Councill..." Furthermore, the Kickapoo chief Little Otter stated that
"a pipe with wampum started from the neighborhood of Detroit & has went to
all the Northern and Northwestern indians..." and that "they are about geting
all the Wawbash Kickapoos to the big village of the Parairie..." (A-613).

Whatever the tenor of these activities, chiefs of the Kickapoo, Wea,
and some Miami and Delaware, responding to proposals of Governor Posey,
414 agreed to settle in villages and pursue agriculture with government technical
and material assistance. In conformity with this arrangement, Posey wrote on
April 24, "They are chusing their situations for villages upon the Wabash,
which I have directed should be at least 25 or 30 miles above the present
line of demarkation of the Indian boundary" (A-615).

In the meantime, a proposal had been made to the government by Nathaniel
Pope, Congressional delegate from Illinois Territory, "to procure a cession
of the lands lying between those ceded by the Kaskaskias Indians on the 13th
of August, 1803, and the Illinois river, so as to include all the lands lying
between the Western boundary of that cession, and the abovementioned river"
(TP 17:482; see also ibid. P. 486). In this connection Governor Edwards
furnished Pope with the following information:

> "As to the Indians who claim the land - I have heretofore trans-
> mitted to the war Dept the notes of Colo Chouteau, which prove

beyond all doubt, that the Illinois Nation of Indians did, and
that their representatives do, now own, the country proposed to
be acquired - The Pottowottomies it is true had for many years
occupied the other side of the Illinois river - but I have
never heard of their having had a single village or settlement
on this side - The Sanguemon country is now occupied, as hund-
ing ground, by the Kickapoos, but they do not pretend to claim
it, and in fact they never occupied it, till about fifteen
years ago, when in consequence of the dreadful violence of the
small pox at their great village, they removed to the Sanguemon,
and built those villages, which we burnt in 1812 - They do not
pretend to any conquest of the country - for they never had a
contest about it - If however they shall be permitted to keep
their present possessions without being reminded of their
total want of title to them - they will ere long begin to
claim them as their own - The Kaskaskias as much own that
country, as they ever did one acre that they ceded to the
United States - " (ibid. p. 487).

415

In a letter which Edwards wrote later on May 12 to the Acting Secretary
of War he modified his original statement of January by saying that the
Chippewa, Ottawa and Potawatomi "occupancy has been _principally, if not exclu-
sively_, confined to the north and north west side of" the Illinois River (ibid.
p. 505; italics - JJ).

As for the Kickapoo, while Edwards is correct in asserting that possession of the lands was not actually contested in battle, the Kickapoo did
begin their movement into the area at least as early as the last quarter of
the eighteenth century.

On February 20, 1817 the War Department notified Edwards to initiate
action which would lead the Indians to acquiesce in the extinguishment of
title to the remaining lands east (south) of the Illinois River (ibid. p. 482).
Although he believed that "no other tribe except the Kaskaskia's can pretend
to have any claims to it, in view of the fact that the Kickapoo had been
hunting in the area "for some years past", Nathaniel Pope, territorial delegate, requested the Secretary of State to authorize "the Governor of the
Illinois Territory to open a negociation with the Kickapoos to obtain a
relinquishment of their claim-" (ibid. pp. 485-6).

Governor Edwards returned to a consideration of the problem once again
on May 12, 1817, when he wrote to the Acting Secretary of War concerning the
nature of the Kickapoo claim:

"The Kickapoos at present occupy the principal part of the Country
416 between the cession of the Illinois nation, (or Kaskaskias) and the Illinois
river - but they have no right whatever to it, except mere occupancy - and
that cession includes the site of their most antient and distant village on
the waters of the Illinois river, which with all other villages that they had
occupied, were destroyed during the war by the troops under my command - The
sites of two other considerable villages, much nearer to our settlements will
be very near the line of that Cession, but may not be included in it - from
the erection of these last mentioned villages to this spring, is only thirteen
years; consequently their possession is of too recent a date to give them any
just pretensions to the land - They may however have been in the habit of
hunting, and even residing upon the lands actually included in the cession
last mentioned. But it is well known that their country was upon the Wabash
& its waters - They are considerably attached to the country they now occupy,
and the longer they are permitted to keep it, the more difficult it will be

to negotiate with them - knowing their want of title to it, they have been
extremely anxious to exchange it for lands in the Missouri Territory..." The
Governor then concluded with this suggestion: "To completely vest the right
in the United Sts a further cession from the Illinois Nation (or Kaskaskias)
seems to me advisable, and I think there will be little difficulty in pro-
curing it-" (ibid. pp. 505-506).

What Edwards is saying is that:

a.) Most of the region between the Illinois River and the Kaskaskia
cession of 1803 is "occupied" by the Kickapoo and the region includes their
villages on the Sangamon.

b.) there are two more large villages of recent date, southwest of
those mentioned above and northeast of the mouth of the Illinois River,
located in the vicinity of the line between the proposed cession and that of
1803.

417

c.) despite the recency of the aforementioned two villages, the
Kickapoo apparently had already been accustomed to hunting for some time, and
probably living, in the lands on which the villages were established.

d.) before coming into the traditional Illinois territory the Kickapoo
country was on the Wabash and its affluents.

Authorization was given to Governors Edwards and Clark by the Acting
Secretary of War on November 1 to negotiate a treaty for the acquisition of
the lands under discussion. On that date the Acting Secretary wrote to
Edwards notifying him of his "commission to treat with the Indians claiming
the lands lying between those ceded by the Kaskaskias in 1803, and the
Illinois River" (A-610). At the same time he sent a letter addressed to both
Edwards and Clark enclosing "a commission for the purpose of treating with
the Illinois, the Kickapoos, the Potawatamies and other tribes of Indians

within the Illinois Territory." He also went on to explain that "The object
of this negotiation is to obtain a cession from the tribes who may have a
claim to it, of all that tract of land which lies between the most Northern
and Eastern point of the boundary of the lands ceded by the Kaskaskias in
August, 1803, the Sangamon and the Illinois Rivers; and which tract of land
completely divides the present settled parts of the Illinois territory from
that part which lies between the Illinois and Mississippi rivers,..." (TP
17:543).

William Clark subsequently declined the appointment as a treaty com-
missioner and was replaced by Chouteau (ibid. p. 563; ASP-IA 2:173).

In the spring of 1817 the Kickapoo were among the Indians coming to
trade at Fort Harrison. According to Thomas Posey, agent at Vincennes, who
wrote to the Secretary of War on May 28, 1817, "Ft. Harrison is considered by
all the Indians as a trading house, or post, for them to resort to. All the
Weas & Kickapoos of course attend there; beside a number of Potewatamies,
Miames, Piankashaws & Delawares whenever they come in from a hunt; upon a
delivery of annuities, councils, treaties &c, they must be fed & have their
arms repaird;..." (A-302). Posey stated that the Kickapoo and the Wea "are
the tribes that are immediately under my agency,..." which included both
Vincennes and Fort Harrison (A-303). Towards the end of the following October
the Kickapoo were also listed with the Sac, Fox, Iowa, etc., as potential
traders at a "factory" which Thomas L. McKenney of the newly established
Office of Indian Trade recommended to be established at Fort Johnson on the
Mississippi opposite the mouth of the Des Moines River (TP 17:540). Apparently the Kickapoo, being centrally located in Illinois, were accessible to
trading establishments on the Wabash and on the Mississippi.

In the summer of 1817 a list of tribes in the Missouri Territory

418

Superintendency, computed as of August 24, included a population of 60 Peoria situated on White (Whitewater) River, probably between St. Genevieve and Cape Girardeau (TP 15:304-305).

The following winter, as indicated above, preparations were made to acquire the lands between the Illinois River and the Kaskaskia cession of 1803. A month after receiving his commission as one of the negotiators of the treaty, Governor Edwards considered the prospects of success on December 6, 1817 in a letter to the War Department. He felt there would be no difficulty "with any of the Indians, except the Pottowottomies, & Kickapoos, who have no just claim to the Territory proposed to be purchased, and whose occupancy of a large portion of it, is of very recent date - The rightful proprietors are the Illinois, which is well known to the former Tribes, and therefore, I think it would be most prudent, and advisable to treat with the Illinois first - Being invested with their title, which the other Tribes know to be good, we should probably have the less difficulty in making an amicable, & satisfactory adjustment with them-" (TP 17:550; see also ibid. p. 576).

419

Referring to the Illinois as "the rightful owners of the land" in their letter to the Secretary of War on October 16, 1818, Chouteau and Clark also stated that they had concluded a treaty with them on September 25, 1818 (ibid. p. 607). This treaty included the earlier cession of the Kaskaskia and made final the cession of all lands claimed by all the Illinois Indians. The commissioners failed, however, to reach agreement with the Kickapoo. As they put it in their letter to the Secretary, "The Other Indians who occupy a portion of the land ceded by this treaty & who have no better claim to it, than recent occupancy, are willing to exchange it for land in this [Missouri] Territory which can be given them, without any detriment to the public interest, but they never could have been prevailed upon to surrender it for any Annuity whatever-". Although the chiefs agreed to the terms of the exchange no formal treaty could be made until the proposed lands were inspected by the tribe and found satisfactory (ibid. p. 607).

Finally, on June 7, 1819 Chouteau and Benjamin Stephenson, after having met with the Kickapoo at Edwardsville, were able to report that agreement had been reached with them on the exchange of lands. The only difficulty was the following, as stated by the treaty commissioners: "The Pattawatamies, who are neighbors to the Kickapoos, instigated, no doubt, by white men [traders who did not wish to lose the business of the Kickapoo by their removal west of the Mississippi], and unwilling to see our settlements approximate to theirs, (as they think they will soon do if the latter cede their land,) have, by every kind of menace, endeavored to deter the Kickapoos from entering into any agreement with us; and they openly declare that, the moment the Kickapoos commence their removal to the west side of the Mississippi, they will waylay, attack, plunder, and murder them;..." (ASP-IA 2:197; A-698). But after the Kickapoo treaty was signed (July 30, 1819), Chouteau and Stephenson wrote that the measures they took "will prevent any further attempt on the part of the Pottawatamies of Illinois, to oppose the removal of the Kickapoo's; And we have now little doubt, but that the Pottawatamies themselves could be easily prevailed Upon to remove to the West side of the Mississipi river, whereby the Indian title to the whole of the lands in Illinois could be extinguished, ..." (A-609).

Commenting on what they accomplished in effecting the treaty with the Kickapoo, which was signed on July 30, 1819, Chouteau and Stephenson stated that the Indians "have relinquished all their lands on the south east of the Wabash river, where it is known to one of the Undersigned [Chouteau?], they

420

many years ago, held undisputed possession, And he believes, from the best
information which his long residence in this country, and his intimate knowledge of the Indians thereof, have enabled him to obtain, that they had an
incontravertable right to a large extent of Country on both sides of the
Wabash river, which they heretofore, had neither abandoned, or relinquished"
(ibid). Apparently the Kickapoo also claimed "most, if not the whole of the
land which was ceded by the Pottawatomies" on October 2, 1818 (ibid). Continuing with their summary of the treaty, the commissioners said that the
Kickapoo "have also Ceded & relinquished a tract of land specially described
in the treaty, which contains between thirteen and fourteen millions of acres,
including the whole of their claim to the Sangamo Country (a large portion of
which they have long claimed and inhabited) and all the land lying between the
eastern boundary of the cession made by the Illinois nation, and the line that
divides the states of Illinois and Indiana." This, according to the commissioners, completes "the extinguishment of all Indian claims west of the
dividing line between the States of Illinois & Indiana, and south of the
Kankakee and Illinois rivers,..." (ibid). They had no hesitation in admitting
that the lands which the Kickapoo agreed to accept west of the Mississippi
were "greatly inferior in quality, and less in quantity than that portion of
the lands which they have ceded, to which, their right was exclusive and in-
disputable" (ibid).

Although negotiations had been concluded with the Kickapoo and Illinois
Indians the Potawatomi had by no means considered that their own claims could
be ignored. On August 25, 1819 Richard Graham, their agent at Peoria, wrote
Secretary of War Calhoun that "all that country bordering on the Illinois &
its waters treated for with the Kaskaskias & Kickapoos is claimed by the
Potawatamies by conquest & Treaty from the Indians then claiming & occupying

421

them - They have occupied since the conquest of it without the shadow of
claim set up by the Kaskaskia and others, who do not reside on the land Sold
by them & claimed by the Potawatamies & who were the nations driven from
them by the Potawatamies about 100 years ago - The Kickapoos reside on the
land, but are there by courtesy acknowledging the right of soil in the
Potawatamies who say the Kickapoos have certain priveleges; among them are
the right to hunt within certain bounds & their assent to any sales the
Potawatamies might made of that district alotted to them-" (A-621).

Apparently Calhoun subsequently wrote to William Clark with reference
to this problem and Clark responded on February 20, 1821. Having no personal
knowledge of the facts in the case Clark prefaced his remarks with the comment, "From the best information I have been inabled to obtain" and continued as follows: "It would appear that the Kickapoo, Potawatomies, Ottaways,
Chipaways, Socks, and other Tribes have a Sort of Common interest in the
Country conquered of the Illinois Nation & I am induced to an opinion, that
the Kickapoo Tribe had the best Claim to the greater part of the tract of
Country which they lately Ceded to the United States; arriseing from being a
party in the Conquest of the Country, and the first who took possession of
that part, in which they have remained ever Since--" (A-139).

Apart from the question whether the lands of the Illinois were
acquired literally by "conquest" Clark was probably right in suggesting that
the Kickapoo had the "best claim to the greater part" of the area they ceded.
In addition, he may well be right when he goes on to state: "The Potawatomies
Claim, it appears is a better one than any other of the Confederated tribes,
to that part of the Ceded Tract which is Situated immediately on the Illinois
& Kankakee River, in which they have hunted for a number of years; To that
part of the Ceded Country their Claim is Considered quite equql to the

422

Kickapoos. For some years past the Potawatomies had temporary villages on the Kankakee River within the bounds of the country ceded" (idem).

The evidence seems to point to a greater degree of activity on the part of the Potawatomi than the Kickapoo in the Kankakee-upper Illinois River region. The Kickapoo, on the whole, seem to have been oriented toward the center of Illinois, the Sangamon River being their heartland. While the area in question appears to be peripheral to the foci of both groups, the Potawatomi give the impression of having been more active in settlement and movement in this peripheral area.

Two years later, on November 2, 1821, the same problem was discussed by Thomas Forsyth at the request of Governor Clark. However, Forsyth did not profess to have first hand knowledge, and he could "only repeat what I have heard from others-" these others being Potawatomi of the Illinois River (A-693). Forsyth recalled that in about 1810 the Potawatomi chief Gomo had told him "that the Kickapoos...well known that the Chipawais Ottawais & Pottawattamies gave them permission to settle and hunt in the Country they now live in..." And Anthony LeClair, a trader at Portage des Sioux, was told the same by the Potawatomi (ibid).

423

Because of Potawatomi resentment against Kickapoo for selling land which the Potawatomi considered rightfully theirs, the latter took reprisals by stealing Kickapoo horses; and it was feared by both Forsyth and Graham that there might be an outbreak of hostilities (A-623, A-688).

On November 16, 1819 agent Graham prepared a report for the Secretary of War on the Indians in the Illinois agency, indicating their general location and population (A-624). In this document the Potawatomi, Ottawa and Chippewa are described as "confederated" and situated in four areas. The population figures, according to Graham, "were obtained from a very intelligent Indian chief some time ago - & from observations of my own & others, beleve it to be very correct-". The following are the location and numbers: Milwaukee-1080; "S.W. shores of Lake Michigan" -180; Kankakee-500; "Illinois & its waters" -3924.

If the foregoing figures are generally correct, then it is obvious that more than half the population was situated in the vicinity of the Illinois River.

The information on the Kickapoo in Graham's report refers to a population of 400 on "Rock River-removed from Sangamo". These are obviously part of the Prairie Kickapoo. They were "seperated from the party who have crossed the Mississippi - they are now hunting with the Saukies & Foxes; & have proposed to confederate with those nations-..." (ibid).

424

For the period 1819-1832 the evidence with regard to the continued
presence of the Potawatomi in northeastern Illinois and northwestern Indiana
confirms the data adduced prior to these dates. If anything their general
situation and geographical locations seem in some respects clearer and more
explicit.

The report of Reverend Jedidiah Morse to the Secretary of War in 1820
states that a Potawatomi population of 3,400 was "Scattered in villages in
the vicinity of Chicago, in the northern part of Indiana, and on the S.
shore of Michigan Lake, and S. near the centre of Indiana" (Morse, 1822,
p. 363).

A party of Long's expedition, in 1823, visiting Dr. Wolcott, the
Indian agent at Chicago, was told by a half-breed Chippewa "that the Indians
who frequent this part of the country are very much intermixed, belonging
principally to the Potawatomis, Ottawas, and Chippewas..." (Keating, 1824,
pp. 169-170). According to Morse there were 500 Chippewa "Scattered in
several villages among the Pottawattamies" (Morse, 1822, p. 363). The
report of Long's expedition also noted a Potawatomi village near the "ford"
of the Des Plaines River, which is about forty miles above the confluence
of the Des Plaines with the Kankakee (Keating, 1824, p. 173).

The narrative of Long's expedition contains a statement on the general
area of Potawatomi hunting as follows: "The hunting grounds of the Potawatomis
appear to be bounded on the north by the St. Joseph, (which on the east side
of Lake Michigan separates them from the Ottawas,) and the Milwacke, which,
on the west side of the lake, divides them from the Menomones. They spread
to the south along the Illinois river about two hundred miles; to the west
their grounds extend as far as Rock river, and the Mequin or Spoon river of

425

the Illinois; to the east they probably seldom pass beyond the Wabash"
(ibid. p. 171). This description of the area encompassed in the Potawatomi
hunting grounds apparently took Chicago as the point of orientation. The
region includes lands extending from the Wabash northward through the area
under study.

That the foregoing statement is generally correct is indicated by a
report from the agent at Chicago, Alexander Wolcott, to John Tipton the agent
at Fort Wayne. Although Potawatomi are not specifically mentioned, Wolcott
discusses the steps he took to establish trading posts for the Indians in
his district. He writes: "I have established a Post at the Great Bend of the
Rocky River, at Milwaukee on lake Michigan ninety miles below [above? JJ]
this place, at Chicago, at the 'Parc aux vaches' on the St. Josephs, at the
forks of the river des Iroquois, a branch of the Kankakee and at Lawton's
House on the Sangarno. These posts are abundantly sufficient &, I think,
most conveniently situated for the accommodations of the Indians of this
district. The Indians who hunt on the Kankakee cannot any of them be more
than forty miles (few of them so many) from one of the three posts St. Josephs,
Chicago, or the river Des Iroquois" (Tipton, 1942, 1:381-2). The Indians
embraced in Wolcott's agency of Chicago and for whom the posts were established were the "Potawatomies, Ottawas, and Chippewas, from the St. Joseph's
round the coast of Lake Michigan to Milwaukee, and those upon the heads of
the Illinois, and upon Rock River" (Cong. Doc. Series No. 181, Document 72,
pp. 3-9, 1828). Tipton's agency included the "Miamies, Eel-Rivers, and
Potawatomies of the Tippecanoe, and heads of the Kankakee" (idem; ibid. pp.
408-9 and map of Fort Wayne Indian Agency, 1824, from Tipton's map).

In 1825 Governor Cass sent to Tipton a "List of Places to be Licensed
for the Indian Trade", indicating the geographical locations for this purpose
within each agency of the Michigan Superintendency (Tipton, 1942, 1:465-7; see

426

also pp. 494-5). However, there are no tribal identifications associated
with the places mentioned. But that Potawatomi are included in the list may
be inferred from this statement by Tipton which he wrote in a letter to
Secretary of War Barbour on June 2, 1827: "The puttowatomies are a powerfull
Nation scattered along the waters of the wabash on the Lake and near the
Canada line..." (ibid. p. 721).

Later that month he wrote Governor Cass: "...Po,ca,gun,Che,co, and
other chiefs from the Kanikee and St. Joseph came in and I delivered them
a quantity of provision which they packed up and set off immediately for
their villages,...a few days (years) more will scarsely leave a trace to
mark the spot where this once powerful nation roamed unmolested" (ibid.
p. 735). An "Abstract of Provisions delivered to the Kankakee Indians and
from other parts of the Fort Wayne Agency..." accompanied the letter; it
contained the names of the chiefs mentioned above in Tipton's letter in
addition to those of other Potawatomi individuals (ibid. pp. 735-7).

427

On February 23, 1828 Tipton, in a letter to Governor Cass, referred
to the fact that "A law has been passed authorising the location of a road
through the puttowotomie Country..." (Tipton, 1942, 2:21). Apparently this
road, which was demanded by the white people of the territory was to extend
"from the Wabash north to Lake Michigan..." (Tipton, 1942, vol. 1,
Introduction, p. 14).

Reference to Potawatomi hunting grounds on the Yellow River affluent
of the Kankakee in Indiana was made on March 8, 1828 in a letter to Tipton
from Sub-agent Lewis Tipton, 1942, 2:26). The following August an abstract
of "Provisions issued to the Potawatamies from 2d to the 6th August 1828
reveals the locations of various groups of that tribe. The places listed
are: Tippecanoe River; lake on Tippecanoe River; Yellow River; Eel River;
Mto-mo-naung; Eel River old town; Wabash; Chippewa Town; Portage of the

Tippecanoe (ibid. pp. 74-76). The area encompassed on this list is between the Wabash and Eel rivers on the south and the Yellow River to the north.

Some of the places on the foregoing list are contained in another Tipton document dated September 6-8, 1828. The latter is a "Pay Roll of the Wabash & Elk Heart Potawatamies for the year 1828" (ibid. pp. 103-105). Additional places mentioned include: "between Kinkiki & River aux plains [Des Plaines-JJ]". Payment was made to the Potawatomi at Tippecanoe Mills.

In April of 1829 some Potawatomi chiefs from the Illinois prairies visited Tipton with an offer to sell their lands some distance south of Chicago. Reporting the incident Tipton wrote: "Seven Potawatamie chiefs with upward of Sixty of their people who live on the prairie in the State of Ill[s]. arrived here a few days Since...They are anxious to sell a large tract of their country in Ill[s]. south of Chicago,..." (ibid. pp. 161-212).

428   Another rather general statement concerning the distribution of the Potawatomi was made by Tipton on September 2, 1830 in a letter to Thomas L. McKenney. He writes: "The Potawattimies are more numerous (than the Miami), and scattered over a larger territory in little bands.--They own land in Illinois, and the Michigan Territory, a part of which, as well as in Indiana, can now be purchased" (ibid. pp. 330 and 400). Again referring, presumably, to the Potawatomi, Tipton in February 1831 wrote, probably from Eel River or Tippecanoe: "The snow at this place has been for a month passed, more than two feet deep and the Indians inform me that it is waist deep in the Prairies on the Tippecanoe and Kankakee north of this" (ibid. p. 396).

BIBLIOGRAPHY

Alvord, Clarence Walworth
    1920 The Illinois Country, 1673-1818. Springfield.

American Historical Review
    1899 Vol. 4, pp. 107-111. New York.
    1900 Vol. 5, pp. 518-542. New York.

American State Papers
    1832 Indian Affairs. Vol. 1. Washington.
    1834   "   "   Vol. 2. Washington.
    1834 Public Lands. Vol. 2. Washington.

Anderson, Melville B. (Translator)
    1898 Relation of Henri de Tonty Concerning the Explorations of
            La Salle from 1678 to 1683. Chicago.
    1901 Relation of the Discoveries and Voyages of Cavelier de La Salle
            from 1679 to 1681. The Official Narrative. Chicago. (Trans-
            lated from Margry, 1875-1866, Vol. I, pp. 435-544).

Bergh, Albert Ellery
    1907 The Writings of Thomas Jefferson. Vol. 16. Washington, D. C.

Biggs, William
    1922 Narrative of the Captivity of William Biggs among the Kickapoo
            Indians in Illinois in 1788. (No publisher.)

Blair, Emma Helen
    1911 The Indian Tribes of the Upper Mississippi Valley and Region of
            the Great Lakes. 2 Vols. Cleveland.

Blasingham, Emily
    1956 The Depopulation of the Illinois Indians. Ethnohistory, Vol. 3,
            No. 3, pp. 193-224 and Vol. 3, No. 4, pp. 361-412.

Bouquet, Henry
    1868 Historical Account of Bouquet's Expedition Against the Ohio
            Indians in 1764. Preface by Francis Parkman. Cincinatti.
    1943 The Papers of Col. Henry Bouquet. Sylvester K. Stevens and
            Donald H. Kent, editors. Pennsylvania Historical Survey, Series
            21655, Northwestern Pennsylvania Historical Series. Pennsylvania
            Historical Commission.

Buell, Rowena
    1903 The Memoirs of Rufus Putnam. Boston and New York.

Charlevoix, Pierre Francois Xavier de
    1923 Journal of a Voyage to North America. 2 Vols. Louise Phelps
            Kellogg, Editor. Chicago.

Chouteau, Auguste
1940 Notes of Auguste Chouteau on Boundaries of Various Indian Nations. Glimpses of the Past, Vol. 7, Numbers 9-12, pp. 121-140. Missouri Historical Society. St. Louis.

Cockrum, Col. William M.
1907 Pioneer History of Indiana. Oakland City, Indiana.

Colden, Cadwallader
1958 The History of the Five Indian Nations. Ithica.

Collot, Victor
1924 A Journey in North America: March-December 1796. Florence.

Congressional Document No. 72, Series No. 81. 20th Congress, 2nd Session. December 2, 1828. Washington.

d'Artaguiette, Diron
1961 Journal of Diron d'Artaguiette, in Travels in the American Colonies, Edited by Newton D. Mereness. New York.

Deale, Valentine B.
1958 The History of the Potawatomis Before 1922. Ethnohistory, Vol. 5, No. 4. pp. 305-360.

Delanglez, Jean
1945 Marquette's Augograph Map of the Mississippi River. Mid-America, Vol. 27, No. 1, pp. 30-53.

Deliette, Sieur (Probable Author)
Memoir of DeGannes Concerning the Illinois Country. Collections of the Illinois State Historical Library (Illinois Historical Collections), Vol. 23, pp. 302-395. Springfield, 1934.

Delisle, Legardeur
1945 Journal of Legardeur Delisle. Stanley Faye, Editor. Journal of the Illinois State Historical Society, Vol. 38, No. 1, pp. 38-57.

Dunn, Jacob Piatt
1894 Slavery Petitions and Papers. Indiana Historical Society Publications. Vol. 2, No. 18. Indianapolis.
1894 Documents Relating to the French Settlements on the Wabash, Indiana Historical Society Publications, Vol. 2, No. 11. Indianapolis.
1902 The Mission to the Ouabache. Indiana Historical Society Publications, Vol. 3, No. 4. Indianapolis.

Edwards, Ninian
1870 History of Illinois from 1778 to 1833; and Life and Times of Ninian Edwards. Springfield, Ill.

430

Esarey, Logan (Editor)
    1922 Messages and Letters of William Henry Harrison. 2 Vols.
          Indianapolis.

Fortier, Edward Joseph
    1909 The Establishment of the Tamarois Mission. Transactions of the
          Illinois State Historical Society for the year 1908. Publi-
          cation No. 13 of the Illinois State Historical Library,
          Springfield.

French, B. F. (Editor)
    1846 Historical Collections of Louisiana. Part 1, New York.

Gage, Thomas
    1931 The Correspondence of General Thomas Gage...1763-1775. Vol. 1.
          Compiled and Edited by Clarence Edwin Carter.

Habig, Marion A.
    1933 "The Site of the Great Illinois Village". Mid-America, Vol. 16,
          No. 1.

Hair, James T.
    1866 Gazeteer of Madison County...Alton, Illinois.

Hamburgh
    1961 Minutes of Mr. Hamburgh's Journal, 1763, in Travels in the
          American Colonies, edited by Newton D. Mereness. New York.

Hamilton, Henry
    1951 The Journal of Henry Hamilton 1778-1779, in (John D. Barnhart,
          Editor) Henry Hamilton and George Rogers Clark in the American
          Revolution. Crawfordsville, Indiana.

Hildreth, S. P.
    1848 Pioneer History: Being an Account of the First Examinations of
          the Ohio Valley and the Early Settlement of the Northwest
          Territory. Cincinnati.

1864 Historical Magazine and Notes and Queries, Vol. 8. New York.

Houck, Louis
    1909 The Spanish Regime in Missouri. 2 Vols. Chicago.

Hunt, George T.
    1960 The Wars of the Iroquois: A Study in Intertribal Trade Relations.
          Madison.

Hutchins, Thomas
    1904 A Topographical Description of Virginia, Pennsylvania, Maryland,
          and North Carolina. Reprinted from the Original Edition of 1778.
          Edited by Frederick Charles Hicks. Cleveland.

Hyde, George E.
    1962 The Indians of the Woodlands: From Prehistoric Times to 1725.
          Norman, Oklahoma.

Illinois State Historical Library, Collections
    1903-1950 Vols. 1-32. Springfield.

Imlay, Gilbert
    1797 A Topographical Description of the Western Territory of North
          America. London.

Indiana Magazine of History
    1938 Vol. 34. Indiana University. Bloomington.

Jackson, Donald (Editor)
    1962 Letters of the Lewis and Clark Expedition, with Related Documents,
          1783-1854. Urbana, Illinois.

Jefferson, Thomas
    1955 Notes on the State of Virginia. William Peden, Editor. Chapel
          Hill, North Carolina.

Johnson, Sir William
    1921-1965 The Papers of Sir William Johnson. 14 Vols. Albany.

Journal of the Illinois State Historical Society
    1931 Vol. 24, No. 1. Springfield.

Keating, William H. (Editor)
    1824 Narrative of an Expedition to the Source of St. Peter's River,
          Lake Winnepeek, Lake of the Woods...Under the Command of Stephen
          H. Long, Major U.S.T.E. Philadelphia.

Kellogg, Louise Phelps (Transl. and Editor)
    1908 The Fox Indians During the French Regime. Proceedings of the
          State Historical Society of Wisconsin. 55th Annual Meeting.
          Madison.
    1917 Early Narratives of the Northwest 1634-1699. New York.
    1925 The French Regime in Wisconsin and the Northwest. Madison.
    1935 LaChapelle's Remarkable Retreat Through the Mississippi Valley,
          1760-61. Mississippi Valley Historical Review. Vol. 22, No. 1,
          pp. 62-78.

Kennedy, Patrick
    1797 Mr. Patrick Kennedy's Journal of an Expedition...in the Year
          1773...In Gilbert Imlay, A Topographical Description of the
          Western Territory of North America, p. 506 ff. London.

Kinietz, W. Vernon (Editor)
    1940 The Indians of the Western Great Lakes 1615-1760. Occasional
          Contributions from the Museum of Anthropology of the University
          of Michigan No. 10. Ann Arbor.

Kinnaird, Lawrence (Editor)
　　1946　Spain in the Mississippi Valley, 1765-1794. 4 Vols. Annual
　　　　　Report of the American Historical Association for the Year 1945.
　　　　　U. S. Gov't. Printing Office. Washington.

Knopf, Richard C. (Editor)
　　1955　Campaign into the Wilderness. Vols. 3 and 4. Columbus, Ohio.
　　1959　Anthony Wayne: A Name in Arms. Pittsburgh.

Krauskopf, Frances (Transl. and Editor)
　　1955　Ouiatanon Documents. Indiana Historical Society Publications,
　　　　　Vol. 18. No. 2. Indianapolis.

Margry, Pierre (Editor)
　　1876-1889　Découvertes et Établissements des Français dans L'ouest et
　　　　　dans le Sud de L'Amérique Septentrionale (1614-1754).
　　　　　Mémoires et Documents Originaux. 6 Vols. Paris.

　　N. D. English Translation of Margry, 1875-1886. Burton Collection,
　　　　　Detroit Public Library, MSS.

Mason, Edward G. (Editor)
　　1890　Early Chicago and Illinois. Chicago.

Memoirs of the Historical Society of Pennsylvania
　　1860　Vol 7. Contains the Military Journal of Major Ebenezer Denny.

Michigan Pioneer and Historical Society, Historical Collections
　　1877-1929　Vols. 1-40. Lansing.

Mid-America
　　1939　Vol. 21, No. 3. p. 209 ff.

Mississippi Provincial Archives. Collected, Edited and Translated by Dunbar
Rowland and A. G. Sanders. Jackson, Miss.
　　1927　Vol. I, 1729-1740
　　1929　Vol. II, 1701-1729
　　1932　Vol. III, 1704-1743

Morse, Jedidiah
　　1822　A Report to the Secretary of War of the United States, on
　　　　　Indian Affairs,... New Haven.

Nasatir, A. P. (Editor)
　　1952　Before Lewis and Clark. 2 Vols. St. Louis.

O'Callaghan, Edmund B. and Berthold Fernow, Eds.
　　1853-1887　Documents Relative to the Colonial History of the State of
　　　　　New York. 15 Vols. Albany.

Palm, Sister Mary Borgias
     1931 The Jesuit Missions of the Illinois Country: 1673-1763.
           Dissertation Presented to the Faculty of the Graduate School of
           St. Louis University in Partial Fulfillment of the Requirements
           for the Degree of Doctor of Philosophy.
     1933 Kaskaskia, Indian Mission Village, 1703-1718. Mid-America,
           Vol. 16., No. 1. pp. 14-25.

Palmer, William P. (Editor)
     1884 Calendar of Virginia State Papers. Vol 4. Richmond.

Paré, George
     1930 The St. Joseph Mission. The Mississippi Valley Historical
           Review. Vol. 17, No. 1, p. 24 ff.

Parkman, Francis
     1894 A Half-Century of Conflict. 2 Vols. Boston.

Peckham, Howard H. (Editor)
     1939 George Groghan's Journal of His Trip to Detroit in 1767.
           Ann Arbor.

Pike, Zebulon Montgomery
     1895 The Expeditions of Zebulon Montgomery Pike, to Headwaters of
           the Mississippi River, Through Louisiana Territory, and in
           New Spain, During the Years 1805-6-7. 3 Vols. Elliott Coves,
           Editor. New York.

Royce, Charles C.
     1899 Indian Land Cessions in the United States. Eighteenth Annual
           Report of the Bureau of American Ethnology. Washington.

Schoolcraft, Henry
     1860 Archives of Aboriginal Knowledge. 6 Vols. Philadelphia.

Shea, John Gilmary (Editor)
     1852 Discovery and Exploration of The Mississippi Valley. New York.
     1861 Early Voyages Up and Down the Mississippi. Albany.

Smith, William Henry (Editor)
     1882 The St. Clair Papers. The Life and Public Services of Arthur
           St. Clair. 2 Vols. Cincinnati.

Steward, John F.
     1903 Lost Maramech and Earliest Chicago. Chicago and New York.

Storm, Colton
     1944 Lieutenant John Armstrong's Map of the Illinois River, 1790.
           Journal of the Illinois State Historical Society. Vol. 37,
           pp. 48-55. Springfield, Ill.

Temple, Wayne C.
     1958 Indian Villages of the Illinois Country. Scientific Papers,
           Illinois State Museum, Vol. 2, Part 2. Springfield.

434

The Territorial Papers of the United States
    1934-1962 Vols. 1-26. Clarence Edwin Carter, Editor. Washington.

Thornbrough, Gayle (Editor)
    1957 Outpost on the Wabash 1787-1791. Indiana Historical Society
        Publications. Vol. 19. Indianapolis.
    1961 Letter Book of the Indian Agency at Fort Wayne, 1809-1815.
        Indian Historical Society Publications. Vol. 21. Indianapolis.

Thwaites, Reuben Gold (Editor)
    1896-1901 The Jesuit Relations and Allied Documents...1610-1791.
        73 Vols. Cleveland.
    1903 A New Discovery of a Vast Country in America, by Father Louis
        Hennepin. 2 Vols. Chicago.
    1904-05 Original Journals of the Lewis and Clark Expedition 1804-1806.
        7 Vols. New York.

Tipton, John
    1942 The John Tipton Papers. Introduction by Paul Wallace Gates.
        Compiled by Glen A. Blackburn. Edited by Nellie Armstrong
        Robertson and Dorothy Riker. 2 Vols. Indiana Historical
        Collections. Vols. 24 and 25. Indianapolis.

Tucker, Sara Jones
    1942 Indian Villages of the Illinois Country. Scientific Papers,
        Illinois State Museum, Vol. 2, Part 1, Atlas. Springfield.

435

United States Senate, Journal of Executive Proceedings, Vol. 1, pp. 128, 131,
135, 146.
    1828 Washington, D. C.

Western Sun
    1810 Vol. 3, No. 35, p. 3 (col. 3 and 4) Saturday, August 25.
        Vincennes.
    1812 Vol. 4, No. 14, p. 3 (col. 1). January 4. Vincennes.

Winsor, Justin
    1895 The Mississippi Basin. The Struggle in America Between England
        and France 1697-1763. Boston and New York.

Wisconsin State Historical Society, Collections
    1855-1931 Vols. 1-31. Madison.

ABBREVIATIONS

The complete reference for each of the following sources is in the bibliography.

A	The letter A, followed by a numeral, refers to a manuscript document. The manuscript collection from which it derives is indicated on the document. The numerals apply to Government exhibits.
AHR	The American Historical Review
ASP-IA	American State Papers, Indian Affairs
ASP-PL	American State Papers, Public Lands
CD-1828	Congressional Document No. 72, Series No. 81, 20 Congress, 2d Session, December 2, 1828.
HM	Historical Magazine and Notes and Queries.
IHC	Illinois Historical Library, Collections
IMH	Indiana Magazine of History
JISHS	Journal of the Illinois State Historical Society
JP	Johnson, Sir William, The Papers of Sir William Johnson
JR	Thwaites, Reuben Gold, Editor, The Jesuit Relations and Allied Documents:...1610–1791
MA	Mid-America
MHSP	Memoirs of the Historical Society of Pennsylvania
MPA	Mississippi Provincial Archives
MPHC	Michigan Pioneer and Historical Society Historical Collections
NYCD	O'Callaghan, E. B., and Berthold Fernow, Editors, Documents Relative to the Colonial History of the State of New York.
TP	Carter, Clarence Edwin, Editor, The Territorial Papers of the United States.
USS-1	United States Senate, Journal of Executive Proceedings, Vol. 1.
WHC	Wisconsin State Historical Society, Collections
WS-	Western Sun

436